A History of American Business

Arthur S. Link
Princeton University
GENERAL EDITOR FOR HISTORY

A History of American Business

SECOND EDITION

C. Joseph Pusateri
University of San Diego

Harlan Davidson, Inc.
Arlington Heights, Illinois 60004

Library of Congress Cataloging-in-Publication Data

Pusateri, C. Joseph.
  A history of American business / C. Joseph
  Pusateri. — 2nd ed.
      p.   cm.
  Bibliography: p.
  Includes index.
  ISBN 0–88295–844–5 : $27.95
  ISBN 0-88295-859-3 (pbk.) : $18.95
  1. Business enterprises—United States—
History.   2. Businessmen—United States—
History.   3. United States—Commerce—History.
4. Capitalism—United States—History.   I. Title.
HF3021.P87   1988
338.0973—dc19   87–32955
                                            CIP

Cover illustration: Selling groceries, San Diego, 1888.
(Courtesy San Diego Historical Society)

Manufactured in the United States of America

92 91 90 89 88   1 2 3 4 5 6 7 EB

CONTENTS

ILLUSTRATIONS

PREFACE TO THE SECOND EDITION

RELATIVELY little change in the Preface to the first edition of this work, written four years ago, seems required now. Once again, I wish to apologize in advance to any readers who may feel that I have given short shrift to their favorite entrepreneur or firm or omitted a discussion of a topic they would have included. The fact that the subject of American business history is replete with significant individuals, issues, and organizations is simultaneously a delight and a hazard for anyone attempting to tell its story. If the historian has even modest ability, the story should be engrossing, because the record of American business enterprise over the past four centuries has been provocative and vital to the nation's development. Yet, on the other hand, the subject is also so vast that it is clearly impossible to convey more than a *précis* of it within the covers of a single volume.

As in the first edition, I have made a conscious attempt to stress the humanity of the business story. Economic decision makers are, of course, human beings and not abstract entries on organization charts, and as such they are both fallible and fascinating. I do not believe the tide of historical events, including economic affairs, is inevitable. Rather, events are shaped by the choices made by individuals in positions of responsibility, drawing upon the incomplete knowledge and the assorted experiences they possess at a critical moment in time. For that reason, readers will continue to find in this second edition elaborations on the role of key business figures in each century of American history and less emphasis on quantification.

After the publication of the first edition, several fellow historians whose judgment I trust greatly suggested that an even more extended treatment of twentieth-century business developments was needed. I hope that this second edition has successfully addressed those recommendations. There is an additional twentieth-century chapter (Chapter 14), and more post-1900 material included in earlier chapters as well. The discussions, for example, of advertising, cable television, the two World Wars, and such firms as Apple Computer, General Dynamics, and Textron, as well as others, are almost totally new.

The appendices that follow the text have been updated too. Several significant business history studies published since 1983 are noted in "Some Suggestions for Further Reading," and the "Chronology of American Business" has been carried forward to 1987. The "Twenty-five Largest Industrial Corporations" now includes comparative listings of companies, ranked by assets, for the years 1917, 1957, and 1986. One change has been made in the "Roster of Fifty Major Business Leaders": Lee Iacocca has been included and life insurance executive Henry B. Hyde has been deleted (the debate over that substitution should be interesting). Unfortunately, after pondering the question for some time, and hearing a good deal of comment about it, I still did not feel I could add a woman to the list. If it had been a listing of the top one hundred, and not just fifty, both Mary Kay Ash of Mary Kay Cosmetics and Katherine Graham of the *Washington Post–Newsweek* media complex may have been worthy candidates for inclusion. Finally, the "Glossary of American Business Terms" has seen some additions too, mainly phrases associated with the recent raiding and takeover phenomena of the 1980s. The fact that a number of business history course instructors have told me that their students have found these appendices useful is indeed gratifying, and caused me to continue them in the second edition.

Once again, it is a pleasurable obligation on my part to acknowledge the indispensable assistance and encouragement of those individuals who made this second edition possible. Besides the many professional colleagues and other readers who offered helpful comments on the earlier version of this work, I want to extend specific appreciation to Maureen Gilgore Hewitt, editor-in-chief, Harlan Davidson, Inc., and her staff. Working with an editor as knowledgable and as patient as Maureen Hewitt is indeed a bonanza for any would-be author.

This work was all the easier to complete because of the lively interest in scholarship consistently manifested and the cordial working environment created by faculty and administrative friends at the University of San Diego. My warm thanks to them all. And most especially, an evergreen appreciation to my wife, Barbara, for her welcome good humor, her unruffled willingness to suffer piles of books and papers strewn about the family room, and very particularly for always being there.

C. J. P.
San Diego, California

I

PANORAMA

In any private-enterprise system, the entrepreneur—the risk-taking businessman—is the prime mover and principal architect of most economic progress. For that reason it is well that we begin by examining the nature of the entrepreneurial function and the form it has taken in the United States. As the cavalcade of American business unfolds in later chapters, the spotlight of history falls successively on quite different types of entrepreneurs. They range from the petty merchant of the struggling seaboard colonies in the 1600s to the battalions of managers in today's large corporations.

We will next see how some scholars have organized their surveys of the past by identifying certain historical stages in the evolution of business. The stage approach not only provides an opportunity to compare and contrast one individual time segment with another, it also supplies a sturdy framework for viewing the panorama of capitalism in western civilization. Hence a discussion of stages should serve as a useful introduction to our subject.

A nation turns to the out-of-doors

No other nation is more definitely awake to the benefits of life in the open air than America today.

The Ford car, which provides reliable motoring at a cost millions can afford, is one of the big and vital factors in this turning to the out-of-doors.

It has made it possible for city dwellers to reclaim precious hours from the routine of work, for recreation and exercise; to find the wholesome and necessary relaxation that only fresh air and sunshine assure.

Runabout . . $260	Tudor $580
Touring . . . $290	Fordor . . . $660
Coupe $520	All Prices F. O. B. Chicago

On Open Cars Starter and Demountable Rims $85 Extra
Full-Size Balloon Tires Optional at an extra cost of $25

FORD MOTOR COMPANY ∴ DETROIT, MICHIGAN

THE UNIVERSAL CAR

MAKE SAFETY YOUR RESPONSIBILITY

CHAPTER ONE

The Entrepreneur

"I know of nothing more despicable and pathetic than a man who devotes all the waking hours of the day to making money for money's sake." So wrote John D. Rockefeller in his 1909 memoirs. He went on to comment about himself: "I was not what might be called a diligent business man."[1] The seeming absurdity of his words lies, of course, in the fact that Rockefeller during his life accumulated one of the world's colossal personal fortunes because of the very business diligence he denied.

Nevertheless, to the chief organizer of the Standard Oil empire, there was no contradiction at all. He said on another occasion: "Mere money-getting has never been my goal. I had an ambition to build."[2] Even more than just a yearning to build a thriving commercial enterprise, though, what the Astors, the Carnegies, and the Rockefellers of America found in the challenge of business was what historian Allan Nevins labeled "the Great Game." Nevins asserted: "They played it with zest and gusto, they enjoyed it even when it was perilous, and they took its ups and downs with equanimity." To Nevins, "the best businessmen have been great adventurers."[3] The story of business in the United States, therefore, might be said to be a chronicle of how well or badly this country's entrepreneurs have played the Game, and what adventures they encountered along the way.

The Role of Business Institutions

Clearly, evolving business institutions have had a special role in our national experience. They have shaped the American economy more significantly than any other single factor. Further, they have been responsible for many of the major societal changes that occurred throughout the country during the four centuries following the establishment of the first English settlement at Jamestown, whether these changes were the physical knitting together of a continent by steel rails in the Gilded Age or the cultural uniformity fostered by the broadcasting and motion picture industries in the twentieth century.

The manner in which business values and philosophy have permeated American culture has been equally significant. The availability of inexpensive property in the new world led to an ethic of upward mobility through hard work alone. That belief quickly became an article of faith for a majority of Americans. Over one hundred years ago, the national gospel of achievement and success through hard work and honest dealing was embodied in the popular series of rags-to-riches books written by Horatio Alger. In the 1980s, it has been characterized, somewhat sarcastically perhaps, by that current acronym for young, upwardly mobile professionals—"yuppies."

Despite the important role of business in American life, standard college textbooks of American history have reflected little of its impact. Such texts have usually focused upon political and diplomatic events, and, more recently, upon social developments, especially the plight of ethnic and racial minorities. When these texts have discussed economic matters, they have often done so in impersonal terms, as forces and movements rather than as the actions of individuals. Businessmen have appeared in American history survey texts primarily in negative tones, usually in examples of colorful buccaneering in the late nineteenth century or as implacable foes of labor organizations in the twentieth.

Forces and movements in history are not impersonal, however; they are the sum total of the particular acts of human beings. Men and women precipitate historical change, and those engaged in the production and distribution of goods and services for profit have been in the vanguard. It was Woodrow Wilson, a president not known as a champion of business interests, who stated: "Business underlies everything in our national life."[4]

The Enterprise Spectrum

As with any history, though, selectivity is necessary. Some business experiences are more notable than others, and these should be emphasized. In the United States today, for instance, there are over fourteen million business units, and they cover a wide spectrum of activities. Approximately ten million firms are sole proprietorships; that is, they are owned and usually managed by a single individual. Most are small and are marked by a limited life span of a few years at best before they are terminated, either voluntarily by their owners or involuntarily by their creditors. Another one-and-a-half million firms are partnerships. In most cases, they, too, are characterized by the modest scope of their operations.[5]

The remaining three million businesses have corporate charters, but here the diversity is enormous. Internal Revenue statistics reveal that a majority of all corporations can claim assets of only $100,000 or less. On the other hand, the top five companies in a recent *Fortune* magazine listing of the 500 largest industrial corporations in the United States (General Motors, Exxon, Ford, IBM, and Mobil, in that order) recorded sales in 1986 that equalled over 8 percent of the gross national product of the whole country. The sales of the complete *Fortune* 500, which number less than 2 percent of all American corporations, were nevertheless equivalent to 43 percent of the entire nation's GNP. General Motors, first on the *Fortune* list, amassed sales in 1986 that exceeded $102 billion, and 1986 was not regarded as a good year for the automotive giant.[6]

It is not possible for any study of American business history to examine the entire enterprise spectrum. Selectivity requires that we remember those firms that have been most representative of any era and especially those that have most shaped the next generation. But the story of any firm is largely synonymous with the stories of its main decision makers. Therefore, when we analyze the record of those business organizations that bore the chief responsibility for stimulating economic change in the United States, it is inevitable that we also seek the human element within.

The Entrepreneur

HISTORY AND DEFINITION

Economic historians have long given a specific name to this decision-making human element—the "entrepreneur." Unfortunately, it is easier to label the element than it is to identify it definitively or to detail its functions to everyone's satisfaction. Peter Kilby has compared the study of business entrepreneurship to the attempts in *Winnie-the-Pooh* to catch the fantastic creature known as the Heffalump. The Heffalump was supposedly an awesome animal that hunters continuously chased but never captured. Moreover, the hunters who did claim to have seen the Heffalump could never agree on an exact description of the elusive beast.[7]

Entrepreneurial Heffalump-hunting began in the eighteenth century. The first use of the word "entrepreneur" appears in the economic writings of Richard Cantillon, an Irishman who made a fortune as a banker in Paris in the early eighteenth century. In 1755, approximately twenty years after his murder by a disgruntled cook discharged from his service, an economic treatise written by Cantillon was finally published. From it has stemmed his reputation as a theorist.

Cantillon coined the word "entrepreneur" in a discussion of the economic return on landholding. He defined an entrepreneur as one who buys factor inputs—the means of production—at set or certain prices in order to sell them later for prices that were unknown when the purchase commitment was first made. Cantillon's definition thus introduced the element of risk-bearing, a quality which became permanently associated with entrepreneurial activity.

The concept of the entrepreneur was further developed in the next century by a Frenchman, Jean-Baptiste Say. Say introduced the threefold division of the factors of production into land, labor, and capital, which became a continuing feature of economic thought. He also broadened Cantillon's idea of the entrepreneur into the individual who combines the three factors of production into a successful and presumably profitable enterprise. An entrepreneur could now be defined as "the person who takes upon himself the immediate responsibility, risk, and conduct of a concern of industry, whether upon his own or a borrowed capital."[8] It seems likely that Say's enhanced appreciation of the entrepreneurial function was a by-product of his own practical business experience in banking, insurance, and textiles. With Say, then, for the first time entrepreneurial activity became synonymous with what we call management.

The modern theory of entrepreneurship is most closely associated with the influential Harvard economist Joseph Schumpeter (1883–1950). Before joining the Harvard faculty, Schumpeter had practiced law and served as finance minister in his native Austria. In 1911, at the age of twenty-eight, he published *The Theory of Economic De-*

velopment, a brilliant work in which he first outlined the role of what he called "creative entrepreneurship." It was for him the primary cause of real economic growth.

In Schumpeter's model, economic activity is repetitive, "running on in channels essentially the same year after year—similar to the circulation of the blood in an animal organism."[9] This circular flow of demand, production, and consumption is broken periodically by changes that force the economy to higher levels of output and a fresh equilibrium. These changes, labeled "innovations," are the result of new techniques applied in organization or production. The creative entrepreneur is the innovator, the prime mover of economic change, who has seen an opportunity and effectively taken advantage of it.

In Schumpeter's view, the creative entrepreneur does not follow the normal course of business routine, but instead forges new combinations from the available tools and techniques. Schumpeter cites five possible ways: (1) the introduction of a new good or a new quality of a good; (2) the introduction of a new method of production or a new way of handling a commodity commercially; (3) the opening of a new market; (4) the acquisition of a new source of raw materials or unfinished goods; (5) the crafting of a new organizational structure in any industry, perhaps through either the establishment or the undoing of a monopoly power position.

He confined the title of entrepreneur to those individuals responsible for new developments. He did not include within his definition those individuals "who merely may operate an established business."[10] Schumpeter discriminated between leaders and followers. The creative entrepreneur whose innovations broke the routine was a leader; others simply followed after, imitating the ideas of the innovator. Soon an equilibrium was once again established as following firms adapted to the altered conditions, and the new became routine. All then awaited the next wave of innovation.

While recent writers recognize the importance of Joseph Schumpeter's work in crystallizing the character of the entrepreneur, they have tended to regard his definition as too narrow. They argue that the modern entrepreneur performs vital business functions not envisioned by Schumpeter—for example, dealing with the issues of governmental relations and of social responsibility—and not apparently included within his strict conception of innovation. For that reason, it is now common to equate entrepreneurship with top management, or even more accurately, with managerial decision making.

In this fashion, one business historian, Fritz Redlich, defined the entrepreneur as the person "who (alone or with others) shapes and reshapes business enterprise, establishes its relations with other enterprises and fits it into the market" and "who directs and determines its spirit and its strategy by making the major decisions."[11]

Another definition of entrepreneurship was explored by Arthur H. Cole. In his 1959 work, *Business Enterprise in Its Social Setting*, Cole stressed the concept of an "entrepreneurial team." In the modern world, according to Cole, "with the increase in the complexity of relationships surrounding business institutions and an increase in the complexity of data needed to operate such units successfully, the multiple or divided quality of entrepreneurship becomes the most important element." He further offered a useful and relatively simple definition of the entrepreneurial team—"those who make, execute, and are responsible for the strategic decisions of a profit-oriented enterprise."[12]

Perhaps the Redlich and Cole definitions are too simple, however, for they may emphasize administrative decision making at the expense of Schumpeter's hallmark of entrepreneurship, innovation. Peter F. Drucker is today's most prolific and influential commentator on the subject of large-scale organizations and their management, and in a recent study he has forcefully argued for a necessary connection between change and the entrepreneur. The Latin phrase *rerum novarum cupidus* means "greedy for new things." For Drucker, authentic entrepreneurs must be *rerum novarum cupidus*. They must, in his words, "see change as the norm and as healthy."[13]

Drucker differs from Schumpeter in that he does not assign the entrepreneur the responsibility for actually initiating change. Rather, Drucker states, "the entrepreneur always searches for change, responds to it, and exploits it as an opportunity." The purposeful and organized search for such opportunities and the exploitation of them, he terms "systematic innovation." True entrepreneurial management, for Drucker, practices systematic innovation; in its absence, an enterprise "inevitably ages and declines." And so too, he warns, does a nation that fails to develop a working entrepreneurial economy.[14]

FUNCTIONS AND QUALITIES

Regardless of the definitions of entrepreneurship, its fundamental task remains the same: to determine the collective objectives of the firm and then to generate an environment suitable for their ultimate accomplishment. This task is often expressed as the function of management. Managerial functions have been classified in various ways, but generally from five to seven different activities are listed. We will cite six: planning, organizing, staffing, directing, controlling, and representing. Although we can describe neat classifications, these supposedly separate functions overlap in practice, and managers find themselves engaged in all or most of them at approximately the same time.

1. *Planning.* The first and most basic of all managerial functions, planning involves deciding upon the objective of an undertaking and choosing the correct means to achieve the goal from among all the alternatives available. It consists of anticipating future events and the actions necessary to cope with them.

2. *Organizing.* No plan of any scope can be executed without an effective organization to carry it out. Hence designing the organizational structure through which planning objectives can be attained is a critical function of management, too. Managers must define and delegate authority and responsibility and impose a logical system on the components of the operation. Simply stated, organizing is a means by which any manager seeks to bring order out of what would otherwise be chaos.

3. *Staffing.* The success of any organization, whether it is United States Steel or the Pittsburgh Steelers, depends primarily on the caliber of its personnel. A manager must secure the right person for every position in the organization's structure, as well as provide for the training, development, and compensation of the individuals recruited. Moreover, staffing is a continuing process, since new positions are created and departing personnel need to be replaced.

4. *Directing.* A key facet of any manager's responsibility is the direction of others, specifically the supervision of subordinates. This directional function embraces guidance, motivation, and communication—in short, all activities which contribute to efficient performance by a firm's personnel. The effectiveness of the supervision provided by top management in any organization is a useful measure of the success of the whole enterprise.

5. *Controlling.* By directing, a manager explains to subordinates what should be done. By controlling, a manager ascertains whether and how well a job was performed. The need for control stems from the inherent imperfection and variability of people and things, proof

of the old axiom that the best-laid plans of mice and men can often go awry. Controlling, to be effective, requires four sequential steps: establishing standards that clarify the conditions which should exist; measuring the degree of progress which has occurred; analyzing whatever variance is discovered if progress has fallen short of the expected norms; and taking corrective action to remedy deficiencies.

6. *Representing.* Finally, an increasingly important function of management in recent years has been the duty to represent the organization in its dealings with outside interest groups. Those groups vary widely in nature and influence, but among the most prominent are governmental agencies and officials, labor unions, financial institutions, suppliers, consumers, civic bodies, and the public in general. Management must present its case in the most reasonable yet telling fashion possible if potential external interference in the internal operations of the firm or any threats to its freedom of action are to be safely forestalled.

Together the above six functions make up the management process. The degree of success with which they are performed is what separates competent managers from ineffective ones. A much less conventional but more colorful prescription for effective management was offered a few years ago by Harold Geneen. Chief executive officer of the International Telephone and Telegraph Company (ITT) for seventeen years, Geneen molded that enterprise into a multinational conglomerate with annual sales in excess of $16 billion and operations in eighty countries. In his 1984 book, *Managing*, Geneen wrote: "If I were forced to try to sum it all up, I would have to say that the best way to run a business with the hope of eventual success is to do it as you would cook on a wood-burning stove." He went on to explain:

> How do you cook on such a primitive stove? Because you know that you cannot control all the elements of fire, wood, air flow, etc., you keep your eye on everything at all times. . . . You do not measure out every spice and condiment. You sprinkle here, you pour there. . . . You dip your finger in and taste it. Perhaps you add a little something extra to suit your own taste. You let it brew a while and then you taste it again. And again. . . . If something is wrong, you correct it. Whatever you do, the most important thing is to keep your eye on it. . . . In the end, you will have a pot roast or a lamb stew that is the very best you could possibly make, a joy to your palate and a tribute to your ability

as a cook. . . . And that is the frame of mind to take into the art of conducting and building a successful business.[15]

Geneen's conviction that the pragmatic manager is the best manager is underlined by what he calls "Theory G," his own axiom that "you cannot run a business, or anything else, on a theory." The notable chief executives of his experience, he contends, "applied their own God-given common sense to dealing with more and more complex realities of the business world, and they learned as they went along." Quite obviously, Geneen's enthusiasm for the sophisticated management science concepts taught in contemporary business schools is well under control.[16]

PERSONALITY AND BEHAVIOR

Is there a basic entrepreneurial "personality"? Are there certain characteristics or motivations that business leaders tend to hold in common? Writing forty years ago, Miriam R. Beard, in her study of business in world history, commented: "The organizer of economic enterprise has generally lacked personality of a sort to capture popular imagination." She added that, as private individuals, entrepreneurs have usually been "too timid, or too busy, or too rationalistic to cut capers."[17]

Writing even earlier than Beard, the German scholar Max Weber proposed one of the most famous theories on entrepreneurial motivation. In *The Protestant Ethic and the Spirit of Capitalism* (1904), Weber argued that the Reformation, and especially the teachings of John Calvin, provided a critically significant psychological motivation for the development of modern entrepreneurship, first in Europe and later in the United States.

According to Weber, Calvin taught that every human being had been predestined to eternal salvation or damnation by the inscrutable will of God. But since God's will was inscrutable, no person could know his or her fate. In an age of religion, however, such as that in which Calvin wrote, whether or not one was among "the elect" was a matter of great moment.

People, therefore, looked for some sign that they could interpret favorably. Many concluded that the achievement of success in one's calling was such a favorable sign. Businessmen thus emphasized the importance of industry, regularity, frugality, and other similar virtues. Not surprisingly, businessmen who practiced these rules of conduct were often successful in their calling. And since they also practiced thrift and shunned conspicuous consumption, their savings resulted in an accumulation of capital that was essential to modern capitalism.

Recent historians have not accepted Weber's thesis without criticism. As Robert L. Heilbroner has remarked: "After all, there was nothing much that a Dutch Calvinist would have been able to teach an Italian Catholic banker about the virtues of a businesslike approach to life."[18] Nevertheless, the Reformation fostered a new religious outlook which played no little part in the rise of the economic system known as capitalism.

The psychology of Weber's grimly determined Protestant capitalist or even Miriam R. Beard's colorless unknown takes on a new perspective in the work of a post–Second World War social scientist, David McClelland. In *The Achieving Society* (1961) and later writings, McClelland focuses on the need for achievement as the reason entrepreneurs are led to exploit opportunities. He describes the need as "a desire to do well, not so much for the sake of social recognition or prestige, but for the sake of an inner feeling of personal accomplishment."[19]

How does an entrepreneur imbued with a high need for achievement behave? McClelland sees several specific traits as distinctive, among them, a preference for taking moderate risks, or what has been called "decision making under uncertainty."[20] When the managers of a business choose to add a new line to the firm's list of products, it is not possible to be certain whether the decision will be correct. Yet, the manager is not a gambler, because knowledge and judgment, rather than a reliance on pure chance, have gone into the decision.

McClelland cites a variety of other behavioral indicators. They include a conviction that one's own efforts will be decisive in attaining objectives, a tendency to be optimistic about the possibilities for success, a desire to have concrete feedback on one's performance, a capacity for anticipating favorable opportunities, and an ability to organize effectively the activities of associates. According to McClelland, these are the characteristics of an entrepreneur. If the need for achievement is widespread in a society, then entrepreneurship will be widespread also.

Thomas C. Cochran, the dean of American business historians, takes a more sociological approach. He offers a persuasive explanation for the distinctive behavior of entrepreneurs. Cochran stresses that a combination of internal and external forces forms the entrepreneur. The most important of these are the personality of the individual, which is the product of childhood and school experiences; the expectations of "defining groups," as Cochran calls them, who hold the keys to one's success; and the operational necessities of the particular enterprise in which the entrepreneur is engaged.

As one demonstration of his thesis, Cochran reinterpreted the rapid adoption of industrial machinery by American manufacturers in the first half of the nineteenth century. Earlier scholars had concentrated upon a shortage of skilled and semiskilled labor in the United States to explain why factory owners here mechanized more rapidly than those in western Europe. Cochran, however, suggests a noneconomic explanation. A labor scarcity did prompt American entrepreneurs to mechanize, but the labor problem was just one part of the story.

Equally important were the attitudes of defining groups, such as competitors, bankers, customers, and even the general public. In the early national period, customers, for example, did not place a high value on expert craftsmanship in manufactured goods; rather, adequate utility and a low price sufficed. Furthermore, the average American in an era of a vigorous westward surge was considerably more migratory than his European cousin. He moved often and usually sold the family's durables or the firm's equipment before leaving his last location. Hence long life was another quality not prized in products turned out by American factories. As a result, relatively inexpensive machine-made articles fabricated by domestic producers competed successfully with better-made but more costly European imports. The expectations of American customers helped to define the strategy adopted by factory owners, investors, and managers.

The personality of the entrepreneur is the final element in Cochran's formula. In the American industrial revolution, that personality was molded by child-rearing concepts and educational and religious precepts that stressed "devotion to work, effective use of time, saving money, abhorrence of debt, and obedience."[21] The famous McGuffey readers, which first appeared in the 1830s, taught this philosophy. They extolled individualism, equality of opportunity, and the sanctity of private property, and featured injunctions such as: "One doer is worth a hundred dreamers" and "When a man resolves to do his work himself, you may depend upon it that it will be well done."[22] Businesslike virtues were the basic stock of the combined preaching of home, school, and church.

Cochran's combination of economic necessity, the influence of defining groups, and the developmental forces shaping the personalities of potential business leaders offers the most complete approach to understanding the formation of entrepreneurs in any era. His conclusions do not contradict the propositions of Weber and McClelland, but instead incorporate them into a larger framework. His interpretation accounts for the individual differences in philosophy and conduct that obviously exist within the business community. Those differences are real, and it is impossible to speak of business opinion as more monolithic than that of any other occupational group.

In general, American entrepreneurs respect private property and the right to acquire it. They praise the virtues of free competition, in theory at least if not in practice, and believe opportunities do exist for whoever is willing to work hard enough to take advantage of them. Beyond such broad inclinations, however, American business leaders are a diverse group.

The entrepreneur is the decisive factor in business history and will be the focus of this study of American enterprise. Business has been the engine of the nation's economy, and the outcome is clear. Whether the economy of the United States thrived or floundered has been and still is today a manifestation, as Cochran put it, of "the long shadow of management."[23]

CHAPTER TWO

The Stages of American Capitalism

THE United States has had a private-enterprise economy ever since it became an independent nation in the late eighteenth century. The American colonial economy, while still subject to the constraints of British imperial regulations, also had a business system in which the managers of individual firms possessed a wide measure of freedom. Such a system has a variety of titles—free market, private enterprise, or, more simply, capitalism. Whatever it is called, however, there is general agreement about its principal features.

The Characteristics of Capitalism

The mainspring of any capitalist system is private property, or, more specifically, the legal right to own it. This right often serves as an incentive to acquire even more property. Because one can retain the fruits of one's own labors, an individual is motivated to work all the harder.

In the United States, the right to property is so basic that it is formally guaranteed to all citizens in the Constitution. The Fifth Amendment explicitly forbids arbitrary interference from the federal government by the commands that no person "be deprived of life, liberty, or property, without due process of law" and that no "private property be taken for public use, without just compensation." Interference by state governments is prohibited both by the Fourteenth Amendment and by the clause in Article I, Section 10, which prevents any state from enacting a "law impairing the obligation of contracts."

A second permanent feature of a capitalist system is economic freedom. It includes freedom of enterprise, the right of firms to enter any markets they choose and to conduct their own operations as successfully as their abilities, resources, and even luck allow them. Conversely, consumers have the freedom to buy the products they prefer and to reject those they do not, if they have the money to pay for their purchases. Similarly, workers are free to pick the employment they find most suitable, if they are adequately qualified for it and willing to accept the wages offered.

Another element of capitalism is its reliance upon competition in the marketplace. The marketplace in a capitalist economy is the point or place where the exchange of privately owned goods and services occurs. There an economic unit, such as an individual or a firm, offers to supply its goods or services in exchange for the products or services of others, or as is more likely in a complex society, for their equivalent value in money. That monetary value is the price of the item being exchanged.

In a condition of pure competition, there would be in theory a large number of producing firms, all unfettered by governmental regulations or actions, each seeking to meet consumer needs and wants more successfully than the others. None of these competing units would be powerful enough to control prices in any significant way. It was this classic simplicity of firms competing in an open marketplace that led Adam Smith in *The Wealth of Nations* (1776), his proclamation of capitalism, to praise the wonders wrought by "the invisible hand." The principle, according to Smith, lay in the fact that individuals pursuing their own self-interest were led by the invisible hand of market forces to promote the broader interests of society as a whole.

It is very doubtful that any golden age of pure competition ever existed in the United States or in any other nation, except in the rarified atmosphere of university economics classrooms. Instead, what has existed and persists today is a changing blend of competitive and noncompetitive, or monopolistic, ingredients that poses a continuing public-policy dilemma, as we shall see. While perfect competition has been the theory of capitalism, imperfect capitalism has been the fact.

Finally, American capitalism is a mixed economic system in which both private and public institutions exert influence. Considerable political debate has swirled around what should be the proper limits to the economic activity of public institutions, namely governmental bodies at all levels. Although the ideological disagreements never cease, they are usually differences of degree only.

Government in the United States—local, state, and national—has consistently exercised some control over or participation in the economic sphere. Laissez-faire has never been public policy in America despite occasional rhetorical flourishes to the contrary by conservative speakers and writers.

The functions of government in the United States have ranged from its acknowledged responsibility for external security to the more controversial application of internal police powers to safeguard the life, property, and well-being of citizens. The latter function includes as much direction of the economy as is politically desirable at any time, especially in the regulation of certain activities of private business. In the twentieth century, the government has stepped into entirely new fields. It has, for example, provided far-ranging social services and has transferred income from one segment of the community to another through such programs as unemployment relief and old-age pensions. The foregoing activity has not escaped frequent challenge from commentators who urge either its expansion or its contraction. The only consensus in recent years has been a broad agreement that the government's newfound functions should not be completely abolished. Even a deeply conservative Reagan administration retained what it called "the social safety net."

Stages in History

The characteristics of capitalism under which business in America now operates have not always existed in their present form. They have evolved over time, and historians have devised stage theories to explain this evolution. Historians have long been fascinated by stage speculations. If each stage or time period appears to have its own distinct character, it is easier to grasp the unfolding of history, especially for the layman.

A danger with these theories, however, is that although they are convenient, they are also highly arbitrary. Each designated stage or segment of history contains certain identifiable characteristics, but none can be indisputably fixed to specific beginning or ending dates. Moreover, the impression frequently remains that the special characteristics of one stage exist discretely and are not part of earlier or later stages. History, of course, is not that tidy.

Nevertheless, explaining history through chronological periods can be valuable if the historian does not insist on rigid breaks between stages. Once we grasp the essence of any span of history—that which sets it apart from what has gone before—we can also begin to ask important questions about the change that has taken place—what or who caused it, how pervasive was it, were there ramifications for other sectors or societies, and what was society's response to it?

Business historians have proposed stage theses in order to understand the emergence and spread of our own economic system and the shifting nature of capitalism. We shall examine three notable theses that have been offered.

N. S. B. GRAS AND THE FORMS OF CAPITALISM

In 1927, Norman Scott Brian Gras was recruited by the Harvard Business School from the faculty of the University of Minnesota. His new assignment was to teach the first courses in business history ever offered at Harvard. Gras established business history as a new and legitimate field of concentration for scholars. He trained graduate students, founded journals, edited case studies, and developed his own stage thesis for the subject. He tied the changes in capitalism to the dominant business form at certain times and cited five specific phases: petty, mercantile, industrial, financial, and national capitalism.

Petty capitalism, according to Gras, was the earliest form. Its chief practitioners were the storekeepers, artisans, and traveling merchants who monopolized nearly five thousand years of business history. Actually, individual petty capitalists outlived their own stage of history, which Gras saw as ending in the eighteenth century. While small business has persisted into the nineteenth and twentieth centuries and still represents a numerical majority of business firms, it is no longer the most significant form of enterprise.

Petty capitalism gave way to mercantile capitalism, typified by the "sedentary" merchant, the more successful of whom were popularly labeled "merchant princes." Gras uses the word sedentary because, unlike the earlier traveling merchant, this new entrepreneur remained fixed to his base of operations, the countinghouse. Another term for the sedentary merchant—since no single facet of business activity confined him—is the all-purpose entrepreneur. He was an importer and an exporter, a wholesaler and a retailer. He owned ships that hauled his firm's cargoes, and he acted as a common carrier for others. He carried on an insurance business, was active in banking and real estate, and, when he found sale goods difficult to acquire from his suppliers, he even engaged in some manufacturing operations. Taken together, the volume of his commercial endeavors was enormous compared to those of the petty capitalist, but no individual business function or product line was sufficiently profitable for him to specialize yet.

According to Gras, mercantile capitalism first appeared during the late Middle Ages in such European cities as Antwerp, Bruges, Florence, Marseilles, and Venice. It reached a peak in England in the mid-1700s and from there crossed the Atlantic Ocean to Boston, New York, Philadelphia, and the other principal port cities of colonial America. These port merchants—such as the Hancocks of Boston and the Browns of Providence—were among the richest members of their society and exercised considerable political sway as well.

This political aspect of their power was not duplicated in Europe. There, a large traditional landowning class existed, which jealously guarded access to political power. Indeed, according to historian Edwin J. Perkins: "This factor explains, in part, why outsiders have always perceived the United States as an excessively business-oriented society, highly attuned to mercantile values; no other society possesses such a long tradition of business leadership in its political system."[1]

In Gras's scenario, industrial capitalism followed mercantile capitalism. During this new era, the all-purpose merchant was gradually displaced by the specialist. This change occurred in two ways. The merchant might begin, for instance, to concentrate on just one of his former activities, perhaps banking or transportation, as the volume of business transacted in that line grew sufficiently to offer the promise of considerable profits.

The other path to specialization lay in the coming of the industrial revolution in the eighteenth and nineteenth centuries. An industrial revolution embodies two specific types of changes: a shift from hand tools to power-driven machinery, and the transition from household and small-shop production to a factory system. The sedentary merchant was often the only person in a community with the financial resources and the business experience to assume responsibility for new manufacturing enterprises.

According to Gras, "the halcyon days of industrial capitalism were over in America by the time of the Civil War, except in the case of important new industries."[2] In his view, after 1865, an intense competition developed between rival manufacturing firms that often tested the industrial capitalists beyond their managerial capacities. The emphasis gradually shifted away from simple growth in output to the control of whole industries, the rationalization of competition, and the imposition of order on formerly individualistic producers.

As the economic demands of the era slowly changed, financial capitalism appeared. According to Gras, it began when firms that planned to combine horizontally into monopolistic cartels or to integrate vertically by acquiring their own distribution channels or raw material sources sought the services of financial intermediaries— or "money middlemen," as Gras called them—to raise needed capital. When the middlemen started to exercise significant influence over the actual management of those business organizations, the stage of financial capitalism had arrived. Gras cited J. P. Morgan and Co. as the inaugurator of this period, and he dated the phase from 1879, when Morgan took on the assignment of selling William K. Vanderbilt's stockholdings in the New York Central Railroad. Gras believed that the influence of the financial capitalist ended in 1933 with the advent of Franklin Roosevelt's New Deal reforms.

Finally, N. S. B. Gras speculated, even as he was writing in the 1930s, on the emergence of a fifth form, which he called national capitalism. He said that it was born in Mussolini's Italian fascist state, but that it would reach its greatest potential in the United States. American national capitalism, although defined only vaguely by Gras, could apparently stop somewhat short of outright socialism. It might take the shape of the centralized planning approach, which historians have often cited as characteristic of early New Deal programs. As Gras phrased it: "Instead of control from New York and Wall Street, we shall have under national capitalism to come under the economic dominance of Washington."[3]

Gras's stages were pathbreaking and interesting, but of limited usefulness to contemporary business historians. His perception of a transition from industrial to financial to national capitalism is particularly questionable. Further, Gras himself offered so many cautions to his model that it stood on shaky ground from the beginning.

Nevertheless, in some of its broader aspects, it still serves a purpose. Spotlighting the relative roles of the petty capitalist and the sedentary merchant in business history remains useful. Gras also called attention to other noteworthy elements in business, such as the emergence of investment banking houses, even if their impact was hardly as overwhelming as his model makes them appear. Governmental regulation of American business did take a quantum leap after 1933, but not to the extent implied in Gras's discussion of so-called national capitalism. His discussion was clearly hindered by his proximity to the economic developments he interpreted, and by his venture into the treacherous terrain of prophecy.

HUGHES'S VITAL FEW

Jonathan Hughes took a different approach in the first edition of his *The Vital Few* (1965). Like Gras, he devised a five-part system, but his stages were functional rather than chronological. These "conceptual categories," as Hughes termed them, were functional in that a "nation lives simultaneously in all these stages . . . just as the population includes people in all stages of life, in the whole range of age distribution."[4]

He proposed five simultaneous stages: idealism, invention, innovation, organization, and stagnation and decline. For all but the last, Hughes identified two specific men in American economic history who exemplified each category. His choices were occasionally surprising.

For the first category—idealism—Hughes asserted that novel ideas inevitably face severe resistance from vested interests. This is particularly true when the changes involve such sensitive areas as religious beliefs or social mores and seem to threaten the economic status quo. To continue to press the ideas in the face of a stubborn and hostile opposition demands, according to Hughes, a systematic idealism which borders on fanaticism. As examples of determined idealists who precipitated economic growth, Hughes named William Penn and Brigham Young. Neither is usually mentioned in histories of conventional entrepreneurship.

Hughes's second category—invention—is more common. The inventor supplies "the wares of economic change" and "produces a new range of choice to the seller or user of economic products."[5]

The historical figures which he selected to epitomize the category were obvious choices—Eli Whitney and Thomas Edison.

Hughes correctly distinguished between invention and innovation. In the latter instance, he quoted Schumpeter's depiction of the innovator as the individual who is responsible for new departures in the economic life of a nation. As exemplars of innovative activity, he offers Andrew Carnegie in steel and Henry Ford in the automobile industry.

The stage which Hughes designates as "organization" is almost indistinguishable from Gras's financial capitalism. In it, the organizer matches corporate demands for capital with society's accumulated wealth that is available for potential investment. Here, Hughes was celebrating financial genius and its application to the reorganization of an industry. For his archetypical figures, he named an inescapable choice—J. Pierpont Morgan—and a somewhat less predictable but not unwarranted selection—E. H. Harriman.

In the second and expanded edition of *The Vital Few*, published in 1986, Hughes enlarged on the fifth of his conceptual categories, now termed "bureaucracy," and he added two new biographies to personify the persistence of the entrepreneurial spirit even in the face of organizational gridlock. He states that at some point in their life, organizations tend to cease growing, and it is then that bureaucracy takes over. Bureaucracy is characterized by "routine administration," which prizes order and stability and "abhors the disruption caused by new ideas." The result is that stagnation sets in and decline begins.

Hughes believes preventing "the apparatus of routine from strangling productive enterprise has become the great problem in giant enterprises as well as in government." As he views it: "The heart of the problem is how to motivate thought, originality, energy, and creative innovation into a social organism—the bureaucracy—whose teleology is routine, perfect routine." As proof that it can be done, however, Hughes profiles two "bureaucratic entrepreneurs" who made a difference. They were Mary Switzer, a professional civil servant who played a major role in the formulation of federal social welfare programs for more than forty years before her retirement in 1970, and Marriner Eccles, for seventeen years chairman of the board of governors of the Federal Reserve System. Hughes offers no apologies for choosing federal officials rather than business figures for his case studies in bureaucratic entrepreneurship, arguing the government of the United States is one of history's most awesome bureaucracies. For Hughes, entrepreneurship within either public or private bureaucracy alters the normal flow of resources and achieves change despite the hostility of entrenched conservatism.[6]

Any stage theory is rife with generalizations that suffer during close scrutiny. Hughes's categories are at least as vulnerable as those of Gras. An example is his blanketed indictment of bureaucracy and his contention that bureaucratic management inevitably breeds gridlock and decline. Nevertheless, the device of simultaneous as opposed to successive stages is another useful way of considering business history, even if we do not always agree with the specific divisions.

CHANDLER AND MANAGERIAL CAPITALISM

No scholar writing in the past two decades has shaped the direction of recent business historiography more than Alfred D. Chandler, Jr. Like N. S. B. Gras, his predecessor at the Harvard Business School, he emphasized administrative and institutional developments. His *Strategy and Structure: Chapters in the History of the American Enterprise* and *The Visible Hand: The Managerial Revolution in American Business* are highly acclaimed. Both books, as well as most of his other publications, investigated the growth and structure of the giant corporation in the United States.

For Chandler, modern corporate enterprise has two special characteristics. It encompasses multiple operating units, each theoretically capable of acting as an independent firm. It is also administered by a hierarchy of middle and top managers whose responsibility it is to monitor and coordinate the units they control. No such enterprises existed in the United States in 1840, but within seventy-five years, according to Chandler, "this type of firm had become the dominant business institution in many sectors of the American economy."[7]

In explaining the appearance of this new phenomenon and its rise to prominence, Chandler, too, posited a stage theory of capitalism. In the first stage—traditional or personal capitalism—owners and managers were identical, as owners made both short-term decisions and long-range plans for their firms. During the colonial period in America the sedentary or all-purpose merchant—Gras's mercantile capitalist—still dominated. He dealt in a wide variety of goods and engaged in a multiplicity of business functions, as we have seen.

Within a half-century after American independence, however, the general merchant had been superseded by the specialist. Firms were established or reorganized to concentrate upon just one or two products. Furthermore, firms now specialized in a single business function, such as retailing, wholesaling, or manufacturing.

The appearance of specialization was directly related to the geographic and economic expansion of the United States in the first half of the nineteenth century. A rapidly mounting volume of cotton exports, a developing grain trade in the trans-Appalachian West, and the transportation revolution that took place during the period all combined to create favorable opportunities for profit. Entrepreneurs could now develop expertise in a narrow market area. Even these specialized firms were still within Chandler's first stage of traditional capitalism, whereas in Gras's system they represented an entirely different phase. In Chandler's system, although the number of individual businesses had multiplied rapidly and their activities had become more sharply focused, the style of their internal administration remained essentially the same. They were still owner-managed, single-unit operations. In other words, Chandler wrote, "as late as the 1840s with very few exceptions owners managed and managers owned."[8]

Gradually, a second stage in the evolution of American enterprise emerged. According to Chandler, this stage took one of two forms—family capitalism or financial capitalism—with vestiges of both persisting into the twentieth century. When a company's growth was primarily self-financed by reinvested earnings, descendants of the founders often retained for a time the decision-making authority. But as the organization grew, it soon became impossible for family members to staff all the key middle- or even upper-echelon managerial slots.

Thus, more and more, salaried managers, unrelated by blood to the firm's founders, exercised day-to-day control. Eventually, the role of the founding family was restricted to membership on the board of directors, whose primary concern was an adequate and dependable return on capital. While they might still have the power to intervene and even unseat a current management team if necessary, they rarely used that power. In this sense, therefore, the period of family capitalism is transitional. As Chandler states: "In only a few of the large American enterprises did family members continue to participate for more than two generations in the management of the companies they owned."[9]

In those instances in which the growth of a business depended upon an infusion of considerable outside capital, financial middlemen, as personified most frequently by investment bankers, exercised for a while the same influence that relatives of founding entrepreneurs had under family capitalism. This was often true in transportation (especially railroads), in public utilities, and in some complicated industrial combinations, such as United States Steel. Chandler's stage of financial capitalism coincides here with the financial capitalism of Gras and the organization category of Hughes. For Chandler, though, this phase is of limited duration and considerably less sweeping than it is for Gras.

The participation of financiers in the active management of these enterprises was usually as short-term as that of succeeding generations of blood relatives in family firms. Bankers eschewed middle-management posts and confined their activities to top-level policy making. But over time, their role became a representational one, in which they showed the flag of their banking house and safeguarded the interests of its customers. Although in theory they could veto the actions of the firm's salaried managers, they usually played no important part in real policy formulation or execution.

Both family and financial capitalism waned in the twentieth century. As confirmation, Chandler cites a study conducted in 1963. By that date, in only 15 percent of the nation's two hundred largest nonfinancial firms did any family or group still exercise even minority control of as little as 10 percent of the stock. Phrased another way, 85 percent of these companies were now controlled by a professional, salaried management team.

Firms in which not only middle- but also upper-tier management positions were staffed by career executives became characteristic of the final stage, which Chandler calls managerial capitalism. These teams or hierarchies of salaried managers had little or no equity holdings in the corporations they administered. Managerial capitalism as thus defined has marked the direction of all advanced market-based economies since the last half of the nineteenth century, emerging at approximately the same time in the United States and in Europe, and only somewhat later in Japan.

The first modern managerial enterprises appeared in the fields of transportation and communication during the 1850s and 1860s, as

railroads flung their complex networks across the continent and telegraph companies linked the nation electronically. Soon after, mass
retailing operations, such as metropolitan department stores and mail-
order houses, grew rapidly in size, resulting in substantial increases
in the number of management personnel required to coordinate the
flow of goods and orders. Even greater sizes were attained, however,
by manufacturing firms in those capital-intensive industries in which
rapid technological advances provided opportunities for mass production, accompanied by significant economies of scale and cost advantages over slower-moving competitors. To take advantage of the
new potential, these manufacturers embarked upon strategies of vertical integration. They extended themselves forward toward the consumer by creating their own marketing and distribution systems and
backward by acquiring their own raw materials and assured supply
sources. Some firms invested heavily in research and development
activities as well, thereby extending their product lines, and/or took
on multinational operations with the establishment of foreign marketing branches or even overseas factories.

The executive hierarchy that was necessary to administer these
expanded organizations soon attained not only a dominance over
them but also a permanence that exceeded the life span of individual
shareholders or managers. The professional executives substituted
their expertise for the market forces that had formerly determined
how resources were allocated and how the flow of goods was coordinated between units that might once have been independent but
now were elements in a single business organization. There had taken
place "the substitution of the visible hand of management for what
Adam Smith called the invisible hand of the market mechanisms."[10]

The Use and Limits of Stages

A more extensive discussion of when and how managerial capitalism
came to the fore in the United States and the resulting response from
other segments of society must await later chapters in this book. No
one stage theory, however, can provide a comprehensive picture of
America's sweeping business scene. At best, stage arrangements pin-
point key features and role models, enabling us to understand a
complicated story more readily.

Chandler's visible hand of management, Hughes's conceptual categories, and Gras's line of capitalists each explain an aspect, and in some instances a vital aspect, but not the whole of the story. Nevertheless, the reader should keep these stage frameworks in mind as the following pages describe in greater detail the development of American enterprise from its old-world origins to the maturing of managerial capitalism.

II

THE AGE OF THE MERCHANT

THE roots of American business institutions can be found in Europe in the Middle Ages. The customs, practices, and techniques developed then were carried to America with every shipload of eager colonists crossing the Atlantic, especially as the colonies themselves were, more often than not, business ventures. Thus it is important for us to consider the old-world origins of American enterprise as well as its new-world beginnings.

There were two distinct tensions in this early history of business in America. The first tension was between entrepreneurs and ecclesiastical authority, to some extent a legacy of medieval experience, while the other was between ambitious businessmen here and governmental decision makers and their constituents in England. In each instance, the primary spokesman for the business position was the colonial port merchant, the dominant entrepreneurial type in America before 1800, and an individual who effectively wielded both economic and political power. For that reason and others that will soon become clear, it is entirely appropriate to label the era the Age of the Merchant.

CHAPTER THREE

Old-World Origins

THE seeds of American capitalism—indeed, of capitalism in general—lay in the economic revival that occurred in Europe beginning in the eleventh century. Since the fall of the Roman Empire six hundred years before, the European economy had been in a virtual state of stagnation. Historians have traditionally associated the political fragmentation and near anarchy which characterized the early Middle Ages with the term feudalism, but feudalism also had an economic side.

Economic Life in the Early Middle Ages

The decentralization of politics in feudal society was paralleled by a commercial and industrial insularity. Probably 90 percent of the European population was rural and drew its livelihood, such as it was, from agriculture. One recent authority on the medieval period has conjectured that a Norman peasant in the tenth century, for instance, probably never saw more than three hundred other people in an entire life span.[1]

In such a situation, commerce was overwhelmingly local, and there existed relatively little interregional trade. Industry was primarily household manufacturing, or what an economist might call "usufacture." Such manufacturing consisted of commodities produced in the home for use by the family itself. Those commodities were invariably the staples of everyday existence—food, clothing, furniture, tools—and were of the simplest type.

Since European enterprise in the years between 450 and 1050 was meager, the prevailing social and economic philosophy expressed a similarly static view of life. Reflecting the religious nature of the era, conventional thought stressed life after death and the promise of an eternal reward in heaven. Whatever afflictions had to be endured on earth, therefore, were temporary and only a prelude to the happiness of heaven. Hence, an individual should be content with his or her lot here on earth and not aspire to more. To seek to rise above one's station by the accumulation of money or property was to risk the loss of eternal salvation.

On two particular commercial activities—lending and selling—the doctrine of medieval religion seemed quite specific, at least on the surface. It was usury for a lender to charge interest, and traditional Christian teaching condemned this practice. It was assumed that a borrower was a human being in need, and to exploit someone in such a condition was to fly in the face of the New Testament injunction to love thy neighbor. Usury was a mortal and inexcusable sin for which the punishment was "excommunication and a ban against burial in consecrated grounds or even prayers said for the repose of the usurer's soul after death."[2]

The seller of goods also faced theological strictures. Christian economic doctrine denounced avarice. Merchants were expected to charge no more than a "just price" for any item. Modern scholars are still in some disagreement as to what church authorities actually meant by the term just price. Early writers, such as Augustine, who had an otherworldly orientation, seem to have defined it as that price sufficient to provide the seller a return that covered costs and the needs of a modest standard of living. Later church fathers, such as Thomas Aquinas in the thirteenth century, appear to have meant the existing market price for an article as contrasted with much higher charges stemming from a special and unfair seller advantage which exploited someone's need.

The precepts of usury and just price thus evolved over time. Nevertheless, official standards did exist, and they influenced business conduct for much of the Middle Ages. Hence they were a vivid reflection of the anticapitalist spirit against which budding entrepreneurs had to struggle.

The Forces of Change

The rigid nature of feudal society began to show cracks in the late eleventh century, cracks that widened considerably as time went on.

A combination of factors precipitated an economic revival, which slowly gathered momentum and finally became self-sustaining. The forces for change included a significant increase in the population of western Europe and a trend toward the consolidation of political power in the hands of fewer and stronger monarchs. The commercial effects of the Crusades also upset the status quo because these religious adventures whet Europeans' appetite for the exotic products and luxuries of the Moslem world and the Far East.

Of all the forces creating change, however, none was more important than the activities of an emergent business community. Although medieval entrepreneurs appeared in a variety of models, one of the most basic was the traveling merchant. Even here, though, there was diversity. He might be a humble itinerant peddler carrying in his backpack a staggering assortment of wares, most of which we would call housewares and notions today.

Another, more prestigious, traveling merchant was the trader who dealt in such valuable commodities as Flemish wool, Russian furs, and Mediterranean spices. Economist Robert L. Heilbroner has described the spectacle of the trader en route as "a small irregular procession of armed men, jogging along one of the rudimentary roads of medieval Europe: standard-bearer with colors in the lead, then a military chief, then a group of riders carrying bows and swords, and finally a caravan of horses and mules laden with casks and bales, bags and packs."[3] It was, clearly, a more imposing sight than that of the lone peddler.

The traveling merchant contributed to the development of urban centers. The commercial revival of the eleventh and twelfth centuries was accompanied by the rise of new towns and cities. As peddlers and traders traveled, they sought shelter and protection at night in the shadow of fortified castles or "burgs" built by feudal princes. While there, the merchants engaged in trade with the local population.

Eventually, the frequent presence of peddlers and traders attracted others, who saw possibilities for profit in supplying the needs of the travelers. Soon the commercial community grew too large to be contained within the walls of the fortress, and it spilled over into the sea outside the burg, the *faubourg*, the French word for suburb. As the *faubourg* itself expanded, it eventually surrounded the old fortress, which disappeared as a separate entity. The residents of the whole area became known as burghers, burgesses, or *bourgeoisie*, depending upon the country in which the town was located.

Medieval Fairs and Long-Distance Trade

The traveling merchant was attracted to particular towns or cities by the great wholesale fairs held there. Thus the fair sites became the most important centers of interregional trade in Europe. The great fairs were much more than the simple weekly market days that served the needs of a strictly local population. They lasted for weeks at a time and drew merchandise from long distances. They were the meeting places of far-ranging merchants, who exchanged their goods at wholesale among themselves, and events of great wonder and civic importance. As historian Fernand Braudel has written: "Fairs meant noise, tumult, music, popular rejoicing, the world turned upside down, disorder, and sometimes disturbances."[4]

Such fairs first appeared in the eleventh century and flourished for more than two hundred years. They declined in importance only after traders gradually chose to operate from fixed business locations in the more successful of the new commercial centers.

A fair was usually authorized by the feudal lord or bishop of the district, who saw the enterprise as an opportunity to collect fees from those renting stalls. The fair often had special privileges in order to attract as many buyers and sellers as possible. If disputes arose over transactions, for instance, they could be settled in the merchants' own courts, thus marking the beginning of the development of commercial codes of law. Even the church's prohibition against usury was often temporarily suspended.

Virtually every area in Europe boasted at least one fair, but the most famous and important of all were those held in the Champagne region of northern France. Actually, there was a series of six different fairs held in the counties of Champagne and Brie, providing an almost year-round opportunity for trading. Visitors were drawn from all over Europe, and as one historian has noted: "Goods were of the utmost variety; cloths and woolens from Flanders and northern France; silks imported from Lucca; furs from Germany; linens from Champagne and Germany. To these the Italians added spices, sugar, dyes, and other luxuries."[5]

By the 1300s the large volume of business that was transacted in the bustling, new mercantile cities of Europe was a decisive factor in the decline of the great fairs. These cities were, in effect, continuous fairs. Traveling traders, weary of the road and attracted by a city's level of economic activity, often settled permanently there. As a result, the traveling trader was transformed into a new type of businessman—the sedentary, or resident, merchant.

The Resident Merchant

The resident merchant still maintained his former scope of operations, but now he sent agents into the field, while he directed affairs from a desk in his countinghouse. Although the merchant may have ceased to travel, his goods continued to roam Europe.

The trade conducted by the resident merchant differed from modern commerce in one important respect. Today merchandise is usually sold before it is shipped, but in the period we are discussing, a merchant regularly forwarded goods to some distant point with no assurance that he could sell them. Trading thus involved speculation or "venturing." As one authority on medieval economic life stated: "It is with good reason that the exporters of English cloth called themselves the Merchant Adventurers."[6]

A multitude of perils faced these adventurous merchants in the High Middle Ages. Among them were shipwrecks and pirates on the high seas, robbers and poor roads on land, the uncertainty of prices in foreign markets, the hazards of extending credit to distant borrowers, problems caused by a thicket of varying political jurisdictions and legal systems, and the slowness of communications in general. The combination of these increased the normal risks run by entrepreneurs.

Resident merchants diversified and shared risks in order to protect themselves as much as possible. When they diversified, the merchants "rarely specialized in one line of business; they dealt in all kinds of commodities and tried to take advantage of all profit opportunities that might present themselves."[7] They routinely formed partnerships to share their risks. These were the most common way to join two or more persons in a single venture or a permanent association, and thus to pool resources for projects either too large or too risky for one person alone.

Partnership arrangements differed widely. Some involved an active partner who managed the business and another who supplied only needed capital. Others were family firms, and many of the famous businesses of the period—such as the great banking houses of Florence operated by the Bardi, Peruzzi, and Medici families—took this form.

The early origins of the modern corporation can also be found in a medieval joint venture arrangement, devised by the Italians, in which shares called *loca* were sold. If the enterprise was the construction of a ship, for example, each shareholder was entitled to a portion of the future income earned by the vessel. A merchant who wanted to reduce his risks significantly might own *loca* in several such ventures.

For further protection, the important merchants of a town often banded together in a merchant guild, which maintained an effective monopoly of the wholesale trade. Outsiders were permitted to do business only with guildsmen, and only members could import certain key commodities. The merchant guild also exercised political power. It controlled the town government and negotiated with similar organizations in other communities. All this occurred with the blessing of the feudal prince of the area, who found a single association of businessmen easier to deal with—and to tax—than a bevy of unconnected individuals.

Guilds even established safeguards against the human nature of their members. Regulations prevented an individual merchant member from gaining an advantage over his peers. Laws against forestalling and engrossing were common.

Forestalling was the practice of buying up goods before they reached the market, perhaps by intercepting them on their way to town. Engrossing was any attempt to corner the market in a particular commodity by purchasing the entire available supply. Prohibitions against both these actions are still common. Such bans were carried over from English common law to become part of the American antitrust heritage.

Bills, Books, and Banks

Medieval merchants developed several other noteworthy business procedures, among them the bill of exchange. The bill was a badly

needed device for making payments in distant locales without transporting gold or silver coin. Shipping hard money was both expensive
and hazardous, and, in some political jurisdictions, was even illegal
because of its scarcity.

The earliest known bills of exchange originated in the commercial
cities of Italy in the last half of the twelfth century. The name derives
from the Latin word for document, *bulla*, and from the fact that a
change from one sovereignty's currency to another was frequently
involved. The bill of exchange was like a promissory note, a buyer's
acknowledgment that he had received goods worth a stated sum in
the local currency and that he had incurred an obligation to pay the
seller a given amount in the seller's own currency at some date in
the future. The transaction actually granted credit, too, since the
customer was allowed a period of time to pay for the merchandise.
The financing charge was hidden in either the difference in the two
money amounts quoted or in a manipulation of the foreign exchange
rates in such a manner that the lender was favored.

The basic bill of exchange soon became more complex, but at the
same time more useful, with the introduction of a third party. Like
a modern bank check, it was an order to a named third party to pay
a specified amount to the seller. Usually the third party already owed
money to the buyer whose purchase had begun the transaction.

An example of this type of transaction written in 1399 has survived.
Jacopo Gosco drew it on the merchant-banking House of Bruges. It
ordered the Barcelona branch of Bruges to pay Domenico Sancio a
sum of money owed to him by Gosco. The document read:

> In the name of God, amen. Pay at usance by this first of exchange to
> Domenico Sancio six hundred ecus at 10s. 5d. (Barcelona) per ecu,
> which six hundred ecus at 10s. 5d. per ecu are for the value received
> (here) from Jacopo Gosco, and charge them to our account. God be
> with you.[8]

If the bill were sent directly to Sancio rather than to the Barcelona
branch, and if it called for payment to him at some future date, he
could choose to use it to secure immediate funds. Sancio could carry
the draft to a local banker and, for a fee subtracted in advance—the
practice of discounting the bill—receive most of his money at once.

In addition to credit instruments such as bills of exchange, other
techniques were introduced that minimized or eliminated the need

to ship gold and silver. One of these was "clearing," in which the amounts owed by and to various merchants were tabulated together, canceling most and resulting in the transfer of specie only as a final balancing. This procedure originated when traders met to settle accounts at the conclusion of the Champagne fairs. Other innovations at this time were also crucial for the future of business. The introduction in the twelfth century of Arabic numerals in record keeping and calculations was a welcome advance from the old Roman system. Figures such as 387 were obviously much easier to work with than CCCLXXXVII.

A new method of bookkeeping, which had appeared for the first time in several Italian cities around the year 1300, also gradually spread. For over a thousand years, there had been no major changes in the prevailing crude system of recording transactions. But as trade grew more complex, a new system became necessary. Double-entry bookkeeping filled the need.

A treatise on the subject by Luca Pacioli was published in 1494. His work, *Summa de Arithmetica, Geometria, Proporcioni, et Proporcionalita*, became one of the classics of business literature. Pacioli advised his readers "to arrange all the transactions in such a systematic way that one may understand each one of them at a glance, i.e. by the debit (*debito*—owed to) and credit (*credito*—owed by) method." Unless this was done, merchants "would have no rest and their minds would always be troubled."[9] It was translated into several languages and was the foundation for all later writings on the subject.

Eventually, most resident merchants assumed banking functions as well. They began as simple money changers, trading local coins for foreign ones, and later accepted deposits upon which they paid interest and also made loans. Gradually, it became difficult to tell whether some merchants dealt more in goods or money.

These banking activities brought the merchants into an apparent conflict with the church's official doctrine on usury. At first, interest charges could be concealed in the exchange rate, but by the late Middle Ages the meaning of usury itself began to change. More and more, it meant an excessive rate of return; a reasonable rate was called interest, not usury. A similarly loose interpretation of the medieval concept of just price emerged.

The growing connection between the church and money lenders— particularly the Italian banking houses of Florence—was an important factor in reducing strictures on them. It has been estimated that, by the year 1250, Florence had eight such firms, and the papacy relied upon them for a variety of services, especially the collection of taxes and tithes and the extension of loans. "The Florentine financier's conquest of the Roman Church," as it has been termed, reached a zenith with the selection of two Medici popes, Leo X and Clement VII. When Protestants "assailed the lavish display and demoralization in the Church in the sixteenth century, they were, in fact, denouncing the business men's influence in Rome."[10] Hence it is not surprising that the earlier disapproval of profit making was effectively eliminated.

The merchant-banker was the big businessman of his time, and, like the human representation of large-scale enterprise in any era, he was not universally admired or appreciated. He often appeared too powerful, too greedy, or too ostentatious for the taste of other segments of society. Geoffrey Chaucer wrote a satiric description of one member of this business elite in *Canterbury Tales*:

> There was a merchant with a forked beard, and girt
> In motley gown, and high on horse sat,
> Upon his head a Flemish beaver hat;
> His boots were fastened rather elegantly.
> He spoke his notions out right pompously,
> Stressing the times when he had won, not lost.
> He would the sea were held at any cost
> Across from Middleburgh to Orwell town.
> At money-changing he could make a crown,
> This worthy man kept all his wits well set;
> There was no one could say he was in debt,
> So well he governed all his trade affairs
> With bargains and with borrowings and shares.
> Indeed, he was a worthy man withal,
> But, sooth to say, his name I can't recall.[11]

In one important sense, though, it can be very misleading to refer to medieval merchant-bankers as big businessmen. While such families as the Medicis did indeed head powerful financial institutions, the actual number of personnel employed in their operations, large as they were for the time, was astonishingly small by modern standards. The Medici bank in the fifteenth century in all its several branches together with the home office in Florence still required the services of less than sixty people to carry on its far-flung activities.

Artisans, Shops, and Guilds

Along with the commercial revival in Europe in the latter half of the Middle Ages, there was a corresponding revival in industrial production. While usufacture—manufacturing in the home for the family's own consumption—remained a major source of basic goods, not everything could be produced in that fashion. Some items required special skills, tools, or ingredients that a rural family did not possess. But as Europe's population increased and the trend toward urbanization gathered momentum, opportunities to specialize increased for persons with particular craft skills. Towns and cities provided enough potential customers for skilled artisans to open permanent workshops and begin producing goods for the new urban market.

Typically, the craftsman operated out of a small shop located at the front of his home. He usually owned his tools and materials and sold the finished wares within the town itself or to customers who lived in the nearby countryside. He was both an artisan and an entrepreneur, since he bore the risks of producing the goods. However, the degree of entrepreneurship inherent in small-shop manufacturing during the Middle Ages was circumscribed. Many craftsmen were closely regulated and well protected by the guilds to which they belonged.

Although a few guilds had a continuous existence from the days of the old Roman Empire, the commercial revival of the eleventh century saw the founding of scores of new guilds. It is estimated, for example, that by the thirteenth century there were over one hundred in Paris alone, including the shoemakers, fishmongers, furriers, jewelers, tailors, ropemakers, and rugmakers, among the more important.[12] Not every medieval artisan belonged to a craft guild, but those in the more important towns usually did. The association was made even easier because persons with the same occupation tended to live in the same section of town or even on the same street.

The guild regulations were designed to spread a comprehensive blanket of protection over the members and to guard them against uncontrolled competition from either outsiders or overly ambitious guildsmen. The goal of the guild was a monopoly of the market for its product. This objective was often easy to achieve because the guild usually had the support of the feudal authorities and municipal officials. As with the merchant guild, taxes were simpler to collect and laws were easier to enforce if a lord dealt with an organization rather than individual artisans. The reasoning was not unlike that of modern corporate executives, who often find a union shop an effective way to maintain production discipline.

With a firmly established guild system, entry into a particular craft was difficult, and it became even more so as time passed. A young aspirant had to undergo years of apprenticeship first. The apprenticeship began with formal articles of "indenture." These defined the relationship between the apprentice and the master.

The apprentice, often a boy eight to ten years old, agreed to obey, to be honest and industrious, and to refrain from such vices as drinking or gambling. The master, in turn, would teach the lad everything about the craft, and feed, clothe, house, and discipline him during the apprenticeship. The length of an apprentice's term varied from two to as many as fifteen years, but gradually, in England at least, seven years became the most common length. The apprenticeship system was tightly controlled by the craft guild, including a limitation on the number of apprentices any master might employ. The limitation supposedly insured that an individual apprentice would not be neglected, but, more important, it regulated the number of new craftsmen who would be future competition for established masters.

When the apprentice completed his term, he became a journeyman (from the French word for day, *journée*). He was now a day or wage laborer, free to travel and to work for whatever master he chose for as long as he chose. Moreover, he could now aspire to be a master with his own shop. But the final step upward to master required more than skill in one's craft. The candidate needed sufficient capital to afford an equipped shop and to meet his guild dues. A wife was almost indispensable as well, since she would keep house and prepare meals for the master's apprentices as well as the family.

The path to the top of many crafts became even more difficult for journeymen as guilds became increasingly restrictive to ward off further competition. Ultimately, almost the only way to achieve the rank of master was to be born into or marry into a current master's family. Little upward mobility was possible for unconnected journeymen because they traditionally received low wages, and guild policies were designed to perpetuate the status quo. The result was a new class in society—the "eternal journeyman."[13]

By the end of the medieval era, guilds had developed into privileged clubs of anticompetitive small businessmen who were primarily concerned with their own protection. Inventions or innovations that might permit one master to gain a step on the others were treated with hostility. Similarly, prices, wages, and maximum hours of work were carefully prescribed in order to prevent an excessive supply of goods, which would depress the market.

Work on Sunday or on holy days was prohibited, for instance, to prevent the less pious from gaining some unfair advantage over their more virtuous guild-brothers. Members were even routinely forbidden from openly soliciting passing customers in the streets by ostentatious actions or displays.

Henri Pirenne, a distinguished medievalist, concluded: "No one was permitted to harm others by methods which enabled him to produce more quickly and more cheaply than they. Technical progress took on the appearance of disloyalty. The ideal was stable conditions in a stable society."[14]

A craft guild could not frustrate change forever. As the export trade in such desirable products as Flemish woolen or Italian silk cloth gained momentum, aggressive merchant-capitalists began to undermine the settled world of the guilds. These merchants were anxious to stimulate production so that they could satisfy the strong popular demand and earn lucrative profits.

One method was to contract with several individual master craftsmen for the entire output of their shops. The merchant supplied the necessary raw materials (the "putting-out system") and any needed working capital and then handled the distribution of the finished product. The craftsmen became dependent upon their merchant employers and on the vagaries of foreign markets. The master now found that he was reduced to the status of a mere wage earner, not unlike a journeyman.

Another method that merchant-capitalists used was to encourage shop production in smaller communities where guilds did not exist or were relatively weak. There, specific steps in the process—such as spinning or weaving in the manufacture of cloth—were performed in workers' homes as well as in small shops. Again, the merchant supplied materials and collected the finished or semifinished product. In that way, the merchant could pay lower wages and offer lower-priced goods in the market. This production approach became known as the "domestic" system. It persisted in some industries and in some countries, including the United States, well into the nineteenth century.

Expansion Overseas

The 1500s represent a major watershed in the stream of western civilization because they contained the convergence of several historical movements. Some, such as the rise of strong national states and the intensification of a capitalist spirit, were already well under way, while others, such as the Protestant revolt against the Roman Catholic Church, represented new surges of enormous significance. The overseas expansion of European nations that took place at the close of the Middle Ages was both the result of important advances in economic history and the cause of others to come.

The immediate impetus for the outward thrust from Europe was the search for new routes to the Far East, which would break a Venetian monopoly of the trade in spices and luxury goods. Recent progress in maritime technology, which made long overseas voyages possible, had made the search more feasible. By 1500 ship design had attained "almost the form it was to retain until the middle of the nineteenth century."[15] Also essential were such aids to navigation as an improved compass, the astrolabe to determine latitude, and better maps and charts.

During the sixteenth century, leadership in discovery and exploration was taken first by the Portuguese and then by the Spanish. In the next century, the English, Dutch, and French took the lead. Throughout the 1400s, the Portuguese probed farther and farther down the west coast of Africa until, at last, Bartholomeu Dias rounded the Cape of Good Hope in 1488. Within the span of only one hundred years, transoceanic voyages became frequent, though still risky. By 1600, "European merchant ships were carrying goods regularly across the Atlantic and the Indian Ocean, even in small quantities across the Pacific; and many of the distant harbours to which they plied were under European control."[16]

The economic consequences of exploration and expansion were enormous and varied. Greater quantities of known commodities were imported from the overseas areas, and products such as tobacco, which were previously unknown in Europe, made their appearance as well. Conversely, old-world goods, especially manufactured articles, reached wider markets than ever before.

The founding of overseas empires in Africa and in Latin America produced a huge inflow of gold and silver. The supply of precious metals was so great that it has been estimated that the stock of bullion in Europe more than tripled in the years between 1500 and 1650. The consequence of this increase was a price revolution. As the quantity of money in circulation climbed, prices doubled and even tripled.

The rise in prices created havoc for wage laborers whose incomes lagged far behind the increasing costs of the goods they wished to purchase. On the other hand, the inflation furnished business with an opportunity for larger profits than ever before. Entrepreneurs benefited from the lower relative wage rates they paid to workers and from the increased value of inventories on hand.

ORGANIZING FOR OVERSEAS INVESTMENT

The new worldwide commerce created ripe fields for the investment of European capital, but to take full advantage of the possibilities fresh forms of business organizations were required. There were two problems: one was the high risk associated with a foreign venture, and the other was the substantial cost of any enterprise. An outlay equivalent to $500,000 or more in modern American currency was needed to dispatch just four ships to the Far East in 1600, and one ship of the four could not be expected to return.[17]

For the English, Dutch, and French, and to some extent for the Spanish, the responsibility for financing overseas activities rested upon private entrepreneurs. In England, for example, the crown lacked the capability to undertake the task. Elizabeth had the inclination and did invest what funds she could in an occasional project, such as a raiding expedition by Francis Drake, but she did not have the resources to make empire building a royal monopoly. The succeeding Stuart monarchs not only had the same insufficiency of resources, they also faced a continuing internal struggle with Parliament throughout most of the seventeenth century that commanded their principal attention.

A new way to accumulate private capital for such ventures grew out of the medieval partnerships of merchant-capitalists. From the early 1600s, the joint stock company—a partnership of capital rather than persons—began to develop. It was the predecessor of the modern corporation and a new plateau in the evolution of business organization.

The joint stock company represented a pool of capital which was administered by the company's officers for the purpose of engaging in some enterprise. There might be many investors, who usually had little interest in managing the affairs of the company, but who shared in the eventual profits. Shepard Clough has summarized the advantages of the joint stock company: "It furnished the public a way of putting its capital to work, even in small amounts, without involving the investors in complicated tasks; it limited investors' liability, and it permitted the stockholder to get cash when needed by the simple expedient of selling some or all of his holdings."[18]

Like the later corporation, another advantage of the joint stock company was its permanence, since it was not dissolved by the death or the departure of the participants. The overseas trade required this degree of permanence. Voyages were lengthy, and the penetration of virgin regions or markets could not promise prompt returns on one's investment.

The joint stock instrument was used successfully to finance Francis Drake's privateering expedition in 1577–1580 against the Spanish. It has been estimated that the venture cost £5,000 and returned a profit of 4,600 percent to its sponsors, who included the queen. Not surprisingly, Drake was knighted after landing in England.

In the seventeenth century, the formation of joint stock companies reached full flower. Companies were formed in England to make rivers navigable, to engage in banking—the Bank of England was founded in 1694—and to secure wealth from intercontinental trade. In the process, the role of merchant-capitalist was central. It has been noted that "everywhere merchants provided the bulk of the capital for overseas voyages, and it was they who carried the companies into the new lands."[19]

AT THE BRINK

In 1600, therefore, private capital and entrepreneurs were ready to lead the way in planting colonies on the coast of North America. Those capitalists who invested in the new world represented a transitional generation. While they were, essentially, the first American entrepreneurs, they were also the human culmination of a six-hundred-year-old business revolution that began when an agrarian feudal society still seemed well entrenched. By the beginning of the seventeenth century, that revolution had produced a business community that had commercial and organizational experience and was financially able to launch the new American empire.

While we have referred to the merchant-entrepreneurs of this era as "capitalists," it should be mentioned that the term "capitalism" was not in use as yet. In his masterly study of European capitalism's development in the late Middle Ages, Fernand Braudel points out that the word "capitalist" probably dates from the seventeenth century. A Dutch tax levied in 1699, for instance, distinguished between "capitalists," who would pay the sum of 30 florins, and others, presumably poorer, who would pay less. On the other hand, "capitalism" was rarely used before the twentieth century. It was not even the subject of an article in the *Encyclopaedia Britannica* until 1926.[20] Whether the word was applied to it or not, by the seventeenth century the system was emerging from a medieval society that had, according to Braudel, "created a favourable environment from far back in time, without being aware in the slightest of the process thus being set in train, or the processes for which it was preparing the way in future centuries."[21]

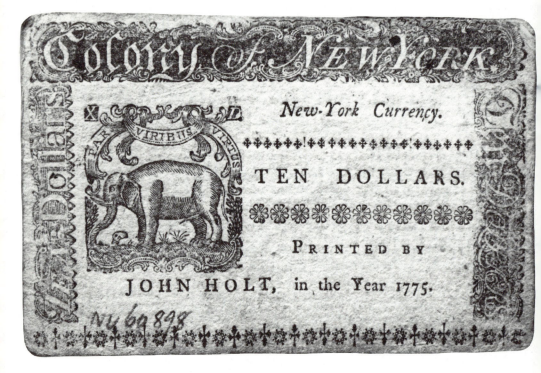

CHAPTER FOUR

New-World Beginnings

THE profit motive was a central factor in the establishment of most of the mainland colonies in North America. Four of the colonies were founded by joint stock companies: Virginia, by the Virginia Company of London, which was made up of prominent London merchants and speculating nobles and landed gentry; Massachusetts, by the Plymouth and the Massachusetts Bay companies; New York (or New Amsterdam), by the Dutch West India Company; and Delaware, by the Swedish New South Company. Several other colonies emerged primarily because individual entrepreneurs, called proprietors, wanted to reap fortunes from real estate investments in the new world. The proprietors of Maryland, the Carolinas, New Jersey, and Pennsylvania were America's first important real estate developers. From its beginning, the history of the future United States was infused with the energy of private enterprise.

England Overseas

In the spring of 1607, three small vessels, dispatched from England four months before by "The Treasurer and Company of Adventurers and Planters of the City of London for the First Colony in Virginia," sailed into Chesapeake Bay. The passengers quickly organized a primitive settlement at a site named Jamestown in honor of their reigning monarch, James I. Although it became the first permanent English settlement in America, Virginia was at the time only the latest in a series of overseas business ventures undertaken by English entrepreneurs.

By 1607 merchant-capitalists in London had accumulated a half century of experience in the use of joint stock companies to promote foreign trade. Predecessors of the Virginia Company were the Russia (or Muscovy) Company in the 1550s, the Levant Company in the 1580s, and, most important of all, the East India Company, chartered in 1600. Merchants who had been active in the Russia and Levant companies were prominent in the formation of the East India Company, and they profited handsomely from the latter's trade with India and the Far East. Successful East India investors and speculators who were envious of that company's success both took the lead in securing the Virginia Company charter from the king in 1606.

These investors hoped to succeed in North America with the same business practices that had been effective in earlier investments. But the Virginia Company—and American business—had to learn a painful lesson about flexibility and adaptability to changed conditions.

In Asia, trading posts or forts were erected at strategic points along the coastline. There the native populations brought exotic local products and exchanged them for European goods. These transactions benefited the shareholders of the joint stock company that financed the enterprise. The company employees sent from England to staff the trading posts were not required to engage in any significant production efforts to support themselves. But this method, which was valid in the operations of the East India Company, proved totally inappropriate in Virginia.

The Virginia Lesson

During its first two decades, the colony of Virginia was a plantation owned by a profit-seeking corporation. Its investors at home presumed that they would soon see ships returning from North America with the same cargoes of precious metals that the Spanish had extracted from Latin America. At the least they expected tradable products that were in heavy demand in Europe, such as those that the East India Company had imported from its overseas posts. As one historian of colonial America has written: "The hard-headed merchants of London and Bristol . . . were convinced that the new world could supply commodities that they were accustomed to buy at great cost and risk from the Mediterranean countries, from the Baltic region, and from Russia."[1] The reality proved otherwise.

Two-thirds of the original Jamestown settlers perished within the first year because neither the company nor its American employees were prepared for the isolation of the outpost, the severity of its environment, or the absence of the riches that the settlers had presumed awaited them. The first settlers dreamed only of easy wealth and were loath to undertake the hard work necessary to build a stable community. Moreover, when profits were not forthcoming, additional working capital was hard to raise in England.

Many stockholders had made only partial payments on their purchased shares, expecting to meet their second installments with the income from the first. But when they earned no profits, they made no more payments, and the company resorted to legal actions in order to force recalcitrant investors to fulfill their obligations. Two hundred and fifty years later pioneer railroad corporations sometimes found themselves in the same situation when speculators in premature enterprises, as they have been called by economists, fled as soon as sweet dreams turned into sour reality.

During the next two decades the Virginia Company fought for its own corporate survival and changed its philosophy and its business strategy as needed. Royal permission to operate a lottery helped it for a while. This would not be the last time in American history that the public's appetite for gambling would produce badly needed revenue for a failing project.

Gradually, company officials in England recognized the need to decentralize authority and control over the affairs of their American colony if they hoped to encourage more individual initiative. The ownership of land, for example, was initially a company monopoly. Now it was used as a device to attract new settlers. Every person who bought a share in the company or agreed to settle in Virginia was entitled to a "headright" of one hundred acres of land along with another fifty acres for each member of his household for whom he paid transportation to America.

To an ambitious Englishman, the attraction of becoming a landowner in Virginia was compelling; the possession of property was the mark of a gentleman in England, where land was scarce and expensive. Political decentralization soon followed the company's abandonment of its land monopoly. Local self-government appeared for the first time in American history in 1619 with the formation of a representative assembly, the Virginia House of Burgesses.

The chief economic problem of the colony was the lack of a marketable product which could be exported profitably. John Rolfe solved the problem in 1613 when he successfully cured tobacco grown from West Indian seeds. Tobacco was an ideal cash crop because it grew well in Virginia's climate and could be grown and processed with the simple tools and unsophisticated labor available in the colony.

There was also a rising demand for tobacco in England. From the time that Sir Walter Raleigh introduced Englishmen to its use in the previous century, they had imported almost all of their tobacco from Spain's colonies in Latin America. Both royal officials and London merchants disliked this dependency. By 1620 the situation had changed. The new Virginia planters secured from the crown a monopoly of the English market in return for the requirement that they export the entire tobacco crop of the colony only to England. At first, the contract appeared to favor the planters, so tobacco production boomed and the population of Virginia began to swell.

Virginia planters by 1627 were exporting over 500,000 pounds of tobacco a year; the result was a gradual decline in the price they received. For the next century and a half, in fact, colonial legislatures were often called upon to battle the chronic problem of oversupply and a depressed tobacco market in England, and they responded with schemes for crop control reminiscent of New Deal farm programs of the 1930s. "By the middle of the 18th century," one historian has written, "many people both in the colonies and the mother country had come to regard Virginia and tobacco as synonymous."[2]

The colony's tobacco boom came too late to save the joint stock company that organized it. Internal quarrels, mismanagement, and a variety of other economic and political woes forced the Virginia Company into bankruptcy by 1624. Virginia itself continued as a royal colony, but the company was dissolved by formal act of James I, who had brought it into existence by charter in 1606.

American entrepreneurs learned valuable lessons from the experience of the Virginia Company. Absentee management had proved a mistake; because of poor communication facilities, a large measure of local control was necessary. Another fatal error was the desire for a quick return on investment from a project that called for long-term, patient development. The company also had inadequate knowledge of the colony's potential—gold and silver were not awaiting collection on Virginia's beaches, and the natives were not able to exchange valuable commodities for European trinkets. Finally, en-

trepreneurs learned that it was important to encourage personal initiative within an enterprise and to merge the individual drive for
the acquisition of wealth with the interests of the overall organization.

The Penn Experience

By the time that it collapsed, the Virginia Company had spent approximately £200,000 in its American venture—a huge sum for the
early seventeenth century—and it had derived no appreciable profits
from the investment. On the whole, other company-operated projects in North America fared little better, and the corporate approach
was soon abandoned. Instead, leadership in new colonization schemes
fell to individual wealthy Englishmen to whom the king assigned
enormous grants of land.

The grantees or proprietors, as they were known, were America's
earliest real estate developers. They hoped to derive their incomes
from either the sale or rental of their land allotments. For one of
the most prominent proprietors, William Penn, the profit motive was
accompanied by a humanitarian concern. Although Penn hoped to
profit from his land (granted by Charles II in 1681), he also saw the
American property as a refuge for oppressed religious minorities,
especially for his own Quakers. It was his "Holy Experiment."[3]

Buyers could purchase parcels of land from Penn ranging up to
twenty thousand acres for the sale price plus an annual quitrent. The
latter was a relic of feudalism, a single yearly cash payment that
freed a vassal from the duty of performing feudal services for a lord.
In Pennsylvania, the quitrent was a shilling per every hundred acres.
Penn also rented farms as small as two hundred acres to settlers
without money to buy their own land.

In the manner of a modern business executive, Penn ardently advertised his own product. He wrote a series of promotional pamphlets
that were translated into several languages in order to reach potential
customers on the European continent. In one, *A Letter from William
Penn*, published in 1683, his readers learned that "the air is sweet
and clear, the heavens serene" in Pennsylvania. In writing about the
city of Philadelphia two years later in another advertisement, Penn
sounded like an eager twentieth-century real estate salesman: "The
improvement of the place is best measured by the advance of value

upon every man's lot. I will venture to say that the worst lot in the town, without any improvement upon it, is worth four times more than it was when it was laid out, and the best forty."[4]

Penn did not repeat the Virginia Company's early mistake of attempting to direct the affairs of his colony from across the Atlantic. Instead, he drafted for his colonists what amounted to a constitution and a bill of rights, the Frame of Government and Charter of Liberties of Pennsylvania. These documents effectively provided home rule for the colony even though Penn in England was still its absolute owner.

In the end, Penn's financial experience as proprietor was not much more successful than that of the Virginia Company. By his own reckoning his Pennsylvania investment resulted in a net loss for him of some £30,000. According to Jonathan Hughes: "When Penn died on July 30, 1718, he was not penniless, although he came close enough."[5] Although Pennsylvania continued as a proprietary colony owned by the Penn family until the American Revolution, the quit-rents, supposedly a key source of income for the proprietors, were not only difficult to collect but also a constant source of political friction with the citizens of the colony. Finally, the new state government formed during the Revolution abolished all proprietary rights and confiscated even the family's private estates.

The Colonial Merchants

Joint stock enterprises such as the Virginia Company and proprietors such as William Penn comprised America's first generation of business firms and businessmen. Nevertheless, they were essentially old-world elements in the economic life of the new American society. The entrepreneurs who lived in the colonies during the seventeenth and eighteenth centuries were more important in the development of a business tradition in the United States.

Numerically, they were a small minority in a population that was overwhelmingly agrarian. As late as the Revolutionary period, up to 90 percent of the people in the thirteen colonies derived their principal incomes from agriculture. Only the remaining 10 percent resided mainly in towns and cities, the loci of the colonial businessman.

Just as in Europe, the new American business community was divided into two categories—merchants and craftsmen. The first category, at least, was broad indeed. It encompassed wealthy export-import traders in cities such as Boston and Philadelphia—the new-world equivalents of the great resident merchant-capitalists of Europe—and small storekeepers in the colonial backcountry. It even included some individuals who are not ordinarily regarded as members of a mercantile class—the tobacco planters of the Chesapeake and the rice and indigo growers of the Deep South.

The colonial merchant presided over a stream of commerce that ran from the outlying farmers of the Appalachian West across the Atlantic to England and Europe, as well as southward to Spanish America and the islands of the Caribbean. At one end of the stream, on the western frontier, the merchant was a country storekeeper who frequently farmed a small plot of his own land at the same time to make ends meet. The storekeeper provided an essential service for his area by accepting crop surpluses from neighboring farmers in exchange for those few manufactured goods that a rural family required but could not produce for itself. Probably a majority of farmers, Stuart Bruchey has suggested, "devoted at least part of their labor and land to the growth of a marketable product—a patch of tobacco or a stand of timber yielding lumber for barrel heads or staves, or tar, pitch, and turpentine (naval stores)."[6]

The all-purpose merchant of the port cities was the central figure in colonial commerce. The port merchant's major role in the economic life of the colonies was the inevitable result of geography, especially in the northern colonies. The South had a climate and soil conducive to the cultivation of the staple crops in demand in England. New England, on the other hand, had rocky topography and poor soil, so the prospects for the development of exportable cash crops were limited. Even in the so-called bread colonies of New York, New Jersey, and Pennsylvania, the grain and flour produced duplicated what could be grown in England. Markets for these colonial products had to be developed elsewhere in order to generate the means to pay for needed imports.

Promising opportunities for colonial merchants to manage trade occurred as markets were found for American products in England, Europe, and Africa, and as an expanding American population consumed an increasing volume of imported goods. If an aristocracy of the soil emerged in the southern colonies, then the North soon had its own aristocracy of the countinghouse.

Business in a Puritan Society

The mercantile class that eventually dominated life in New England suffered some early bruises on its journey to commercial and social leadership. Massachusetts Bay was a Puritan commonwealth, founded by conservative Calvinists for whom religious considerations permeated all aspects of everyday life, including the economic. As good Calvinists, the Puritans of Massachusetts Bay naturally stressed the virtues of thrift, hard work, and sobriety, and regarded a measure of material well-being as a signal of salvation. Such beliefs coincided well with the accepted standards of conduct for business success, and to that extent Calvinist precepts supported the operations of New England merchants.

On the other hand, the Puritan ethic also had its restrictive side. Although one should strive for success in one's vocation, the goal ought not to be personal gain but rather the greater glory of God. Restraint was even more essential for the merchant, as the Puritans, going well beyond European Calvinism, regarded trade as a morally dangerous field of human endeavor. Bernard Bailyn has described the supposed predicament: "The soul of the merchant was constantly exposed to sin by virtue of his control of goods necessary to other people."[7] Rather than take advantage of this economic position, the Puritan businessman was expected to be content with simply a just price for his merchandise, ironically a viewpoint little changed from that of the medieval church fathers hundreds of years before the Protestant Reformation.

The inherent conflict in Puritan thinking became evident with the trial of Boston merchant Robert Keayne. Born a butcher's son in England, Keayne became a prominent merchant tailor in London. Because of his religious beliefs, he immigrated to Massachusetts in 1635. He quickly set himself up in business there as an importer of English manufactured goods and profited because the demand for such goods was much greater than the supply.

Then, in 1639, Keayne's world collapsed. He found himself facing the highest court in the colony, accused of charging excessive prices for items as mundane as a bag of nails, gold buttons, thread, and a bridle. The accusations claimed that the merchant reaped "above six-pence in the shilling profit; in some above eight-pence; and in some small things, above two for one."[8] Keayne was fined by the civil court, and then had to defend himself before the religious authorities of the colony. Even though he had a reputation as an ardent supporter of the church and a generous benefactor of charitable causes, Keayne barely escaped excommunication, and suffered instead a stern and embarrassing reprimand.

Keayne never believed that he had committed any wrong, civil or religious. Shortly before his death in the 1650s, he composed a detailed (50,000-word) defense of his conduct years before. In it he maintained that he had acted no differently from his peers then and since. It was apparent that Keayne never really understood that he and the Puritan establishment that condemned him were reading the same Calvinist text in two different ways.

According to Keayne, he always adhered to Calvinist teachings and never succumbed to "an idle, laxie, or dronish life," but was subjected to public attack nonetheless.[9] The business success that should have marked him as among God's chosen was instead the basis for his condemnation. His enemies charged that he put his own self-interest above that of the common good and so was guilty of avarice.

The Keayne episode also reflected the divergent old-world backgrounds of the antagonists. The early civic and religious leaders of the Puritan colony traced their roots back to the independent farmers or tenants of rural England. The merchant community of Boston was, in general, city-bred, raised in London and the other chief ports of England, and possessed previous business experience at some level. Bernard Bailyn has explained the tension in this fashion: "Freed from the complexities and competition of the Old World cities and trained in some aspect of the production and distribution of goods, the merchants experienced a release of energies in America which frequently struck the Puritan leaders as brashness and insubordination. Conflict between men who had risen through the struggles of city life and the leaders of the Puritan Commonwealth was implicit from the start."[10]

Eventually Puritan religious fervor declined in New England, especially after the Stuarts were restored to the throne in 1660. Despite the warning of clerical voices that "worldly gain was not the end and design of the people of New England," talk of trade rather than the Bible dominated conversations in Boston by the late seventeenth century.[11] A capitalist spirit and a merchant elite gradually superseded the authority of the pulpit.

In keeping with the new spirit, handsome residences were constructed and filled with European luxuries as visible evidence of accumulated wealth. Moreover, material affluence led to political power as the emergent merchant princes of New England filled the posts of local selectmen, judges, and colonial legislators. The new oligarchy even perpetuated itself through extensive intermarriage. The trend was reinforced by the tendency of widows and widowers to remarry within their own class. Richard Wharton, for example, married daughters from three different leading commercial families—Tyng, Higginson, and Winthrop.

Most appalling to ministers of the old order was that the new generation of businessmen no longer regarded membership in a Puritan church as an essential feature of their lives. They even exhibited a tendency to affiliate with the Church of England, emulating the English merchants with whom they traded. By the 1700s they could be described as "cultivated, imaginative, acquisitive individuals who as gentlemen of commerce moved easily across international borders in their social and business pursuits."[12]

The House of Hancock

A vivid picture of the operations of colonial port merchants can be drawn by focusing on the career of Thomas Hancock of Boston. He exemplified the most successful of that entrepreneurial class.

Thomas Hancock was born in Massachusetts in 1703 and was the son of a minister. He was the uncle of John Hancock, the signer of the Declaration of Independence. In his teens, he was apprenticed to a Boston bookbinder, learned the trade, and eventually opened his own shop on Ann Street where he sold and bound books. His business ability brought him success from the start, but, as was often the case with colonial merchants in America, his expanding volume of trade was matched by an increase in indebtedness to his British suppliers. American importers depended on their agents in England for credit as well as merchandise.

By the late 1720s Hancock had taken on other lines of goods and was engaged in a general import-export business. Some of the capital that permitted the expansion seems to have come from a fortunate marriage to the daughter of another prosperous merchant. Necessity also played a major role in the diversification of his operations. A persistent shortage of hard money in the colonies required Hancock and other merchants to accept payment for goods in kind. Thus, as his business grew, so did the variety of items he accumulated in trade.

Hancock, like most port merchants, operated a general store not only to sell the manufactured goods he imported but also to dispose of the odd items he accepted in return for the imports. Textiles and clothing made up the largest portion of the merchandise he sold, but hardware, provisions, rum, and tea were also important. By mid-century, books, his original merchandise, occupied only "a tiny corner" of the store and accounted for less than 1 percent of its overall sales.[13]

While Hancock sold at both wholesale and retail, the former gradually predominated. His American market stretched along the Atlantic coast and into the interior areas of New England as well as to other merchants in Boston itself. Sometimes rural customers forwarded orders for merchandise by small coasting vessels, and the shipments were returned in the same fashion. Thus Hancock's firm was a colonial prototype of later mail-order houses.

Customers routinely expected to obtain credit on their purchases. Terms of six months to one year were common, and longer periods were negotiable. Although a 6 percent interest charge was usually assessed on overdue accounts, merchants seldom made vigorous efforts to collect the unpaid balances. A combination of poor communications and the chronic specie shortage forced merchants such as Hancock to accept on their books accounts receivable that were as slow as the molasses the merchants sold. These colonial merchants were in turn equally dilatory with their own suppliers in England. Accounts often remained unpaid for years.

The commercial activities of the House of Hancock had two distinct but related sides. On the one hand, there was the "home trade," and, on the other, were its foreign operations, which consisted of the export of American products to England, the European continent, Africa, or the West Indies. The long voyages and other uncertainties characteristic of sales in such overseas markets made personal supervision impossible and increased the business risks considerably. Hancock therefore relied upon partnerships with other merchants to reduce his potential for financial loss, and he depended on agents in overseas ports to make many on-the-spot decisions for him.

Competent agents in foreign ports were the most important factor in successful long-distance trading. Hancock undertook few ventures without the assistance, at the distant point of sale, of a representative who possessed the authority to make rapid business decisions. On the rare occasions when he had no commercial counterpart in a particular trading area, he relied instead on the good judgment of the Yankee ship's captain who transported the shipment or on a designated "supercargo," a traveling agent who accompanied the goods on board ship. The latter individual was often a young relative or a friend's son just embarking upon a business career.

Agency transactions were usually handled in the following manner: Hancock shipped a cargo such as whale oil to his London agents, Kilby and Barnard. They in turn sold the oil in London and charged the Bostonian a commission for services. Along with the whale oil, Hancock usually sent an order for a return shipment of goods. Kilby and Barnard purchased the requested merchandise, charged a commission for that task also, and then arranged for transportation back to Boston.

If the value of the whale oil was less than the cost of the returning goods, a common situation, the London firm advanced the difference to Hancock. Over time, English agents carried American merchants on credit for considerable sums. Often too, the Englishmen asked Hancock to purchase American goods for them, a service for which Hancock charged his own 5 percent commission. The purchases in America were apparently made as much to help settle the long-outstanding debts of colonial traders as to acquire wares for sale in England.

The prices that merchants charged on both sides of the Atlantic varied with the terms of individual transactions. The lowest prices were offered for cash sales. On credit sales, Hancock's markups might reach 100–200 percent above his cost, depending upon the length of credit extended. The actual profit, however, was not as substantial as the high markups implied.

An importer such as Hancock had to take into account not only the cost of goods sold but also the burdensome freight charges that stemmed from the poor transportation system in the colonies. Freighting might add as much as 20 percent to the original cost. A merchant also had to account for credit losses in the form of uncollectible receivables and the relatively slow turnover in the firm's inventory. Of course, if a wholesale merchant such as Hancock set his markup at two or three times the cost of the merchandise, the further markup imposed by the country storekeeper who sold at retail meant high prices indeed for colonial consumers.

Like their British counterparts, American port merchants engaged in a variety of other business activities. Among these was the assumption of banking functions. Since there were no banks in the colonies before the late eighteenth century, merchants acted in their place. Other businessmen often left money on deposit in Hancock's care because he had a reputation for integrity and financial stability. The House of Hancock in turn allowed the depositor to remove his funds on demand, and it honored any bills of exchange drawn on the depositor's account. In keeping with normal banking practice, Hancock invested the funds deposited with him in everything from the securities issued by the colonial government to lottery tickets—in the latter usually without much success.

Hancock added real estate speculation and the conduct of manufacturing and mining operations to his various business activities. He purchased properties in both Boston and rural New England, and even secured title to a pair of remote islands off Nova Scotia in the hope of developing future settlements there. The Nova Scotia project was a failure. At one time or another, Hancock was also a partner in a copper mine, an iron ore mine, a paper mill, a rum distillery, and a shipbuilding enterprise.

The success or failure of any manufacturing or mining investment that Hancock made seemed to depend upon the technical talent he found to supervise operations. Since Hancock lacked such expertise himself and since he chose not to give up his mercantile activities in order to acquire it, the ventures were profitable only if he found an experienced and competent manager. In the American colonies, where the industrial revolution had not yet occurred, such specialized talent was still in short supply. Hancock's biographer, noting the checkered results of the merchant's industrial enterprises, commented accurately that they were undertaken "half-a-century too soon."[14]

Thomas Hancock died on August 1, 1764, at the age of sixty-one. His nephew John succeeded him as head of the firm, but he proved to be a better politician than businessman. At the time of his death, Thomas Hancock left a fortune of some £100,000, one of the largest estates of the colonial period.

Hancock's scope of operations was typical of the major all-purpose merchants of his era. Stuart Bruchey has summarized the almost awesome range of responsibilities among this class of businessmen:

In changing contexts provided by government action or inaction and by rising and falling markets in peacetime and war, merchants had to decide such questions as what commodities to invest in and where to buy them, where and when to ship them and in what assortments, whether to consign their goods to ship captain, supercargo, or resident merchant, whether to invest in vessels or freight spaces, what goods to have purchased as returns, whether to invest part of the proceeds of the outward cargo in bills of exchange, where to dispose of return cargoes: by reshipment or by sale in the local market, and, if the latter, what credit terms to give and what men to trust, and finally, how to employ the proceeds of business: i.e. how to balance investments between ships, or shipshares, commodities, warehouses, bonds or notes, real estate, and, later, stocks.[15]

The multiplicity of entrepreneurial decisions required of a colonial port merchant was alleviated only by the slower pace of the ordinary business day. There were few separate transactions in any one day, and so he was free to spend a good deal of time outside his countinghouse. He regularly joined his peers at a favored merchants' exchange or coffeehouse and inspected potential real estate purchases or other investments. But slow-paced day or not, the port merchants of the pre-Revolutionary years represented the first important resident businessmen in what would soon become the United States.

The Southern Entrepreneur

To understand the nature of the business community that emerged in the otherwise agricultural region of the southern colonies, one must appreciate the geography as well as the economy of the area. Indeed, the South can be regarded as two distinct sections, the Chesapeake Bay colonies of Virginia and Maryland, and the Lower South colonies led by South Carolina.

BUSINESS IN THE CHESAPEAKE BAY COLONIES OF THE UPPER SOUTH

In the Upper South, rivers were navigable by oceangoing vessels for a considerable distance inland, thereby allowing ships to dock at the sites of principal plantations and to load tobacco destined for England directly from the growers' own wharves. The large planters who consigned cargoes to English mercantile houses did not, however, confine themselves only to raising tobacco. They were also resident agents, or "factors," for smaller growers, buying their crops and in turn selling to them the small number of imported commodities required on their farms. Thus the Chesapeake entrepreneur was typically both planter and merchant.

Edward Dixon of Hanover County, Virginia, furnishes one such example. He owned two plantations, which employed slave labor to raise tobacco crops. In addition, his account books for the 1740s show that he dealt with well over four hundred customers. They purchased from him items ranging from sugar and rum to hardware and textiles, and paid for the merchandise with the tobacco they grew on their own small farms.

Most sales were credit transactions, as smaller planters were usually unable to pay the full costs of their commodity purchases in any other way. The chain of credit extended all the way to England. An English firm forwarded cargoes to the planter-merchant, who then distributed the goods to other local farmers. The latter were expected to pay the debts they incurred with their tobacco crops, which the planter-merchant collected and shipped to London or Liverpool along with his own. Historian Paul G. E. Clemens, in a study of the Maryland experience, has written that this group of entrepreneurs was "an elite that rivaled the landlords of New York's Hudson Valley, the great sugar planters of the West Indies, and the gentry of England."[16] The important port merchants of New England might be added to that list.

During the 1720s, agents of Scottish merchants began to set themselves up in the interior of the Chesapeake region. They offered a range of services beyond the capabilities of most planter-merchants. These Scottish factors collected tobacco in central warehouses, exchanged it for British imports, extended credit terms, and engaged in other activities of assistance mainly to smaller growers. The local planter-merchant system was thus paralleled by another focused upon a resident agent for a mercantile firm in Glasgow. Scottish agents became increasingly important with the approach of the American Revolution and as the lands of many Tidewater planters became less and less productive after decades of tobacco cultivation.

Possibly the most lucrative profits earned by the Chesapeake's planter-entrepreneurs flowed neither from growing tobacco nor serving as a resident factor for other growers, but from success in land speculation. The concept of land as a commodity to be purchased and then resold at a profit was not a characteristic of the European economic system. Yet it quickly became a mania in America. Here, land was plentiful, cheap, and used lavishly.

When continuous cropping gradually depleted the fertility of a piece of land, it was simpler and more economical to acquire fresh property than to rebuild the productivity of the old. But the land-speculating planter was not just looking for new lands on which to raise tobacco, he was seeking large parcels that he could sell rapidly to others at a handsome profit. Between 1743 and 1760, for example, the Virginia colony awarded some 3 million acres of land in its Appalachian West to individual speculators and to others organized in joint stock companies. Among the latter was the Ohio Company, a cluster of Virginia planters (including George Washington's half brother) along with a prominent London merchant, who were granted the right to 500,000 acres along the Ohio River if they would settle one hundred families in the area within seven years. Four years later, a second such joint stock enterprise, the Loyal Land Company, received from the colonial government of Virginia another 800,000 acres in the same area. The resulting American penetration of the Ohio Valley was a fundamental cause for the renewed hostilities between England and France that later historians called the French and Indian War.

TRADE IN THE LOWER SOUTH

In the Lower South, the streams did not permit upriver navigation by oceangoing vessels, so trade developed in ports along the seacoast. These principal ports were Wilmington in North Carolina, Savannah in Georgia, and, most important of all, Charleston in South Carolina, the region's commercial capital. Whereas tobacco dominated Chesapeake agriculture, rice and indigo accounted for more than 75 percent of exports from the Lower South.

Planters usually placed their crops in the hands of Charleston-based factors, who operated in much the same manner as the tobacco factors of Virginia and Maryland. Often factors in the Lower South were simply agents of a London mercantile house, but sometimes they were planters themselves.

Charleston planter-factors, in addition to marketing their own crops, shipped the rice and indigo harvests of other growers. They also imported British goods, which were usually wholesaled to back-country storekeepers. Henry Laurens of South Carolina symbolized this category of southern entrepreneur. He owned plantations in South Carolina and Georgia and was also a Charleston factor who later entered politics and was eventually elected president of the Continental Congress. Fittingly, he succeeded another leading businessman, John Hancock, in that office.

Laurens dabbled in the slave trade, too. He solicited consignments of African slaves from British traders, sold the black cargoes in Charleston, and sent the proceeds, minus his commission, back to England in either freight or bills of exchange. Laurens occasionally exhibited a troubled conscience over this phase of his business activities, but he persisted nevertheless.

The New England merchant—contrary to a common misconception—played little part in the international slave trade. Richard Hofstadter pointed out that in the mid-eighteenth century probably 90 percent of the slaves imported into the southern colonies were transported in English, not Yankee, ships.[17] And often the consignee of the English shipper, who met the human cargoes in America and dispersed them at a profit, was a southern planter-entrepreneur, such as Henry Laurens.

The Colonial Artisan

As with the term "merchant," the expressions "artisan" and "craftsman" encompassed a wide variety of individuals. Included under these headings were "trades requiring minimal skills such as coopers, tailors, cordwainers (shoemakers), and weavers as well as elite craftsmen like silversmiths and instrument makers."[18] Edwin Perkins has estimated that artisans headed from 7 to 10 percent of colonial American households. While their numbers were not large, their services were nonetheless essential.

Although both employed handicraft techniques, artisans could be distinguished from those persons involved in usufacture—producing simple goods in homes for family use—in that artisans were specialists, earning most or all of their incomes from particular crafts. In the backcountry, itinerant craftsmen made the rounds of farms and small villages. They carried with them their own materials and tools, perhaps to make and mend shoes or to repair metal objects. Moreover, the traveling craftsman also acted as a peddler and carried a small stock of sale goods.

In the larger towns, an artisan established himself in a small house, usually with his shop on the ground floor and the family living quarters in the rear or on the second floor. As a small businessman, he owned his shop, tools, and raw materials, designed the product, managed his employees, who generally consisted of a few apprentices and journeymen, and retailed the final output. A major portion of his sales were "spoken" goods, items ordered by and prepared for specific customers. In the principal cities of the colonies, where a larger population formed a wider potential market, many shopkeepers also kept a modest inventory of merchandise on display for drop-in customers.

Craftsmen too were enmeshed in the credit net. Since hard money was always scarce, credit accounts were often established for buyers, though sometimes merchandise might be exchanged for other goods or for the services that a customer might be able to provide. A leading authority on the handicraft system, Carl Bridenbaugh, summarized the situation: "A long chain of credit stretched from the London magnates to the colonial urban merchants and from them through the craftsmen to the consumers, who were often themselves artisans."[19]

The milieu of the colonial artisan was marked by the appearance of the nation's first businesswomen. It was not unusual for a craftsman's wife and daughters to help out in the shop and on occasion to keep the books as well. There were, moreover, a small number of craft lines in which a woman might acceptably become an artisan herself. These consisted primarily of dressmaking, hairdressing, embroidery, and millinery. Much less frequently, one might encounter a woman in a craft not normally associated with clothing or delicate decoration.

The wife of Benjamin Franklin's older brother, James, carried on the latter's printing business after his death. For a colonial widow to continue in her deceased husband's business was not regarded as socially improper. Nevertheless, most crafts, as well as mercantile occupations, remained closed to women under normal circumstances. One result was to force some into the unsavory alternative of prostitution. A newspaper in South Carolina carried this lament by a woman identified only as Eliza: "Were there a probability of women of small fortunes and genteel education to gain a subsistence, . . . we would not see one tenth part of those poor wretches, who are constantly parading this populous town."[20]

The colonies faced a chronic shortage of skilled labor. The problem persisted throughout the period, and it was not eased by the restrictions that Great Britain imposed on the emigration of skilled workers. Of course, the shortage worked to the advantage of those artisans who were already in the colonies, as it meant higher wages and an easier access to the status of master than was the case in guild-ridden Europe. The demand for their skills was so great that the formation in America of guilds designed to limit entry or control production proved nearly impossible.

The one feature of the guild system that was retained here was the requirement of an apprenticeship period. As in Europe, young boys were contracted to master craftsmen by articles of indenture calling for terms of service of usually four to seven years. There were actually two forms of apprenticeship: one was "voluntary," in which an agreement was usually reached between the boy's parents and the shop owner; the second was compulsory, as each colony bound out bastards and orphans in order to give the youngsters a livelihood and to prevent them from becoming public charges.

Good apprentices, however, were hard to find. Masters placed advertisements in newspapers seeking them. A notice in Boston in 1769 read: "Half a dozen Boys is wanted, about 14 years of age, to learn the Art of Hackling Flax and Weaving Linnen."[21]

When an apprentice completed the required term of service, he became a journeyman. Free now to work for any master and to offer his skills in any locale, the American journeyman found higher wages than his European counterpart. The added income permitted him to accumulate a small but sufficient starting capital to open his own shop. The phenomenon of the eternal journeyman was not characteristic of colonial skilled workmen who had any measure of ambition, ability, and character.

Undoubtedly, the colonial era's most famous and perhaps rebellious apprentice was young Benjamin Franklin. Not being interested in pursuing his father's trade of candle- and soap-making, and showing too strong a longing to go to sea instead, Ben in 1718 was apprenticed at the age of twelve to his older half-brother, James, one of Boston's few printers. It became James's responsibility then to feed, clothe, and house the younger boy during his term of service and to teach him the art of printing.

Five years later, the seventeen-year-old Ben Franklin, already a well-trained printer, quarrelled with his brother and became very impatient to be on his own. He decided to violate his apprenticeship contract by running away from his now-irksome situation. Without informing anyone of his plans, he boarded a ship in Boston harbor bound for New York. Some weeks after his arrival, he moved on to Philadelphia. There he first took employment as a journeyman printer and later set up his own successful shop, eventually becoming the most important printer-publisher in the city. Ironically, Franklin's success was achieved, W. J. Rorabaugh has observed, "in violation of custom and contract, by leaving home, by running away. An example of wrongdoing richly rewarded was the legacy that Benjamin Franklin left to later generations of apprentices."[22]

Gradually, as the number of colonial artisans increased, voluntary associations, such as fraternal societies, developed, too. Ordinarily, their thrust tended to be educational and benevolent rather than economic, especially since they were frequently composed of both masters and journeymen.

One association that undertook a wider program was the Carpenters' Company of Philadelphia, founded in 1724. Its stated purpose was "obtaining instruction in the science of architecture, and assisting such of their members as should by accident be in need of support."[23] But in addition to its stated work, the company also formulated a "Book of Prices," which fixed the scale of charges for all new carpentry in the city. An appointed committee determined appropriate price schedules and settled disputes between members and their customers or between the members themselves. A carpenter had to be a master for six years in order to qualify for membership in the company.

This example in Philadelphia was copied both before and after the Revolutionary War by carpenters' associations in other cities. But, in general, most organizations of artisans were more inclined to social services than to economic action. The chief regulatory controls exercised in the colonial years stemmed from the actions of public authorities, not guildlike associations.

Municipal governments singled out particular crafts and occupations for price or fee regulation. These trades were considered to be so essential to the general interest that they were licensed and treated in effect as public utilities. Among the licensed trades and professions were bakers, butchers, cartmen, coopers, physicians, and surgeons. This type of regulation remained a permanent feature of American life.

The Ladder of Wealth

Recent historians studying colonial tax and probate records have provided us with some perspective on the relative wealth of businessmen in America's pre-Revolutionary society. At the top of the economic ladder stood the major urban merchants and large landholders. They represented perhaps 10 percent of the white population but held as much as 65 percent of the personal wealth in the colonies.

Much more numerous was the colonial middle class. It probably constituted over half of the white population, but its share of the total personal wealth was only 20 percent. The middle class included the ubiquitous yeoman farmer, the small storekeeper, and the master craftsman, as well as a modest number of urban professionals, such as doctors, lawyers, and ministers.

At the bottom of the ladder was the colonies' poverty class—indentured servants, other unskilled workers, slaves, and apprentices. Only the last group had a very realistic expectation of in time rising above their lowly status, although one former indentured servant did actually become a signer of the Declaration of Independence.

Alice Hanson Jones, in her in-depth statistical sampling of colonial probate records, *Wealth of a Nation to Be*, found that on the eve of the American Revolution the privately held wealth (excluding slaves and servants) of the thirteen colonies probably reached the impressive aggregate total of $4.8 billion in dollars of 1978 purchasing power, or about $8,100 per family. Her conclusion is that by 1774 the American colonists "had attained substantial wealth which compared favorably with that of 'ordinary people' in England and Europe and, on average, may have been not far behind that of England even when the wealth of the lords and barons is included."[24] And for the ambitious entrepreneurs on the middle and upper rungs of the colonial economic ladder, the last quarter of the eighteenth century would offer even more promising opportunities for the employment of their talent and initiative.

FOUNDED A.D. MDCCXCV.

CHAPTER FIVE

Business in a Revolutionary Era

As British subjects, American colonists lived under an array of limitations, prohibitions, and encouragements that were designed to knit England's empire together as a functioning whole. But this formal imperial system was more economic than political, and it rested lightly on the shoulders of most Americans. Indeed, it was the most liberal empire in world history. Until 1763, one recent study points out, "the only visible restrictions on colonial freedom were in matters of trade—its direction and organization, both between the colonies and alien countries. In all other matters, the mainland colonists enjoyed local autonomy and practical freedom in dealing with their own affairs."[1]

The Imperial System

The underlying philosophy of the British imperial system was mercantilism, a vague doctrine that dominated European economic policy from the close of the Middle Ages into the nineteenth century. It has been described as "little more than a shared perception among those who controlled northern and western Europe . . . that foreign trade could be made to serve the interests of government—and vice versa."[2] Its objective was to strengthen the power of the nation-state, both through economic self-sufficiency and through the increase in the stock of precious metals, or bullion, held by the state treasury. Colonies had a valuable role to play in this campaign for national greatness, for they provided gold and silver as well as other vital raw materials.

England's regulation of colonial economic life dated from the mid-seventeenth century, in a series of laws known as the Acts of Trade and Navigation or, more simply, the Navigation Acts. This legislation regulated commercial life in five ways. The first protected British shipping interests by requiring that vessels engaged in commerce within the empire be owned and crewed by British subjects. Another, the Enumerated Products Act of 1660, designated specific colonial commodities that could be exported only to England or other destinations within the British Empire. Tobacco, sugar, and indigo comprised the original list of "enumerated articles"; later, the list also included, among other commodities, rice, molasses, furs, and naval stores (pitch, resin, tar, and turpentine).

The purpose of the enumerated articles list was clear. It was intended to guarantee England access to inexpensive raw materials, some of which London merchants could then profitably reexport. In 1750, tobacco ranked highest among products that the American colonies exported to England, and most of it was reexported to the European continent. At the same time, colonial shippers were barred from seeking directly their own markets in Europe.

Another type of imperial regulation concerned imports into the colonies. The Staple Act of 1663 required that most goods transported from Europe to the colonies should first be cleared through an English port. Firms in the mother country thus obtained a virtual monopoly over shipments to America. Other regulations were designed to maintain the colonies as producers of raw materials and as consumers of British manufactured goods. The colonies were forbidden to export fur hats, woolen goods, or finished iron and steel products, but at the same time subsidies were offered to suppliers of such items as indigo and naval stores.

Finally, part of the Navigation Acts was the Molasses Act of 1733, which levied prohibitive tariffs on molasses, rum, and sugar imported to the colonies from the Dutch and French West Indies. But, since the foreign West Indies were an expanding market for exports from the mainland, the act was never enforced. Moreover, the Dutch and French West Indies were important sources of imports that were cheaper than those from the British West Indies. Although nonenforcement wreaked no great hardship on the American colonies, there was one significant consequence of the Molasses Act's hollow threat. As one study has phrased it: "For the first time a key act of Parliament was openly ignored by both colonists and British officials. An irreversible precedent had been set."[3]

BURDENS AND BENEFITS

The British imperial system worked to the benefit of some businessmen in the colonies, but to the disadvantage of others. Requirements that trade within the empire be carried in British vessels certainly stimulated the growth of the shipbuilding industry and merchant marine interests in New England. By the beginning of the American Revolution in 1775, one-third of the ship tonnage registered under the flag of Great Britain was built in the American colonies.

Some businessmen benefited from Parliament's policy of subsidizing the production of specific colonial products. The bounty paid on naval stores encouraged the growth of that industry, especially in North Carolina. In turn, the availability of these commodities within the colonies worked to the advantage of those American entrepreneurs who provided shipping services for producers.

Balanced against the benefits were the burdens of the system on the business community. Colonial merchants faced high costs for the goods they imported via England as well as for the enumerated goods that they exported. Non-British imports, which composed about 15 percent of all imports, as well as protected English manufactures, were more expensive. Exports, such as tobacco and rice shipped by the planter-entrepreneurs in the South, were reexported from England only after British merchants had added warehousing charges and commissions on the cargoes. These extra costs of handling and reshipping probably would have been incurred even without the restrictions of the Navigation Acts. Blood and language bound Americans to England, as did the ability of its mercantile houses to offer financing. Even after the Revolution—and without the Navigation Acts—most American tobacco was still exported to Britain.

Another disadvantage of the imperial system was that colonial merchants paid higher prices for shipping services than they would have if foreign vessels had been allowed to compete for the American carrying trade. Yet, this burden on colonial exporters, whose goods bore a higher and thus less attractive price tag, must be balanced against the benefits received by those other colonials (or in some instances the very same persons) who built and owned the protected ships.

Parliament also passed legislation that attempted to control American industry. The Woolens Act of 1699, for example, prohibited the export of woolen cloth beyond a colony's borders. Its purpose was to defend English manufacturers of woolen goods against both American and Irish competition, though the latter was probably the greater threat. The Woolens Act prevented a potential, rather than actual, industry from emerging in the American colonies, which lacked the skilled labor to compete effectively with low-cost English goods.

The Hat Act of 1732 was similarly inspired. It forbade the exportation by water of beaver hats from their colony of origin. In a provision designed to restrict the size of an artisan's operations, the act also limited to two the number of apprentices employed in any hat shop. Historians differ on the effects of the act, but, because it is likely that American hatters were already in the export trade, the full development of the American hat industry was probably impaired.

The third in the series of parliamentary actions dealing with colonial industry was the Iron Act of 1750. It prohibited the colonial production of finished iron products and encouraged the production of pig and bar iron by eliminating tariff duties on them. The law was never seriously enforced. As a result, as Carl Ubbelohde has written: "No matter how rigidly restrictive the statute reads in the law books, it appears to have had little or no direct effect on the development of the colonial iron industry."[1] Because of America's abundant iron-ore deposits and the vast hardwood forests that provided a low-cost source of charcoal fuel for furnaces and forges, colonial output of bar and pig iron in the 1770s had already exceeded that of the British Isles.

THE IMPERIAL SYSTEM BREAKS DOWN

Historians have debated endlessly the relative balance of benefits and burdens in the British imperial system and have, in the process, employed increasingly sophisticated econometric tools. It is nonetheless clear that, had the Navigation Acts been strictly enforced, the economic burden would have been considerably heavier upon the colonial business community. British policy makers did not have the will to do so and, rather than provoke a political controversy with the American colonies, they instead preferred to pursue a policy of "salutary neglect."

The year 1763, however, was a major turning point in British policy. The Treaty of Paris, which ended the Seven Years' War, gave England dominance in North America. France withdrew from Canada and thus removed a threat that had bound the American colonists closely to the mother country.

The war with France left England with a larger empire as well as a huge public debt, about half of which was incurred in defense of the American colonies. Although the colonists were not asked to retire that debt, they were expected to shoulder a significant share of the expense of garrisoning ten thousand English regulars in North America. To raise these revenues, George Grenville, who became prime minister in 1763, imposed a new series of taxes and reformed the administrative system.

Under Grenville and his successors, Parliament passed a succession of revenue measures, which included the Sugar Act of 1764, the Stamp Act of 1765, the Townshend Acts of 1767, and the Tea Act of 1773. The Sugar Act actually reduced the high duties on molasses and sugar from the foreign West Indies levied by the Molasses Act of 1733, but it included strict enforcement provisions to insure collection. The Stamp Act, a form of taxation in use in England since the 1600s, required that all legal documents, newspapers, liquor licenses, and even decks of cards and college diplomas bear purchased stamps.

Colonists responded violently to the Sugar and Stamp Acts. Ultimately, when the opponents of these acts organized a boycott of British imports, it was clear that Grenville had miscalculated. The laws hit hardest those groups in the colonies who were the most articulate and best organized and who could mount the most effective counterattack—lawyers, merchants, newspaper editors, and tavern keepers.

In Boston, New York, and Philadelphia, almost a thousand merchants agreed not to trade with England until the detested legislation was repealed. These nonimportation agreements were enforced in many places by patriotic gangs who called themselves the Sons of Liberty and who included a mixture of smaller businessmen—storekeepers and shopkeepers—as well as clerks, journeymen, apprentices, and unskilled day laborers. Their leaders were usually lawyers and some larger merchants.

Even in the smaller port towns, business support for the protests was strong. Benjamin W. Labaree has shown that in Newburyport, a town on the Merrimack River forty miles north of Boston, a merchant aristocracy dominated the community's economic, social, and political life. This aristocracy supported the colonial cause, and Newburyport "was virtually without Tories." The "interdependence of political freedom and property rights" was stressed in resolutions drawn up in business-controlled town meetings. One such resolution argued: "That a people should be taxed at the Will of another, whether of one man or many, without their consent is Rank Slavery. For if their Superior sees fit, they may be deprived of their whole Property upon any frivolous Pretext, or without any Pretext at all."[5]

The colonial actions produced the desired reaction in England, where mercantile houses were already suffering from a postwar slump. Unwilling to risk their profitable American markets further, British exporters prevailed upon Parliament to repeal the offending statutes. When a stubborn Parliament tried again in 1767 with a fresh combination of duties known as the Townshend Acts, a renewed boycott by American businessmen slashed imports by a third in 1768 and to less than half that amount a year later. Again British merchants pleaded with Parliament for relief, and the Townshend Acts were repealed in 1770.

A period of relative calm followed. It was not shattered until British officials rendered service to the East India Company, which, after a century and a half of prosperity, was finally faltering because of mismanagement. Its only real assets were 17 million pounds of tea and its political influence. The Tea Act of 1773 was the result of both.

The act imposed a duty of three pence per pound on tea, but also allowed the East India Company to sell its wares through its own agents in the colonies rather than at auction in England, where American wholesale merchants purchased tea through their English agents. This privilege would enable the company to undersell merchants who imported tea legally from England, as well as others—probably the majority—who smuggled it from Holland. The Tea Act allowed Parliament to undermine colonial taxation protests. If the tea was cheap enough, British ministers reasoned, Americans would buy it, taxed or not, and put aside such abstract principles as no taxation without representation. In effect, it was a scheme to drive a wedge between the consumer and the business community in the colonies.

By 1773 Americans were consuming over a million pounds of tea per year, of which less than a quarter entered the colonies legally.

The implications of this widespread evasion of the law, which re-spectable merchants engaged in, were historic; this evasion repre-sented "a significant contribution to the breakdown of law and order throughout the ports of North America, where the Revolution's first seeds were sown. Violent resistance to the hapless customs officers became a common practice, deplored by a few but condoned by the multitude."[6]

Merchants affected by the Tea Act joined with such radicals as Sam Adams of Boston in a cry of outrage. In their public clamor, the merchants stressed the danger for the entire colonial economy. Par-liament was about to devastate the tea trade in America; if it could thus undermine one form of commerce, it could do the same to all others.

When the East India Company cargoes began to arrive in American seaports in the autumn of 1773, vigorous retaliation began. Violent mobs met the company agents in Philadelphia, New York, and Charleston and forced them to resign. In Boston, however, the agents were the two sons of the royal governor, Thomas Hutchinson, and they resisted the patriots' threats.

Consequently, on the evening of December 16, about fifty men, vaguely disguised as Indians, left a mass meeting of eight thousand assembled at the Old South Church, boarded the tea ships, and threw forty-five tons of the East India Company's best into Boston Harbor. The destroyed tea was valued at some £9,000.

Historians now generally believe that, while such prominent mer-chants as John Hancock opposed the landing of the tea, most also were against violence. "Their vehicle of action," wrote Arthur Meier Schlesinger, "was a legal gathering of the towns; further than that the majority of them, at the beginning, had no desire to go: popular tumult and the destruction of life and property were not normally in their program to secure relief from a commercial grievance."[7] Thus, few merchants were probably among the "Mohawks" who made a teapot of Boston Harbor; the overwhelming majority of the participants were probably the same artisans and day laborers who composed the rank and file of the Sons of Liberty. In one respect, at least, the propertied merchant class had an effect in what Bernhard Knollenberg has described as the "orderliness" of the Boston Tea Party, in which, he noted, "no one plundered or injured the rest of the cargo on any of the ships."[8]

In a set of measures that the colonists called the Intolerable Acts, the reaction of the British government to the Boston Tea Party was swift and harsh. The acts were passed to punish the offenders in Massachusetts by forcing payment of damages to the East India Company and restoring London's political control in America. One of the measures closed the port of Boston until the company was reimbursed for its loss, and, as a result, put that city's import-export merchants out of business.

The Wartime Business Community

Although there may have been general agreement among colonial businessmen about the need for protest against a Stamp or Tea Act, there was no consensus on the subjects of war against the mother country or the ultimate step of independence. Many Americans who had been patriots before the events of 1775–1776 became Tories thereafter. The decision often simply reflected the locale of their business operations. Those firms and entrepreneurs in British-held areas remained Loyalist, and those on the other side of the battle lines supported the Revolution. It was frequently as simple as that and followed the line of least resistance, sometimes regardless of personal feelings.

Some Loyalist merchants chose to go into voluntary exile rather than aid the rebels. More than two hundred left Boston for Canada or England when British troops evacuated the city in March 1776. Of those Tories who stayed in patriot-controlled districts, many "made the most of a difficult situation by becoming passive spectators or secret abettors of the British in the struggle."[9]

A major factor in the experience of American merchants during the Revolution was the removal of British restrictions on colonial commerce. The war disrupted the normal overseas trade with England and allowed the new United States to develop a direct trade with Europe. Nevertheless—war or no war—the bilateral commerce with England was never completely curtailed. A British army occupied New York from 1776 until the end of the war, and Loyalist merchants there profited. Philadelphia businessmen similarly traded with England while that city was occupied in 1777 and 1778.

For patriots, the principal wartime trading partners—especially between 1778 and 1782—were France, Spain, and Holland. In pay-

ment for European goods, American importers offered mainly tobacco, a product that was so much in demand in France that the
French intervention has been characterized as the culmination of
King Tobacco Diplomacy. Other means of payment were the loans
that European governments extended to the Continental Congress
and the expenditures of the French armed forces in America. In the
latter case, French purchasing agents bought supplies from local
merchants with bills of exchange drawn on the Paris government,
which the merchants then used to buy imported goods.

A lucrative but risky business opportunity—and a product of wartime conditions—was privateering. Both the Continental Congress
and individual states authorized privateers to raid the British merchant marine, and the business of privateering was usually in the
hands of port merchants, who frequently formed partnerships in vessels to reduce the possiblity of loss. Partnership shares, in fact, circulated like stock in modern corporations.

American raiders haunted the busiest British shipping routes, especially in the Caribbean, and captured prizes and inflicted heavy
losses on the enemy war effort. By 1781 over five hundred privateering vessels were in service and operated principally out of ports
in Massachusetts and Pennsylvania. Privateers not only inflicted damage on British commerce, but also supplied the former colonists with
captured goods that helped compensate for the loss of normal peacetime trade with England. Privateering also stimulated the shipbuilding industry in the United States, and it added to the American maritime register those ships taken from Britain.

A pervasive problem that Americans faced during the Revolution
was their failure to devise a successful financing of the war. Without
constitutional authority to tax and unable to borrow large sums from
the public—who were uncertain of the war's outcome and who had
little capital in any event—the Continental Congress relied heavily
on the printing of paper money. During the Revolution, the Congress
issued some 200 million dollars in Continental currency; the states
meanwhile issued an equal sum. An obvious result was a spiraling
price inflation, as the volume of paper money in circulation climbed
faster than the available supply of goods.

Opportunities for business profits nonetheless remained. If a merchant acquired a supply of goods, he could charge as much as the
market could bear, and reports of profits of 600 percent or more
were not uncommon—especially in sales to purchasing agents for the

Continental Army. Merchants met accusations that they were profiteering at the nation's expense with the response that they had little
alternative but to charge high prices. They paid dearly to their own
suppliers, particularly farmers, the risks of trading in wartime were
great, and the paper currency would probably soon depreciate. As
one economic historian put it, "In a time of inflation nearly everyone
found it hard to draw a sharp line between profiteering and pru-
dence."[10]

The economic conditions of the Revolutionary era engendered a
new class of aggressive entrepreneurs, who soon took their place
alongside the established merchant elite. One such example was Jer-
emiah Wadsworth of Connecticut, a leading war trader. The son of
a Hartford minister, Wadsworth in 1775 became a purchasing agent
for the Continental Army. Three years later, Congress appointed
him commissary general for the military. In that post, he earned a
salary based on a commission of one half of one percent of total
expenditures—hardly an incentive for reducing public outlays. When
this dubious commission system aroused open resentment, he resigned his position, went into business on his own in late 1779, and
began to collect supplies to sell to the army. Wadsworth meanwhile
invested in a privateering brig—*General Wayne*—as well as in other
maritime projects. By 1781, Wadsworth and a partner had contracted
with the French forces fighting in America for provisions such as
"One Thousand Hundred Weight of Wheat Flour and Two Hundred
Sacks of Rye Flour" and "Two Thousand Four Hundred Bushells of
Pulse." In partial payment, he and his associate received "all Profits
arising from Prizes which shall be taken by the Vessels of the French
Fleet and Consigned to either or both of them."[11]

Wadsworth remained a major figure after the end of the war. He
actively invested in real estate in both New England and the West
and in government securities. He also became the second president
of the Bank of New York, the single largest stockholder in the Bank
of North America, and, in the 1790s, a director of Alexander Hamilton's Bank of the United States. Wadsworth was typical of a group
of young businessmen for whom the American Revolution offered a
springboard to economic success and national stature. Their rise partly
replaced the entrepreneurial leadership lost in the emigration of
Loyalist businessmen during the war.

Robert Morris and the Business of Finance

During most of the war, the new nation endured an inflation fueled by a badly depreciated paper currency. Prices reached $100 for a pair of shoes and $1,500 for a barrel of flour, if paper rather than hard money was offered in payment. Although wartime inflation inflicted severe hardship on those with fixed incomes, such as soldiers in the Continental Army, or on laborers, whose wages lagged far behind price increases, not everyone found the situation financially disastrous. Debtors met their obligations in cheaper dollars; farmers and merchants refused to sell supplies unless prices were sufficiently high.

In early 1781, Congress attempted to correct this situation. It appointed Robert Morris, a leading Philadelphia merchant, as superintendent of finance, a post that he held until late 1784. Morris was the son of a Maryland tobacco factor; as a teenager, his father apprenticed him to an important Philadelphia mercantile house, where—with the formation of Willing and Morris in 1757—he became a full partner.

He was a somewhat reluctant signer of the Declaration of Independence and a member of the committee of the Continental Congress that dispersed contracts for military provisions—where he made sure that his firm shared handsomely in the available opportunities. At the beginning of the war, therefore, Morris was optimistic about business prospects. As he stated in 1776, "There never has been so fair an opportunity for making a large fortune since I have been conversant with the world."[12] During the first three years of fighting, a third of all government contracts were assigned to Willing and Morris.

Morris has been described as having "a warm, outgoing personality whose considerable talents were exercised with tremendous energy and perseverance," and a practical, rather than philosophical, mind. His investments extended to commerce, land speculation, manufacturing, privateering, and governmental securities. He was involved in "at least nine major partnerships and numerous lesser engagements, not to mention an extensive network of mercantile correspondents."[13] Morris was quite likely the foremost merchant in Revolutionary America.

Within a few days after taking office as superintendent of finance, Morris proposed that Congress charter the nation's first commercial bank. In January 1782, the Bank of North America thus opened its doors in Philadelphia with Morris's old partner, Thomas Willing, as its first president. Patterned after the Bank of England, the Bank of North America served as a depository for public and private funds, acted as the fiscal agent for Congress, and thereby accepted monies owed to the United States and made payments on behalf of the nation. It also issued bank notes, redeemable in specie on demand, which circulated as currency and at par, testifying to the confidence of the business community in Morris' institutional brainchild. By 1783 the Bank of North America returned to its stockholders annual dividends of 14 percent on their investments.

Morris's aims as superintendent of finance paralleled the programs of Alexander Hamilton as secretary of the treasury ten years later. But, unlike Hamilton, Morris confronted crippling opposition in Congress and in the states, and, in late 1784, he resigned his office and returned to private business activities—which he had never entirely left. During his last months as superintendent of finance, for instance, he opened America's trade with China. Morris and his partners fitted out a new ship, the *Empress of China*, with forty tons of ginseng (a root prized in China for its medicinal qualities and supposed ability to guarantee fertility), brandy, wine, tar, turpentine, and $20,000 in coin. His share alone amounted to almost $60,000.

The *Empress of China* sailed from New York City in February 1784. After a four-month stay in the port of Canton, it returned to the United States in May 1785 with a cargo of tea, silks, chinaware, and other exotica. The partners realized a profit of $37,000, substantial enough to encourage an ongoing trade with the Far East.

In his later years, Morris engaged in a wide variety of ventures, some highly speculative. Eventually, his affairs became so confused that George Washington chose not to offer him the new position of secretary of the treasury in 1789. During the 1790s, Morris's income never quite seemed to keep pace with his borrowings, and by 1798 he was in default for millions of dollars. He was arrested and imprisoned for unpaid debts for three years. While in Philadelphia's debtor prison, he was visited by George Washington, among other distinguished visitors, and his predicament helped to publicize a growing movement in the country to abolish imprisonment for unpaid debts. Once released, he lived out the balance of his life in obscurity. Nevertheless, Morris left an enduring contribution. He was the first in a long line of private capitalists, eventually including such figures as Nicholas Biddle, Jay Cooke, J. P. Morgan, and Andrew Mellon, who would for a time assume responsibility for the public financial affairs of the nation.

Peace and Hard Times

The American Revolution was completed in 1787 and 1788 with the drafting and ratification of the Constitution. That document had a major impact upon business development in the United States, and, in turn, the economic and business conditions of the 1780s played a crucial role in the framing of the Constitution itself.

For all practical purposes, hostilities ended with the signing of a preliminary peace treaty by British and American negotiators at the end of 1782. At that point, it was permissible for businessmen on both sides to reopen a normal peacetime trade. The commercial pattern that developed in the 1780s, however, was as abnormal as it was normal. It was inevitable that England would again become a major trading partner, despite the recent unpleasantness. American consumers were accustomed to British-made goods; American merchants preferred their long-established suppliers. British firms, equally anxious to hold their market in the United States, extended credit on purchases. The problem arose in paying for those imports in the United States.

Because the value of American exports was less than the value of goods imported, a substantial trade deficit resulted. The deficit was worsened because England now taxed tobacco from the former American colonies, and thereby decreased consumer demand, and because France had, in 1785, formed a "monopsony," a single governmental buying agency, which contracted with Robert Morris for all tobacco purchases. The decline in competition depressed prices that American growers received.

Although tobacco was the most important American export, other prewar sources of income also declined. Shipbuilders in the United States found, for instance, that their vessels were now regarded as foreign and were, therefore, barred from most of the carrying trade in the British Empire. In the 1770s, Massachusetts alone built an average of 125 ships per year, but by 1785 its output was no more than twenty. American merchants now found, moreover, that mercantilist restrictions impeded trade not only with the British West Indies but also with French and Spanish possessions in the area.

During the 1780s, the trade deficit forced a migration of specie overseas to meet commercial obligations, a development that further diminished an inadequate money supply and depressed prices. Business bankruptcies rose alarmingly during the hard times of the mid-1780s, with the severity of the depression tempered only by the fact that a fair-sized segment of the economy was still engaged in self-sufficient farming and was thus less susceptible to the pressures of the market economy.

By the mid-1780s, a consensus had emerged that the money supply needed to be expanded, but a sharp disagreement arose over how the expansion should be accomplished. One faction, composed principally of wholesale merchants in the port towns, favored commercial banks as the proper means. Three such banks existed by 1787—Morris's Bank of North America, the Bank of New York, and the Bank of Massachusetts. Each issued bank notes that it lent to borrowers and redeemed in specie on demand. These notes provided an expanded currency, but under conservative restraints, as the three banks did not deal with the average citizen, even within their own immediate locales.

The opponents of these "merchants' banks" complained that they benefited only an elite group. Although the major opponents—farmers who sought long-term credit and an increase in the money supply to raise agricultural prices and to ease debt repayment—were not in a position to organize commercial banks of their own, they did expect assistance from state governments. Despite strong oppositon from most merchants and other creditors, seven states issued paper currency during the decade, and others failed to do so only after considerable debate. The reasons behind the strong opposition of the merchant community were obvious, for although importers had to pay their foreign suppliers in coin, they themselves received depreciated paper currency from their own customers.

The paper-money controversy was among the more important factors leading to the drafting of a new document of fundamental law for the nation in 1787. The Constitution was intended to remedy the weaknesses in the Articles of Confederation, weaknesses that in the minds of many businessmen were in no little part responsible for the economic problems of the postwar years. It is clear that they supported the calling of the Philadelphia Convention and the ratification of its handiwork in considerable numbers, but the exact extent of business support and leadership in the movement for a new Constitution has been a matter for significant scholarly debate.

Business and the Constitution

In 1913, Charles A. Beard published his classic work, *An Economic Interpretation of the Constitution*. In it, he argued that the Constitution was the work of leaders whose primary concern was their property interests. The group consisted of merchants, manufacturers, speculators in western lands, and government bondholders, all of whom believed they stood to benefit from a stronger central government and from more restraints on the states. They were acting, supposedly, out of a sense of pocketbook patriotism.

While Beard initiated a useful discussion of the economic forces behind the Constitution, his analysis was grossly oversimplified, and it even misread a good deal of the evidence. A succession of later historians have challenged Beard's conclusions. The most exhaustive refutation is offered by Forrest McDonald's *We the People: The Economic Origins of the Constitution* (1958). According to McDonald, Beard's fundamental mistake was that he applied a single generalization to every state—that personal property interests (or "personalty" in Beard's phrase) always supported the Constitution and were the dynamic element in its drafting and adoption.

McDonald sees a much more complex picture. Almost all free Americans—slaves and indentured servants being excluded—belonged to one of four broad occupational categories: farmers, nonagrarian producers, mercantile interests, and members of professions. Within each of those four categories, there was a variety of subgroups, all with their own sets of self-interests. If we examine only McDonald's second and third occupational categories—nonagrarian producers and mercantile interests—we find that they composed the business community of the new United States.

The second category—nonagrarian producers, or, more loosely, manufacturers—was the largest of the nonagricultural occupations, but the group with the least political power. It should be divided into three subgroups: craftsmen and artisans, small manufacturing industries—long part of the old colonial economy—and relatively new "capitalistic" manufacturing enterprises.

Craftsmen and artisans, McDonald points out, carried on their business activities as part of some other line of economic endeavor. A country blacksmith, for example, served the farmers in his area; ship carpenters served urban shipbuilders and owners. Politically, they were often allied with those interests to which they were economically tied, and, McDonald concludes, "men engaged in service occupations were of little weight in the contest over ratification."[14]

Another subgroup, small manufacturing industries, included lumber, paper, and flour mills, rum distilleries, and similar operations. Immune for the most part to British competition because of the expense and difficulty in transporting their bulky products long distances, they were hardly affected by the constitutional issue. The businessmen who headed these firms usually took no special position on the question unless they held valuable interests in other fields as well.

A final subgroup of nonagrarian producers was the new capitalistic manufacturing ventures, which were the first wave of the industrial revolution in the United States. They organized early forms of the factory system, recruited a larger number of workers than seen in the past, and dared to enter fields that British producers had formerly dominated. The number of businesses fitting this description began to multiply in the late 1780s, notably in the iron and textile industries. Because they faced stiff British competition, the protection that a strong central government might provide was attractive, and many of these entrepreneurs supported the ratification of the Constitution.

McDonald divides mercantile interests into four subgroups: tradesmen, factors, wholesale merchants, and shippers. Tradesmen were the retail storekeepers of America. They shared certain common business values, but they were not united on the issue of the Constitution. In larger cities, tradesmen usually supported ratification because of the economic difficulties that their seaport communities had experienced since the end of the war; in the countryside, storekeepers tended to support whatever position prevailed in their community. The one important exception was those tradesmen who were either substantial creditors or debtors. Creditors in states with strong paper-money movements favored the Constitution and its restrictions on state-issued currency; tradesmen with heavy debts assumed the opposite position.

The actual number of businessmen who were factors was small; the majority of factors were English and Scottish citizens. But for those Americans who did act as resident factors, chiefly in the southern states, the Constitution had both benefits and drawbacks. Because factors were agents for British mercantile houses, they tended to view political issues in overseas terms. Although they worried about the possible enactment of import tariffs by the new federal government, they reacted positively to the Constitution's clauses easing the collection of prewar debts owed by Americans to British merchants. As a result, the support of resident factors in the campaign for the new Constitution was ambivalent and not significant.

Wholesale merchants, although closely bound by ties of economic and personal relations, were separated into two camps, which were distinguished by whether or not an individual entrepreneur was engaged in shipping as well as trading. Those whose operations were confined to import-export transactions had a fundamental stake in the maintenance of a free-trade policy, and thus found themselves at odds with the aims of new manufacturers seeking tariff protection. Nevertheless, traders still saw economic advantages in the adoption of the Constitution. They were well aware that in any renewal of fighting with England (a not unlikely event in view of America's precarious independence) the port cities would be the enemy's first targets. A stronger central government appeared to promise a more formidable defense establishment and the diplomatic authority to preserve the peace. For these and other reasons, wholesale traders consequently were willing to support the Constitution despite their nervousness about keeping the channels of foreign commerce free of restrictions.

That segment of the mercantile community with substantial investments in the carrying trade had no such hesitancy. Shipowners were angered that Algerian pirates, in the absence of anything resembling a United States Navy, attacked their merchant vessels with impunity. The indirect financial costs of this impotence were also painful, as English underwriters charged the American merchant marine discriminatory insurance rates. Shipping interests also resented the effective closing of the British West Indies to American carriers, the limits placed by the French on products sold in their Caribbean possessions, and Spanish restrictions in the same area. Retaliatory tariffs and embargoes seemed to be the only answer, and "the Constitution made it possible to conduct such a cold war on the national level, where success seemed more likely."[15]

In sum, Beard's simple division of political factions into only real and personal property interest groups has not withstood historical scrutiny. McDonald counted twenty different interest groups; other scholars have been equally critical of Beard's thesis. Yet it can be said that the most economically and politically powerful citizens supported the Constitution. At the time, a young John Quincy Adams voiced the belief that the Constitution seemed "calculated to increase the influence, power, and wealth of those who have it already."[16]

To many, a dangerous development in the 1780s was the growing tendency of states to impose tariffs or other impediments on interstate commerce, whether the source of the commodities was a foreign nation or a neighboring state. The Constitution's prohibition of state import and export duties and the clause lodging the power to regulate interstate and foreign commerce in the Congress of the United States had an impact on business that cannot be overestimated. A single, huge free-trade area was created that encompassed the entire nation. The size of this enormous market gave encouragement for aggressive entrepreneurs to undertake large-scale production and distribution of goods.

Further contributions to the creation of a barrier-free national market were the constitutional clauses that forbade states from "impairing the obligation of contracts," granted to Congress the power to enact uniform bankruptcy laws, established a postal service, standardized weights and measures, and promoted "the progress of science and useful arts, by securing for limited times to authors and inventors the exclusive right to their respective writings and discoveries" through copyrights and patents.[17] The Constitution also empowered Congress to formulate uniform naturalization rules, which thereby eliminated a possible thicket of state regulations and indirectly assisted economic growth by stimulating immigration.

Interstate business benefited from several constitutional restrictions upon a state's ability to intervene in the economy, especially in bans on the coining of money and the issuance of paper currency. The Constitution's establishment of a federal judiciary system similarly aided businessmen involved in interstate commerce, for the Constitution clearly gave the federal courts jurisdiction over cases involving citizens of different states and over legal disputes arising under its provisions. More than likely, the federal judiciary would prove a friendlier and less biased forum for nonresident businessmen than the courts of another state. The economic authority that the Constitution left to the states was essentially internal police powers— the right to enact rules and laws that, as in colonial days, comprised principally the licensing, inspection, and similar regulation of local business activities.

The new Constitution thus created a political and legal climate conducive to economic risk-taking. Some years ago, two historians cited the Constitution and the assembly line as the enduring achievements of American civilization. They went on to state that the pair were inextricably linked, essentially "parts of each other." As Broadus and Louise Mitchell wrote, "without a workable plan of living together as citizens, we could not have industrial mass production for a vast free market. Without government we could not have goods. Without the invention at Philadelphia in 1787 there would have been no invention at Detroit a century and a half later." There was a necessary sequence, the Mitchells concluded, in which "the order of priority was first the charter and afterward the commerce."[18]

III

THE AGE OF TRANSITION

DURING the seventy-five years between George Washington's inauguration in 1789 and the end of the Civil War, the American economy underwent a remarkable transition that laid the basis for world leadership. A dramatic westward movement across the continent was paralleled by equally dramatic transportation innovations. The advent of the Erie Canal, the appearance of steamboats on the Ohio and Mississippi river systems, and the railroad's penetration of the barrier of the Appalachians strongly contributed to the creation of a national market for the products of American factories.

Two other developments had an important effect on businessmen during this era. The dominant entrepreneur of the period before 1800, the all-purpose merchant, now gave way to the specialist. Because of an enlarged market, entrepreneurs after 1800 concentrated on a single business activity and developed expertise in factory production, the distribution of a particular line of merchandise, or other entrepreneurial specialties. In addition, business, beginning with the railroads, faced an unprecedented problem in the final decades of the period—the challenge of managing large-scale corporate enterprises. The response to that challenge became the foundation on which the modern American business system would eventually be built.

CHAPTER SIX

The Twilight of the All-Purpose Merchant

THE ratification of the Constitution, and its implementation with the inauguration of George Washington as president in 1789, marked the opening of a new era in American history. At the same time, another era was coming rapidly to a close. The age of the general-purpose merchant was now in decline, and the specialized firm emerged to replace him in all areas of business activity.

Adam Smith had already predicted the transition in *The Wealth of Nations*. He wrote that the extent of specialization in an economy depended upon the width of the market, that is, aggregate demand. Growth in the actual or potential demand for goods and services stimulated the development of more specialized economic activity, and specialization in turn translated into increased productivity per business unit. He illustrated the effects of the division of labor—and of a gain in productivity—by using his famous example of the operation of a pin factory. According to Smith, ten workers in such a factory, each responsible for a different and distinct step in the production process, could make more than forty-eight thousand pins a day. But if each was required to work separately on the entire production task, he reasoned, "they certainly could not each of them make twenty, perhaps not one pin a day."[1] Smith used the example of pin making to demonstrate the broad implications of productivity gains that would result from a greater division of labor. He envisioned "specialization not only by skills but also by occupations, functions, firms, and industries."[2] In the United States during the half century after Washington took the presidential oath of office, the transition from the all-purpose merchant to the business specialist was directly related to a "widened" market at home and abroad for American goods and services.

Widening the American Market

In 1790, the home market for American goods was small and scattered, separated by primitive roads and poor communications. The United States had a population of 3.9 million persons, but the distribution of that population was only 4.5 inhabitants per square mile (as opposed to sixty-four per square mile in 1980). Most Americans lived in rural areas; only two hundred thousand were urban. No city had a population of over fifty thousand residents, and only eight towns numbered even eight thousand or more. Philadelphia, the country's largest city, had forty-five thousand citizens.[3]

During the next fifty years, however, a population explosion, and a substantial expansion of the home market, occurred. By 1840, settlement had spread westward, and the population had doubled with each succeeding generation. Between 1790 and 1840, the American population grew from about 4 million to over 17 million; population density roughly doubled to 9.8 persons per square mile. The largest American city in 1840, New York, boasted a population of 313,000; Philadelphia, now second in size, was over 200,000; and Baltimore and New Orleans were both 100,000. At the same time gross domestic product in real terms (in constant prices) grew at an average of 4.2 percent yearly, a rate that surpasses the twentieth-century rate of about 3.2 percent.

During the same period, there was a notable increase in the proportion of workers in occupations other than agriculture, from 17 percent in 1800 to 37 percent four decades later. Although part of this change was the result of new manufacturing employment, the bulk of the shift from agriculture was into the service sector of the economy. In Peter Temin's words: "Some of the new service workers must have been domestic servants in the growing cities. Many of them were engaged in commercial and transport activities. To the extent that workers were being transferred from agriculture to commerce and related activities rather than manufacturing, it would be more correct to speak of a *commercial revolution* than an industrial revolution for this period."[4]

In an analysis of American economic growth before the Civil War, Paul A. David has described three distinct periods of ten to fifteen years each in which the rate of growth suddenly accelerated. The first in this series of surges, or "long-swings," began in the early 1790s, extended into the opening decade of the 1800s, and was associated with developments in Europe. The second "burst of accelerated growth" got under way in the early 1820s, continued through the middle of the next decade, and was probably related to the rapid expansion of manufacturing in the United States, especially in the cotton textile industry. A final "long-swing," which began in the late 1840s and ended before the Civil War, was also heavily influenced by industrial development and the emergence of railroads as major factors in the economy during the 1850s.[5]

Two unrelated events in 1793 played major roles in triggering David's surges of growth: the outbreak of war between Great Britain and the new revolutionary government in France, and, in the United States, Eli Whitney's invention of the cotton gin. For the business community, the consequences of these events were far-reaching.

Foreign Trade and Domestic Cotton

Because Europe engaged in twenty years of almost continuous warfare after 1793, the United States, as the world's most important neutral nation, reaped a profitable commercial harvest. It enjoyed a rising demand for exports; more striking still was the effect upon the reexport trade. Goods produced elsewhere were transported to American ports and reloaded onto American vessels for a final trip to Europe. Since the ships of a neutral nation were supposedly not subject to seizure in time of war—since "free ships make free goods"— all major belligerents in the war looked to the United States to transport commodities from their colonies in the Western Hemisphere. Reexports from the United States thus grew at a staggering rate, from less than $1 million to almost $60 million between 1790 and 1807.

An extraordinary prosperity, which was felt immediately in the Atlantic seaport cities, especially in the northeastern states, was the result. Boston was practically rebuilt in this period. As one contemporary observer wrote, "The great number of new and elegant buildings which have been erected in this town within the last ten years strikes the eye with astonishment, and proves the rapid manner in which the people have been acquiring wealth."[6]

According to Douglass C. North, the major effects of this war-created prosperity were "the growth of subsidiary, complementary, and residentiary types of economic activity induced by export industries."[7] The most important subsidiary activity was shipbuilding, for the profits from the export and reexport trade were so large that shipowners could earn back the construction costs of their vessels in just one or two voyages. With the boom in shipbuilding came growth in dependent businesses, such as sail making and ropeworks.

The "complementary" activities that developed to serve foreign traders, according to North, included new banks, commission merchants, and marine insurance companies. Although banks provided services for other types of undertakings, it was the carrying trade and overseas commerce that were the initial factors which stimulated their establishment. "Residentiary" activities, according to North, were those related to the increased urbanization resulting from commercial growth. A variety of locally oriented manufacturing and service businesses now appeared to accommodate a larger urban population.

Just as important, there was a greater demand for foodstuffs to feed the urban population. Because this growth in demand required greater agricultural production, the reduction of transportation costs was essential. In 1790, the transportation of a ton of goods across the Atlantic cost, on the average, nine dollars; the same shipment, however, could not be transported even thirty miles on land for that price. The enlarged urban demand for cheap foodstuffs stimulated a long period of innovation in transportation between 1790 and 1840—most immediately, in a rush to construct turnpikes and to improve roads, usually between coastal cities and interior towns. President Thomas Jefferson's proclamation of an embargo in 1807 in retaliation against new English and French restrictions upon trading rights of the United States as a neutral signaled the approaching end of this era of war profits, and, with America's own declaration of war on England in 1812, the era ended permanently.

The second key factor in widening the American market in the early nineteenth century and in thereby stimulating entrepreneurial specialization was the rapid growth in the cotton trade. A prerequisite to its development was the emergence of a mechanized cotton textile industry in Great Britain during the preceding century. Technological innovation—the invention of Kay's flying shuttle, Arkwright's water frame, Hargreaves's spinning jenny, and Crompton's "mule"—caused a tremendous increase in the output of yarn and cloth, and, in the process, of British consumption of American cotton.

Before the Revolution, cotton was an insignificant part of southern agriculture. According to Stuart Bruchey, the extent to which cotton "figured among American exports as late as 1784 may be gauged by the reported seizure of eight bags of American cotton by the customs officers in Liverpool on the ground that so much cotton could not possibly be the produce of the United States."[8]

Two varieties of cotton were grown in the United States—Sea Island and Upland. Climatic limitations restricted the former to a narrow strip along the South Carolina and Georgia coast, and it was therefore never the major source of supply for British mills. Although Upland, or short-staple, cotton could be grown throughout most of the South, it seemed to hold little promise because of the large amount of manual labor necessary to remove seeds from the fiber. Before 1793, it took one worker an entire day to clean only one pound of Upland cotton. The invention of Whitney's gin in that year multiplied the output of a single laborer fifty times.

The effect was a decrease in the production cost of raw cotton at the same time as the demand for it was soaring in England. Cotton quickly became the principal export of the South. By 1811 its dollar value was over 50 percent greater than that of tobacco. In 1801, southern production had already reached 48 million pounds; within twenty years, it was 180 million pounds; and, just ten years later, it had doubled once again. As early as 1815, cotton constituted one-third of the value of all American exports; by the 1830s, this proportion was more than one-half.

The British textile industry depended upon raw cotton from the southern United States for up to 80 percent of its needed supply. In that regard, Jonathan Hughes has commented: "It was quite an incredible situation that a single commodity could so dominate the American economy's position in the world."[9] Moreover, while British consumption of American cotton remained high, factories in the United States were also absorbing larger and larger quantities. By mid-century, domestic manufacturers in the North were consuming about a third of the South's crop.

As with the commercial prosperity generated by the European wars of the Napoleonic period, cotton prosperity had an extensive effect on the American economy. It induced new investments in transportation facilities to collect and forward the cotton grown in the South, factories to turn out finished cotton textiles, and a variety of financial and marketing mechanisms to facilitate its efficient distribution. All of these developments represented fresh opportunities for business specialization.

Financial Specialization and the House of Brown

After 1790, specialization developed gradually in all sectors of the economy, but it manifested itself perhaps earliest in finance, an area to which many of the old general-purpose merchants turned as an alternative to their traditional way of doing business. In theory, the traditional firm could have incorporated a division of labor by simply employing specialists and erecting a departmentalized structure. But such a change would have also necessitated expanding the firm beyond the imagination of most entrepreneurs of the time. They took for granted a small management group, comprised of a few family members or trusted acquaintances, an organization that firms had followed since the Middle Ages. Rather than expanding the internal structure, it seemed preferable to reorganize by concentrating on one business function or a single line of goods once the widened market had made that strategy economically feasible.

General-purpose merchants who chose finance as a specialized field focused upon private banking activities or founded publicly chartered commercial banks and insurance companies. Vincent P. Carosso has distinguished between private and publicly incorporated banks. Private banks accepted deposits, made loans, and traded in foreign exchange, but the fact that they "were partnerships and did not issue their own notes (paper money) distinguished them from incorporated banks. Lack of a charter also made it unnecessary for private banks to submit to state or federal inspection or disclose the amount of their capital, two privileges they guarded jealously."[10] One example of a private bank was the related partnerships first organized as Alexander Brown and Sons, later as Brown Brothers & Co., and today as Brown Brothers Harriman Co.[11]

The House of Brown, as it was generally known in the nineteenth century, was founded in 1800 in Baltimore by Alexander Brown, an Irish linen merchant who immigrated to the United States in the late

1790s. Brown quickly established himself as a typical all-purpose merchant, and he pursued a variety of business activities. During the next twenty-five years, as all four of Alexander Brown's sons became active in the firm, its emphasis began to change, especially after it opened a Liverpool branch in 1810. Liverpool had become the leading cotton port in England, and, as that commodity came to dominate American exports, it was with mercantile houses there rather than in London that shippers in the United States dealt.

By the 1840s, the Browns had centered on the "monied business," the provision of financial services for the foreign trading community, and had largely divorced themselves from the wholesaling of goods on their own account. The House of Brown now moved its headquarters to New York City and established branch offices and agencies in Baltimore, Boston, Charleston, Mobile, New Orleans, Philadelphia, and Savannah, as well as Liverpool. The firm was considered "the foremost international banking-house serving the Anglo-American foreign trade sector."[12]

The Browns supplied three primary financial services: the extension of advances to American exporters in return for the consignment of cotton shipments from southern ports; the issuance of letters of credit to American importers of British manufactures; and the purchase and sale of foreign bills of exchange. The letter-of-credit function that the House of Brown performed was a key service for American importers seeking to buy goods in England. Armed with this guarantee of their credit, American merchants were in a stronger position to bargain for lower prices from British manufacturers. The discounts that merchants could thereby receive from sellers, who treated the letter as the equivalent of cash, were larger than the commissions paid to the Browns for issuing the documents. Only a very few Anglo-American financial houses had the prestige to provide this type of service, and the Browns were one of that small number. By the 1830s the capital accumulation of the House of Brown exceeded even that of its leading British rival, Baring Brothers & Company, Ltd., of London.

The Course of Early Commercial Banking

The mercantile class dominated the beginnings of chartered commercial banking in the United States. The inauguration of Robert

Morris's Bank of North America in 1782 was a model for new institutions in New York and Boston that involved prominent port merchants. The Bank of New York opened in June 1784, its charter drawn up by Alexander Hamilton, who first sent the bank's cashier to Philadelphia to study operations of the Bank of North America. When, in Boston, the Massachusetts Bank began business a month later, the shareholders also asked Thomas Willing, the Philadelphia bank's president, for advice about commercial banking.

Willing replied that it had been just as new to his own associates. He described banking as "a pathless wilderness," and admitted that "all was to us a mystery." The path that the Philadelphians chose through the wilderness was consistent with their earlier experience. "Educated as merchants, we resolved to pursue the road we were best acquainted with," Willing explained. "We established our books on a simple mercantile plan, and this mode, . . . pointed out by experience alone, has carried us through so far without a material loss or even mistake of any consequence."[13]

Altogether, twenty-two state-chartered banks were organized between 1781 and 1798, including two each in Boston, Baltimore, and Philadelphia. Moreover, following Hamilton's *Report on a National Bank* in 1790, Congress incorporated the First Bank of the United States in 1791. Shares of both state banks and the national bank usually had a face value of $400 to $500, and, as one historian of the industry wrote: "A good deal of vision and courage was required for the investment in enterprises of an unheard-of type. Those qualities in conjunction with wealth could then be found in America only in the merchant class."[14]

The first banks were conservative enterprises funded and directed by members of the mercantile community, who sought both new investment opportunities and a means of supplying greater outside financing for their own trading ventures. From 1789 to 1816, however, over two hundred more banks commenced operations, most of them after Congress refused to recharter the Bank of the United States in 1811, when its original twenty-year charter expired. Congressional opposition was based on the constitutional scruples of Jeffersonians and antagonisms from some smaller state banks, which resented the competition and economic power of the Bank of the United States. These state banks exerted considerable influence in Congress.

The banks founded after 1800 tended to be less conservative than those of the Federalist period of the 1790s. They were, moreover, distinguished by geography, politics, and the customers they served. Outside the leading commercial cities, country banks came into existence, and their chief goal was the promotion of their areas. Banks were divided by lines of political party—Republican or Federalist— and by the nature of their clientele. Names such as Merchants Bank, Mechanics Bank, or Boatmen's Bank, which have survived to the present day, originally signified the type of people with whom the institution dealt.

A suspension of specie payments in 1814 by all but the most stable banks in New England and New York, and the overall monetary confusion that the profusion of new state banks posed, stimulated support for central control of the American banking system. The fruit of this popular demand was the chartering of a new national bank, the Second Bank of the United States, by Congress in 1816. The lobbying activities of a number of prominent businessmen, led by Stephen Girard of Philadelphia, reinforced public sentiment and played a key role in enacting the charter.

The son of a French merchant, Girard settled in Philadelphia in 1776 and started a foreign trading firm. By 1805 he owned six ships (each named after a European Enlightenment philosopher) and engaged in a worldwide commerce that involved voyages to China, India, and Malaya. When the Bank of the United States lost its federal charter in 1811, Girard was its largest stockholder. He and a group of associates, including John Jacob Astor of New York, immediately began convincing Congress to approve a new national bank.

Girard meanwhile bought the old Bank of the United States building and, in 1812, established in it a banking business of his own. The Girard Bank was wholly owned by its founder and appeared to be "the old Bank of the United States unchanged: customers found themselves in the same handsome room and dealing with the same staff."[15] The Girard Bank was technically an unincorporated private operation, but it functioned like any state-chartered commercial bank.

When the Congress finally passed a national bank bill in 1816, Girard subscribed to $3 million of its stock. President James Madison appointed him as one of five governmental directors of the institution. But Girard's interest was promotional rather than managerial, and he resigned the office in December 1817 when he became convinced that the Second Bank of the United States was falling into the hands of reckless speculators and corrupt politicians. He remained its largest stockholder, and eventually his conservative approach won out when, in 1823, the bank was reorganized, and the able Nicholas Biddle assumed its presidency.

After 1815, Girard gradually withdrew from trading ventures and confined himself to managing his investments in banking and real estate. He was regarded in his own lifetime as personally unlikable, a cranky, one-eyed Scrooge who seemed to be a lonely miser. But when he died in 1831, the city of Philadelphia discovered that he had left the bulk of his fortune to various civic and philanthropic works, including a school for orphan boys, which received $2 million on the condition that a clergyman never visit it. Girard raised philanthropy to a new level of giving.

Nicholas Biddle became president of the Second Bank of the United States in 1823 after having served as a member of its board of directors. He was an American aristocrat—sophisticated, traveled, and well educated. He wrote poetry and prose and had edited the western exploration journals of Lewis and Clark. Most important, he was an excellent economist and an expert in banking operations. Under Biddle, the potential power of the bank to regulate the nation's banking system was for the first time realized.

Managing the Second Bank of the United States was a complex administrative challenge. The bank supervised the activities of twenty-two separate branches, which handled a volume of business substantially larger than that of major mercantile houses. It was "the first prototype of modern business enterprise in American commerce."[16] Nonetheless, the bank employed only a small number of persons to administer its affairs. Biddle and two assistants supervised the activities of the branches, each of which was managed by its own cashier selected by and responsible to President Biddle. They were usually men who had formerly worked in the Philadelphia headquarters, who had Biddle's confidence, and who might be more immune to local influence.

While Biddle controlled and coordinated, he also attempted to combine the formulation of central policy with a measure of decentralized responsibility. He consulted with subordinates before making policy decisions, and he preferred suggestions to outright orders. He has been described as "forceful and strong-willed but at the same time urbane, even-tempered, and considerate of the well-being and interests of his collaborators and subordinates."[17] If the bank was a prototype of a later American business organization, Biddle was an early example of a modern business executive.

The eventual downfall of the Second Bank of the United States—following Biddle's ill-fated entrance into national party politics and his alliance with the anti-Jacksonians Henry Clay, Daniel Webster, and the Whigs—need not be described here in its dismal detail. One historian, Robert V. Remini, has stated that the bank died needlessly. It had simply been "caught in a death struggle between two willful, proud, stubborn men"—Andrew Jackson and Nicholas Biddle. In Remini's words: "Between them they crushed a useful institution that had provided the country with a sound currency and ample credit. At any number of points during the long controversy they could have compromised their differences and allowed the Bank to continue to serve the nation. Instead they preferred to sacrifice it to their need for total victory."[18]

When the bank's federal charter was not renewed because of Jackson's presidential veto, Biddle sought to prolong its life by securing state incorporation in Pennsylvania in 1836. But the bank experienced difficulties during the depression of the late 1830s, and Biddle resigned in 1839. The bank permanently closed its doors in 1841, and Biddle died three years later with suits filed by unhappy stockholders still pending against him.

The Course of Early Insurance Specialization

Insurance firms were another specialized business that grew rapidly in the fifty years after the ratification of the Constitution. Marine insurance firms emerged first and most prominently, a natural development because the practice of insurance—although conducted informally—for seafaring vessels against the numerous perils of long voyages was well developed by the eighteenth century.

American shippers largely relied on British underwriters, and similar services were only gradually offered in the United States. At first, the procedure was haphazard. A shipper who wanted insurance sought out a broker, often a merchant or even a tavern keeper, who then established a rate or premium and wrote a policy. The broker retained the policy and invited other businessmen to sign for a specific portion of its face value.

When the face value was fully subscribed, the voyage was insured. In those cases in which the vessel arrived safely, the premium money was divided proportionally among the underwriters according to their subscriptions. If the vessel met with some disaster, it was the responsibility of the broker to collect the needed sums from the underwriters and to reimburse the policyholder for the loss. For his services, of course, the broker expected a commission.

After a broker and a group of underwriters had done business together for a period of time, it was natural for them to think in terms of establishing a more formal association of some sort. The earliest such association was Thomas Willing & Co., started in 1757. As its broker or agent, it employed the services of William Bradford, the proprietor of the London Coffee House, a favorite Philadelphia wharf-side meeting place for merchants. But the Willing group was only a temporary association, and it was not until 1792 that a permanent, incorporated marine insurance firm appeared.

The new organization was the Insurance Company of North America (INA). Its principal promoters were Samuel Blodgett, Jr., who had made one fortune in the China trade and later another in real estate speculation in the young District of Columbia, and Ebenezer Hazard, a prosperous Philadelphia merchant with a perfect name for the insurance business. They had first intended to form a "tontine" (a lottery insurance device named after a seventeenth-century Neapolitan banker, Lorenzo Tonti, in which the winners of a pool of money would be those who survived a stipulated number of years), but when they found little interest in that scheme, they decided instead to establish a chartered insurance company. With some of the investors active in the Bank of North America, its name was apparently modeled on that institution.

Designed to engage in marine, fire, and life (which was still new) insurance, INA chose in 1792 to concentrate only on the first. It planned to remedy the twin weaknesses in the old underwriting system—delay and shortage of capital. Formerly, Americans were unable to "take on short notice the large risks that the London companies could underwrite with a stroke of a pen."[19] With a pledged capital of $600,000, the Insurance Company of North America was no longer just a peripheral endeavor for local businessmen.

The first INA policy was issued on the *America*, a ship making a voyage from Philadelphia to Londonderry. The firm accepted a risk of $5,333.33 for a premium of $120. Its second policy insured the cargo of the *America* for $3200 at a premium of $72.50. The language of these policies offers some insight into the range of dangers that might be encountered at sea and the scope of protection extended: "Touching the adventures and perils which we, the said underwriters are contented to bear and take upon us, they are of the seas, men-of-war, fire, lightning, earthquake, enemies, pirates, rovers, assailing thieves, jettisons, letters of mart and counter-mart, surprisals, takings at sea, arrests, restraints and detainments of all kings, princes, and peoples of what nation, condition, or quality soever."[20] The success of the INA stimulated competing firms to enter the field. Twelve marine insurance companies operated in the United States by 1800 and forty by 1807.

In 1794, the INA decided to add fire insurance to its services, but it was not the first to offer that protection. Fire insurance first appeared in England in the late seventeenth century after the great London Fire of 1666, which burned for four days and destroyed 85 percent of the buildings in the city. In America, after some unsuccessful attempts, fire insurance existed continuously as an enterprise after the founding in 1752 of the Philadelphia Contributorship for the Insurance of Houses from Loss by Fire. Among its founders was Benjamin Franklin.

Americans followed the common English practice of placing a firemark—cast of lead—on the front of any insured building. The assumption was that volunteer fire companies, the first of which Franklin had established in 1736, would see the mark and work all the harder to put out the blaze. The extra effort would result because some members of the volunteer companies would themselves be participants in the Contributorship, a mutual insurance organization, and because it offered rewards to fire fighters who saved company-insured property. In reality, the effect of the firemark at times was to cause rival companies to spend time fighting each other for the privilege of putting out the fire.

By 1781 the Philadelphia Contributorship had $2 million worth of insurance in force. The INA, on the other hand, was the first to offer fire insurance nationwide, rather than in a single city. In this way, it could spread its risks and avoid being ruined by a single urban conflagration. Again, the INA's success encouraged competitors, and, by 1810, an estimated forty fire insurance companies were operating in the United States.

Life insurance grew more slowly. Few policies were written before 1840, often only on the lives of ships' captains whose vessels were protected by marine insurance companies. Life insurance did not grow until the rapid urbanization of the middle and late nineteenth century, when new mutual companies employed "feverish promotion programs" and other aggressive marketing methods and led the way into a period of even greater growth.[21]

Securities and Early Wall Street

More important for the future than for the moment was the emergence of a specialized market for securities. At first, a security holder with bank stock or government bonds to sell would deposit the certificates with an auctioneer, who often dealt in merchandise rather than in those intangibles. Informed of a pending sale, potential purchasers would congregate around the auctioneer's table in a well-frequented coffeehouse, as he offered the securities in question. It was a disorderly system, and, understandably, steps were eventually taken to regularize it. On May 17, 1792, a group of merchants met under a buttonwood tree on New York City's Wall Street and pledged themselves to establish what amounted to a guild of securities dealers and to eliminate the old-style auctioneer. They soon constructed a building of their own at the corner of Wall and Water streets, a private club and auction room known as the Tontine Coffee House, where only members could participate in its stock offerings.

Nevertheless, activity remained at a modest level. Most brokers were men with primary interests elsewhere, either in mercantile or other financial ventures, and their security dealings were still a minor segment of their business concerns. The day before the Hamilton-Burr duel in July 1804—during which activity was temporarily halted at the Tontine, as prayers were offered for Hamilton's safety by the Federalist membership—"trading took place in four United States debt obligations, three banks, three insurance companies, and three bills of exchange."[22] Such was the nature of the market until well after the War of 1812, when newly available canal stocks and an influx of European capital helped spur further expansion.

In 1817, the Tontine Coffee House market received a full-fledged constitution from its members and a new name, the New York Stock & Exchange Board. There was now an initiation fee of twenty-five dollars and the threat of expulsion for those selling fictitious certificates. Although canal and similar internal-improvement stocks attracted the attention of brokers in the 1820s, the first "thousand share days" did not occur until the advent of railroad listings on the board during the next decade.

Meanwhile, a market developed outside the board. Since the price of board membership was high, it was largely restricted to the city's financial elite, and those unable to join "remained on the periphery of the emerging securities market." As interest in securities trading grew in the 1820s, nonmember brokers became more numerous: "During warm weather they would trade in the open air, and former Board members who had lost their seats would mix with newly arrived hopefuls and older men who were never able to make it to the Board. Since they gathered in the streets, Wall Street thought it best to name them after their condition: they were known as curbstone brokers."[23]

A pattern was evolving—the Stock & Exchange Board (later the New York Stock Exchange) became the center of Wall Street's securities market, while the curbstone brokers (later the New York Curb Exchange and, in 1953, the American Stock Exchange) gained temporary control of those stocks not traded inside the formal surroundings of the board. Thus an important new cadre of specialized middlemen emerged by the second quarter of the nineteenth century, securities brokers who linked enterprises requiring investment capital with those persons who had available funds for speculation.

The Last of the All-Purpose Merchants

When John Jacob Astor, probably the richest man in America, died at the venerable age of eighty-five in 1848, his fortune was conservatively estimated in excess of $20 million. Although he had spent the major portion of his business career in the world of the all-purpose merchant, he earned the bulk of his fortune from a single specialized pursuit, what Thomas Cochran has called "the great business of real estate."[24] Astor devoted himself to real estate investment only after he had made a surprising decision—to abandon all of his successful trading activities. Astor thus represents the transition that occurred within the American business community during the Jeffersonian-Jacksonian years. He was in his lifetime "one of the last of the great general merchants and one of the first of the great specialists."[25]

Astor was born in the city of Waldorf in the German Rhine country, and he later spent four years in London, where his brother made musical instruments. In 1784, at the age of twenty, he immigrated to America with seven flutes and $25. After his marriage to the daughter of a ship's captain—she provided him a dowry of $300 and excellent commercial connections in New York City—he opened a shop in the home of his new in-laws, selling musical instruments and imported toys, and—at first, as a sideline—engaged in the fur business.

Astor had learned something about the fur business from encounters with fellow passengers during the voyage to America and from a brief employment with furriers in New York City. He then began to operate on his own by buying furs from trappers and small traders, who brought their pelts down the Hudson River. His next step was to venture into the backcountry himself. Leaving his wife in charge of the shop, he traveled "up the Hudson, visited the Catskills, traded in the Adirondacks, and around Lake Champlain. He sold trinkets to the Indians in western New York and took his pay in furs."[26]

By the 1790s, furs had become Astor's primary occupation. He soon ceased his own backwoods trips, relied instead on agents to make purchases for him, and began to engage in other available opportunities in the customary manner of general-purpose merchants of the time. Astor prepared furs for sale at home and overseas; he was also a heavy importer of goods from abroad and an investor in ships, government securities, and western lands.

Since a line of oriental merchandise was an expected portion of any general merchant's inventory, Astor soon entered the China trade, too. By 1809 he had five ships crossing the seas to Canton, exchanging furs, Hawaiian sandalwood (cut especially for him through an arrangement with Island chiefs), and specie for teas, silks, chinaware, and spices. Astor's biographer, Kenneth W. Porter, thus described the complexities of trade between China, Europe, and the United States after the War of 1812:

> At New York the China cargo is unloaded. Some of the goods are sold at auction, some over the counter of Astor's own shop, some are shipped as freight to other ports in the United States and to the West Indies. Some, perhaps in company with furs from the Great Lakes and

the Missouri, are shipped to Hamburg and Le Havre. [Still other] vessels clear for the Mediterranean, and sail away through the Straits of Gibraltar and on to the eastern end of the great inland sea. Here at Smyrna part of the China cargo is exchanged for Turkey opium. The brig then turns back on her course to Gibraltar, where the remainder of her China cargo is exchanged for quicksilver, specie, and lead, and the vessel clears once more for her home port.[27]

As Porter summarized them, Astor's intersecting trading patterns encompassed "the interior and the west and east coasts of North America, the west coast of South America, the Hawaiian Islands, Canton, England, the Mediterranean, both Northern and Southern Europe—indeed all parts of the commercial world."[28] In 1808, Astor organized the American Fur Company and used it as a vehicle in a ruthless drive aimed at achieving dominance in the fur trade. Small competitors were simply crushed; more efficient rivals were brought into Astor's company as employees or limited partners. Astor planted trading posts from the Great Lakes to the Rocky Mountains and erected a system of several departmental headquarters.

But, even as the American Fur Company was achieving supremacy, Astor withdrew from the business and sold his interests in it and in all his other mercantile activities by 1835. Porter speculated that Astor's retirement from trade was inspired by ill health and old age, and, equally important, by a desire to concentrate his energies on a nearby lucrative field of endeavor—Manhattan Island real estate. Over a span of a half century, but particularly after 1835, Astor's Manhattan dealings amounted to "hundreds, even thousands, of transactions, buying, selling, leasing, renting, and lending money on real estate security."[29]

He bought the Park Street Theatre, built the three-hundred-room Astor House Hotel, and acquired substantial property in what is now Greenwich Village. But, in general, he disdained buying higher-priced land in the heart of the city and instead selected low-priced lots on the outskirts, where land was close enough to profit from rising urban demand. He understood that, as New York's population increased, the city would expand northward, and he profited handsomely from the resulting rapid escalation in land values. Shortly before his death, Astor is reputed to have somewhat wistfully remarked: "Could I begin life again, knowing what I now know, and had money to invest, I would buy every foot of land on the Island of Manhattan."[30]

Astor behaved in the accustomed manner of the traditional all-purpose merchant in his operation of an import-export business and in his involvement in fur marketing. But he also made the transition to new specialized forms of investment and activity; he purchased a share in the Tontine Coffee House, took an active role in capitalizing the Second Bank of the United States, held directorships in four insurance companies, was a major participant in financing the first railroad to lay tracks from New York City, and, above all, became the greatest landlord in the nation's most populous city. In so doing, John Jacob Astor personified a changing entrepreneurial community and represented the new as well as the old in American business.

CHAPTER SEVEN

Innovations in Transportation and Distribution

HAROLD D. Woodman has written that the United States by 1815 "had the potential to become a rapidly growing capitalist society" with "a number of revolutionary qualitative changes."[1] These changes occurred after 1815 across a broad spectrum of business activity, but nowhere with more far-reaching impact than in the transportation and distribution of agricultural and industrial goods.

Innovations in transportation dramatically reduced the costs of moving goods, encouraged their shipment over longer distances, and made possible, for the first time, national markets. As transportation improvements widened the size of the American economy, numerous opportunities for entrepreneurial specialization also developed. Firms began to provide specialized marketing services, as an assortment of middlemen appeared who replaced the old general-purpose merchants. Commission merchants, freight forwarders, brokers, factors, and jobbers participated in a more efficient distribution of both agricultural commodities and manufactured goods; now firms could often concentrate upon only one or two product lines.

The Beginnings of the Transportation Revolution

Private enterprise took the lead in initiating the transportation revolution. As was the case elsewhere, seaport merchants were key figures. At first, they aggressively sought to extend their markets into the backcountry and hinterlands through improved roads. State governments acted slowly, as few of them could afford either to assume the financial burden or to solve the political dilemma of determining which section of the commonwealth would be favored with better roads. As a result, politicians usually allowed private entrepreneurs, in return for the right to collect tolls, to take on the double task of constructing new hard-surfaced roads and of maintaining them.

A turnpike corporation, chartered to build a road between any two specific points, generally raised the necessary capital by selling stock to the public, used the power of eminent domain to obtain land and construction materials, and exacted tolls from its users. The turnpike boom began with the organization of a company to construct a road, completed in 1794, between Philadelphia and Lancaster, Pennsylvania. The success of the Lancaster Pike inspired the construction of other turnpikes, most of them in New England and the Middle Atlantic states. By the 1820s, for example, New York State had chartered over two hundred companies that controlled four thousand miles of highway, and Pennsylvania had authorized nearly ninety more. In New England, the approximate cost of building 135 turnpikes in this period has been estimated at $6.5 million. In some cases states did more than just charter the turnpike companies. A number of states also invested directly in the enterprise itself. Pennsylvania was the most active, contributing about one-third of the capital invested in its turnpikes. Thus began a common approach in internal improvements—a "mixed enterprise" combining private and public resources.

Cities as well as states stimulated the construction of transportation facilities by priming the pump with public funds. Between 1820 and 1860, Baltimore supported railroad development with $20 million. Other communities followed suit, although on a less generous scale. In reality, the early nineteenth century was no golden age of *laissez-faire*. Writes one historian, "from Missouri to Maine, from the beginning to the end of the nineteenth century, governments were deeply involved in lending, borrowing, building, and regulating."[2]

In the long run, turnpike investments were seldom profitable. Although the improved roads were a boon to individual travelers, they did not generate sufficient long-haul freight traffic to provide adequate earnings. Shipping freight overland, even on turnpikes, still entailed a relatively high unit cost as compared to water transportation. It was less expensive, for instance, to send low-value, bulky agricultural products, such as wheat, flour, and hemp, down the Ohio and Mississippi rivers to New Orleans and then by ship to eastern seaboard cities—a distance of three thousand miles—than three hundred miles overland to Philadelphia or Baltimore by whatever roads were available. It has been suggested that, in New England, probably no more than a half dozen of the region's more than two hundred turnpikes were even moderately successful.

Nevertheless, as with all internal improvements, a distinction is necessary between private profits and the so-called social rate of return. Some types of economic activity, such as the construction of new transportation facilities, are sometimes more profitable to society as a whole than to those businesses responsible for their operation. Douglass North has offered a simple illustration of the concept: "A railroad that costs $100 million earns $10 million annually in net income. The private rate of return in ten per cent. It also increases the income of farmers along its route, however (as a result of lower transportation costs), by $10 million annually. The social rate of return is twenty per cent."[3] Historians have generally conceded that the transportation revolution did in fact return economic benefits to society beyond the direct profits earned by the companies immediately involved. The turnpike movement is a case in point. It flourished during the twenty-five years after the completion of the Lancaster Pike in part because stockholders of the turnpike companies had other business interests that profited from a better road system. The merchant-capitalist, who took the lead in the formation of turnpike companies, thus had more in mind than the tolls collected on the new roads.

The Corporation Comes of Age

An important aspect of the turnpike era was that, almost without exception, the companies were chartered corporations. Indeed, before 1820, when the corporation was still new to the American scene, those firms that were engaged in turnpike development and in commercial banking held the majority of the charters issued by state legislatures.

A corporation is a group of persons authorized by law to act as a unit for some stated purpose. It is, in legal language, an artificial person who can sue and be sued, own property, and transact business. Moreover, unlike a partnership, which ceases to exist with the death of any partner, a corporation has an existence beyond the life of an individual stockholder.

Because a large number of people—including many small investors—can purchase shares in a corporation, large-scale accumulations
of capital for major enterprises in the nineteenth century became
possible. Limited liability of corporate stockholders for the debts of
a business also spurred capital accumulation. In the event of a business failure, stockholders were usually only liable to the extent of
their investments, and the rest of their assets were safe from attach-
ment.

A corporation charter is a grant from a political sovereignty. Today,
the formation of a corporation only requires the completion of a
simple form and the payment of a small fee. But in the early days
of the American Republic, state governments, and sometimes Congress, granted charters by legislative enactment.

Prior to the Revolution, few corporations were established. Almost
all of these served religious, educational, and charitable purposes or
were vehicles for the legal organization of towns, boroughs, and
cities. Only seven business corporations existed in the colonial period, as compared with over three hundred created by state governments in the first twenty years after the Revolution. One reason
why business incorporations were so rare was that, in general, the
scope of authority of colonial legislatures was limited to local matters
and concerns. Anything of broader proportions fell within the jurisdiction of the crown and Parliament.

This situation changed significantly following independence. Over
two-thirds of the corporations formed between 1781 and 1801 were
concerned with domestic transportation improvements, such as turnpikes, bridges, and navigation. This was not surprising. Such undertakings had a public-service character that was vaguely similar to
colonial corporations, and they required substantial amounts of invested capital in projects that were often highly speculative. The
trend continued after 1801. Of more than two thousand corporations
chartered by special act of the Pennsylvania legislature before the
Civil War, 64 percent were in transportation, and only 11 percent
in insurance, 8 percent in manufacturing, and 7 percent in banking.[4]

Gradually, the demand for corporate charters became so great that
state legislatures were in danger of being swamped by the requests.
State legislators discovered that, by abandoning the special act policy
and instead by enacting general incorporation laws, they could save
time and also respond to growing criticism that special acts produced
political corruption and monopoly. In 1811, New York State enacted

a limited general incorporation law that applied to manufacturing concerns, and Connecticut followed with a similar statute in 1817. Both, however, were unsuccessful. They were weak laws that permitted organizers of a corporation to obtain private charters—an alternative invariably chosen if they had political influence—that often granted exclusive privileges, tax exemptions, or the right of eminent domain. In 1845, the Louisiana constitution forbade private charters and required incorporation under general statute. The following year, Iowa copied the Louisiana provision, and by 1861 thirteen states had the same mandatory feature in their incorporation policies. Nevertheless, before the Civil War, chartering by special legislative action remained the most common means of establishing a corporation.

As the nineteenth century progressed, mercantile and manufacturing businesses took advantage of incorporation with increasing frequency. One encouraging development was the United States Supreme Court's decision in 1819 in *Dartmouth College v. Woodward*. Although the Constitution prohibited any state from impairing contractual obligation, it did not define a "contract." In *Dartmouth College*, Chief Justice John Marshall, speaking for the court, ruled that a corporation charter was a contract within the meaning of the Constitution. No later legislature, therefore, could alter the terms granted in any charter.

Actually, the court's holding was somewhat less than absolute. In a concurring opinion, Justice Joseph Story suggested a path around the Constitution. If a state legislature wanted some control over its corporations, it need only reserve to itself, as part of the original contract, the right to revise or withdraw charters once they were issued. But as long as a reliance on private chartering rather than on general incorporation law continued, eager promoters could evade even that safeguard.

The Supreme Court was by no means finished with the matter of emerging corporate organization. Under both John Marshall and his successor as chief justice, Roger Taney, the court repeatedly took positions that significantly fostered the growth of capitalism in the United States. That posture was understandable. According to one constitutional historian, "the conviction that the individual was the *raison d'être* of civil society and the agent of national progress" united law and economics in the nineteenth century.[5] The creative entrepreneur, it was firmly believed, required positive support from government to serve the welfare and progress of society.

The Taney Court provided further elaboration on the contract clause in the *Charles River Bridge v. Warren Bridge Co.* (1837) case. The proprietors of a toll bridge between Boston and Cambridge claimed that their state charter was a contract that prevented the Massachusetts legislature from authorizing the construction of a new free bridge nearby. Although the Charles River Bridge operators argued that their charter gave them a tacit monopoly, the Supreme Court held that such a monopoly could not be inferred; public grants should be strictly construed. There was, however, an even more important meaning to the decision, for it supplied the legal basis for "endorsing and promoting creative destruction." If the court had ruled in favor of the existing toll bridge, economic development might have been endangered. Such a ruling might have imposed a moratorium on any innovations that threatened competition to existing enterprises or services. By ruling for the state's right to charter a new free bridge that would serve as severe competition for the old, writes Stanley Kutler, it offered constitutional support for "public policy choices favoring technological innovation and economic change at the expense of some vested interests."[6]

Two years later, in 1839, the Taney Court again addressed the subject of corporate operations. In *Bank of August v. Earle*, a lower federal court had held that a corporation chartered in one state had no automatic right to operate in any other state. Clearly, if that ruling stood, it would have barred corporations from interstate commerce. Taney rejected the lower court's contention that a corporation had no existence beyond the limits of the state in which it was formed. He instead assumed a middle position. Corporations could do business under interstate comity within other states, unless legislation specifically excluded them. In the absence of such legislation, a state was presumed to have permitted "foreign" corporations within its borders. Eventually, after the Civil War, even a state's power of prohibition by positive action was weakened considerably when the Supreme Court began to regard corporations as "persons" protected by the Fourteenth Amendment's due process guarantees.

Innovations in Transport by River and Canal

Early in the nineteenth century, two other transportation innovations in the United States played a significant part in reducing shipping costs. The development of the steamboat and the construction of an extensive canal network were major factors in forging a truly national home market and in thereby stimulating business specialization.

In 1807, Robert Fulton successfully demonstrated the commercial feasibility of steamboats when his *Clermont* completed a trip up the Hudson River from New York City to Albany. Equally important to the future economic expansion of the nation, Fulton and his business associate, Robert R. Livingston of New York, a drafter of the Declaration of Independence and the former United States minister to France who negotiated the Louisiana Purchase, founded the Mississippi Steamboat Company in 1809. They had built at Pittsburgh the first steam-powered craft to operate on western waters. Named *New Orleans* for its intended destination, the vessel was 138 feet long and carried a tall smokestack, two masts with schooner sails, and a pair of side wheels. It eventually arrived at New Orleans in early 1812 and then spent the next two years chugging between that city and Natchez before it sank on a river snag in 1814.

The *New Orleans* was just the first of many boats that would operate on western rivers. Some 750 were in service by the 1850s, and steamboating had become "the most important agency of internal transportation in the country."[7] It was not until after the Civil War that the railroads finally wrested transportation leadership away from steamboats and ended their golden age on America's river systems.

From a business standpoint, steamboats had a relatively low threshold of entry. They could operate without the expense of constructing and maintaining a right of way, and a large investment was not required. On western rivers a medium-sized freight steamboat might cost only $20,000 to build, though the floating palaces which operated later on the Mississippi and catered to passenger travel could entail $200,000 or more.

In the East and on the Great Lakes, steamboats mainly provided passenger service. Corporations there gradually became the more important form of ownership, as steamboat lines appeared that offered a regularly scheduled packet service. In the West, however, regular service was more difficult because of fluctuating depths of rivers. Unlike the East, freight was the basis of the steamboat business in the West. Captains usually waited for the accumulation of a complete cargo before sailing and would not accommodate a small number of passengers and shippers by adhering to a scheduled departure.

Hence the tramp steamboat that was free to go wherever the water was highest and the cargoes most available was more common in the West. Packet lines did not appear until after 1840 and then only on the heavily used Ohio and Mississippi river systems. As a result, the single owner, or the small partnership, remained in the forefront of the steamboat business, at least in the West. The low threshold of entry effectively guaranteed competition, which, together with productivity increases occasioned by improvements in boat construction, caused freight rates to fall substantially. The per-ton rate between Louisville and New Orleans, for example, declined from twenty dollars before 1820 to just six dollars in 1849.

One way to view the economic effects of innovations in transportation such as the steamboat is through the concept of "cost externalities." These are the reduced average unit costs that firms experience as a result of events and developments outside their own actions. As cost externalities accrue for businesses, profits increase and some strategies or operations that were not profitable before become sound policy. Cost externalities that were available to commercial users of steamboats were an important inducement to business expansion during this period. As for the boat owners themselves, recent evidence shows that direct profits were more than satisfactory. One study of forty-five steamboats that operated from Louisville in 1850 placed the average rate of return on invested capital from 8.5 percent to 24 percent.[8] At these levels, steamboating offered returns as good as or better than such economic alternatives as investment in cotton plantations or early western railroads.

Just ten years after Fulton's *Clermont* steamed up the Hudson River, another transportation innovation was in the making, as the New York state legislature authorized the construction of the Erie Canal from Albany to Buffalo, a distance of 364 miles. Only one hundred miles of canals then existed in the entire country, largely because of the twin obstacles of heavy capital requirements and the need for canal engineering skills that were simply unavailable in the United States. Moreover, the short canals that had been constructed were not noticeably successful. Thus, the Erie Canal project was a considerable act of faith on the part of New Yorkers.

Even before its completion in 1825, the Erie had given strong evidence of success on those sections that were already open, as traffic and tolls rose every year. The success of the Erie Canal encouraged similar enterprises elsewhere and touched off an era of canal mania. In the words of one modern authority: "The building

of a canal between the Hudson and Great Lakes in the 1820s captured the imagination of all Americans because it was the first breach
in that great barrier to western expansion, the Appalachian Mountains. Like the first transcontinental railroad of half a century later,
the canal proved to contemporaries that the methods of modern
science and industry could overcome all such barriers to the expansion of the nation and thus provide the means to bind together the
sectors of an enormous country."[9]

Canals differed in terms of ownership from turnpikes and steamboats. Although the capital necessary for the construction of a turnpike or a steamboat might be as high as a few hundred thousand
dollars, a canal project of any scope required an investment in the
millions. Since such sums were simply not available from private
investors, an estimated 70 percent of all capital expenditures for
canals between 1815 and 1865 came from state governments, which
directly owned all major canals.

The federal government also played a role in the building of some
canals. After declining to aid New York in the Erie's construction,
Congress was persuaded by the Erie's success to support later projects. The Corps of Engineers was authorized to conduct terrain surveys for canals, and stock was purchased by the federal government
in a few enterprises. Significantly for the future, the practice of distributing millions of acres of federal lands for rights-of-way and for
sale by the receiving companies began with canal grants in five states,
thus setting the precedent for the even more generous encouragement given a few decades later to railroad development.

Cost externalities in this instance were also significant. The new
all-water route between New York City and Cleveland formed by
the Hudson River, the Erie Canal, and Lake Erie caused shipping
costs to drop sharply and allowed business firms on the Atlantic Coast
access to untapped markets in the old Northwest. The attractive
freight rates also stimulated regional economic specialization. The
Northeast was now rapidly industrialized; the West became more
market-oriented, less reliant on subsistence agriculture, and concentrated on the cultivation of staple crops for shipment to eastern
cities or overseas.

Innovations in Transport by Ocean

Between 1815 and 1860, a series of innovations in maritime transportation also took place. The first was the introduction of transat-

lantic packet lines, which differed from other vessels engaged in foreign commerce because they sailed on established schedules. Entrepreneurs in New York City took the lead. In January 1818, the Black Ball Line, organized by five New York import merchants and named for the large black ball printed on the sails of its vessels, became the first successful Atlantic packet service. Its ship, the *Courier*, sailed from Liverpool, while another, the *James Madison*—despite forbidding Atlantic winter weather—left New York on schedule.

Soon the Black Ball Line had four ships in operation, each of which made three round trips per year, one more than ordinary vessels usually completed. On voyages to Liverpool, Black Ball packets carried cotton and wool bales and barrels of flour and fruit; on the return voyage to New York City, they carried textiles, wine, miscellaneous manufactured goods, and immigrants. Competing packet lines did not appear until 1822. In January of that year, a New York newspaper announced: "The owners of the ships *Meteor, Panthea, Manhattan*, and *Hercules*, intend one of them to sail from this port on the 25th, and from Liverpool on the 12th of each month."[10] The owners of this second line, like the first, were seaport merchants and friends and relatives of the Black Ball principals. New York City's early success made it difficult for other American seaports to compete, and packet lines were slow in developing elsewhere. The packet was a key factor in New York City's dominance in American foreign trade in the antebellum era. By 1860 New York Harbor handled one-third of the nation's exports and two-thirds of its imports.

Gradually, other changes occurred in maritime operations. Vessels became larger, more streamlined, and much faster. The cargo ships of the 1850s were at least three times as large as those thirty years earlier. The fabled American clipper ships were remembered as much for their beauty as for their remarkable speed. The clippers had their greatest success on long ocean hauls to destinations such as the Far East and, after the discovery of gold in California in 1848, the Pacific Coast. In 1854, the *Flying Cloud* set a record from New York around Cape Horn to San Francisco of eighty-nine days and eight hours that remained for decades. Other ships made the same trip in two hundred days.

But the era of the clipper ship was brief. As the California traffic declined in the late 1850s so did the clipper's popularity. As George Rogers Taylor pointed out, "The truth of the matter is that the clipper was a large and expensive ship of relatively small carrying capacity; her narrow wedgelike hull, though perfect for speed, carried relatively small cargo for each registered ton. . . . Historical writers, bemused by the romantic appeal of these fast and beautiful ships, have often given them far more attention than their importance justified."[11]

The gradual application of steam power to ocean transportation soon threatened the era of the sailing ship, whether packet, clipper, or simply tramp trader. That innovation was slow in coming, as technical problems in engines, hull construction (wood or iron), and means of propulsion (paddle wheels or screws) needed to be solved. Although steamboats operated on American rivers after 1807, not until the 1840s did transatlantic steam service become completely developed.

A turning point in the history of oceanic steam service came in 1840, when Samuel Cunard, aided by a subsidy from the British government, began a steam-packet line between Liverpool and Boston. In 1848, Cunard added New York City to his line's American destinations and posed a serious threat to the profitability of American sailing packet companies. First-class passenger traffic and high-value freight quickly shifted to the new steam service and left the slower sailing ships with low-value bulky freight and immigrants. America's recognized artistry in the designing of sailing ships had the unanticipated effect of slowing the nation's adoption of the next generation's innovation—steamships—and, consequently, Great Britain wrested leadership in ocean travel.

An aggressive and ambitious New Yorker, Edward Knight Collins, offered the first significant American challenge to Cunard's success. Born in 1802, Collins was a commission merchant before he decided in 1831 to concentrate upon maritime activities.[12] He first established the Dramatic Line of sailing packets (so named because its ships honored famous actors), and then, in 1841, began actively lobbying Congress with a proposal to subsidize American steamship service to compete against Cunard.

When the federal government approved his plan in 1847, Collins organized the United States Mail Steamship Company, or, more commonly, the Collins Line. In return for an annual governmental subsidy of $385,000, Collins agreed to construct five steamships of at least two thousand tons, each capable of conversion to warships in an emergency. The five steamships were then to complete twenty round trips each year between New York and Liverpool.

Collins's vessels were designed to be the largest, fastest, and most luxurious on the Atlantic, but they were also—with construction costs running beyond original estimates—the most expensive. When the Collins Line began operation in 1850, a bitter competition with Cunard ensued. As each sought to garner the other's market share, freight and passenger rates halved. Collins attracted a large share of the market because his steamships were slightly faster than Cunard's and because passengers preferred their comforts and service. But the Collins Line operated at a loss, and Collins was forced to seek larger and larger federal subsidies. Indeed, as a result of ardent lobbying, the annual government contribution reached $858,000.

Obviously attracted by grandiose plans, Collins became committed to the construction of a huge paddle wheel steamship of four thousand tons, the *Adriatic*. It cost over a million dollars to build, an unprecedented sum, but was so inefficient to operate that it made only one trip. Disillusioned with its expensive investment, Congress terminated all subsidies to Collins in 1858, and the line collapsed soon thereafter. The remaining ships were sold at auction to pay creditor claims. As for Collins, he resisted other merchant-marine ventures and spent his remaining years investing in mining properties before his death in 1878.

Maritime leadership thus indisputably passed into British hands. The decision of Congress to abandon the subsidy program—but only after the Collins Line had received over $4 million—a drop in the California trade in the late 1850s, the Civil War's devastating effect upon the cotton trade, an increase in shipbuilding costs in the United States, and British superiority in the building of new iron-hulled ships all combined to place the American merchant marine in a state of permanent decline. In 1863, the American share of the total tonnage of vessels entering harbors in the United States dropped below 50 percent. By the beginning of the First World War, American ships transported just 10 percent of the foreign commerce of the United States.

Nonetheless, a definite improvement in the productivity of ocean shipping occurred during the antebellum period. The greater speed and cargo-carrying capacity of the merchant fleets of both Britain and the United States—as well as the competition between them—forced freight rates down and created cost externalities for American shippers. In the case of cotton during the 1820s, for instance, transportation accounted for 10 percent of the delivered price in England;

but, by the 1850s, that proportion had declined to less than 3 percent. The decline in ocean shipping costs widened the market and stimulated domestic production in much the same way as had innovations in internal transportation.

A New Breed of Middlemen: The Cotton Factors

The all-purpose merchant of colonial times had carried on an unspecialized trading business for two principal reasons. First and most important, since his markets were small and scattered, he was forced to handle a broad variety of merchandise to achieve any significant volume of trade and return on his efforts. Second, the all-purpose merchant dealt in commodities that were generic, and they necessitated no special knowledge or expertise in handling or distribution.

But, as we have already seen, the expansion of commercial possibilities in the half century after 1790 stimulated entrepreneurial specialization that was not previously possible. A "new breed of middlemen" emerged, as Glenn Porter and Harold C. Livesay have written, who "coordinated the flow of goods, allocated capital to farmers and manufacturers through the extension of credit, backed improvements in transportation, and served as primary economic integrators at least through the Civil War years."[13] Porter and Livesay point out that the businessman who made the transition from general-purpose merchant to more specialized middleman or wholesaler both gained and lost in the process. He gained a new expertise in his specialty, and likely operated more efficiently. On the other hand, he was now tied to the vicissitudes of a limited range of merchandise and could not spread his risk across a broad assortment of commodities. Any sudden and unfavorable changes in the market for his chosen product line would leave him exceedingly vulnerable.

Most old-style merchants, as part of the transition, dropped their retail activities altogether to concentrate only upon wholesaling. They then further focused only upon one or two types of goods. The specialized wholesaler after 1815 more and more chose to act as a broker, factor, or commission agent; frequently, he did not hold title to the commodities he handled, but instead acted only as a conduit.[14] The reason for that departure from past practice was that, because the volume of goods handled and the number of customers serviced had increased so markedly, the capital required for outright purchases was now beyond the financial capabilities of independent middlemen.

The rapid rise of the cotton trade provides an example of these tendencies. The most important middleman involved in the financing and marketing of that southern staple was the cotton factor, who was based in the towns and cities of the cotton South. In the early days of the Cotton Kingdom, planters hauled their crops to ports such as Charleston, where they were sold for cash or exchanged for manufactured articles. That system, however, was cumbersome. It required the planter to supervise the process in person and tended to force him into quick sales, often at disadvantageous prices. Planters therefore came to rely instead upon a system of agents, often beginning with an "inland factor."[15]

As cotton production moved into the interior of the South, the inland factor became located in market towns, such as Atlanta, Montgomery, Memphis, or Shreveport. The marketing system began with planters, who transported their crop to the warehouse of the nearest inland factor. There the crop remained until the factor shipped it to the next link in the chain, a coastal factor based in a port city, usually Charleston, Savannah, Mobile, or New Orleans. The cotton factor's specialty was choosing the exact moment for the sale of a planter's crop—a crucial decision, since prices might vary by as much as five cents per pound or more in a single season. Indeed, the factor's own income depended upon his timing, because the size of his commission was tied to the proceeds of the sale (the usual commission was 2.5 percent); if the factor failed to secure as high a return as a planter expected, he would change agents with little hesitation.

Marketing a planter's crop was only part of a factor's responsibility. He also served as the planter's purchasing agent. Throughout the year, supplies for the plantation were ordered as they were needed through the factor. He had to be as skilled at finding the lowest prices for the planter's purchases—ranging from rope or bagging to such personal luxuries as books and wines—as he was at locating the highest price for cotton.

Factors also extended credit to their clients—in general, in the form of advances against a cotton shipment not yet sold or even a crop not yet picked. The planter might have such privileges as writing drafts on the factor or having the planter's other creditors present their bills directly to the factor for payment. The overall functions of a cotton factor were not unlike those of the Scottish tobacco or

Charleston rice factors before the Revolution, except that the antebellum cotton factor was an independent entrepreneur rather than the resident agent of a Glasgow or London mercantile house.

Disagreements inevitably arose between planters and factors. Planters were dismayed at their growing indebtedness. Factors were concerned that accounts remained unsettled from year to year. Ralph Haskins summarized the feelings on both sides: "It was commonplace to speak of 'years of bondage,' of 'endless schackles of debt,' and of 'planters harnessed to the factor's plow.' But the system of advances did not favor one side exclusively. If many planters found it well-nigh impossible to escape indebtedness, creditors had their own problems."[16] These included, besides chronic nonpayment of debts, a bewildering tendency on the part of some planters to accept advances and then coldly to ship their crops through other agents.

In any event, "within the first two decades of the nineteenth century the cotton factorage system had settled into a pattern which would vary little throughout the antebellum period—and even beyond."[17] Because of the importance of the cotton trade for the American economy in these years, the factor may have been the nation's most important specialized middleman.

A New Breed of Middlemen: The Westerners

The marketing system for western agricultural products functioned similarly. While the factor served as the market entry point in the South, the country storekeeper performed the same function in the growing trans-Appalachian West.[18] Like the factor, the storekeeper performed three functions. He was a retailer of eastern or European manufactured items and processed groceries. The storekeeper also accepted the produce of local farmers in exchange for his sale goods, and he then shipped that produce to eastern or southern coastal cities and to Europe. By his willingness to accept almost anything grown or raised in the West—furs, meats, wheat, flour, beeswax, hemp, whiskey, and more—he was able to dispose of the wares on his shelves to a population that lacked available cash to purchase them. The storekeeper in the New West was, moreover, a source of necessary working capital for farmers, as a large percentage of sales were on credit. There was, however, a cost accompanying those credit sales. Markups of 75 to 100 percent were considered normal and necessary, in view of the number of long-unsettled accounts that country merchants found on their books.

In serving as the conduit by which western produce reached its market, the storekeeper of the West differed from the southern cotton factor only in that he took actual title to the goods he transferred, while the factor operated on a commission basis. The storekeeper tended to rely upon Atlantic Coast wholesale houses for the largest portion of his merchandise, even after Ohio and Mississippi Valley wholesale centers had developed. Many Westerners were convinced that they could do better by making their purchases in the East rather than in Cincinnati, Louisville, or St. Louis, thereby eliminating interior middlemen.

The storekeeper who bought heavily in Philadelphia, Baltimore, or New York often made an annual trip East to select his stock in person. He thus insured that the right goods were chosen and was able to accompany the merchandise on its trip westward. But the journey also required an investment of money and of time—at least six weeks. Nevertheless, to the country merchant, the long trip East was a sound business decision.

While merchandise moved westward from the Atlantic seaboard, the agricultural products of western farms travelled in the opposite direction. In 1815, the only feasible route to the East for bulky western produce was the Ohio-Mississippi river system. Even by shipping grain in a more concentrated form—as flour, pork, lard, or whiskey—direct shipment eastward through the Great Lakes was not possible before the construction of the Erie Canal. But, as John G. Clark has concluded, with "the stimulus of the Erie Canal and the canal systems of Ohio, Indiana, and Illinois, the major focus of the grain trade shifted from the Ohio-Mississippi route to the Great Lakes."[19]

The growth in the grain trade between 1830 and 1860 fostered the development of freight-forwarding and commission-merchant firms in the larger river and lake towns of the New West. They facilitated the movement of farm products eastward and of manufactured goods westward. Since transportation was not yet integrated on a national scale, these firms offered various services for interstate commerce. They handled such details as supervising necessary transfers, insuring shipments, and storing goods until the next leg of the trip. It was not uncommon for a freight-forwarding company to have a stock of merchandise on hand to sell, either on its own account or on consignment for others. It thus also assumed a wholesaling function. Such firms, in return for promised shipments of grain or other products, extended credit or cash advances to country storekeepers, who were able, in turn, to extend the same credit to farmers.

An example of the distribution system occurred in 1828, when James Aull, a storekeeper in Lexington, Missouri, shipped nine barrels of beeswax down the Missouri River to a St. Louis firm of forwarding agents, Tracy and Wahrendorff. Aull instructed them to oversee the transfer of the barrels from the keelboat, in which the beeswax arrived at St. Louis, to another riverboat, which was destined for New Orleans. There it was placed in the hands of a different agent, James Breedlove. In New Orleans, Breedlove had the responsibility to transfer the beeswax to a coastal vessel sailing for Philadelphia, where the shipment was consigned to a commission merchant, Robert Toland. He finally sold it and credited the proceeds of the sale, minus his fee for services, to Aull, who not incidentally owed fees as well to his St. Louis and New Orleans agents. Aull might alternatively have instructed Tracy and Wahrendorff in St. Louis to sell his shipment to retailers in that city rather than forward it on to another point: Aull chose this alternative to sell over six hundred gallons of honey in St. Louis because he feared that the containers might leak if transported any farther. The decisive factor was the country merchant's own estimate of the market in which he could secure the best price for his goods, and there he ordered his agents to sell the shipment.

As the production of grain in the United States moved steadily westward—by the 1850s, it was centered in Illinois, Indiana, Ohio, and Wisconsin—Great Lakes cities such as Chicago, Cleveland, and Buffalo replaced New Orleans as the chief forwarding points. In these cities, wheat and flour were collected from storekeepers and farmers alike. Eventually, the wheat might reach a miller in Rochester, New York, or perhaps an overseas destination as far-flung as Rio de Janeiro, after first passing through the Erie Canal and the port of New York. At Great Lakes forwarding points, huge elevators were built for the temporary storage of the grain, and their users received warehouse receipts in return for shipments, with the receipts circulating as currency.

The Chicago Board of Trade was organized in 1848 to systematize the buying and selling of the increasing volume of those receipts, as more than 8 million bushels of wheat passed through Chicago in the year 1859 alone. At the same time, the device of trading in future contracts was slowly introduced and became a key feature of the modern commodities exchange. "Informal transactions in grain futures outside the Chicago Board of Trade finally gained respectability among the majority of hitherto chary commission merchants, and in 1865 the business was permitted inside the hallowed halls of that institution."[20]

Along with the use of the "to arrive" contract—later known as futures trading—the new marketing system also introduced uniform grading standards, which made it possible to complete trades by telegraph without the necessity of forwarding samples, grain inspections, and expanded warehouse and elevator facilities. The system, one historian of the subject has commented, "represented a pragmatic response that was initiated by millers, merchants, shippers and grain dealers and was ultimately accepted by the legal order— all striving for both greater profit and predictability in a market-oriented age."[21]

The Role of the Jobber

The activities of specialized middlemen who handled the flood of agricultural products flowing eastward was connected to another distribution system that had its own specialists who coordinated a stream of imports and domestic manufactures moving in the opposite direction. As the volume of imported goods from Great Britain soared after 1815, and as American factories became more firmly entrenched, many eastern wholesale merchants who had formerly dealt in a diversity of merchandise instead specialized. They usually handled one or two major lines of goods, such as drugs, dry goods, or hardware, on a commission basis for a British exporter or for a New England factory owner. But the final link to the retail storekeeper was another specialized intermediary—the jobber.

The jobber filled a gap between the growing number of specialized commission agents on the one hand and the thousands of general storekeepers on the other. The retailers who purchased merchandise in New York or Philadelphia, either in person or through a forwarded order, found it increasingly inconvenient to negotiate with a growing assortment of specialized merchants to secure the yearly stock they required. The jobber simplified the process. He purchased his own inventory in large lots from auction sales or commission agents and importers, and then resold it in the smaller quantities requested by local retailers.

As the century progressed, jobbers began to advertise their wares extensively and to send salesmen on the road to solicit business. Furthermore, they offered credit terms to inland retailers that extended as long as twelve months—arrangements that were not possible if storekeepers had instead bought goods at auction in the East. It has been estimated that, by 1860, jobbers were distributing at least 80 percent of the dry goods sold in the United States. They were also "the most important link in the distribution chain for such commodities as hardware (including simple hand tools), groceries, shoes, plumbing and building materials, and drugs."[22]

Porter and Livesay have cited a Philadelphia wholesale drug firm, Troth and Company, as one example of a successful jobber. Founded in 1815, the firm bought and sold an assortment of goods that were then loosely regarded as "drugs," including medicines, paints, and glassware. Troth purchased its inventory from importers and domestic manufacturers; it sold to retailers and physicians located mainly in the nation's interior. Troth, like all jobbers, kept a substantial stock of goods on hand that it could ship in small quantities to customers, who themselves maintained only a modest amount of items on their shelves.

During the early 1840s, Samuel Troth, the firm's principal owner, estimated that he was dealing with about three hundred customers, usually on credit terms of six months or more. For working-capital-poor storekeepers in the West, this extension of credit was indispensable for their survival. General stores and other retailers, who formed a substantial portion of Troth and Company's trade, became accustomed to dealing with several jobbers—dry goods, shoes, hardware, and others along with drugs—for supplies. The jobber, as a new form of wholesale merchant, was an entrepreneurial response to a changing market situation. Such adjustments were, however, a part of the mercantile tradition. "By adapting to the shifting needs of trade," one historian has put it, "merchants had remained the dominant force in the Western economy since the late Middle Ages and they remained so in pre–Civil War America."[23]

Continuity and Communication

The distribution network that evolved before the Civil War persisted
for decades afterward. It replaced the simpler personal world of the
all-purpose merchant with a more complex one. Yet, despite the
widening market and the shift to commercial specialization that it
made possible, as Chandler has observed, the "internal administration" of American business enterprises "continued to be carried out
along traditional lines."[24] Partnerships thus remained the dominant
ownership arrangement for large firms, and, although corporations
existed in the fields of commercial banking, insurance, and transportation, they composed a small part of the business community.
The day-to-day management of new specialized companies differed
little from the mercantile firms that they had superseded. The owner
or owners still closely supervised the operations of the firm, which
had a small all-male staff. Countinghouse employees usually included
only a few bookkeeper-clerks and an equal number of porters.

Managerial practices had undergone little change in another respect. Double-entry bookkeeping, virtually unchanged since its Italian origins in the fifteenth century, still was the common form of
accounting. Modern cost accounting appeared as an administrative
tool during and after the 1850s, first in the larger industrial manufacturing concerns. But, in an age of commercial capitalism, "ordinary mercantile double-entry bookkeeping methods were adequate
for the external nominal and financial transactions of merchants and
traders."[25] Initial expansion of specialized companies in the nineteenth century, according to one historian, actually simplified the
businessman's managerial responsibilities. Chandler argues that, while
the new middlemen "handled more transactions and dealt with more
suppliers and customers than did the older general merchants, . . .
the transactions were more of the same kind and with men in much
the same business. Transactions became increasingly routinized and
systematized."[26] Moreover, accurate information on just one or two
merchandise lines was far easier to secure than on an extensive variety of goods traded in many different ports.

While the improvement of transportation reduced shipping costs,
improvements in means of communication decreased "information
costs"—that is, the costs, to both buyers and sellers, of obtaining
accurate and timely information for sound business decisions. Although handwritten letters delivered by government surface mail

remained the primary means of business communication in the mid-nineteenth century, the mail benefited from general advances in the speed and regularity of both land and water transportation. The Post Office Act of 1792 had established steep postage rates. A single-page letter sent less than thirty miles cost six cents; the same letter mailed to a destination more than four hundred miles away cost twenty-five cents. As late as 1843, it still took eighteen and a half cents to send a letter from New York City to Troy, New York—even though transporting a barrel of flour the same distance cost six cents less. Public pressure prompted Congress to alter its approach—which had been that the Post Office should be self-supporting—and, during the 1840s, it agreed that "there was no more need for the Post Office to be self-supporting than for the army and navy to pay their own way."[27] Rates were gradually reduced, and, by 1851, a letter sent nearly across the continent cost three cents.

Easier access to post offices also elevated the quality of mail service. The number of offices multiplied from seventy-five in 1790 to over twenty-eight thousand by 1860. And, as new systems of transportation were introduced—steamboats, steamships, and railroads, in particular—the government used them as mail carriers with significant improvements in speed and service. In 1799, it took the news of George Washington's death a week to travel from Virginia to New York; forty years later, mail from Washington reached Boston in forty hours. And the majority of mail was business correspondence.

Newspapers and magazines were another form of communication that underwent change. The combination of a high level of literacy, cheaper postal rates and better service, a growing urban population, and technological achievements in printing and the manufacture of paper sparked a rise in circulation and in the number of periodicals available to Americans. The number of newspapers in the United States thus grew from under one hundred in 1790 to over fourteen hundred a half century later.

The expansion of the media had a major impact on the business community. More than ever before, newspapers featured local and national news, but, more significantly, they carried important commercial information, such as shipping schedules, prices, and bank exchange rates. Specialized business magazines also began publication, and they contained not only statistical data but also discussions of contemporary business topics. One recent historian has summarized the overall effect: "Because news flowed faster and more regularly, business decisions were made on the basis of better information—far better than that available to colonial merchants—and transactions were conducted with greater speed and efficiency. More rapid communication helped make possible more rapid turnover of capital and a dramatic increase in the volume of trade, which, in turn, helped bring about increased specialization of business functions and processes."[28]

The most revolutionary development in information transmission before the Civil War undoubtedly was the invention and widespread adoption of the telegraph. Nearly instantaneous communication now became possible. Samuel F. B. Morse, an artist and college professor, was, of course, responsible for the first successful commercial application of the electromagnetic telegraph. He began work on an instrument in the early 1830s and obtained a patent in 1841. Two years later, he persuaded a reluctant Congress to appropriate $30,000 for the construction of a demonstration line between Washington and Baltimore.

The line was finished and operating in 1844, but, in spite of proof of the telegraph's technical feasibility, Congress and the Polk administration had already lost interest. Morse then turned to the private sector for support, and, within months, promoter-entrepreneurs such as Amos Kendall and Ezra Cornell had involved themselves in telegraphic ventures, and a line was established between New York and Washington. Its success awoke both the business community and the public to the potential of Morse's invention.

Rival companies were quickly organized, and the intense competition stimulated a rapid rise in telegraph mileage, which, by 1860, reached a total of sixty thousand miles. A year later, communication was established with the West Coast. The transcontinental connection was the work of an emerging force in the industry, the Western Union Company, which was incorporated in 1856. Later, through a series of swift consolidations, Western Union virtually eliminated its competitors and, by 1866, had achieved a near-monopoly position.

There is little doubt about the profound impact of the telegraph on American society in the nineteenth century. As one historian has written, "there was hardly an individual or an institution which escaped its influence, for the whole tempo of life was quickened with the development of the telegraph industry."[29] For American business enterprise, the telegraph not only sped the distribution of vital information but also made possible the close coordination of operations required in large-scale corporate enterprises, first in the fostering of major railroad systems and later in the emergence of giant industrial organizations.

Innovation and Change

Thus the years between the inauguration of George Washington and the sundering of the Union by civil war witnessed continual and far-reaching innovations in transportation, marketing, and communications. The consequences of reductions in freighting costs and travel time and a more efficient flow of information reinforced each other and encouraged entrepreneurs to take advantage of the profit potential inherent in an integrated national market, thereby lessening American dependence on foreign trade as the engine of economic growth. Products from all regions—Northeast, South, and West—moved more expeditiously and cheaply than ever before, a greater specialization in production and marketing was established based on local and regional comparative advantage, and the groundwork for even more massive changes to come was well laid.

CHAPTER EIGHT

The Industrial Revolution in America

"About 1760 a wave of gadgets swept over England."[1] So began an anonymous English schoolboy's description of the transition from an agricultural to an industrialized economy. The term that describes this process—the "industrial revolution"—was coined by early nineteenth-century French observers, who were impressed by a succession of remarkable technological innovations and the rapid development of the factory system of production in England. They were convinced that the "changes brought about by the economic revolution were as fundamental in their effect on British life as were those wrought by the political revolution which had changed French life after 1789."[2]

While this term has become a permanent part of the historical vocabulary, it remains somewhat misleading. Above all, historians reject the implication that the industrial revolution was a sudden, cataclysmic conversion that began about 1760. Rather, they view it as less a single event than a gradual process. Whatever its timing, it is clear that the nature of this economic transformation was revolutionary. As a historian of technology, Melvin Kranzberg, has observed: "In the sense that the process of industrialization thoroughly transformed every aspect of society, then it is proper to describe it as a revolution: it certainly revolutionized men's ways of living and working, and in the process gave birth to our contemporary civilization."[3]

Britain, America, and Industrialism

The industrial revolution began and progressed differently everywhere. Great Britain was the first nation in which the industrial sector of the economy outstripped the agricultural sector in terms of value of goods produced. For industrial entrepreneurs, Britain had a large internal market that was free of the feudal restraints that hampered trade on the European continent. Moreover, a colonial empire supplemented the domestic market and provided both a source of valuable raw materials and, to a lesser extent, another market for finished goods.

Other factors in the early industrialization of Britain were important. Enough risk capital was available to finance investments in mechanization; and Britain had a sound monetary system, good land transportation, an impressive merchant marine, and favorable governmental policies. Moreover, public opinion was sympathetic to industrial development. Kranzberg has pointed out, "Not only the government but the entire society must develop values, attitudes and institutions favorable to industrialization. Specifically, these would include a desire for material progress, the approval of social mobility, a willingness to accept new ideas and techniques, and an appreciation of technological advance as leading to material betterment."[4]

Americans shared similar values and attitudes. Yet the wonder of the advent of the industrial revolution in the new world is not that Great Britain preceded the United States, but that the United States was able to follow so closely behind. American industrial advances were as rapid as those of any other nation—with the exception of Great Britain—in spite of serious obstacles, including the difficulty of competing with England's well-established manufacturing sector.

There was little doubt that Britain was determined to keep its technological leadership. Parliament enacted laws prohibiting the export of any "textile, metal-working, clock-making, leather-working, paper-making or glass manufacturing equipment," and similar legislation prevented any skilled worker from leaving the British Isles and entering "any foreign country outside the Crown's dominions for the purpose of carrying on his trade."[5] In 1785, the Privy Council enforced this law by requiring that ships' captains submit, before sailing, a list of passengers by name, age, occupation, and nationality to port officials. Any British mechanics on board were arrested, and penalties were as high as a year's imprisonment and heavy fines. Despite such strict regulations, however, British authorities never successfully halted the emigration of skilled mechanics.

The sparse and scattered population of the United States, its high internal transport costs, and its shortage of investment capital also hindered the process of industrialization. Yet the United States could rely on several material advantages. These included numerous waterpower sites, ample coal and iron deposits, and extensive forests to provide the charcoal used in iron production. Other advantages had to do with the American labor force. Thomas Cochran has described the presence of "exceptionally flexible workbench artisans— men who knew how to use tools and could improve on old processes." While skilled workmen in Europe tended to concentrate upon a single craft, American artisans "moved readily from making furniture or hoes to erecting textile machinery and ultimately to fashioning parts for steam engines; or from building houses to constructing paper mills; or from working for wages to becoming independent entrepreneurs."[6]

Still another stimulus to investment in manufacturing was a favorable public policy on the part of state and federal government. States frequently granted subsidies, tax exemptions, loans, and even temporary monopolies to new manufacturing firms, and, as we have seen, state corporation laws were instrumental in large-scale enterprises. During the first twenty years of the nineteenth century, eight states chartered over five hundred manufacturing corporations, almost two-thirds of which were in Massachusetts and New York alone. The national government also contributed to the promotion of industrial development. Before the Civil War, its involvement was primarily confined to protective tariffs levied on imports, a form of assistance that most economic historians now agree had little effect in the growth of domestic manufactures. Another, more passive, form of assistance was the absence of regulatory legislation that restricted the freedom of entrepreneurs.

A final important factor in industrialization was that entrepreneurs in the United States were, by the late eighteenth century, prepared to undertake the financing and management of manufacturing enterprises. They perceived their opportunities and willingly accepted the accompanying risks. In an age of mercantile capitalism, many members of America's first generation of industrialists, not surprisingly, were successful merchants who possessed the business acumen and the risk capital necessary to begin successful manufacturing firms. This mercantile influence, Victor Clark wrote, "pervaded all manufactures . . . and was so omnipresent that we might describe the antebellum period as a time when manufactures were integrating out of commerce."[7]

The American industrial revolution began at the end of the eighteenth century. In 1790, the production of manufactured goods in this country was still in the handicraft stage, and it consisted of household manufacturing, small shops, and local mills. Along with handicraft was the "putting-out" system, which encompassed both household and shop production and was important in the making of clothing, hats, shoes, and textiles. In the case of shoes, merchant-capitalists of the early 1800s had leathers and linings first cut in a central shop in order to reduce wastage. These materials were next distributed to "outworkers" in homes or smaller shops, who finished the shoes by stitching, binding, lasting, and soling them. The merchant-capitalist then collected and marketed the completed product.

The putting-out system was, in essence, a handicraft form of production, and, with the introduction of machines, it gradually disappeared. For the merchant who depended on the system for his stock of merchandise, it had disadvantages. There was a lack of quality control over a large number of scattered laborers, and delivery dates for the finished goods were often uncertain. Nevertheless, for those industries in which manufacturing was not easily mechanized, the putting-out system persisted into the late nineteenth century.

Over time, factory-produced goods gradually displaced household manufactures and reduced small-shop output. Factory goods also eventually diminished the volume of imports flowing into the United States, a process that economists describe as "import substitution." From 1810 (the first year for which reasonably reliable data is available on manufacturing) to 1860, the value of American industrial output rose from approximately $200 million to about $1.9 billion. Seen from another standpoint, about 75,000 Americans worked in factories in 1820; forty years later, the number stood at 1.5 million. Although the majority of the population was still engaged in agricultural pursuits in 1860, the industrial revolution had clearly gathered great momentum.

Textiles, the Pioneer Growth Industry

A great deal of antebellum industrial growth occurred in consumer-goods industries. The federal census of 1860 revealed that, measured in terms of value added by manufacture, the cotton-goods industry ranked first. The emergence of cotton textiles as the nation's first "growth industry" was only logical. Cloth was a basic necessity for any family, and it provided a substantial market opportunity for would-be manufacturers. Furthermore, because the value of cloth per pound was high, it eased the disincentive of high transportation costs. The new technology for the factory production of cotton yarn and cloth that had already been introduced in England and Scotland by 1790 was susceptible to being "borrowed" by enterprising Americans. These factors were present even before Eli Whitney's invention of a cotton gin in 1793 and the emergence of the American South as the world's largest producer of raw cotton.

Hence, it was in cotton textiles that the factory system first developed in America. Although there is no universally accepted definition of a "factory," it possesses the following general characteristics: (1) it sells a substantial portion of its output in a regional or national, as opposed to strictly local, market; (2) its operations, carried on within one building or a group of adjacent buildings, involve a considerable capital investment in machinery and other equipment, which are usually power-driven; (3) its laborers work at the factory site rather than in their homes or at other scattered locations, and they are subject to shop discipline.

Cotton textiles became located especially in New England. That region was blessed with an affluent merchant class who possessed capital to invest and the administrative and marketing experience and the entrepreneurial energy to apply to new ventures in manufacturing. The fact that New England farming did not have as high an economic return as agriculture in the South or Midwest also created a labor supply that was more willing to work in other occupations.

The immediate challenge that an American textile-mill operator had to confront was the production of a cotton yarn strong enough to be woven into cloth. In England, the problem had just been solved by Richard Arkwright's invention of the water frame, patented in 1769. The frame enabled a worker to spin a relatively strong yarn in considerable quantity by a combination of waterpower-driven rollers and spindles. Since the water frame was too large and too expensive to be installed in any homes or small shops, a factory setting was necessary. By 1771 Arkwright had secured the financial backing of Jedediah Strutt, a successful merchant, and soon had factories operating at a number of locations. Labor did not pose difficulties, as machine tenders required no special skills. Workers in an Arkwright mill could learn most tasks in little more than a few weeks; machines, in essence, had replaced skilled labor. In the process, Arkwright made a fortune for himself. He was eventually knighted in 1786 and became the textile industry's first great magnate.

SAMUEL SLATER AND EARLY AMERICAN INDUSTRIALIZATION

One employee of an Arkwright-equipped cotton mill was Samuel Slater, born in 1768 in Derbyshire, England. At the age of fourteen, he was apprenticed to Jedediah Strutt as a clerk, but within a few years Slater had risen to the position of a mill overseer. He has been described as a "steady, persevering, self-contained, blunt young man, capable of new enterprise, and with infinite concern for detail."[8] It was Samuel Slater who brought the industrial revolution to America.

By the late 1780s Slater believed that his chances of becoming a factory owner would be considerably greater in the United States than in England. Disregarding the laws forbidding English textile mechanics from emigrating, he committed the details of the Arkwright system to memory, disguised himself as a farm laborer, and made his way to London, where he boarded a ship for New York. It was 1789, and he was twenty-one years of age.

Upon his arrival in the United States, Slater found immediate but unsatisfactory employment in a struggling New York City textile mill. By chance, he met a ship's captain who knew of other experiments in manufacturing that the Brown family in Rhode Island was conducting. The Browns presided over a successful mercantile house that carried on trade in British goods, West Indian products, and African slaves.

One of the firm's principal owners, Moses Brown, had also become interested in textiles, and he purchased some crude American machinery that, when put to the test, was faulty. Thus, when Slater wrote to Brown on December 8, 1789, his letter was one of the most momentous pieces of correspondence in American business history. Slater wrote in part: "A few days ago I was informed that you wanted a manager of cotton spinning, etc. in which business I flatter myself that I can give the greatest satisfaction, in making machinery, making good yarn, either for stockings or twist, as any that is made in England; as I have had opportunity, and an oversight, of Sir Richard Arkwright's works, and in Mr. Strutt's mill upwards of eight years."[9]

Moses Brown replied quickly. If Slater would come to Rhode Island and improve the Brown machinery, he could become a partner in the rejuvenated enterprise and receive "the credit as well as the advantage of perfecting the first water-mill in America."[10] Without even bothering to draft a reply, Slater boarded a ship for Providence, eager to pursue Brown's offer.

A partnership was then organized that was called Almy, Brown, and Slater. William Almy (Moses Brown's son-in-law) and Smith Brown (another relative) agreed to supply Slater's machines with all the raw cotton required and then to handle the marketing of the finished yarn. On December 20, 1790, Slater's newly constructed machines, installed in an old mill in Pawtucket, Rhode Island, were finally put into motion, and the industrial revolution was under way in the United States.

The labor force of the spinning mill primarily consisted of local children between the ages of seven and twelve. By the second month, seven boys and two girls were employed six days per week for a weekly wage of as much as sixty-seven cents. Wages were ordinarily paid, however, in goods, usually yarn, food, or other supplies.

As production expanded and the number of mills multiplied, Slater cast a wider net. He published advertisements in newspapers in Rhode Island and Massachusetts that encouraged families—especially those with five or more children—to apply for work. In 1793, he established a Sunday school in his own home for his youthful employees. At first he taught the school himself, but later he hired students from what is now Brown University as teachers. What later generations would see as an evil of the industrial system—child labor—was to Slater a virtue. Child labor instilled discipline, good work habits, and a respect for authority in young people; it provided families with additional income.

Mechanics and overseers were the only skilled workers in Slater's mills, and they were often the fathers of the children employed there. Slater made a point of hiring men for skilled positions who brought additional members of their families to the factory with them. Not infrequently, these men, once they accumulated experience in the Slater system, would start businesses of their own, forming a new generation of manufacturers—in much the same way that Slater had used his knowledge of the Arkwright methods.

Slater's mills only spun yarn and did not weave it into cloth. Almy and Brown, both of whom possessed a mercantile background, took complete charge of marketing; Slater insured that his partners had an acceptable commodity to sell. Since Americans were not familiar with the use of cotton yarn, it was necessary to persuade them to choose it over wool or linen made from flax, a task that called for some marketing expertise.

As sales increased, additional production facilities became necessary. In 1793, a new mill was constructed on the Blackstone River north of Providence, and, in 1799, Slater built a mill of his own at Rehoboth, Massachusetts, which he operated simultaneously with the other factories. More mills followed, including one established in 1806 in a new Rhode Island community that was named Slatersville.

Slater's decision to launch some independent ventures was largely prompted by disagreements with his commercial partners. A fundamental difference was that New England merchants preferred a family partnership as a form of ownership. According to one recent study, Almy and Brown were most comfortable in a firm "in which ownership was synonymous with management and family connections usually meant more than skill in the employment of personnel and the choice of partners."[11] As a result, Slater was always treated as somewhat of an outsider.

The apparent success of Slater's enterprises had the inevitable effect of fostering competition. By 1810 there were over sixty spinning mills operating in the United States and more in the process of construction. Many of these new mills were founded by men who had gained their training under Samuel Slater.

Even after Francis Cabot Lowell introduced the power loom in 1813 and combined spinning and weaving in a single factory, Slater continued to confine operations at his mills to cotton yarn "spun by water." Nevertheless, he did employ the putting-out system to broaden the market for his product. During the 1820s, for example, a Slater mill at Oxford, Massachusetts, sent its yarn to over five hundred hand-loom weavers, who usually worked in their own homes. When they returned the cloth to Slater, he carefully examined each piece, and, if it was poorly woven, he docked the weaver's pay and scolded him for an unsatisfactory performance. Not until 1823 did he introduce the power loom in one of his mills and gradually reduce reliance on the putting-out system.

Despite his pioneering role in bringing the industrial revolution to the United States, Slater was still in some ways an entrepreneurial conservative. He retained preindustrial attitudes toward the administration of his own enterprises. Slater declined to adopt the corporate form of ownership despite its clear advantages for organizing larger businesses. He preferred the simpler relationships associated with partnerships of relatives or close friends. Moreover, he attempted to maintain a personal oversight of all his operations even when they had become widely dispersed because he was reluctant to delegate authority to others.

By his death in 1835, Slater, despite some financial reverses in his last years, still owned mills in Rhode Island, Massachusetts, and New Hampshire. He fathered the cotton-textile industry in the United States and laid the groundwork for the nation's future industrial growth by introducing the factory system. He was not the first to attempt the transfer of British technology to the United States, but he was the first to achieve commercial profitability. A key factor in Slater's success, along with his genius for production, was the steady infusion of capital from established merchants—a factor that was also crucial in the second stage of the history of American cotton textiles.

FRANCIS CABOT LOWELL AND THE WALTHAM SYSTEM

The step from yarn to cloth was a bottleneck that prevented American mills from introducing mass production. On the other hand, in England, the bottleneck had been eliminated by 1810. Beginning with the designs of Edmund Cartwright in the 1780s and continuing with the improvements of Thomas Johnson and William Horrocks, the British textile industry developed workable power looms by 1813, when some 2,400 were already operating in England and Scotland.

The man most instrumental in introducing the power loom to the United States was Francis Cabot Lowell. He was born in 1775, the son of a prominent Massachusetts attorney and judge who had also been one of the organizers of the state's first bank in 1784. Because his father was married three times—to a Higginson, a Cabot, and a Russell—the son "grew up in an extended-kinship group second to none in Boston and its satellite towns on the North Shore, a family connection based upon several generations of merchant-shipowning."[12] Young Lowell attended Harvard, where he excelled in mathematics, before joining a partnership in the import-export business with his uncle, William Cabot, in 1793. During the next two decades he was an all-purpose merchant and, in the process, entered into ventures with most, if not all, of Boston's business aristocracy, including Nathan Appleton and Lowell's brother-in-law, Patrick Tracy Jackson.

In 1810, Lowell decided to take his family to England for an extended stay because of his own and his wife's frail health. It seems likely, however, that business considerations were also paramount. The Napoleonic Wars had led both France and England to impose restrictive measures on American trade, and the Jefferson and Madison administrations in Washington, beginning in 1807, retaliated with the Embargo and Non-Intercourse Acts. The damage inflicted upon the nation's foreign commerce left American merchants open to alternative investment opportunities and aware that domestic manufactures would no longer face the usual British competition. Moreover, the growing possibility of an Anglo-American war in the near future only intensified the desire to diversify into fields other than overseas trading.

During a two-year stay in the British Isles, Lowell traveled to manufacturing centers in England and Scotland. As a prominent American merchant, he was given the opportunity to observe closely textile factories in operation, including those that employed the new power looms. It took him little time to make up his mind.

Lowell returned to Boston in 1812 convinced that he could duplicate British power looms and establish a new level of manufacturing in the American textile industry. According to one historian, David J. Jeremy, Lowell "offered almost optimum reliability as a vehicle of technology transfer. His family background, financial involvement, and his keen mind honed on Harvard mathematics and mercantile risk taking, combined with a personal inspection of the state of the art in British factories, made his judgment almost impeccable."[13]

In late 1812, Lowell began work on two fronts. In an attic room on Boston's Broad Street, he began constructing a power loom with the assistance of a British-born Yankee mechanic, Paul Moody, and, by 1814, they had assembled a working machine. Nathan Appleton later recalled "the state of admiration and satisfaction with which we sat by the hour, watching the beautiful movement of this new and wonderful machine, destined as it evidently was to change the character of all textile industry."[14]

On a second front, Lowell sought out his friends in the mercantile community of Boston and won pledges of a substantial starting capital. Patrick Tracy Jackson also agreed to assist Lowell in the active management of the new enterprise, which, in February 1813, was incorporated as the Boston Manufacturing Company. The new corporation was one of the pivotal business firms in American economic history. As a historian of the industry, Caroline Ware, has written: "The most important thing which could have happened to the cotton industry was that, after twenty-five years of slow growth and small scale experimentation, it should have been taken up by men with the best business imagination in the land, unhampered by its traditions, concerned with making fortunes and building states, not with manufacturing cotton cloth."[15] Although Ware probably does not give enough credit to the progress of the Slater mills, the Boston Associates, as they became known, undoubtedly brought the factory system to an entirely new level of organization.

The Boston Manufacturing Company was initially capitalized at $100,000, but, within a few years, this figure was increased to $400,000. These sums, unprecedented for the time, were necessary because of the greater investment in fixed assets that power-loom weaving required and because of the large scale of production. The new firm soon constructed a mill at Waltham on the Charles River, a short distance from Boston. It measured ninety feet by forty-five feet and was four stories high; its size was greater than anything ever seen in New England.

Production began in December 1814 at what some historians regard as the first modern factory in the United States. All within a single factory, the Waltham mill integrated and mechanized the manufacturing process from the raw material to the finished product, coarse cotton cloth. Within the mill, production flowed upward. On the ground floor, the carding machines combed, stretched, and prepared the raw cotton for the spinning frames on a middle floor and for the looms on the top floor.

The power loom and the integrated factory—because they enabled American manufacturers to compete with Britain after 1815—have been called "virtually a life-saving innovation" for the textile industry.[16] Under the putting-out system, mill owners paid hand-loom weavers three to seven cents per yard; the direct expense of power-loom weaving was, on the average, only one cent per yard. While many manufacturers who kept the putting-out system failed during the depression after 1815, the Boston Manufacturing Company prospered.

In 1817, just weeks after the premature death of Francis Cabot Lowell at the age of forty-two, the company distributed a 12.5 percent dividend to its shareholders. In the following years, dividends were even better, so much so that, by 1822, stockholders had received over a 100 percent return on their original investments. The substantial profits earned at Waltham spurred the Boston Associates to seek further expansion. But, by 1821, all available water-power sites near Waltham were in use, and so a search began for a new location.

Paul Moody discovered a promising site on the Merrimack River, about twenty-five miles north of Boston. When Moody reported his find, Patrick Tracy Jackson began to envision a manufacturing center—much larger than any single mill—that would include multiple factories operating on an unprecedented scale, and he had little trouble convincing the Boston Associates to reinvest their Waltham earnings. Construction began in 1822. The stockholders organized a new corporation, the Merrimack Manufacturing Company, with a capitalization of $600,000. Since the site was isolated, workers were transplanted to it and housed in a new community for which Nathan Appleton suggested the name Lowell. By the fall of 1823 Lowell was in production.

In the following years, a succession of textile companies was established at Lowell—each growing out of the success of its predecessors, each controlled by the same small group of Boston entrepreneurs. By 1836 investment in the eight principal firms in the area was over $6 million, and Lowell mills employed over six thousand workers.

As important were the general management concepts that Lowell and his colleagues introduced. Collectively, these have become known as the "Waltham System." Its key features were: the integration of all stages of production within a single plant; a substantial capitalization, which made possible larger-scale operations; the selection of mill managers for their overall administrative ability rather than their experience with textile manufacturing alone; the concentration upon only one standardized product in each factory, which facilitated high-volume production runs and low unit costs, and necessitated little skill on the part of workers; the marketing of the product through a single "selling house," instead of a large number of commission agents; and the employment of a unique labor force of young women who were housed in company-owned dormitories.

The most publicized feature of the Waltham System was its solution to the problem of securing factory labor—the dormitory or boardinghouse plan. This plan involved the active recruitment of young New England farm girls, who were housed in company-owned dormitories located near the mills. In order to break down the resistance of conservative Yankee families to sending their unmarried daughters to work and live in a distant factory town, the dormitories were under the charge of matrons of unquestioned character and under stringent rules designed to protect the virtue of their residents.

Francis Cabot Lowell devised the plan to recruit a labor force and to demonstrate that the degradation of factory workers seen in Great Britain need not be repeated in the United States. In their heyday, Lowell's dormitories were showpieces, and they attracted numerous distinguished observers, including many from Europe, who marveled at them. The workers at Waltham and Lowell were the first generation of American women who sought employment outside the home. Thomas Dublin, who has done the most detailed study of the subject, has concluded that women worked at the mills less because of necessity than because they "offered individual self-support, enabled women to enjoy urban amenities not available in their rural communities, and gave them a measure of economic and social independence from their families."[17] In a typical Lowell mill of the 1830s, more than 85 percent of the employees were female, most of whom were between the ages of fifteen and thirty.

Women worked in the mills from eleven to thirteen hours per day, six days a week. The work schedule, although extremely arduous by modern standards, was not uncommon for a young woman who grew up in a farm family. Moreover, the pace of operations within the factory was not especially taxing in the early years.

This idyllic setting began to change in the 1830s. Twice in that decade, women workers at Lowell participated in a "turn-out," or strike, once to protest a wage reduction in 1834 and again in 1836 against an increase in dormitory rates. During the 1840s, workers were the victims of management-imposed speedups (increasing the operating speed of the machines the women tended) and stretch-outs (assigning additional machines to an individual worker). Thereafter, the number of women from New England found in the mills began to decline, in part because of worsening conditions, but also because alternative career options—especially in teaching—were now available. Irish immigrants quickly filled these mill jobs, and they had little control over employment or working conditions.

Although the Waltham System established integrated factories in the United States, it made little attempt to integrate the administrative structure of the various companies. Decision-making authority was, in essence, triangular in the Lowell mills. The chief executive officer of each firm, who held the title of treasurer, resided in Boston. He was selected for his administrative experience—invariably acquired in a mercantile background—rather than for any special expertise in textile production. The treasurer's responsibilities were to purchase raw cotton for the mills, to maintain the accounts of the company, and to evaluate the efforts of the mill superintendent.

The mill superintendent or agent, the second leg of the administrative triangle, supervised the day-to-day operations of the mill. He was responsible for efficient production and for the management of the work force. Through detailed reports, the superintendent kept in constant contact with the treasurer, his immediate superior.

The final leg of the triangle was the mill's selling house. Although, in theory, it was responsible only for marketing the final product, in reality it exercised internal decision-making power. Its knowledge of the market and its readiness to advance the textile firm further working capital against future shipments enabled the officers of the selling house to dictate the type and quantity of cloth each mill manufactured. Thus, even in the most advanced segment of antebellum American industry, little centralized managerial control existed.

Not all textile mills adopted the Waltham System. Some smaller and older spinning mills in southern New England still relied on the putting-out system rather than bear the high cost of installing power looms and the other technical improvements associated with Lowell operations. Gradually, the reluctant were converted, but, even then, the power loom that they usually adopted was not the type pioneered by Lowell and Moody. Instead, it was one introduced into the United States by an immigrant Glasgow textile mechanic, William Gilmore. His machine was somewhat simpler in design than the Lowell-Moody loom, and, most important, it was available at a lower cost.

The textile industry played a decisive role in America's industrial revolution. In 1832, a survey of American manufacturing carried out under the direction of the secretary of the treasury found that 106 companies had assets of \$100,000 or more. Of these, eighty-eight were textile firms.

Continuous Processing and Interchangeable Parts

A good deal of the technological progress associated with the industrial revolution in the United States stemmed from American adaptations of British innovations. Nevertheless, there were two important innovations that originated in the United States: continuous processing and the assembly of products using interchangeable parts.

Continuous processing—or, as it was later called, assembly-line production—first occurred in the automated flour mill developed in the 1780s by Oliver Evans, a Delaware-born mechanical genius. In most mills, workers performed the back-breaking work of lifting grain to the top of a gravity system, which then fed it between millstones; they hoisted it up once more to store it in a silo. Evans sought a way of accomplishing these tasks with less human effort.

He designed and patented a system of interconnected machines that eliminated all hauling and heavy labor by means of buckets, hoppers, and conveyor belts. His invention performed every necessary mill operation without the aid of manual labor, and it required the services of just a single supervisor. The inherent advantages of Evans's automated mill were so plain that the techniques were widely adopted in the following years—often with complete disregard of the inventor's patent.

Immediately before the Civil War, the continuous-processing concept appeared again in the pork-packing houses of Cincinnati. At a "disassembly" line, a row of laborers at fixed stations butchered carcasses that hung from hooks and moved on overhead rails at a predetermined speed. Each worker carried out a single task, such as splitting the animal or removing specific parts. The minute division of labor and elimination of wasted motion resulted in a significant increase in productivity. The automobile assembly lines in Henry Ford's plants in Detroit several decades later had their roots in the early advances in continuous processing of the antebellum years.

The production of goods that use the principle of interchangeable parts necessitates that the parts be manufactured with such accuracy that any two pieces will be identical. The final product can then be assembled with little or no hand tooling of the components. The advantages of this method were threefold: (1) because the machines were driven by water or steam power, a saving in human labor was made possible; (2) the tending of the power-driven machinery required less skill than was necessary to tool parts by hand; (3) and, a broken component could be replaced from a standard stock of spares. The chief deterrent to the widespread use of the system was the expense of developing the necessary machine tools.

For many years, full credit for the innovation in the United States was given to Eli Whitney, the nation's most famous antebellum inventor. More recently, however, historians describe Eli Whitney's part in interchangeable manufacture, at least in part, as a legend.[18] Whitney first became interested in interchangeable parts during the unhappy aftermath of his invention of the sawtooth cotton gin. Whitney's brainchild had an enormous impact on the South. One Whitney biographer described it in this way: "His gin reduced labor fifty-fold without putting anyone out of work. Indeed, his invention would make employment for thousands—Negro slaves on the land, women and children in the factories, eager white men in the shops and the countinghouses. The United States would grow rich."[19] The gin also firmly fastened the institution of slavery upon the South and, perhaps, in the long run made inevitable the Civil War.

Although Whitney's gin changed the course of southern agriculture and American history, it worked no magic on his own personal fortunes. In 1793, he had formed a partnership with Phineas Miller, a South Carolina plantation manager, to secure a patent from the federal government and to begin manufacturing gins. The partners foolishly expected that they could produce sufficient gins to clean all the South's cotton for a "commission" of one pound in every five, essentially the system that grist mills had long employed. But Whitney and Miller were never able to maintain exclusive control of their gin, its patent notwithstanding, because of production delays, the ease with which other manufacturers could duplicate the simple concept, the outrage of cotton planters at what they regarded as an exorbitant charge by would-be monopolists, and the importance of the gin for the South's economy.

Consequently, Whitney and Miller found themselves embroiled in an almost endless series of costly and time-consuming lawsuits to enforce their patent rights, while little revenue actually flowed into the firm's coffers. By 1798 Whitney was frustrated and disillusioned, and—more out of a sense of desperation than entrepreneurial enthusiasm—at this point he then chose to begin a new manufacturing venture.

A foreign-policy crisis offered an unexpected opportunity. In 1797, after the "XYZ Affair," diplomatic relations with the revolutionary government in France soured badly, and the United States soon found itself fighting an undeclared naval war in the Atlantic; rumors abounded of a French invasion force that threatened American shores. George Washington, then in retirement, was hastily called back from private life to command an expanded American army, and Congress rushed to provide the troops with adequate arms.

Whitney, perceiving an opening for himself, wrote to the secretary of the treasury on May 1, 1798. He proposed to supply the government with at least ten thousand muskets within a short time. The treasury, eagerly accepting the offer without examining it too closely, contracted with Whitney for the delivery of four thousand muskets by the end of September 1799 and another six thousand a year later. The government promised to pay him regular cash advances with five thousand dollars immediately to assist in initial production. The price was set at $13.40 per musket.

No established arms manufacturer had ever turned out such a quantity of weapons in so little time, and, in Whitney's case, he needed to equip a factory, secure raw materials, and recruit workers. Not surprisingly, he failed badly in meeting his deadlines. He did not deliver even the first five hundred muskets until September 1801, and the full contract was not completed until 1809, long after the French crisis had passed.

When pressed about the protracted delay, Whitney responded in 1799 that he was producing his muskets by means of a new manufacturing principle. "One of my primary objects," he wrote, "is to form the tools so the tools themselves shall fashion the work and give to every part its just proportion—which when once accomplished, will give expedition, uniformity, and exactness to the whole."[20] It was the first indication that he planned to make his muskets with interchangeable parts. Whitney's claims—and, in 1801, his demonstration in Washington (before an audience that included John Adams and Thomas Jefferson) of ten different lock mechanisms fitted into the same musket—were enough to sustain the patience of government officials, and they continued their cash advances.

Unfortunately for Whitney's reputation, recent scholarly research has cast serious doubt on his originality in arms production. His armory at Mill Rock, Connecticut, introduced little that was actually new, but instead heavily borrowed from other producers. Three sources played a larger role in bringing interchangeable parts to American manufacturing. One was the efforts of Simeon North, a Connecticut farm-implement manufacturer turned armsmaker.

North too was awarded a series of contracts by the army beginning in 1798. The 1813 contract that he signed, calling for the production of twenty thousand pistols, carried a unique provision. It stipulated that "the component parts of pistols are to correspond so exactly that any limb or part of one pistol may be fitted to any other pistol of the twenty thousand."[21] It was an unprecedented requirement, insisting upon manufacturing employing the principle of interchangeable parts. Pursuant to the contract, North developed what was probably the first milling machine ever designed to turn out uniform weapons. However, he completed only a small number of pistols before governmental officials altered the model specifications.

A second source was the work at the federal government's own Springfield, Massachusetts, armory, especially under the direction of Roswell Lee (1815–1833). Even more significant was the progress made by John H. Hall at Harpers Ferry, Virginia (now West Virginia). In 1826, Hall, according to most historians, successfully produced in quantity the first fully interchangeable parts for shoulder weapons ever manufactured in the United States, Whitney notwithstanding. Yet most modern writers do not simply dismiss Whitney's role in fostering what British observers later called "the American system of manufacturing." Until his death in 1825, he produced arms for both federal and state governments at his Mill Rock factory. Although more significant technical advances were probably made elsewhere, Whitney's prominence and his gift for publicity made him invaluable as a popularizer of the system.

American arms production reached its zenith in the nineteenth century with the career of Connecticut-born Samuel Colt. At the age of sixteen in 1830, he went to sea on a ship engaged in the Asian trade. It was while watching the helmsman spin the ship's wheel that he conceived the idea of a pistol with a revolving cartridge cylinder. He secured a patent for his invention in 1836, but he did not become a successful manufacturer for yet another decade.

With the coming of the Mexican War in 1846, Colt received a $25,000 government order for his guns. At first he contracted with Eli Whitney's son for the assembly of the pistols in the Whitney family factory in Connecticut, but later, ending that association, Colt opened his own armory in Hartford. He eventually installed there over a thousand belt-driven machines that allowed him to produce a revolver that was 80 percent machine-made. In 1851 Colt exhibited five hundred of his guns to impressed British observers at the Crystal Palace Exposition in London, the first World's Fair. Soon after he became the initial American manufacturer to establish an overseas branch factory when he began operations in England on the banks of the Thames River. When Samuel Colt died in 1862, he was the world's most famous weaponsmaker. Even more, Colt had brought the American innovations of mass production and interchangeable parts to a new, higher level of industrial development.

The use of the principle of interchangeable parts was readily transferred from muskets to other products, such as watches and clocks, sewing machines, locks, bicycles, typewriters, and agricultural implements. The common characteristic of its spread was the design and use of highly specialized machinery in production. Eventually, with the rise of an important group of machine-tool firms, the manufacture of this machinery became an industry in itself. As Nathan Rosenberg has written: "The machine-tool industry, then, came to constitute a pool or reservoir of the skills and technical knowledge essential to the generation of technical change throughout the machine-using sectors of the economy. Precisely because it came to deal with processes and problems which were common to an increasing number of industries, it played the role of a transmission center in the diffusion of the new technology."[22] As a result, new, lower-priced manufactured goods were now available in a mass market. Where only the wealthy could purchase hand-tooled mechanical items, ordinary people could now buy items that previously they had either done without or accepted as hand-me-downs from affluent neighbors. And, the wider market encouraged even more innovations in succeeding years.

Steam, Iron, and Coal

In large part, the availability of sufficient waterpower dictated the concentration of textile mills at sites such as Lowell, Massachusetts. Because of easy access to waterpower, manufacturers became interested only slowly in the use of steam engines in production. The indefatigable Oliver Evans experimented regularly with such engines, and, in 1802, he successfully installed one in a Philadelphia mill that he operated. Its success launched him in business as an engine builder, and he was probably the first person in the United States to specialize in that activity. It is estimated that, by his death in 1819, some fifty Evans engines were used along the Atlantic seaboard. Nevertheless, as late as 1850, the use of stationary steam engines in industry was not common. These engines were expensive in fuel, and mechanical breakdowns were frequent. Moreover, eastern manufacturers placed the annual expense of steam power at four times or more that of waterwheels or turbines. As the years passed, engines were improved, the cost of fuel (principally coal) became less, and new waterpower sites were more difficult to find. By 1870, therefore, steam had caught up with water as a means of driving industrial machinery, and it thereafter drew rapidly ahead.

The increased use of steam engines was linked to the development of the iron industry in the United States. Advances in iron manufacturing reduced the cost of engines and improved their efficiency and reliability. But the history of the iron industry before 1860 stands in sharp contrast to that of textiles. Both witnessed important British innovations during the last quarter of the eighteenth century, but, while American textile operators quickly adopted these breakthroughs, ironmasters in America abandoned their old-fashioned methods more slowly.

The British innovations included the use of coked coal to smelt iron ore into pig iron and the development of puddling and rolling techniques to refine the pig iron into usable wrought iron. The coke in England, which replaced charcoal in blast furnaces, turned England from a net importer of pig iron to a major world producer. And, while English forests were depleted, reducing the amount of charcoal that could be gleaned from timber, there was no lack of coal for coking. Puddling allowed pig iron to be heated and worked in a furnace that used mineral fuel rather than charcoal, and rolling eliminated the tedious pounding of pig iron on a forge with trip hammers.

American iron manufacturers were slow to employ these innovations. Timber was plentiful in the United States, while its supplies of soft bituminous coal (from which coke was produced) were located west of the Alleghenies, and facilities to transport it to seaboard manufacturers did not exist before the mid-nineteenth century.

On the eastern slopes of the Alleghenies in Pennsylvania, there were massive deposits of a different type of coal—anthracite. It was known as "stone coal," because of the difficulty igniting it, and its development awaited technical solutions to this problem. By the 1830s, however, the mining of anthracite had become commercially feasible, and, for the first time, American ironmasters used a mineral fuel rather than charcoal in the smelting process. The production of pig iron rose—without an accompanying price increase—as anthracite became the most popular form of fuel. In 1830, nearly all American pig iron was produced with charcoal; by 1865 three-quarters of it was made with hard anthracite coal. But the importance of anthracite was short-lived, and, by 1875, coke began to surpass anthracite as a fuel for blast furnaces.

The ascendancy of anthracite ought not to be dismissed as only a brief episode in the industrial progress of the United States. Alfred Chandler has hypothesized that anthracite made possible a revolution in ironmaking. The availability of cheaper iron and of a usable mineral fuel for steam engines stimulated the manufacture of more iron products and increased the size and number of factories that produced these items. Moreover, as Chandler concludes, "On the basis of the fuel, iron, and power thus generated by the opening of the anthracite fields, manufacturers could lower costs and undersell British imports and, of more importance, undersell the small local manufacturers scattered thoughout the nation's largely rural areas."[23]

One notable aspect of the antebellum iron industry's history was the appearance, for the first time, of integrated firms. Until the 1840s, firms limited their functions either to smelting iron ore or to refining pig iron. Smelting was carried out at rural "iron plantations," which encompassed as much as ten thousand acres or more of land. The extensive acreage was necessary because of the use of forest-derived charcoal in blast furnaces, and the rural location of iron ore deposits also determined the country setting of these smelting operations.[24]

The substitution of anthracite for charcoal spelled the end of the old iron plantation, as blast furnaces were easily located in urban settings. The size of firms increased as well. Nonetheless, mineral fuels did not by themselves promote integration. Before 1840, small foundries, forges, and mills, usually serving local markets, remained modest operations because of lack of entrepreneurial ambition, insufficient capital, and the poor state of transportation facilities.

The transformation of the iron industry began in the 1840s. The catalyst was the growth of railroads, which stimulated demand for metal rails. But the rail market was a fierce competitive arena; British mills offered a low-cost product that American refiners could not match. A few American manufacturers thus concluded that, only by reducing their costs substantially and by maintaining a steady production volume at high levels, could the British invasion be overcome.

A small number of producers began the integration of the smelting and refining phases of iron manufacture as a way to achieve these goals. For example, Benjamin Jones integrated his mill by buying blast furnaces, thanks to an infusion of outside capital provided by James Laughlin, a Pennsylvania commission merchant. As a result of this expansion of operations, the capitalization of the reorganized Jones and Laughlin firm rose from $20,000 to $175,000 by 1861, an increase that came both from Laughlin's financial support and reinvested earnings. By 1860 the largest ironworks in the United States were all integrated rail mills, including Pennsylvania's Montour Iron, which employed some three thousand workers. Firms that were not integrated found themselves unable to keep even a modest portion of the rail market.

Integrated mills were, in fact, the future of the American iron industry. They produced their own pig iron—thus eliminating the need to purchase that supply from an iron broker—and they sold directly to the ultimate consumer, in this instance, a relatively limited number of railroads. In this fashion, the giant integrated steel enterprises of the post–Civil War era would operate successfully.

Cyrus McCormick and the Selling of the Reaper

A variety of new agricultural implements also widened the market for the products of the iron industry and extended further the dimensions of the American industrial revolution. Cast iron and steel plows, seed drills, rice threshers, mowers, and other devices fostered the development of the "farm-servicing" industry, which, by 1860, had become one of the ten most important in the American economy. But "the most continuous, concerted efforts by tinkers and inventors," as one historian writes, "to improve the methods of production and reduce labor costs" occurred in the cultivation of wheat.[25]

Before 1830, the short harvest season was the main bottleneck to any major expansion in wheat output. Harvesting was still a manual process that involved the use of hand sickles or cradles—and that was not only arduous but also expensive. The average farm laborer could cut only about two and a half acres per day, and, during the short harvest period, larger farms relied upon outside labor, which they paid at the prevailing wage rates. A relatively high labor cost and the continued uncertainty of having an adequate number of workers were incentives for the wheat farmer to adopt labor-saving implements once they became available and mechanically and economically practicable.

The answer to the wheat farmer's problem appeared in the 1830s with the development of the first, still fairly primitive, reapers. The businessman thereafter most closely associated with them was Cyrus Hall McCormick. Along with McCormick, others—Obed Hussey, McCormick's own father, or perhaps another tinkerer of the period— also played a small role in the invention of the reaper. Cyrus McCormick's major contribution was, rather, his innovations in marketing and organization-building through which the reaper became widely popular. McCormick has also been credited with everything from a doubling of wheat acreage in the United States to the winning of the Civil War for the North. Perhaps equally important for our purposes, McCormick represents a transition figure who bridged the gap from the antebellum industrial revolution in the United States to the emergence of large-scale corporate enterprise.

Cyrus H. McCormick grew up on his father's farm in Virginia's Shenandoah Valley. Actually, Robert McCormick, the father, owned not a small farm, but an estate of twelve hundred acres, nine slaves, and eighteen horses. "He had," according to his son's biographer, "earned the right to indulge his passion for mechanical experiment without fear for the material comfort of his family, in case his inventions did not find a ready market."[26] For years, Robert McCormick worked on a device to reap wheat. But it was his son Cyrus who, at the age of twenty-two, by modifying his father's design, produced a working model in 1831. Not until 1834 did the younger McCormick finally apply for a patent, apparently spurred on by reports that Obed Hussey, a brilliant but erratic inventor, had assembled his own reaper model and was already attempting to sell copies to farmers. Curiously, despite his patent, McCormick then put aside his reaper for the rest of the decade and devoted most of his time to a fruitless venture in iron manufacturing. But, after 1840, Mc-Cormick abandoned his debt-ridden iron business, made a series of needed improvements on his reaper, and began selling a modest number to eastern farmers. By the mid-1840s, however, he recognized that his real market lay in the prairies of the trans-Appalachian West, where wheat farming was rapidly finding a new locus and where a shortage of wage labor made the reaper especially valuable.

McCormick also saw that his Virginia workshop was too small and poorly situated to take adequate advantage of western demand. The addition of transportation costs to the selling price of the machine might either deter customers from a purchase or induce them to buy a lower-priced competitor's model. McCormick, it has been pointed out, "was one of the first American industrialists to face the necessity of making a major move in order to be closer to his markets."[27]

In 1848, he closed his Virginia operation and moved westward to the growing city of Chicago. Previously, he had assembled reapers in his own shop and also licensed a few other manufacturers to produce them. Now, licensing agreements were terminated, and McCormick produced all reapers bearing his name from a single factory in Chicago.

In 1849, he envisioned selling as many as fifteen hundred reapers during that year's wheat-growing season. At the same time, he faced the challenge of marketing a complex and expensive product to interested but cautious customers. He pioneered a marketing strategy that, to an unprecedented degree, relied on heavy advertising and a network of salesmen who were responsible for demonstrating the ease of operation and the reliability under the pressures of a hectic harvest season of the McCormick reaper. Eventually, this sales force became more than just peddlers of machinery. A system of company agents was established, each, in effect, a franchised dealer for McCormick implements who was closely regulated by the central administration in Chicago.

The agents had multiple duties. They not only demonstrated and sold equipment, they also had to stand ready to service it when breakdowns occurred. Furthermore, since the reaper and similar McCormick products were expensive, a policy of selling on credit was introduced early. The price of the basic reaper in the 1850s, for example, was $115 cash, or $120 if purchased on credit. If a farmer bought on credit, he was expected to pay thirty dollars down and the balance after the next harvest, an arrangement that placed an additional burden on the company's agents, since they were required to evaluate the credit worthiness of buyers and collect past-due accounts from recalcitrant farmers.

No such elaborate marketing structure existed in any other field. As Harold Livesay has stated, "The success of this system of sales and service, the first of its kind, and not simply the productivity of his factory carried McCormick to the top of the farm machinery industry and kept him there despite fierce competition and the expiration of his patents."[28]

As the years passed, McCormick left more of the day-to-day management to his brothers William and Leander and later to salaried managers. Nevertheless, he remained unwilling to relinquish too much control, even as he dabbled in politics, religion, world travels, and other investments. As a result, by the time of his death in 1884, the firm remained ostensibly powerful, but was growing less and less efficient. In its prime, however, McCormick's organization was responsible for innovations that would serve equally well later manufacturers of other durable goods—notably, the twentieth century's most important consumer durable, the automobile.

The Crystal Palace

It might be said that the American industrial revolution came of age in the eyes of those overseas in 1851. Prompted by a suggestion from Prince Albert, Great Britain issued an invitation to the world, proposing that all nations present their manufactures at a grand exhibition housed in a huge London hall later known as the Crystal Palace. Before it closed its doors, some 6 million people visited the Crystal Palace Exposition, and American products unexpectedly were among the most popular and impressive attractions.

For the first time, the ingenuity and quality of manufactured goods from the United States won worldwide attention. Among American achievements, Charles Goodyear's India rubber articles, Gail Borden's food items, Samuel Colt's revolving pistols, and Cyrus McCormick's reaper all won medals and awards. With considerable pride, an American observer at the Crystal Palace reported: "The number of inventions exhibited . . . was in the highest degree creditable to us, and elicited from distinguished sources in Great Britain the admission that to 'the department of American notions' they owed the most important contributions to their industrial system."[29] American industry had come of age and was prepared to eclipse the world's manufacturing leader, Great Britain.

CHAPTER NINE

Railroads and the Challenge of Big Business

THE economic growth of the United States would not have been possible without the development of improved transportation facilities. Fortunately, new and better means of moving goods and people appeared one after another during the first half of the nineteenth century. None had an impact as permanent and far-reaching as the railroad, which an early Ohio school board called "a device of Satan to lead immortal souls down to Hell."[1] The railroad quickly overcame such initial fears of the unknown and won enthusiastic, even wild, acceptance during its formative years.

The Pioneer Roads

The British again led the way. In England, the world's first railroad began operating in 1825 between the North Sea port of Stockton and the coal-region town of Darlington. The distance was a modest twelve miles, but it was a beginning.

Concrete steps toward the establishment of a pioneer railroad were not taken in the United States until 1827. Entrepreneurial responses to potential commercial threats triggered the opening of the railroad era in the United States, and, as in other sectors of economic activity, merchants led the way. In Baltimore, the business community feared the damaging effects upon the city's trade that might result from New York's new Erie Canal. Therefore, a group of business leaders headed by Phillip E. Thomas, a hardware merchant and bank president, secured from the Maryland legislature a charter to incorporate the Baltimore & Ohio Railroad in February 1827, and, on July 4,

Charles Carroll, the sole surviving signer of the Declaration of Independence, turned the first spadeful of earth.

The businessmen wanted to construct a line that tied Baltimore to the Ohio River two hundred miles away. It was a visionary scheme, since no railroad of that length existed in the world or was even contemplated at this early stage of railway history. By 1830 only thirteen miles of track had been laid, despite the original grandiose predictions, but it was sufficient to begin service. In 1853, the B&O was finally completed to Wheeling on the Ohio River. Nevertheless, the construction of the B&O encouraged the development of railroads elsewhere.

In Charleston, South Carolina, businessmen imitated their counterparts in Maryland by turning to a railroad scheme to gain access to the produce of interior areas, especially a rich cotton-growing region that funneled most of its output by river to Savannah. The Charleston & Hamburg Railroad connected Charleston with a town on the Savannah River across from Augusta, Georgia. The 136-mile line was completed in 1833, and it was momentarily the longest railway in the world. The company also had the distinction of operating the first locomotive built in the United States, an engine named Best Friend of Charleston purchased for $4,000 from the West Point Foundry in New York City.

A group of Boston merchants also played a pioneering role in railroad history. Like the businessmen in Baltimore, these merchants perceived a threat from the Erie Canal, and their answer was the Boston & Lowell Railroad, chartered in 1830, and the Boston & Worcester and Boston & Providence, incorporated in the following year.

Although the early railroads anticipated public assistance, they were nonetheless private enterprises. This pattern persisted. Railway mileage multiplied quickly during the 1830s with over three thousand miles of track laid, a third of which was concentrated in New York and Pennsylvania. During the next ten years, mileage more than doubled despite a depression during the first half of the decade.

Technical advances occurred also. These included the rise of major engine-building firms, such as the Baldwin Locomotive Works of Philadelphia. Matthias Baldwin was a jeweler's apprentice and toolmaker who, in 1831, built a miniature indoor steam locomotive and train for a Philadelphia museum. The exhibit attracted so much favorable attention that the officials of a local railroad commissioned

Baldwin to build a full-sized engine for their line. By 1835 he had produced five such locomotives, and, by his death in 1866, he had made approximately fifteen hundred. He achieved the latter figure even though, because he was a staunch and outspoken abolitionist, his engines were boycotted in the South. Baldwin's firm continued into the twentieth century and became the largest engine builder in the world.

The Pace Quickens—the 1850s

The railroad did not have a significant effect on the American economy until the 1850s. During that decade, track mileage more than tripled, and the Mississippi Valley was linked to the Atlantic seaboard. Chicago attained national prominence as a major rail center; eleven lines entered the city, and the first major north-south trunk line, the Illinois Central, was extended southward from Chicago. The federal government promoted railroad construction on a trial basis by offering grants of public lands, and the Illinois Central ultimately received a total of 2.5 million acres.[2]

In the same decade, the railroad industry triumphed over competing forms of transportation. Railroads had easily surpassed turnpikes in moving passengers and freight, but canals were another matter. For freight, canal rates per ton-mile were lower than those of competing rail lines, but as the differential gradually narrowed to less than two cents by the end of the decade, the other advantages inherent in rail transport were decisive.

Railroads could be built in areas that could never be served by a canal, and they supplied year-round service as well. A typical canal was closed for three to five months a year in the North because of winter weather, periodic flooding, low water in summers, or the need for repairs. The Erie Canal was usually open completely only from May through November, and shippers were forced to rely on alternate transport during the remaining months.

During the period 1853–1859, freight traffic on the Erie Canal peaked and then began to decline in the face of competition from two railroads, the New York Central and the Erie. Rails carried the lighter, more valuable shipments, while those that were bulkier and less costly remained for a time with the slower canal boats. The greater speed of the railroad (three to four times as fast as canals) meant that passengers preferred it whenever they had a choice.

Railroads successfully challenged steamboats, too, during the 1850s. Train travel had several advantages over water. It was not unusual for the rail distance between two cities to be considerably less than that on existing waterways. The rail mileage between Cincinnati and New Orleans, for example, was 922 miles, but a steamboat using the Ohio and Mississippi rivers had to travel 1,484 miles. The shorter distances helped offset the advantage that a riverboat might have in a lower average freight rate per ton-mile.

Passengers, especially, enjoyed the faster speeds and shorter distances. In 1860, a steamboat trip from Cincinnati to New Orleans took eight days, compared with two-and-a-half days by train. Yet a rail passenger did sacrifice something in comfort; trains of even a later era were hard pressed to match the amenities of the elegant floating palaces that plied the major rivers of the West.

The railroad possessed one further advantage over the steamboat in its ability to lay track to virtually any location. Even branch lines leading directly to an individual manufacturer's factory site became possible. Moreover, some cities, such as Columbus, Ohio, and Springfield, Illinois, that never had access to significant steamboat service grew rapidly with the advent of the railroad.

The Trunk Lines Cometh

In the 1850s, an embryonic concentration movement occurred as a number of smaller lines were absorbed into larger systems. By the mid-1850s four of those systems had pierced the Appalachian barrier, tying Atlantic coastal cities to western commercial centers. The four trunk lines, as they were known, were the Erie, the New York Central, the Baltimore & Ohio, and the Pennsylvania Railroad.

The first was the Erie, and it was plagued by debt and financial manipulation. Although it was organized in 1833, the line was not completed from the Hudson River to the small hamlet of Dunkirk on Lake Erie—a distance of 483 miles—until 1851. The Erie was then the world's longest railroad.

The New York Central, the state's second line to the West, was an amalgamation of smaller roads. As late as 1850, rail service from Albany to Buffalo consisted of a loose connection of eight different lines operating along the route. There was even a four-block break in Rochester between two of the lines that was intended to benefit local teamsters and liverymen.

The dominant force in bringing about integration of the various rail companies was Erastus Corning. In addition to his iron business and his political activities as a mayor of Albany, a state senator, and, later, a congressman, Corning invested in railroads. Since 1833, he had been president of the Utica and Schenectady, one of the component roads. In that position he received no salary but more than made up for that omission because his iron firm supplied almost all the railroad's rails, spikes, and other hardware.

Corning skillfully maneuvered through the New York legislature a law that authorized the combination of all the railroads into a new corporation to be known as the New York Central, formed in 1853. Corning became its first president. Its capitalization—$23 million— was considered so vast a sum that it amazed the nation. Under Corning, the consolidated system made immediate improvements in its service, purchased new locomotives and cars, and rapidly increased its passenger and freight revenues.

In his new office, Corning continued to profit from his insider's position. According to his biographer, "by the end of July 1855, New York Central purchases on the Erastus Corning & Co. books stood at $1,098,407.30," of which almost $700,000 had been spent for rails. The *New York Times* estimated in the 1860s that "the privilege of supplying the Central with iron was worth at least $250,000 a year to its president."[3]

Corning's eleven-year tenure as president of the New York Central—he resigned in 1864—was marked by one principal mistake: he failed to recognize the importance of securing his railroad's own connection with New York City. He relied instead on steamboats on the Hudson in good weather and the independent Hudson River Railroad in the winter, when ice blocked all water traffic between Albany and New York City. Corning owned an interest in a steamboat business there, which accounted for at least part of his decision not to acquire the Hudson River line despite its relatively inexpensive price.

Cornelius Vanderbilt did not overlook the same opportunity. He gained control of both the Hudson River Railroad and its main competitor, the New York and Harlem, and thus virtually strangled the Central by denying it winter access to New York City. The outcome of the struggle was inevitable. In 1867, the incumbent directors of the New York Central, including Corning, were ousted, and a Vanderbilt-chosen group was installed. It was the end of Cornings's leadership role in the railroad's history and the beginning of the Vanderbilt era for the New York Central.

The Pennsylvania Railroad was probably the best managed of all the trunk lines that emerged during the 1850s. It, too, had been the result of some municipal paranoia. The business and civic leaders of Philadelphia were worried about their growing loss of trade to New York City and frightened by a projected extension of the Baltimore & Ohio to Pittsburgh, which created the prospect that further trans-Allegheny commerce would be diverted away from the Quaker City.

The Pennsylvania Railroad was chartered in 1846 to defeat the B&O threat. Characteristically, the railway's first board of directors consisted of six merchants, four manufacturers, two financiers, and one merchant-manufacturer. As in most other ventures of this period, the commercial elite of a city provided the leadership for a new and daring enterprise.

Among the first acts of the Pennsylvania's directors was the employment of J. Edgar Thomson as chief engineer. It was an outstanding decision, because Thomson became one of the premier railroad men of the century. He already had considerable experience on the Camden & Amboy and the Georgia Railroad before he accepted the Pennsylvania post. Within three years, Thomson was named general superintendent, and, in 1852, he became the railroad's third president, an office that he held until his death in 1874.

The Pennsylvania soon bore his imprint. "In his quiet composed manner, Thomson determined the road's strategy, oversaw its day-to-day affairs, and dominated its strong personalities," who included a rising young Scotsman named Andrew Carnegie. He forged, in the words of his biographer, "a personal fiefdom, a business empire he ruled with paternalistic devotion."[4] In the process, he delighted shareholders with high prices for their stock and an uninterrupted flow of dividends, which averaged a healthy 10 percent yield over the period of his tenure.

Unlike other railroad magnates of the period, Thomson's power lay in his management expertise rather than in any considerable personal stock ownership. He thus personified a future generation of railroad officials who concentrated upon efficient operation rather than stock manipulation. Thomson was not, however, completely oblivious to investment opportunities. He was a partner in the ownership of timber lands, coal deposits, steel mills, and construction companies, all of which provided materials or services to his railroad.

By 1855 Thomson had finished the line to Pittsburgh, the Pennsylvania's original objective. Then, in 1858, the Pennsylvania secured an interest in a western road, the Pittsburgh, Fort Wayne, and Chicago, giving itself a secure connection all the way to Lake Michigan. Following the Civil War, Thomson continued to pursue an expansionist strategy, which, at the time of his death, had resulted in an overall domain of some six thousand track miles or 8 percent of the nation's total. In those years, Thomson presided over the greatest transportation company in the world.

The fourth of the trunk-line systems forged during the 1850s was the Baltimore & Ohio, the oldest of America's pioneer railroads. In 1852, the B&O reached Wheeling on the Ohio River, the goal that it had set for itself more than twenty years before. Passenger and freight service between the Chesapeake Bay region and the Ohio was now available. A trip that previously had taken several days by stagecoach on the Cumberland Pike could now be made in less than twenty-four hours.

Governments, Railroads, and the Nation

Although railroads were profit-seeking private enterprises, they also relied on the public treasury for at least a portion of their financial support. In 1860, for example, railway investment totaled over $1 billion, but 25 percent represented public funds.

This governmental assistance took a different form for railroads than it had with canals. The government assumed nearly three-quarters of canal-construction costs, principally at the state level, and direct ownership and operation was common. On the other hand, railroads relied less heavily on public aid and were usually privately owned even when governmental support was secured.

This difference existed in part because most lines appeared at a later stage of the transportation revolution than canals, and at a time when private sources of risk capital were more abundant. Moreover, railroads did more than collect tolls, like canal operators; they also provided the vehicles for the movement of passengers and freight.

This was a more complex task, and one that few governments were willing to undertake.

The most frequent types of state and local government aid were liberal provisions inserted in the charters of railroad corporations and money or credit for construction. Charters granted companies the power of eminent domain, tax exemptions, authority to issue whatever amount and class of securities they wished, and sometimes a monopoly on rail-transportation rights between designated points. With direct financial aid, states invested heavily in railroad promotion. As early as 1838, state debt incurred for this purpose amounted to nearly $43 million.

The state of New York issued $3 million in bonds to subsidize the construction of its Erie Railroad, and some western states were even more enthusiastic. Missouri lent almost $25 million to seven different rail lines, and slightly lesser amounts were forthcoming from other states in the region.

Local governments probably provided an equal or even greater amount of support in the antebellum period. Philadelphia assumed a debt of $8 million, or about $20 per person, for various railway ventures. The per capita debt of New Orleans for the same purpose was even higher, about $23 for every resident. Usually the funds were used either to purchase stock in a railroad corporation or to buy the bonds issued by a company.

Federal assistance to railroads took the form of tariff reductions and land grants. In the period from 1830 to 1843, Congress reduced the tariff on foreign iron rails. American railroads thus saved millions of dollars, though the windfall was not unopposed. Lobbying by domestic iron manufacturers resulted in a higher duty in 1843, only to have Congress slash it once again in 1846.

In 1850, a coalition of southern and western interests pushed through Congress a bill sponsored by Stephen A. Douglas of Illinois that granted land to Illinois, Mississippi, and Alabama for railroad construction. The proposed line was to extend from Illinois to Mobile, Alabama. The grant consisted of a two-hundred-foot right-of-way plus six alternate sections of land for each completed mile of track. When he signed the bill into law, President Millard Fillmore took the first step in a policy direction that generated controversy for decades.

During the 1850s, the federal government granted over 22 million acres to eleven western and southern states. As a result of the acreage that those states gave to the Illinois Central Railroad alone, only 15 percent of its construction cost was borne by shareholders. Most of the expense was met by the sale of bonds secured by the granted federal land. Forty-four other railroads shared in the congressional largesse during the 1850s.

The most generous federal grants, however, were made after the Civil War. By 1871 approximately 175 million acres had been distributed to various railroads, about 35 million of which were eventually forfeited because the roads were never built. The most famous recipients were the transcontinental lines built after 1865. The Northern Pacific, for example, received 42 million acres.

In all, there were seventy-nine land-grant railroads, and it has been estimated that they earned nearly $500 million from the sale of their acreage. But, in return, the land-grant roads had to transport government freight, mail, and military personnel at reduced rates, and not until 1946 did Congress abolish the last of those rates. In 1945, the House Committee on Interstate and Foreign Commerce calculated the United States had saved $900 million because of the lower rail charges—almost double the amount that the railroads probably earned from land sales.

Nevertheless, historians have often criticized the policy of granting public lands to promote railroad construction as dubious generosity. It supposedly encouraged hasty, slipshod, and sometimes unnecessary building. The federal government might have achieved its goal through the guarantee of railroad bonds rather than by land grants. But the subsidies did make the completion of a nationwide rail network possible sooner than it would otherwise have occurred, and they helped significantly in the rapid settlement of the American West.

Some recent economic historians, primarily those trained as economists rather than historians, have been unsatisfied with generalizations about the economic impact of railroads; they have insisted instead on exact measurement of the difference railroads made. This attempt to convert historical generalizations into numerical quantities has, however, only generated a continuing scholarly argument.

The best-known efforts were those undertaken by Robert Fogel and Albert Fishlow.[5] They developed estimates of the social savings for railroads that have been the focus of considerable dispute. Both calculated the savings by seeking to determine what additional costs society would have had to pay in transport charges if railroads had not been in existence and alternate means of moving goods and people, primarily by water, had to be employed.

Fishlow placed the social savings for the year 1859 at 4 percent of the gross national product (GNP). Fogel estimated a savings of about 5 percent of the GNP in 1890. He concluded that without the railroads, the GNP of the United States in 1890 would not have been attained until 1892. Their separate but similar conclusions were that railways were important to but not indispensable for American economic growth in the nineteenth century.

These calculations and conclusions have been the target of widespread scholarly challenge and criticism. One critic, Jeffrey G. Williamson, has reexamined the year 1890 and reckoned the social savings at 21 percent of the GNP.[6] The issue of the exact impact of the railroad upon the American economy is, therefore, still an open question.

The Golden Age of Railroading

The railroad systems of both the North and the South played a key role in overall strategy and in battlefield operations during the Civil War. Troops and supplies were continually shuttled between the various combat theaters during the four years of the sectional struggle. But although rail communication was essential to the war effort, the Civil War momentarily stalled any expansion of track mileage in the United States. The delay was only temporary, and the period from 1865 to 1915 became America's golden age of railroading.

Track mileage doubled between 1865 and 1875, and the nation's first transcontinental rail line was completed in 1869 when the Union Pacific and the Central Pacific met near Ogden, Utah. By 1900 five transcontinentals linked the Pacific Coast with the Mississippi Valley, and overall track mileage had grown from 35,000 miles in 1865 to 193,000. By the First World War there were 254,000 miles of track, and rail service became available to almost every city and town in America.

A variety of technical inventions and improvements made this dramatic expansion of the rail network possible. Locomotives were larger and more powerful; specialized freight cars, including refrigerator, tank, and coal cars, were developed; and passenger cars that offered greater comfort became available, especially George Pullman's sleeping and dining cars. In addition, George Westinghouse's air brake, a shift to steel rails, and the nationwide adoption of a uniform track gauge also contributed to the establishment of a national rail system.

Although positive accomplishments and impressive growth marked the fifty years after the Civil War, the period was also, in the words of one historian, "one of retrogression for American railroads." Railway corporations were too often guilty of "inflated construction costs, incompetent managers, stock manipulations, rate discriminations, and general corruption" on a continental scale.[7]

During this period, the government supervised only slightly the marketing of corporate securities, and railroad promoters had a full field of opportunities for ethically marginal practices. One of the most controversial was the construction company device that historian Edward C. Kirkland described as "less concerned with moving dirt than with moving securities."[8]

A railroad contracted with a construction company for the building of its line with the usual payment in stocks or bonds. The price set in the contract was often considerably higher than the actual cost of building the road, and the owners of the construction company would thereby turn a tidy profit, especially when the corporation handling the construction was controlled by insiders within the contracting railroad.

The device was in common use after the Civil War, but it became notorious through the activities of the Crédit Mobilier, the construction company for the Union Pacific. The chief stockholders and managers of the railroad were the principal owners of the Crédit Mobilier, which "earned" large profits. The affair became a national scandal because some prominent members of Congress and the Grant administration shared in the lucrative arrangement.

Such practices necessitated overcapitalization, which later caused a serious problem for the lines involved. Even in good years, it was difficult for these railrods to earn enough income to meet the interest payments or to distribute dividends on the excess securities. This "watered stock" accounted for as much as $2 billion of the industry's $7.5 billion debt in the early 1880s. It was also the basis of a perennial debate over what railroads claimed was an adequate return on the investment carried on their balance sheets and what shippers considered unjustifiable profits.

Because of such devices as the construction company, however, risks were taken in railroad development that otherwise might not have been taken. It was frequently more profitable to build the roads than to operate them. For example, many western lines were routed through unsettled areas ahead of normal demand for transportation services. Hence, in return for tolerating some irregular practices, the railway network in the United States was probably completed sooner than would have otherwise been possible.

In general, the business ethics of even the most stalwart industry leaders of the period were much lower than modern standards of conduct. It was an age of bare-knuckled capitalism, and no episode better illustrated that dismal fact than the brawl between Cornelius Vanderbilt and the Erie's notorious triumvirate—Daniel Drew, Jay Gould, and Jim Fisk.

Vanderbilt gained control of the New York Central in 1867, and he ran it afterwards with reasonable efficiency, even though the capitalization was inflated to benefit himself and other insiders. Despite the watered stock, Vanderbilt's company paid a regular dividend, cut the travel time between New York City and Chicago from fifty to twenty-four hours, eliminated the numerous train changes previously required to make the trip by creating a single system almost one thousand miles long, and built the Grand Central Terminal in New York City.

He was less successful in his attempt to win control of the financially distressed Erie. At its helm was Daniel Drew, a Bible-reading stock-market operator. Drew was a former cattle drover who reputedly fed his animals salt followed by all the water they could drink on their way to market so that they weighed in at an artificially heavier poundage. This devious ploy was, some believe, the origin of the term "watered stock."

For a number of years, Drew, as treasurer of the Erie, used his office to manipulate the railroad's stock for his own benefit. Then he allied himself with Jay Gould, who was an even shrewder market manager, and Jubilee Jim Fisk, a flashy Civil War blockade runner and partner in the Boston dry-goods firm of Jordan, Marsh & Company. Between 1864 and 1872, the trio inflated the Erie's common stock from $24 million to $78 million without adding significantly to the real value of their railroad property. The Erie became the "scarlet woman of Wall Street" and did not pay another dividend to its shareholders until 1942.

When Vanderbilt reached out for the Erie in 1868, he purchased 100,000 shares of its common stock, but still lacked control. Fisk and Gould, he soon learned, had discovered a printing press in the cellar of the Erie offices and were churning out a flood of new stock certificates, a maneuver that Fisk justified as freedom of the press. Gould hurried to Albany where, working with Senator William Marcy Tweed of Tammany Hall, he bribed legislators into legitimizing the whole affair. Charles Francis Adams, in his account of the Erie affair, bemoaned the level of politics at a time when "the halls of legislation were transformed into a mart in which the prices of votes were higgled over, and laws made to order were bought and sold."[9] The market price of an assemblyman was supposedly $15,000.

At one point in the struggle, Drew and his partners fled New York for New Jersey to avoid a Vanderbilt-inspired arrest order. They established themselves at Taylor's Hotel in Jersey City, and fortified it with guards and three cannon to ward off any Vanderbilt assaults. Fisk took charge and issued periodic warlike communiqués to the press from "Fort Taylor."

Eventually, the opposing forces made peace. The Erie group returned some of Vanderbilt's losses, and the Commodore abandoned all efforts to take over the Erie. A few years later, Drew himself was forced out of the Erie and into bankruptcy by his previous allies. In 1872, under pressure from an exasperated board of directors, Gould left the Erie for greener pastures in the West. In the same year, Jim Fisk was a shooting victim in a sordid quarrel over the attentions of a former mistress.

The Erie episode undoubtedly represents the worst side of Gilded Age railroading. Yet it reflects a pattern of thought of many industry leaders. According to one recent study, "railroad officials of the era pictured themselves as sovereign rulers wielding vast authority over their economic domains while beset on all sides by the same vicissitudes and dangers that assailed their public counterparts."[10] Competitors became enemies against whom war must be waged either to conquer new territory or protect one's own.

The First Big Business

During the festivities that accompanied the completion of the Baltimore & Ohio to St. Louis in 1857, the mayor of Baltimore, Thomas

Swann, exulted over America's railways: "Look at the great enterprises . . . the New York and Erie, the Central Pennsylvania, and the Baltimore & Ohio Railroads. What country on the face of the earth can boast of such enterprises?"[11] Swann was correct. No other country could match the span of the great railroad corporations. More important, the railroads also represented the birth of big business in America.

The consequences were far-reaching. Although the railroads brought fundamental economic changes by "increasing the volume and regularity of transportation, adding to the national income, and becoming a brand-new market for American industry," they were, according to Alfred D. Chandler, even more important as creators of "new patterns of economic and business action and new institutional forms."[12] Railroad executives became pioneers in modern management techniques because they had to contrive methods to deal with unprecedented problems in finance, business administration, and labor, competitor, and governmental relations.

The unique challenges that railroads faced required them to formulate novel entrepreneurial responses. Those challenges first appeared during the 1850s, because, earlier, no single company had operated a system of sufficient size to strain traditional business methods. But by 1855 more than a dozen companies operated rail lines that exceeded two hundred miles in track length. Effective coordination of such a sprawling enterprise posed a considerable administrative puzzle.

In capital investments, railroad corporations also dwarfed other business enterprises of the time. In the early 1870s, the Pennsylvania, under Thomson, boasted a $400 million investment. Even the largest textile mills required a capital of only $500,000. Size can also be measured by the extent of an organization's work force. In the 1850s, a trunk line such as the Erie employed four thousand workers, while manufacturing firms had only a fraction of that number.

Although unprecedented size was the principal factor in stimulating new business policies and procedures, so also were the needs to insure passenger safety, prevent traffic snarls, set adequate rates, and handle the substantial revenues generated by the larger volume of business. These businesses required a more specialized executive who was experienced in railway operations and devoted full time to his administrative assignment. Thus the merchants, bankers, and other businessmen who were the original railroad promoters gave way to a new type of industry leader, the salaried professional manager. A separation developed between ownership (as represented by share-holders and their representatives on boards of directors) and man-agement (represented by the career executive who now assumed control of railroad operations). Thus the separation so common to big business in the twentieth century appeared in the railroad in-dustry in the nineteenth.

The eastern trunk lines took the lead in designing new adminis-trative structures to cope with their unique problems.[13] The Balti-more & Ohio, the Erie, and the Pennsylvania each conceived plans for a more efficient management of their operations during the crit-ical decade of the 1850s. These plans were largely designed by the new professional managers—Benjamin H. Latrobe of the B&O, Dan-iel C. McCallum of the Erie, and J. Edgar Thomson of the Pennsyl-vania. All were civil engineers who turned from building their roads to administering them. Not surprisingly, as Chandler has noted: "They approached their brand-new problems of building an administrative structure in much the same rational and analytical way as they ap-proached that of building a railroad or a bridge."[14] Their innovations began with what was probably the first detailed organization manual for any American business, the *Organization of the Service of the Baltimore & Ohio Railroad*. Its principal author was Benjamin H. Latrobe, chief engineer of the B&O.

The scheme elaborated in the manual separated the activities of the company into two independent departments: finance (or, as the manual described it, "the collection and disbursement of the reve-nue") and operations ("the working of the road"). The treasurer of the corporation headed the finance department, and a general su-perintendent, who was invariably a professional engineer, was in charge of operations. Managers of subdepartments reported to the treasurer and superintendent. In the operations department, these middle managers included a master of machinery, a master of the road, and a master of transportation, each with his own precisely delineated duties.

The B&O plan was refined in the 1850s by the Erie Railroad, which, by 1851, had become the country's largest system. Since the Erie's size prevented any individual from overseeing its entire length of some five hundred miles, the road was broken down into five divisions, each of approximately one hundred miles and under the control of a division superintendent.

To carry out their new management design, the board of directors appointed Daniel C. McCallum as general superintendent in 1854. He was an engineer by training and began his tenure by promulgating a set of "general principles of organization and administration" that delegated responsibilities and granted sufficient power to implement them effectively. He emphasized a steady flow of information to provide managers with the current data necessary for successful decision making.

McCallum's information system included hourly, daily, and monthly reports. The daily reports, the core of the plan, were required from all conductors and station agents and dealt with every facet of train and traffic movement. The collected statistics passed through the Erie's administrative hierarchy until they reached the general superintendent, who used them to evaluate the comparative performance of the five divisions and to set rates for the line.

McCallum's efforts attracted favorable attention. The *American Railroad Journal*, for example, discussed his work in detail, and it even offered readers a lithographed copy of McCallum's organization chart for the price of one dollar. Unfortunately for McCallum, the Erie fell into the hands of Gould, Fisk, and Drew in the following decade, and any interest in efficient management soon dissipated. A disappointed McCallum then left the company to enter a bridge-building firm.

J. Edgar Thomson tested and improved the innovations of Latrobe and McCallum on the massive Pennsylvania system. Thomson divided his line into geographic divisions, as the Erie had been, each headed by a superintendent who reported to a general superintendent who had overall authority for the railroad's fortunes. In particular, Thomson established a specific line and staff structure in which superintendents held formal control in their divisions, but were assisted by staff executives who developed standards and procedures for various specialized tasks.

The Pennsylvania created a third major department in addition to finance and operations. This was the traffic department, whose responsibility it was to obtain and process, but not actually move, freight and passengers. The decentralized, divisional line and staff organization perfected on Thomson's Pennsylvania closely resembled the more famous administrative structure devised by Alfred Sloan for the General Motors Corporation in the 1920s, as we shall see.

Bankers and Railroad Finance

The railroad industry stimulated new directions both in financing large-scale enterprises and in dealing with labor forces of unprecedented size. Raising needed capital was a first step in launching any railroad project. Although governmental assistance helped, the private investor provided the bulk of support.

In the early days of railroading, the private investor was usually a person who profited directly from the road's construction; that is, businessmen, shippers, and other citizens living along the proposed route. Later, when the needs for capital exceeded local resources, the investor who lived at a considerable geographic distance—either in the populous Northeast or in Europe—contributed the required funds. Distant investors usually wanted only a secure and regular return, and therefore they often bought bonds rather than common stock. When they chose stock, they bought the new preferred version, which offered a priority on dividends, though frequently no voting rights.

As the distant bond or stockholder became the object of railroad promoters' attention, financial intermediaries, such as stock exchanges in the seaboard cities and especially in New York City, became more important. In 1835, only three railroads were listed on the New York Stock Exchange, and by 1840 there were only ten, but a decade later thirty-eight lines were being traded. During the 1850s, American railroad securities became the glamour investment, especially in England. Overseas investors held approximately $52 million in railway securities in the early 1850s, but even that sum seemed small by 1869, when foreigners owned $243 million in those American bonds and stocks.

Along with the expansion of security exchanges, the spread of the American railroad system was largely responsible for the emergence of another key financial intermediary, the investment banking house. Vincent Carosso, the institution's biographer, has written that "by the outbreak of the Civil War, investment banking in the United States . . . had achieved a significant degree of maturity and specialization.''[15] The leading houses could handle million-dollar issues and were located in the principal commercial cities of the East.

As Carosso has also noted, the investment banker tended to play one role in periods of prosperity and another during the depressions of the 1870s and 1890s. During a prosperous period, the banking house supplied the necessary capital for railroad expansion and improvement. In harder times, investment bankers performed "rescue" services; they negotiated and arranged reorganizations of debt-ridden and floundering railroad corporations.

Moreover, the investment banker served two entirely separate sets of clients. He was the agent for railroads and other enterprises that sought new or additional capital. He was also the broker for private individuals and institutions with funds to invest. Thus the investment banker linked the supply of capital with the corresponding demand.

The bankers maintained close ties to the railroad companies and often accepted seats on boards of directors. A banking house could thus assure its investing customers that it was watching the property in which they had placed their money. The banker-director therefore influenced policy, usually by supporting and fostering more conservative and cautious solutions to competitive problems.

The earliest firm to achieve importance in the investment banking field was Jay Cooke & Co., founded in 1861. During the Civil War, the Treasury Department turned to Cooke when it received a poor response to the bonds it was offering to finance the Union effort. Cooke organized an effective campaign that emphasized a flag-waving patriotism and an appeal to the small investor. Until Cooke's bond-selling drive, the smaller investor had never been an important factor in the market for securities in the United States.

This success during the Civil War brought Cooke's firm to the forefront of investment banking houses. Confident of his abilities, Cooke looked for new opportunities and found one in western railroads. In 1870, he marketed the securities issued by the Northern Pacific Railroad—a proposed transcontinental line—and he agreed to serve as both its fiscal and purchasing agent. He handled financial transactions and secured necessary equipment and supplies, often using his own firm's funds.

This time the Cooke magic failed. European investors were wary of so risky a project, and domestic customers, including the small investor to whom he had so skillfully appealed during the war, were, in general, uninterested as well. The Northern Pacific had none of the patriotic associations of the wartime bond issues. With the railroad's indebtedness to the firm standing at over $5 million, Jay Cooke & Co. was forced to close in September 1873. The failure created a financial panic on Wall Street and ushered in a major depression.

Other investment banking houses appeared during the 1860s and 1870s. Abraham Kuhn and Solomon Loeb transformed their Cincinnati mercantile business into a New York City banking firm. Although the two brothers-in-law succeeded in their new venture, the firm attained real prominence only after the Frankfurt-born Jacob H. Schiff became a partner in 1875. Schiff eventually headed the firm, although it was still called Kuhn, Loeb & Co.

The colossus in American investment banking was John Pierpont Morgan, undoubtedly the most famous and most powerful banker in the history of the United States. He was the son of Junius Spencer Morgan, a partner in the prominent London banking house of George Peabody & Co. In 1860, the younger Morgan organized his own firm in New York City and operated as a Peabody agent in America. During the 1870s, Morgan participated in a series of partnerships that culminated in the establishment of Drexel, Morgan & Co. in 1871 at 23 Wall Street, which became the business address for Morgan operations for decades.

His partner, Anthony J. Drexel, was already well known as a Philadelphia banker. The alliance with Morgan provided him with both a New York and an English connection. When Jay Cooke failed in 1873, the way was open for Drexel, Morgan to assume leadership in American investment banking.

Morgan's intense involvement with the railroad industry began in 1879 when he was approached by William H. Vanderbilt, who had two years before inherited 90 percent of the New York Central's common stock from his father, Commodore Cornelius Vanderbilt. The son was experiencing a growing disenchantment with the responsibilities associated with the active management of the Central and wanted to sell a substantial portion of his stock. Morgan agreed to form a syndicate to purchase 250,000 shares from Vanderbilt and then to sell those same shares, mainly in Europe, without forcing down the price of the railroad's stock on the exchange.

The syndicate that Pierpont Morgan and his father put together bought Vanderbilt's shares at $120 each and sold them at $130. Most of the stock was purchased by English investors, who now held a major interest in the New York Central, and Morgan became the guardian of their investment by assuming a directorship on the rail-road's board. The firm of Drexel, Morgan also served as the fiscal agent for the Central. The episode, according to one historian, "meant an entirely new direction and consideration in the matter of railroad and other corporate finance, where ownership would be spread widely and bankers would become managers as well as financiers of railroads and other businesses."[16]

Thereafter, the House of Morgan played a continuous role in rail-roads. Morgan and his firm later refinanced Jay Cooke's millstone, the Northern Pacific; settled a budding territorial war between the New York Central and the Pennsylvania (Morgan personally presided over a peace conference convened on his yacht, the *Corsair*); created regional rail associations to eliminate cutthroat competition between lines; and reorganized and consolidated an array of distressed rail-roads, including such stalwarts as the Baltimore & Ohio and the Chesapeake & Ohio. In one such consolidation, he merged over thirty separate lines into one new organization, the Southern Railway Company, which thereby became the largest and strongest system in the South.

Morgan's aims in any reorganization plan were to safeguard bond-holder interests, restore the ill railroad's battered credit, and put the entire operation back on a profitable basis. Through the presence of Morgan-designated trustees, he then maintained a close watch on the property even after the formal reorganization was completed. When one set of railroad men objected to this banker control of their line, Morgan reputedly retorted, "Your roads! Your roads belong to my clients."[17]

Each rescue venture brought Morgan sizable fees and enhanced prestige and influence. He could, as Jonathan Hughes states, "by the force of his personality and logic, simply bully the railway tycoons."[18] By the end of the century Morgan's concept of order had been im-posed upon warring railroads in all regions of the nation.

Railroads and Unionism

Railroads were also the first major business organizations to expe-rience the problems inherent in dealing with sizable labor forces. By 1900 rail employment exceeded 1 million workers, a significant proportion of whom were banded into national craft unions, or brotherhoods, as they were termed in the industry. Because their members tended to be highly skilled, the unions held strong bargaining positions as compared to laborers in most other occupations. Thus railway employees were not only the first to work in substantial numbers for large-scale corporate enterprises, but they also, through the vehicle of their unions, set a pattern for the troubled history of organized labor in America.

Rail unions achieved a national scale during the Civil War. The Brotherhood of Locomotive Engineers, formed at a convention in Detroit in May 1863, was the earliest to appear. Its strategy was not militant. Indeed, its policy has been described as winning management approval by "elevating the character" and raising the efficiency of its membership. The employer would supposedly be so pleased with the improved performance "that he would of his own free will provide better recognition of labour and higher pay."[19] These roseate visions changed, however, as the hard realities of labor-management relations in the Gilded Age became apparent.

Railroad managers, like most other businessmen of the time, looked with disfavor on what they regarded as union attempts to alter the status quo. They cited natural market forces—the inexorable laws of supply and demand—as the controlling factors against which both management and labor were purportedly powerless to contend. They preferred to bargain with their workers as individuals rather than collectively, and they viewed national union officials as outside agitators intent upon disturbing the proper course of events. And, if events did take an unfortunate turn and a labor stoppage resulted, railroad managers expected and usually received assistance from all levels of government, assistance that often was the key to breaking the back of a strike.

Other national unions soon followed the example set by the Engineers. The Order of Railway Conductors was formed in 1868, and the Brotherhood of Locomotive Firemen appeared in 1873. The Engineers briefly abandoned their nonmilitant strategy in 1876–1877, but fruitless strikes against the Boston & Maine and the Philadelphia & Reading only caused them to reverse course once more. In the latter strike, they unsuccessfully opposed one of the more formidable union-busting railroad executives, Franklin B. Gowen, and his self-proclaimed crusade for the "right of the individual laboring man against the tyranny of trade unions."[20] The Engineers retreated to their former conservative stance and refused thereafter to take any leadership responsibility or even to offer measurable assistance in the great railroad strikes later in the century. The other two brotherhoods followed a similar cautious policy.

On two occasions attempts were made to bring all railway workers together into a single industrywide union. Each instance resulted in a major work stoppage that culminated in federal intervention. The first occurred in June 1877 when dissatisfied workers met at Allegheny City, Pennsylvania, across the river from Pittsburgh, and formed the Trainmen's Union. The new union mounted a strike against depression-era wage cuts imposed by some of the important roads. The strike began in the East and swept westward to such rail centers as Chicago, Omaha, and St. Louis. About two-thirds of the country's track mileage was affected, including all the trunk lines that connected the Atlantic Coast with the Mississippi.

In Pittsburgh, the struggle was especially ugly. A unit of the state militia dispersed one body of strikers, killing twenty-six in the process, only to find itself besieged in a roundhouse from which it eventually withdrew under fire. It temporarily abandoned the city to a riotous mob, and the ensuing destruction of property totaled in the millions of dollars.

Militia units were soon deployed in other states, and President Rutherford Hayes sent federal troops to Illinois, Indiana, Maryland, Missouri, and West Virginia. They were dispatched in answer to urgent appeals from state governors and calls from federal court judges. It was the first significant occasion in American history in which the army had been ordered out to suppress a strike in time of peace.

Unfavorable public opinion, unyielding company managements, internal disunity among the railway workers, and the vigorous application of governmental force all combined to defeat the strikers. When the railroad strikes of 1877 failed, the embryonic Trainmen's Union died as well. Only the conservative brotherhoods remained to represent the interests of rail employees, but their activities were confined to their own specialized membership, a distinct minority of the entire railroad work forces.

Not until the 1890s was another attempt made to organize an industrial union for railroad employees. In 1893, Eugene V. Debs, secretary-treasurer of the Locomotive Firemen, resigned his office and began a new labor organization, the American Railway Union (ARU). Debs's goal was to lead a union of all railway workers, regardless of their specific job or skill level. He theorized that this "one great union" should include so great a percentage of the industry's labor force that no individual company would dare to refuse the ARU's legitimate demands.

A short but successful strike against the Great Northern line in April 1894 gave some initial impetus to Debs's union. Its membership reached about 150,000 that spring despite the opposition of the older brotherhoods. Overconfidence fostered by its Great Northern victory probably accounted in large part for the ARU decision to involve itself in the Pullman dispute.

The so-called Pullman strike actually had three separate phases.[21] It began as a walkout by workers at the Pullman Palace Sleeping Car Company, located in the "model town" that George Pullman had conceived and constructed near Chicago. The employees were seeking the recision of wage cuts imposed in that depression year or else a reduction in rents that they paid for Pullman-owned homes. George Pullman proved intransigent on both counts, and the employees appealed to the ARU for support, since about 35 percent of them were already members.

The strike moved into its second phase when the ARU voted a boycott on the handling of any trains containing Pullman-made cars until that company came to terms with its striking workers. The effect of the boycott was first felt in the Chicago area, but it spread rapidly to wherever ARU strength existed, eventually encompassing a wide area west of the Mississippi River.

Historians have raised questions about the wisdom of the ARU's tactics. Some have argued that public sympathy turned against the union as a result of the boycott, since the public saw little justification for interference with the normal operations of the railroad lines, which were not directly involved in the Pullman dispute. The railroad managers seized upon that innocent-bystander rationale as an effective device to undermine union support and entice government intervention.

The struggle reached its third and final phase when the various lines began to discharge any workers who refused to handle trains with Pullman cars attached. The impasse became a general railway strike as other ARU members walked off their own jobs when one of their fellow workers was fired. Management then turned to Washington for support.

The administration of President Grover Cleveland and particularly the attorney general, Richard Olney, were more than willing to assist.

When Debs and the union refused to obey a federal court injunction that forbade continued interference with railroad operations, Cleveland succumbed to Olney's insistent urgings and, in early July 1894, authorized the use of the army to enforce judicial orders. Debs was arrested and indicted for contempt of court on July 7, and a few days later the ARU offered a weak proposal as a last resort. It expressed a readiness to call off the strike if all discharged union members could return to their old jobs. The proposal, plainly an admission of defeat on the part of the ARU, was quickly spurned by the companies.

By mid-July 1894 the Pullman strike had ended in a union debacle. The railroads, with the invaluable backing of the courts and the military, crushed both the strike and the American Railway Union, which soon disappeared entirely from the labor scene. After serving six months in prison for contempt, Debs emerged to spend the rest of his days furthering the cause of socialism in the United States.

Federal action in the 1877 and 1894 strikes proved, according to one scholar, that "serious disruption of the transportation system could not be long ignored or long tolerated. The inconvenience and hardship, not to mention outright danger to the public was too great. Almost inevitably the halting of important railroad services by labor disputes provoked federal intervention in one form or another."[22]

Even Grover Cleveland recognized that a repetition of the Pullman experience was unacceptable to the nation. Shortly after the strike ended, he appointed a special presidential commission to investigate the causes and to recommend corrective legislation. The United States Strike Commission, as it was officially called, interviewed over one hundred persons before issuing a report. It found blame on all sides— Debs and the ARU, George Pullman, and railroad management. It concluded that boycotts and strikes were "barbarisms unfit for the intelligence of this age," and it recommended the establishment of a permanent arbitration board to settle labor disputes within the railroad industry.[23]

A version of the commission's recommendation eventually became law. In 1898, Congress passed the Erdman Act, which provided for voluntary submission of railroad labor disputes to mediators, and, if mediation attempts failed to achieve a settlement, then the dispute could be submitted to a board of arbitration. While the Erdman Act was rarely used for more than a decade after its passage, it did represent the federal government's first attempt to settle labor-management differences without strikes and the use of military force.

The railroad industry thus again broke new ground for big business in the United States, this time in employer-employee relations.

Competition and Cooperation

The massive investments in roadway, stations, and rolling stock that railroads required meant a substantial long-term indebtedness that had to be funded annually. Thus high fixed costs that did not vary with the volume of traffic carried plagued railroad corporations whether they ran one train or fifty a day. They needed a constant level of traffic sufficient to cover at least their "sunk" costs, which could amount to two-thirds of the total expenditures of the company.

Moreover, growth after 1865 left many lines with excess capacity—the ability to carry more traffic than they usually handled. Hence, if railroads could secure extra freight or passengers, these would help cover fixed costs and generate profits without adding to operating expenses. Railroad managers set their charges with these special cost factors in mind.

. If traffic was predominantly in one direction, shipments on the return trip received especially favorable rates. Carload lots also had lower rates, since it cost the same to move a fully loaded car as it did a half-empty one. Locations that lacked alternative rail or water routes usually paid higher tariffs than points with a more advantageous setting. A railroad might have multiple rate schedules, some for areas in which competition existed, and others that were significantly higher for noncompetitive sections.

A personal form of discrimination was common as well. Sometimes one firm received a lower rate than another for essentially the same service. The firm with the greater bargaining power, usually because of the heavier volume of its freight shipments, frequently paid the published rate but then received a secret refund or rebate under a negotiated agreement with the rail line. Naturally, such discriminatory practices, when they came to light, were greeted with intense indignation by unfavored shippers and their governmental spokesmen.

Thus a railroad's profits depended upon a steady volume of business, and any attempt by a competitor to cut into that volume by slashing prevailing rates threatened financial ruin for one or the other. Nevertheless, rate wars were common in the years following the Civil

War. They were usually initiated by weaker roads in desperate need of additional revenue. They recurred, it was said, with the certainty of "small pox or the change of seasons," climaxing in a trunk-line rate war in 1876–1877 that reduced freight charges between the seaboard and the Mississippi Valley by as much as two-thirds in some instances.[24]

Conservative railroad managers did not like such chaotic events. They prized stability of revenues above all other objectives. Consequently, they tried to eliminate destructive price competition. But the managers faced a philosophical dilemma when they employed anticompetitive cartels for this purpose. On the one hand, railroad men prided themselves upon being supporters of the free-market system, but on the other hand they sought ways to avoid the turbulence that unrestrained competition could create. A semantic answer to the dilemma was to distinguish between supposedly legitimate or healthy competition and predatory or cutthroat actions. The distinction was primarily in the eye of the beholder.

The campaign to eliminate recurrent rate wars evolved through three broad stages. In the first, competing lines entered into informal "gentlemen's agreements." Essentially uncomplicated alliances, these rate and traffic agreements were often arranged at periodic industry conventions and gatherings. These agreements multiplied after 1865, but they were invariably short-lived. In periods of rising receipts, competing companies were more inclined to abide by the stipulated rate schedules than they were in harder times when it was more difficult to attract sufficient traffic to meet fixed costs. Sometimes subordinate officials of a railroad began rate cutting without the awareness of the top executives. It was one side effect of the huge size to which major railway corporations had grown.

When informal alliances failed to eliminate rate wars, a second stage of cooperative endeavors occurred. In this stage, tightly organized pools replaced the old gentlemen's agreements in most areas of the country. They were regional associations with formal structures, administrative officers or commissioners, and specific percentages and procedures for the division of revenues among the members.

The first important pool of this type was formed by about two dozen southern railroads in 1875. The Southern Railway and Steamship Association was in large part the brainchild of Albert Fink, a senior vice-president of the Louisville and Nashville. Born and educated in Germany, Fink was an engineer by profession. He became the cartel's general commissioner and was quickly recognized nationally as the chief advocate of such associations as a means to end internecine rate battles.

Fink's plan was to divide traffic among the participating companies. The share allocated to any single road would be based on past data with an annual readjustment, if necessary. The Southern Railway and Steamship Association was so successful that Fink was invited by the managers of the eastern trunk lines to form a similar organization for them and their western connections. The result was a Joint Executive Committee that included representatives of the various roads that made up the pool. They voted on policy questions, but, if they were divided, Fink, as chairman, decided the issue.

From the beginning, pools were the targets of severe public criticism. They were accused of being combinations created to extract monopoly profits from helpless shippers. Fink replied that pools did not increase rates, but rather simply prevented them from falling to disastrous levels. The only thing shippers lost was an opportunity to exploit the railroads during rate wars, he argued.

The inherent weakness in any such cartel, whether formal or informal, was its unenforceability at law. Under common law, it was regarded as a conspiracy in restraint of trade. Fink sought to change that interpretation by ardently lobbying Congress to legalize pooling. His efforts were unsuccessful, and the Interstate Commerce Act of 1887 included an explicit prohibition of railroad pools.

The third and final stage was one of consolidation, the creation of giant, self-sustaining rail systems. To many managers, there seemed to be no other choice. As a Burlington officer saw it: "The consolidation of small roads into larger roads, and then the combination of the large roads themselves is the solution to the railroad problem."[25]

The process of consolidation and system building took various forms. Outright purchase of or at least investment in competing lines was employed in many cases; in other instances, the property was leased. The construction of entirely new track mileage was a third option, and, in the 1880s, 75,000 miles were laid in the United States, the most laid anywhere in a single decade.

The cost of expansion was very high, however, and investment banking houses thus acquired even more influence in railroading. Only those firms could muster the huge capital requirements of empire building. Even then the effort so drained the resources of a number of roads that they were unable to withstand the depression of the 1890s. They were placed in receivership as a result and underwent a financial and administrative reorganization, usually engineered by a banking house such as J. P. Morgan & Company.

By 1906 the process of consolidation was largely complete. Of the nearly 230,000 miles of track in the United States, about two-thirds had come under the control of only seven interest groups—Vanderbilt, Morgan, Gould, Edward C. Harriman, James J. Hill, the Rock Island, and the Pennsylvania Railroad. America's railways had moved from a condition of being "overbuilt, financially undernourished, divided into hundreds of poorly integrated corporate entities, and ridden by rate wars which reduced the profits of the best-situated roads drastically and drove the weaker ones to the wall of bankruptcy" to a condition in which only seven groups of rail lines claimed 85 percent of the industry's earnings in 1906.[26]

The Railroad Influence

The railroad was perhaps the most important influence in nineteenth-century America. Its development and growth represented a commitment of the entire nation. According to Henry Adams, the railroad necessitated the involvement of "capital, banks, mines, furnaces, shops, powerhouses, technical knowledge, mechanical population, together with a steady remodelling of social and political habits, ideas, and institutions to fit the new scale and the new conditions."[27]

The main influence that railroads exerted on the American economy was the furnishing of a relatively cheap and serviceable means of transport for both passengers and freight. They also were a prime factor in hastening the westward migration that occurred after the Civil War. But their importance was clearly not confined to these vital roles. As we shall see, railroading was the first business that was placed under systematic government regulation both at the state and the federal levels, and lessons learned from this experience were eventually applied in other sectors of the economy. Moreover, as the country's first large-scale business operations, railroad corporations were pioneers in tackling the novel administrative and competitive challenges associated with their unprecedented size. They set a course that was soon followed by the future giant enterprises that were about to appear on the business scene.

IV

THE AGE OF MANAGERIAL CAPITALISM

AMERICAN business, in the century after the final shots of the Civil War, was one of the world's great success stories. By 1900 the United States had taken over first place in international industrial leadership, outdistancing all its economic rivals, including Great Britain. Then, during the twentieth century, America's lead broadened as a scientific and technological revolution called into being whole industries that were unknown just a few years before.

The business expansion of the post–Civil War era also created a new form of capitalism—managerial capitalism. Business direction now became the province of salaried, professional managers, as the widening gap between nominal ownership and actual control of large corporate enterprises was apparent to all. Managerial capitalism resulted in new attitudes toward all aspects of business behavior, including the venerable goals of profit maximization and the growth of the firm; relations with government, labor, and the consumer; and the role of the corporation in a world setting. Its fruits are both yesterday's achievements and today's challenges.

CHAPTER TEN

Industrialization: Expansion and Extension

"IF our civilization is destroyed, as Macaulay predicted, it will not be by his barbarians from below. Our barbarians come from above. Our great money-makers have sprung in one generation into seats of power kings do not know."[1] In those bitter words, Henry Demarest Lloyd, Chicago journalist and reformer, portrayed what he, in 1894, regarded as a frightening specter—the rise of big business in the United States.

As we have seen, large-scale corporate enterprise made its debut in the American railroad industry, but it was the spread of big business to the industrial sector that truly arrested national attention because it remade the country's economic landscape. The creation of industrial organizations of unforeseen size was the most significant historical development in the half century after the Civil War. By 1915, the American business scene had assumed much the same shape that it retains today.

The process by which big business came into being can be viewed from two standpoints. The first is overall expansion or aggregate growth. By the onset of the First World War in 1914, American manufacturing had taken such enormous strides that its output equaled the combined total of America's three closest rivals—Great Britain, Germany, and France.

The second standpoint is somewhat more analytical. By the end of the period 1865–1915, a number of key industries in the United States were highly concentrated; that is, they were dominated by oligopolies, a small number of very large corporations. Although growth in individual plant size was required with the introduction of more sophisticated technology, great size in the overall company was attained by organizational extension. A firm either assumed additional business functions beyond the production of a manufactured article or combined with competitors in cartels and mergers designed to reduce price competition or restrict output. In the parlance of the business historian, therefore, a strategy of extension meant vertical integration, horizontal combination, or often a mixture of both.

The Civil War and Business Expansion

The role that the Civil War played in the industrial expansion after 1865 has been the focal point of considerable historical debate. The case for the Civil War as a major economic watershed, which both marked and stimulated the nation's transition from a predominantly agricultural and commercial society to a new era of industrialization, was made by Charles A. Beard and Louis M. Hacker. Hacker contended that the Civil War had been responsible for "a real leap forward," and that, although there was a "start toward industrialization" before 1861, it seemed doubtful that "the process would have been accelerated had it not been for the war itself."[2]

More recent studies of the data for the Civil War period do not support the Beard-Hacker thesis. They show that increases in commodity output averaged only 2 percent during the wartime decade, the lowest growth rate for any ten years in the entire century. Thomas C. Cochran found similar figures when he compared industrial measures such as pig iron, coal, and copper production and other indicators during the war with those of both the antebellum and postbellum years.[3]

Nevertheless, Paul Uselding is still cautious about discarding Beard and Hacker too quickly. He warns that the wartime inflation (consumer prices soared by more than 70 percent in the North between 1860 and 1864) "had the usual effect of transferring resources from wage recipients to profits; hence the war put capital in the hands of industrial entrepreneurs, and may well have helped finance the postwar expansion."[4]

In sum, few, if any, historians are ready to accept the Beard-Hacker view in its undiluted form, but there is still some reluctance to dismiss it entirely. During the Civil War, a probusiness federal government created a national banking system, raised protective tariff duties, enacted a contract labor law, and awarded generous land grants to western railroads. Admittedly, though, the effects of such actions in the political sphere cannot be measured easily, so the question of the Civil War and its legacy for American business remains an unsettled issue.

The impressive expansion of American industry between 1860 and 1910 can be accurately measured, however. Agriculture was the dominant sector in the economy in 1860 and contributed about 60 percent of total value added in commodity production, while industry contributed only 38 percent. But, by 1880, the two shares were roughly equal, and, by 1910, industry claimed three-quarters of the total. Since gross agricultural output actually grew in those years, industrial expansion was rapid. In the early years of the twentieth century, the United States boasted one-third of the manufacturing capacity of the world.

The industrial expansion of the postwar years also had its geographic ramifications. The manufacturing belt shifted westward to include the Great Lakes states as the rise of the steel industry influenced the location of new factories. The patterns of American foreign trade were also altered. The huge domestic market created by the transportation revolution in the first half of the century plus a sharply rising population (it increased from 31 million in 1860 to 76 million in 1900) meant that the United States was less dependent than ever before on overseas suppliers and foreign buyers. Although the dollar value of our imports and exports did show increases in this period, international trade, as a percentage of the gross national product, actually declined. Shifts in the types of goods bought and sold occurred as well. Manufactured articles, which accounted for only 15 percent of American exports in 1860, had grown to almost 45 percent by 1910.

The specific industries that spearheaded the expansion of manufacturing shifted also. The processing of farm products and the production of traditional consumer goods, such as cotton and wool textiles, led the way in 1860, but, in the late nineteenth century, industries that had not even been in existence before 1860 became prominent. One historian has said that their emergence precipitated "a second industrial revolution" in the United States with quite different characteristics from the first.[5] Three of these "infant" industries merit our special attention as brief case studies in industrialization—steel, petroleum, and telecommunications.

The Age of Steel and Mr. Carnegie

The growth of steel was so spectacular that the industry became a symbol for the age and was basic to the expansion of manufacturing as a whole after 1865. As late as 1867, the United States produced only 1,643 tons of steel ingots; three decades later the annual tonnage was over 7 million and the nation was the source of more than 40 percent of the world's output.

A newly developed technology dramatically transformed prewar iron producers into the steel giants of the future. Before 1856, steel was a luxury item, made only in small quantities for cutlery and certain expensive tools. But, in August of that year, Henry Bessemer read a paper before a meeting of the British Association for the Advancement of Science at Cheltenham, England, in which he outlined a process for making steel in large batches by forcing a blast of air on hot pig iron to burn out the impurities. Eventually the process brought Bessemer royalties of about $5 million and, like Richard Arkwright, a knighthood.

At approximately the same time, William Kelly, an American iron-master, discovered the same method of producing steel. Eventually the competing patents of Bessemer and Kelly were consolidated, but it took a decade of testing the process before large quantities of steel began to pour out of the famous pear-shaped converter with its accompanying discharge of brilliant flames and showers of sparks.

The demand for steel was spurred by postwar railroad building and the dissatisfaction of railroad managers with the durability of iron rails. The increased weight and speed of locomotives forced frequent rail replacements, which created delays and added to operating costs. In 1863, Pennsylvania Railroad officials, noting that some European lines had begun using more durable steel rails, ordered 150 tons from England. When the first shipment proved its worth, other American railway companies soon followed the Pennsylvania's lead.

Because these British rails were labeled "Bessemer Steel," all steel made by the new process "tended to become identified with the name of Bessemer while Kelly's faded away."[6] Rails formed the backbone of the emerging steel industry until the 1880s, and they consumed nearly all the Bessemer output. Although Bessemer rails cost twice the amount of iron rails in the 1860s, the price differential had disappeared by 1880, and demand for iron rails evaporated.

Alexander Holley was America's first steelmaster and made a valuable contribution to the steel industry. He was the son of a cutlery manufacturer who had also served as governor of Connecticut. The young Holley was graduated from Brown University in 1850 and undertook various engineering assignments. He went to England in 1862 on a commission to study naval armaments.

The journey was the turning point in his life. While in England, he examined Bessemer's Sheffield plant and, according to his biographer, was deeply impressed by the awesome sight of the converter in operation.[7]

In 1864, Holley joined a partnership that secured control of the Bessemer patents, and the following year he opened an experimental works at Troy, New York. He was instrumental in forming a group that acquired both the Bessemer and Kelly rights, and then licensed new producers and furnished them with plans and technical advice. Before his death in 1882, he had become the nation's foremost steel plant engineer and designer. Of the eleven Bessemer plants in 1880, Holley designed six (including Carnegie's renowned J. Edgar Thomson Works in Pittsburgh), consulted in the building of three more, and supplied the inspiration for the remaining two, which copied his ideas.

The Bessemer process did not have a monopoly on steel production. In the 1860s, two pairs of brothers—Charles and Frederick Siemens in England and Emile and Pierre Martin in France—developed the open-hearth process. It utilized a furnace with a shallow bowl in which a charge of molten pig and scrap iron was cooked by exterior heat. Because the process worked more slowly than a Bessemer converter, open-hearth steel could be sampled and adjusted to more exact specifications than were required in rail making.

Open-hearth steel was not widely accepted until the 1890s. By then railroad construction had slowed, which reduced the demand for rails, and it had become clear to engineers that the Siemens-Martin process was more useful for steelplates and structural shapes. Furthermore, unlike the Bessemer process, it was able to use, as its raw materials, scrap iron and more of the Lake Superior ores.

For most Americans in the last quarter of the nineteenth century, Andrew Carnegie personified the story of the steel industry in the United States. The diminutive Carnegie (five feet, four inches tall and only 130 pounds) was born in Dunfermline, Scotland, in 1835. His father was a hand-loom weaver whose craft became obsolete with the rise of steam-powered mechanized mills. The impoverished Carnegie family migrated to the United States in 1848 on borrowed passage money to seek a new beginning. Nevertheless, Carnegie always retained a sentimental love of Scotland and, in his later life, spent a considerable portion of his time at his own palatial Scottish castle and presided over an estate of some thirty-two thousand acres and two thousand tenants.

Carnegie began his work life as a bobbin boy in a textile mill and progressed from there to a series of jobs—messenger boy, telegrapher, and private secretary to Thomas A. Scott, superintendent of the Pennsylvania Railroad's Pittsburgh division. When Carnegie eventually left the Pennsylvania in 1865, he himself held the post of division superintendent, succeeding Scott.

Carnegie could not have chosen a better training ground than J. Edgar Thomson's railroad system, probably the most complex and sophisticated large-scale enterprise in the world at that time. From that railway experience, Carnegie learned some tough-minded entrepreneurial principles for the future. Harold Livesay has described them: "Install whatever arrangements are necessary to know all costs all the time; to customers who can opt for a competitor's services, keep the price barely above costs and rely on volume to make a profit; with shippers, charge the limit; promote cost-conscious subordinates and fire the others; if business volume strains capacity, drive your men and equipment as hard as you can before hiring or buying more; buy what pays for itself and nothing that doesn't."[8]

In the immediate years after he left the Pennsylvania, Carnegie dabbled in a variety of investments and speculations. Despite considerable financial success in those activities, Carnegie put them all aside in 1872 to concentrate solely on steel manufacturing. He had invested as early as 1866 in a firm that produced Bessemer steel in modest quantities, but it took six years before he was convinced that the future lay in steel. By then an adequate supply of phosphorus-free Lake Superior ores was assured, and he had seen in person the high-volume manufacture of Bessemer steel in England.

Carnegie now set out to build an entirely new steel plant that would be the most advanced in the world. He employed Alexander Holley to supervise the construction of the mill at a location twelve miles south of Pittsburgh. He named it the J. Edgar Thomson Steel Works in order to win the goodwill of the Pennsylvania Railroad. As Joseph Frazier Wall has written in his masterly biography: "Carnegie fully appreciated that he was even more dependent than before on railroads, now that he was primarily a manufacturer rather than a financier. The railroads were the customers for his one major product, steel rails, and they must also carry the raw materials to his plant and the finished products to their market."[9]

Carnegie's unswerving demands were that the costs of production should be regularly reduced and that earnings should be reinvested in new equipment and continued plant expansion. He was a pioneer in using vertical integration within the industry. Vertical integration may be defined as the location, within one firm, of a sequence of processes in producing a good. These processes include obtaining raw materials, manufacturing the articles, and marketing the final product.

A large steel manufacturer such as Carnegie required enormous quantities of raw materials. To guarantee himself a reliable supply, he integrated backward by acquiring extensive iron-ore deposits and ample coking-coal reserves and producing the pig iron that went into his Bessemer converters and open-hearth furnaces. Carnegie's organization even ran its own fleet of lake steamers and an intracompany railroad between Pittsburgh and the Great Lakes. Carnegie Steel integrated forward also by dispensing almost entirely with the services of independent wholesalers and establishing instead company-owned sales offices in the nation's principal cities. He referred to the overall strategy as "everything being within ourselves."[10]

By 1900 Carnegie's mills were the most efficient steel producers anywhere. They were out-producing the entire British steel industry, and they accounted for a third of American output. When Carnegie finally agreed to sell his steel empire to Morgan's newly organized United States Steel Corporation in 1901, the price was $480 million. Carnegie's personal share was $225 million. Carnegie had originally invested $250,000 in the J. Edgar Thomson Works thirty years before.

The Kerosene Age and Mr. Rockefeller

Colonel Edwin L. Drake was neither a colonel, a geologist, nor a petroleum engineer. He was an unemployed railroad conductor who was by chance chosen to oversee the drilling at Titusville, Pennsylvania, of America's first producing oil well. As Harold Williamson, the historian of the petroleum industry, observed: "Drake presented only two visible assets for the task: he was immediately available, and his services would come cheaply, since he could obtain a railroad pass to Titusville."[11]

As early as 1767, a Moravian missionary had reported oil springs in the Titusville area and Indians who used the skimmings as an ointment for everything from rheumatism to toothaches. In 1855, Benjamin Silliman, Jr., a chemist at Yale University, analyzed petroleum samples from the Titusville springs. His report set in motion the events that led to the emergence of a new industry. Silliman confirmed that petroleum could be refined into a satisfactory illuminant—safe, bright-burning, and inexpensive—and he estimated that as much as 90 percent of the crude oil had commercial value.

On the basis of the Silliman report, a corporation was chartered— the Pennsylvania Rock Oil Company of Connecticut—and Edwin Drake was sent to Titusville. It is not clear who first thought of drilling into the earth for oil, but the idea came from the techniques used by salt-well drillers, some of whom had bored holes up to one thousand feet deep by 1830. The salt-well drillers often encountered unwanted yields of crude oil, which they usually disposed of as a waste product.

Drake, who was dubbed Colonel by his corporate sponsors to impress the local citizenry, arrived in Titusville in late 1857. After numerous delays, his well had reached a depth of sixty-nine feet on August 28, 1859, when crude oil was at last discovered floating a few feet below the level of the derrick floor. Drake took nearly two years to drill the sixty-nine feet, the costly and exasperating penalty which his company paid for hiring an amateur to perform the task. Drake earned only a modest return for his work, eventually squandered his small savings, and lived in poverty and obscurity until his death in 1880.

The reaction to Drake's oil strike was immediate: "Like the discovery of gold in California . . . Drake's well ignited a rush into western Pennsylvania that . . . quickly gave the area in and around Titusville all the characteristics associated with a mining boom."[12] Production soared from two thousand barrels in 1859 to almost five million ten years later.

Ralph and Muriel Hidy have noted that oilmen practiced "cultural borrowing" to a remarkable extent.[13] They borrowed the techniques of salt-well drillers to raise the crude and the processes of coal-oil refiners to extract kerosene and such by-products as naphtha, lubricants, and paraffin wax from the raw petroleum. The oilmen used existing transportation facilities—wagons, barges, and especially railroads—and marketed the final product through established distribution channels. Even the lamps in which kerosene was burned had been developed for coal-oil use just a few years before.

Refineries sprang up in northwestern Pennsylvania as well as in other nearby locations such as Pittsburgh, Philadelphia, and Cleveland. Small refineries in the 1860s could be built for as little as $200 and even the larger units seldom cost more than $15,000. But this period was also chaotic for aspiring petroleum entrepreneurs because prices fluctuated wildly and business failures multiplied. As the Hidys described this early period: "Lack of balance between functions was chronic: first production would outrun the throughput by refiners; then manufacturing capacity would exceed both current production of raw material and the rate of consumption of finished products. Oilmen knew from bitter experience that their business was wasteful, risky, hazardous, and unstable."[14]

Several oilmen took steps to discipline the unruly industry. On January 10, 1870, five men in Cleveland, Ohio, signed a document that represented the opening of a new chapter in petroleum history. The men were Stephen V. Harkness, Henry M. Flagler, Samuel Andrews, and two brothers, William and John Davison Rockefeller. The document was the articles that incorporated the Standard Oil Company of Ohio.

Although Standard Oil was not the instrument of a single individual, John D. Rockefeller was the key figure in its history. Physically unimposing—approximately six feet tall, with reddish-brown hair, a slight build, and a reserved manner—he was a fine family man, devoted to his wife and children. He was also a fervent Christian (Baptist), abstemious in his personal habits, and generous in his philanthropies. Yet this seemingly model citizen was also the object of violent hatred. The paradox reveals the concern that Americans felt for the new corporate society with which they were coping and their tendency to personalize abstract grievances.

Rockefeller was born in western New York State in 1839. His father engaged in a variety of occupations, usually that of an itinerant patent-medicine salesman. Even after his son had become wealthy, the father continued to travel the medicine-show circuit, billing himself as "Dr. William Rockefeller, the Celebrated Cancer Cure Specialist." With the head of the family absent for long periods, a substantial responsibility fell upon John as the eldest son. He thus acquired resourcefulness and the ability to lead, and developed a lifelong passion for order and stability.

The Rockefeller family moved to Ohio in 1853, and, two years later, John secured his first full-time employment as an assistant bookkeeper for a commission house in Cleveland. In 1859, he became a partner in a wholesale firm that dealt in agricultural products. The firm was successful from the start and generated sufficient profits to allow the partners to dabble in other opportunities, one of which was petroleum.

Rockefeller avoided the wildly speculative drilling and production side of the industry and invested instead in a new Cleveland refinery. By 1867 he terminated his original wholesale business and concentrated entirely on petroleum refining in a new partnership called Rockefeller, Andrews, and Flagler. Rockefeller and Henry Flagler provided the capital and management expertise, and Samuel Andrews, an experienced petroleum refiner, supervised technical operations.

From the time of its incorporation in 1870, the Standard Oil Company embarked on a strategy of relentless expansion. Its history during the Rockefeller years fell into four broad, overlapping phases. The first of those phases—"confederation"—lasted from the inception of the business until the end of the 1870s. Chronic overproduction had occurred throughout the oil industry, which resulted in bitter competition and a slashing of everyone's profits. The Standard Oil executives responded by eliminating the "wasteful" competition. By aggressive competitive pressure, they persuaded other refiners either to cease operations or to join Rockefeller's company in a loose alliance.

Standard Oil possessed two substantial advantages over its competitors: it was a more efficient manufacturer, and it had developed close ties with the railroads that carried its freight shipments. The railroads were willing to grant discounts or "rebates" to a major shipper like Standard Oil, and these were decisive in any competitive battle. Rockefeller later justified the rebates as a benefit to all parties involved and to the nation: "The railroads, rather, were the ones who profited by the traffic of the Standard Oil Company, and whatever advantage it received in its constant efforts to reduce rates of freight was only one of the many elements of lessening cost to the consumer, which enabled us to increase our volume of business the world over because we could reduce the selling price."[15]

In the second phase of its history—"consolidation"—Standard Oil welded its loose alliance into a tighter combination of corporations that had central control and a rational organization. During the 1880s, Standard Oil and its affiliates refined over 80 percent of the kerosene sold in the United States. They also manufactured more than one hundred by-products, including lubricants, gasoline, naphtha, paints, wax, varnishes, and petroleum jelly.

Before the process of consolidation was complete, Rockefeller and his associates began a third phase in their organization's growth, "vertical integration." They took this step for defensive reasons—to provide an assured supply of crude oil, to reduce dependence on railroads, and to meet a rising tide of overseas competition. They purchased oil-field properties, constructed trunk pipelines to carry both crude and refined oil, built tanker fleets, created foreign marketing subsidiaries, and established a nationwide system of domestic, licensed dealers.

By 1890 the fourth phase—"public attack"—was well under way. Critics accused the company of employing the worst forms of competitive tactics, including ruthless price-cutting, industrial espionage, subterfuge, and even sabotage. Rising citizen concern contributed to the passage of the Sherman Antitrust Act by Congress in 1890, and incessant criticism of the petroleum giant resulted in a federal antitrust suit in 1906.

In May 1911, the Supreme Court ordered the dismemberment of the Standard Oil combination. Thirty-three subsidiaries were severed from the parent corporation and reorganized as independent companies with no common officers or directors. Ironically, the court's holding that Standard Oil was an illegal monopoly occurred when the organization was losing rather than retaining its control of the industry. In fact, Standard Oil's share of the market was the smallest it had been since the 1870s. Several factors contributed to this decline: the opening of new crude fields in the Southwest faster than even Standard Oil could keep pace; the rise of aggressive, integrated rivals, such as Pure Oil, Gulf, and Texaco; a reduced demand for kerosene, Standard's staple, and an increased demand for gasoline and fuel oil; and a top management marked by advancing age and conservatism. Standard Oil's share of the nation's refining capacity was reduced to 60 percent by 1911.

Rockefeller himself had retired from the active management in 1896, and, until his death in 1937, he was mainly concerned with the philanthropic distribution of his vast fortune. He described his approach as "scientific giving," and his gifts eventually totaled $550 million.

In his biography of Rockefeller (written in 1953 and still the best available on the subject), the late Allan Nevins praised Rockefeller's "single-mindedness, his sharpness of insight, his cool disdain of emotional factors; his instinct for the future, . . . his breadth of ambition, and his skill . . . in finding novel weapons to attain his ends—his strategic ingenuity, in short." Yet even Nevins's appreciation of Rockefeller's life and work is tempered by the unanswered questions he posed: "Did the deadweight Standard Oil hung upon business ethics (for though it would be hard to prove that it depressed the current code, it certainly did nothing to raise it) outweigh the great constructive innovations of the combination, and the example set by its efficiency and order?"[16]

The Early Telephone Age and Mr. Vail

Between 1865 and 1915, the population of the United States almost tripled, from 36 million to 101 million inhabitants. During the same period, the population became more urbanized. In 1860, only about 20 percent of Americans lived in urban areas, but this figure had reached 40 percent by 1900, and, in 1920, a majority of the population was classified as urban. This rising concentration of people in cities created huge potential markets for both new and old industries. One set of entrepreneurs who took advantage of the urban opportunities were those involved in the spread of the telephone network.

On March 7, 1876, Alexander Graham Bell, a Scottish-born teacher of the deaf, received a patent to develop a "harmonic telegraph." In the process, Bell invented the telephone and became the holder of probably the single most valuable patent in the history of any industry. A successful leather merchant, Thomas Sanders, and a wealthy Boston lawyer, Gardiner Greene Hubbard, had supported Bell's experimentation, and a firm—the Bell Telephone Company—evolved out of that informal arrangement and was organized in July 1877. Hubbard managed the business, and Bell was its "electrician."

Two months before, Hubbard had distributed handbills that were the first telephone advertisements. They promised that the Bell firm was "prepared to furnish Telephones for the transmission of articulate speech through instruments not more than twenty miles apart." The handbills added that "conversation can easily be carried on after slight practice and with occasional repetition of a word or sentence."[17] In July 1877, when Bell Telephone was formed, there were only about one hundred telephones in use, but within a year the number reached eight hundred. All of them were two-party connections linking only a pair of specific locations; workable exchange equipment had yet to be developed.

Bell, the inventor, gradually withdrew from the growing business. He had little interest in administrative affairs, and he wished to follow other paths. By 1881 he had severed all ties to the Bell Telephone Company except for his ownership of two thousand shares of its stock and some later appearances in its defense during patent litigations. Bell had invented the telephone, but others invented the telecommunications industry.[18]

Hubbard wanted to avoid the investment of massive amounts of capital that he would have needed to build telephone networks all over the country. Instead, he planned to sell franchises to local companies, which would pay royalties for the use of the Bell patents. Locally owned companies would be required to raise their own starting capital and to manage their own operations.

Before Hubbard proceeded with his scheme, however, further corporate reorganizations took place. In April 1880, a new Massachusetts corporation was chartered—the American Bell Telephone Company—and control passed to a different group of Boston investors led by William H. Forbes, the scion of a prominent family whose financial interests ranged from banking to railroads. But as Hubbard stepped out of the picture, he performed one key service that was crucial to the future history of the Bell organization—he hired Theodore N. Vail as its general manager. Vail transformed a struggling Gilded Age enterprise into a twentieth-century giant.

Vail had first found a career in the railway mail service and became its general superintendent in 1876. His experience with the mail— he was regarded as the country's leading expert on its delivery— convinced him of the necessity for good nationwide communication systems. Hence, in 1879, he resigned from his post in Washington and accepted Hubbard's offer of the general manager's duties.

Forbes and Vail came from different backgrounds—conservative Boston Brahmin versus aggressive Midwesterner—and had different business strategies. Forbes favored a cautious policy with most profits distributed in generous dividend payments to his friends in Boston, who made up a sizable portion of the stockholders. Vail, on the other hand, was an ardent expansionist; he argued that the company should retain most earnings to finance future growth.

Even though Vail had to overcome Forbes's misgivings, he accomplished a great deal in the 1880s. In 1882, he arranged for American Bell to buy a controlling interest in the Western Electric Manufacturing Company of Chicago, the largest such firm in the United States. Vail was looking ahead to the 1890s, when the Bell patents were due to expire and the company would undoubtedly face outside competition. Integrating backward by acquiring valuable equipment-manufacturing capacity was the means of both guaranteeing a dependable source of supply and assuring Bell future patentable technology. A recent study of the integration decision concluded: "By the second decade of the twentieth century—when the Bell System had become a highly integrated functional organization in which specialized managers and engineers planned, implemented, operated, and maintained a nationwide communications network on a continuous round-the-clock basis—Western Electric had become the linchpin of the enterprise."[19]

Vail turned his attention also to the local licensees. New franchise holders were required to give American Bell an equity position in their businesses. In this way, Vail's organization had a permanent stock interest in the local companies even after American Bell's patents ran out. His clear aim was to "take possession of the field."

Finally, Vail regarded the creation of an efficient long-distance service as of critical importance to American Bell's future. It would tie the local licensees together and cement Bell's dominance over them and the telephone industry. Thus, in February 1885, a new subsidiary of American Bell was chartered in New York (where corporation laws were not as restrictive as in Massachusetts) to build and operate a long-distance service. The subsidiary was the American Telephone and Telegraph Company (AT&T). The presence of the word "telegraph" in the name left open the possibility that American Bell might also enter that field in the future.

By 1885, therefore, Vail had nearly completed the structure that the Bell System would have for the next century. Vail resigned from

American Bell in September 1887 because of continuing differences with Forbes and the unlikelihood that he could advance to president. Six years later, the last of the basic Bell patents expired, and American Bell was immediately faced with a new competitive situation. Substantial areas in the United States were still without telephone service, and local investors could now finance independent companies. Vail had hoped to prevent this by a rapid expansion, but the slow-growth policy of the Forbes group left the door open for competitors.

The independents proliferated rapidly and usually received encouragement from a public alienated by American Bell's image as a greedy monopolist. Bell fought back by refusing to allow the independents to purchase equipment from Western Electric or connect to its long-distance network. It also began a rapid extension of service in a race with the independents for new territories.

American Bell needed an infusion of new capital to finance this belated expansion. Since the restrictive Massachusetts corporation laws made this difficult, the solution was to convert the New York subsidiary, AT&T, into a parent company by shifting all of American Bell's assets to it. The transfer was completed in December 1889. AT&T continued to operate the system's long-distance lines in addition to assuming American Bell's former functions.

Despite Bell's counterattack, AT&T's share of the market steadily declined. By 1907 the nation had 6 million phones and only 3 million were Bell's. In that year also, AT&T's unending need for additional capital finally resulted in a shift in control. The Boston-based directors, who had been in charge since 1880, were replaced by a Wall Street syndicate headed by J. P. Morgan. Theodore Vail was installed as president.

Since his resignation in 1887, Vail had pursued a number of diverse opportunities that ranged from Colorado mining to hydroelectric development in Argentina. His wife had died in 1905, followed soon after by his only son. Thus a lonely, saddened Vail was ready for a new direction in his life, and the Morgan syndicate supplied it with the offer of AT&T's presidency.

Although Morgan men held seats on the AT&T Board, the investment banker did not interfere with Vail's operational authority. Both men believed that the Bell System should be the single force in the industry. Vail referred to the concept as "universality," which meant a publicly accepted monopoly.

He continued AT&T's campaign against the independents by emphasizing lower rates and better service so that consumers, when they had a choice, would voluntarily choose Bell. At the same time, he gradually bought out more and more of the independents when their profits declined. Morgan made Vail's campaign easier through his ability to shut off the flow of commercial credit to the underfinanced independents, which made them vulnerable to a takeover bid by Vail. Vail broadened AT&T's scope through the purchase in 1909 of a 30 percent interest in Western Union. This stock gave AT&T working control of the telegraph company, and, in 1910, Vail became president of Western Union, too.

The universality campaign did not go unchallenged in an era when the public clamor over the monopolies reached a peak. Journalistic critics and reformers turned their attention increasingly to telecommunications, and some called for outright nationalization of the industry. Vail responded to the threat by preaching a doctrine of regulated monopoly.

He called for public oversight of AT&T through regulatory commissions. The business of providing telephone service for a community was, he contended, a natural monopoly, and competition enforced by the government would mean only needless duplication of facilities and equipment. In return for the freedom to operate as a monopoly, however, AT&T would willingly submit to regulation by state and federal agencies.

Vail's proposal for a regulated monopoly did not deter convinced trustbusters, who had the support of many independent company officials. In January 1913, George W. Wickersham, attorney general in the lame-duck Taft administration, informed Vail that the Justice Department was considering an antitrust prosecution. Woodrow Wilson would enter the White House in only two months, and Vail decided that, in view of Wilson's vigorous antitrust rhetoric during the presidential campaign of 1912, an accommodation must be sought.

He instructed AT&T vice-president Nathan C. Kingsbury to begin negotiations with the Wilson administration. The eventual outcome, announced in December 1913, was the so-called Kingsbury Commitment. By its terms, AT&T agreed to dispose of its interest in Western Union, purchase no more independents except with the prior approval of the Interstate Commerce Commission, and allow the existing independent companies to connect with Bell System lines. Vail had staved off a possible antitrust action at the cost of abandoning AT&T's drive toward an absolute monopoly in telecommunications.

By the time of Vail's death in 1920, one writer has observed, "AT&T was a thriving concern, a quasi-monopoly which had come to terms with both the government and the public. . . . The independents would remain, and in time AT&T would work in harmony with them, in much the same fashion as the whale lives with smaller animals in the sea."[20] Bell's share of the market had stabilized at roughly three-fourths of all the nation's telephones by 1920, and, because of Vail's leadership, AT&T was on its way to becoming the largest private corporation in the world.

Integration and Combination

Industrialization did not mean simply producing more in the same way. The firms that became synonymous with the phrase "big business" blended technological and organizational innovations to increase the output of their factories and, at the same time, to increase productivity and lower unit costs. These innovations, whether they were improved machinery or a better plant design, brought "mass production" to American industry, and big business first appeared in the new mass-production industries.

Corporations employing mass-production techniques soon found it necessary to extend their operations beyond the single function of production by a forward integration toward the purchaser of the firm's goods or a backward integration toward the basic materials that would eventually make up the finished product. In some instances, vertical integration was preceded by horizontal combination. Two or more firms that produced similar products joined into one new and larger organization. Through this process of extension, those industries that formed the core of the national economy emerged into the modern multifunction business enterprise.

Alfred Chandler broke new ground in American economic history with a famous article published in 1959 in the *Business History Review*. In his essay, he explained the sudden appearance of corporate giantism in the late nineteenth century. Chandler's classic article, "The Beginnings of Big Business in American Industry," highlighted vertical integration as an important avenue to great size. Previous historians had emphasized only horizontal combinations in their discussions of big business.

Chandler argued that, "where the product tended to be somewhat new in kind and especially fitted for the urban market," manufacturers first chose to integrate vertically, but when the products to be marketed were "established staple items, horizontal combination tended to precede vertical integration."[21] The firms whose products fell into the former category were a varied lot, but they usually had a common problem—the existing distribution system, populated by independent middlemen, did not meet their special needs. With more goods to sell—because of the new mass-production innovations—firms had to develop more effective ways to distribute these goods to buyers. A few examples should illustrate this point.

BEEF, BANANAS, AND CIGARETTES

Agricultural processing firms were among those that chose to integrate forward by marketing their own goods. These goods included beer, flour, tobacco, and bananas, among other products, but the best-known case is that of the meat-packing industry and Gustavus Swift.

Mary Yeager, the author of the most complete study of the industry's origins, has written that, "before the introduction of the refrigerator car in the 1870s, the meat-packing industry was ruled by Mother Nature with a mighty invisible hand."[22] Because of its highly perishable nature, ready-to-market "dressed" beef was almost never shipped long distances, such as from western ranges to eastern urban markets. Instead, live cattle were transported, a method that was expensive and wasteful, since 60 percent of a steer was inedible. In addition, cattle usually lost weight on a long trip, and some died before reaching their destination. On the other hand, if only the salable portions of beef were shipped, they would require much less space than live animals.

Gustavus Swift took the lead in upsetting the old order. A New Englander by birth, Swift was a partner in a Boston wholesale meat house in the early 1870s. In 1875, he left Boston for Chicago, ostensibly to buy cattle for his firm, but he was already mulling over ways to gain a competitive advantage. The edge he sought was to sell dressed beef from cattle slaughtered in high volume in a Chicago packing plant.

He formed a partnership with his brother Edwin in 1878, and then contracted with an engineer to design a new type of refrigerated railroad car (those few already in use had proved generally unsatisfactory). When the major railroads to whom he offered the design refused to invest in construction of the cars—the lines had sunk a considerable sum into livestock equipment and pens and were not inclined to see them become obsolete because of Swift's novel ideas— he undertook the building and ownership of the cars himself. Swift next reached an agreement with the Canadian Grand Trunk Railroad to have his cars hauled to eastern markets. Since the Grand Trunk had only a modest investment in livestock facilities, it was not threatened by Swift's plans. Competitive pressures eventually forced the other railroad companies to follow suit.

In addition to developing a workable refrigerator car, Swift had to overcome the inadequacies of the existing distribution system. Eastern wholesale butchers and livestock dealers attempted to inspire boycotts of Swift meat by spreading tales of impurities and poor taste in beef slaughtered days before and a thousand miles away. To combat the opposition, Swift energetically promoted the dressed-beef concept by personal contact and extensive advertising. Moreover, he created a network of refrigerated warehouses or "branch houses" to store his beef, since independent jobbers had no such facilities and were reluctant to invest in costly refrigeration apparatus. From these branch houses, Swift's salesmen fanned out to call on local retailers and convince them of his product's high quality.

The combination of high-volume production with innovations in distribution translated into a significant cost advantage. Swift was able to set a price up to seventy-five cents per hundred pounds cheaper than his competitors who still relied upon the shipment of live cattle. Then as his methods took hold and demand increased rapidly, he established additional packing plants in Kansas City, Omaha, and other locations.

By 1881 Swift Bros. & Co. shipped almost $200,000 worth of beef weekly, owned over 150 refrigerator cars, which cost up to $6,000 each, and operated thirty-four branch houses. The most obvious proof of success, however, was the fact that Chicago's other leading packers all quickly adopted the innovations and extended their own operations to include elaborate distribution chains. Within a decade after the Swift brothers formed their partnership, oligopoly had come to meat-packing, and four principal integrated firms were responsible for half the entire national meat supply.

Other firms that processed agricultural products applied similar innovations to their own manufactures. In 1899, for instance, Andrew Preston, Lorenzo Baker, and Minor Keith incorporated the United Fruit Company. They had already popularized an exotic tropical fruit, the banana, in the United States. In order to do so, they had acquired their own banana plantations to assure an adequate supply, refrigerated steamships to preserve the fruit on the long trip from Central America, and climate-controlled storage houses in the United States to hold the bananas until they were sold. United Fruit's fully integrated structure allowed it to dominate the banana trade for years.[23]

United Fruit made many positive contributions in the Latin American countries in which it operated. Hospitals were built, water and sanitation facilities constructed, schools established, and employment provided for the local population. But there was a dark side to its presence too. As one historian of the region, Maurice P. Brungardt, has written, United Fruit also "throttled competition, overthrew governments, bribed presidents, blocked railroads, ruined planters, bankrupted cooperatives, opposed organized labor, dominated workers, and exploited consumers. Such influence by a U.S. corporation in the comparatively weaker nations of Latin America left a legacy of distrust and bitter hatred that the U.S. government and other U.S. companies still have trouble overcoming."[24]

James Buchanan Duke introduced vertical integration in cigarette production. This product played a minor role in the tobacco industry until 1883, when Duke cut his firm's production costs by replacing conventional hand rolling with machine manufacturing. He further solidified his industry leadership by purchasing bright-leaf tobacco directly from farmers, which eliminated the role of the tobacco broker as a middleman. In addition, "Buck" Duke's firm, which was incorporated in 1890 as the American Tobacco Company, spurred the marketing of its cigarettes through aggressive, imaginative advertising and through regional distribution centers. After American Tobacco introduced a full-line policy of selling a variety of related products, the firm, by 1900, produced 80 percent of all cigarettes, plug and smoking tobacco, and snuff made in the United States.[25]

SEWING MACHINES AND ELECTRIC LIGHTS

Agricultural-processing firms were not the only ones to pioneer growth through vertical integration. Some businesses that produced durable goods followed the same course. The McCormick Harvesting Machine Company—described in an earlier chapter—was one of these. Another was the Singer Manufacturing Company.

In January 1852, Isaac Merrit Singer and Edward Clark formed a partnership to manufacture a sewing machine for which Singer had received a patent the year before. Singer was a man of considerable mechanical ability, but also a notorious lecher and profligate—he fathered twenty-four children by five women, only two of whom he married. Clark, however, was a respectable New York lawyer and an able manager. It was he who brought a practical business sense to the partnership (incorporated in 1863) and created the organizational structure.[26]

After resolving a patent dispute with Elias Howe, who invented an earlier but less workable version of a sewing machine, by the formation of a patent pool in 1856, Clark turned his attention to the problems inherent in the high-volume production of Singer's machine. At first the firm relied upon independent manufacturer's agents to market its products, but the existing middleman system did not meet the requirements of this new and complex product. Independent agents had little knowledge of the technical details of the machines, and they were not prepared to offer extensive sales demonstrations or follow-up repairs. They were also incapable of assisting customers with the credit necessary to finance the installment purchase of a machine selling for the then lofty price of $110.

Instead, the Singer Company opened its own branch sales outlets. Each was staffed with a female demonstrator, a mechanic to handle servicing, a salesman to do the actual selling, and a manager who, in addition to supervising the others, dealt with credit and collections. Clark summed up his firm's approach: "The business we do is peculiar, and we have adopted our own methods of transacting it."[27]

Vertical integration also occurred in producers'-goods industries. Like the reaper and sewing machine, the products were often technologically complex and required a specially trained sales and service force. Some producers created manufacturer-owned marketing organizations because they calculated that operating their own sales offices would be less expensive than paying commissions to outside brokers or agents. In addition, they could vigorously promote sales of their own brands, since outside commission agents handled the competing products of a number of firms and lacked the incentive to promote one particular make.

The experience of the electrical-equipment industry offers another version of growth by integration. Steady progress in perfecting an incandescent lamp was made after the Civil War. Thomas Alva Edison produced the most significant work in this field. Although Edison was only thirty years old when he turned his attention to electric lighting in 1877, he had a number of successful inventions to his credit—a stock ticker, the multiplex telegraph, and the mimeograph, among others. The year before, Edison had established a laboratory at Menlo Park, New Jersey. It was one of the first industrial-research laboratories in America, and, as one scholar has pointed out, it marked a contradiction between the myth that grew up about Edison and the reality of Menlo Park. Wyn Wachhorst has observed that, "ironically, while much of the Edison symbol derives from the image of a lone individual succeeding through extraordinary physical, mental, and spiritual powers, Edison actually initiated the kind of team research . . . that served as a pilot model for the huge industrial research laboratories such as those later organized by General Electric or Bell Telephone."[28]

Edison's breakthrough came in October 1879, when a vacuum bulb using a carbonized cotton thread as a filament burned for over thirteen hours. But Edison was clearly aware that the incandescent bulb was only one item in a larger system yet to be designed. His goal had always been to distribute electricity over a wide urban area from a central station.

The Edison Electric Illuminating Company was organized in 1880 to light the financial district of New York City. It had the backing of a group of investors led by J. P. Morgan, who asked Edison to install an individual power plant in his own home (although a short circuit burned a part of Morgan's library, the banker still supported the inventor). Edison's company purchased property on Pearl Street in a dilapidated New York City neighborhood for its central power station. Six large dynamos were installed that were so formidable in size that Edison named the model Jumbo, after P. T. Barnum's celebrated circus elephant. On September 4, 1892, service was begun. A newspaper account of the day described the scene: "In store and business places throughout the lower quarters of the city there was a strange glow last night. The dim flicker of gas, often subdued and debilitated by grim and uncleanly globes, was supplanted by a steady glare, bright and mellow, which illuminated interiors and shone through windows fixed and unwavering."[29] Within four years there were fifty-five other city lighting plants that used Edison's system.

The electrical-equipment industry was now "so big that its financial and administrative problems were . . . best solved by lawyers, financiers, and promoters rather than by inventors." The several Edison corporations were combined into the Edison General Electric Company, in which the inventor held only a 10 percent interest. Edison gradually withdrew from the electrical industry altogether, a choice he made, by his own statement, "to free my mind from financial stress, and thus enable me to go ahead in the technical field."[30] In truth, he returned to inventing (a profession that he had virtually created) in part because the sophisticated technology of electricity had already left him too far behind.

The Edison General Electric Company concentrated upon the manufacture of electrical apparatus for power generation and paid little attention to the operation of utility companies. Its industry leadership was soon challenged by a pair of emerging competitors, the Thomson-Houston Electric Company and the firm of George Westinghouse, which he founded in 1884 and named after himself. All three experienced rapid growth in part because "the demand for interior lighting from a central station source had been well established by the gas companies. The incandescent electric light was about the same as gas in cost and much superior in quality."[31]

All three companies faced the same basic marketing problem. The product they offered was complex and expensive. Furthermore, improper installation might mean not only inefficient operation but also a real danger to the user. The manufacturers therefore had little alternative but to organize their own marketing departments, which were staffed with trained personnel who could handle sales as well as proper installation, instruction, and repair services.

In 1892, two of these three integrated manufacturers agreed to merge. Edison General Electric and Thomson-Houston exchanged their stock for that of the new corporation, the General Electric Company. The new corporate name dropped any reference to Edison, to the chagrin of the disgruntled inventor. At the turn of the century, therefore, the electrical-equipment industry was dominated by a duopoly of two major integrated firms, General Electric and Westinghouse.

GROWTH BY COMBINATION

The second form of extension that various firms chose was that of horizontal combination, frequently followed by vertical integration. These firms combined because they wanted to control prices and competition within their industries in order to prevent the erosion of profits.

A continuing deflationary trend in the economy, which began with the depression of the 1870s, intensified the search for a limit to competition. Using 1873 for a base price index of 100, prices in 1890 stood at only 78, a decline of 22 percent. By 1896 the index had fallen to 71, a decrease of another 7 percent. In simplified terms, an important cause of this continuing decline in prices was a surge in the output of goods without a corresponding increase in the supply of money.

To combat falling prices, many businesses increased their production levels in the vain hope that such a step would generate more earnings, especially to cover the high fixed costs imposed by enlarged plant capacity and the introduction of expensive technology. Instead, they glutted the market and aggravated the basic problem they wanted to solve. Thus they eagerly sought a means of stabilizing prices and "rationalizing" intraindustry competition.

Manufacturers tried to achieve their goal initially by working through loose combinations, such as pools and trade associations. In doing so, they followed the pattern set by the railroads, which faced similar problems, and pooling had the same inherent weakness for both groups. The cartels depended upon the cooperation of all their members, and, if one or more refused to abide by the terms of the original agreement, there could be no recourse to the courts to enforce the "contract."

John D. Rockefeller referred to pools as "ropes of sand." His unsatisfactory experience with them during the 1870s led him to conclude that a tighter form of combination was imperative. Samuel C. T. Dodd, Standard Oil's legal counsel, suggested the requisite form. Dodd was probably the first great practitioner of corporate law in the United States and served as Standard Oil's principal attorney from the 1870s until after the turn of the century. He recommended adapting an old device, the trust agreement, to a fresh use—the formation of a closely knit industrial combination. A board of trustees controlled a majority of the voting stock in the companies that made up the Standard Oil alliance. In return for the surrender of their stock, the original holders were given trust certificates, which entitled them to share in the combined earnings of all the companies that made up the trust.

The Standard Oil Trust was contrived in 1879 and revised in 1882. In the latter year, the board of nine trustees, who included John D. and William Rockefeller, Henry M. Flagler, and John D. Archbold, exercised control over forty different firms and at least 80 percent of the nation's refining capacity. Within the trust framework, Rockefeller and his fellow trustees could wield sufficient power over the entire family of companies to carry out a thorough consolidation. They closed poorly located refineries, built new ones where and when needed, and began the process of vertical integration.

The precedent of the Standard Oil Trust was quickly followed in other manufacturing fields. The pattern was repeated by the appearance of trusts in the cottonseed-oil (1884), linseed-oil (1885), whiskey (1887), sugar-refining (1887), and lead-smelting (1887) industries. Nevertheless, despite its initial success, the trust device was relatively short-lived. Suits charging that trusts were illegal restraints of trade were brought in a number of states—an Ohio Supreme Court decision in 1892 precipitated the dissolution of the Standard Oil Trust—and the passage by Congress of the Sherman Antitrust Act in 1890 certified their demise. The word "trust," however, continued in the popular parlance of the time as a synonym for any substantial business combination.

After the abandonment of the trust, a third form of horizontal combination soon appeared—the holding company. In most states, permission for one corporation to hold or own the stock of others required a special legislative act. However, in 1889, the state of New Jersey amended its general incorporation laws in order to permit holding companies. The change allowed corporations chartered in the state to own stock in other corporations whether they were chartered in New Jersey or elsewhere. New Jersey now became the haven for companies that had given up their trust structures and wanted a viable substitute.

In 1899, the Rockefeller group increased the capital stock of the Standard Oil Company (New Jersey) from $10 million to $110 million. Jersey Standard, as it became known, then exchanged its stock for that of the constituent companies that had made up the Standard Oil Trust. Its directors were essentially the same men who had conducted the affairs of the trust.

A FLOOD OF MERGERS

The ultimate form of horizontal combination is an amalgamation or merger, which joins firms together into a single enterprise. Although mergers have occurred throughout the last one hundred years, business historians have recognized certain periods of especially intense activity. Four particular "waves" have been identified: the first took place during the 1895–1904 interval; the second occurred in the 1920s; the third reached its peak in the 1960s; and the fourth has swept the 1980s.

During the five years from 1898 to 1902, more than 2,600 firms were absorbed by mergers; about 1,200 disappeared in 1899 alone. This sudden flood of mergers occurred for several reasons. One factor was the trend of Supreme Court antitrust decisions, which seemed to support the legality of mergers.

The rise of a market for industrial securities was an indispensable factor. Before the 1890s, the stocks of only a few manufacturing firms were publicly traded. During that decade, however, industrial stocks became extremely popular. The successful profit record that many of the new mass-production corporations maintained, even during the depression years from 1893 to 1897, impressed investors. Conversely, widespread failures among railway companies disappointed investors and encouraged them to shift to industrials.

Promotional factors were at work, too. Investment bankers and other merger underwriters found that they could market the securities of a newly formed combination at a price considerably higher than its per-share net worth. Investors were willing to pay the price because they expected the merger to succeed, the enlarged enterprise to pay attractive dividends, and the price of its watered stock to rise even further. Promoters could thus entice manufacturers into mergers by paying higher prices for ownership interests than the firms were actually worth, and the promoters themselves earned substantial profits from their management of the stock offering.

In her 1985 analysis of the great turn-of-the-century merger wave, Naomi R. Lamoreaux stressed more fundamental factors. She determined "the consolidation movement was the product of a particular conjunction of historical events: the development of capital-intensive, mass production manufacturing techniques in the late nineteenth century; the extraordinarily rapid growth that many capital-intensive industries experienced after 1887; and the deep depression that began in 1893."[32] After failing to halt the damaging price warfare accompanying the depression-driven decline in product demand by any other means, manufacturers in these industries turned, almost as a last resort, to outright consolidations.

To merge was one matter, but for the merger to succeed was quite another. Probably only half the mergers between 1885 and 1905 could be classified as successful. These were usually found, according to Glenn Porter, "in technologically advanced industries which achieved genuine economies of scale."[33] Mergers were least successful in labor-intensive or low-technology industries where the threshold of entry was not particularly high. Examples include clothing, lumber, printing, and textiles. Mergers also failed if the costs of consolidation had been excessive because plants and equipment were acquired at inflated prices. The consolidated firm was required to charge too high a price for its output in order to secure an adequate return on investment. As a result, new competitors quickly entered the industry, underselling the merged organization, and forcing down its market share.

When mergers did succeed, they dominated their industries. Economists employ "concentration ratios" to measure the degree of competition in an industry. One of the most frequently cited is the ratio that represents the percentage of total sales in an industry accounted for by the four largest firms. Using that measure, in 1901, about one-third of the value added in American manufacturing was accounted for by industries where the ratio was 50 percent or higher.

Where the level of concentration remained low, one manufacturer could cut his price without noticeably affecting others. But once the number of firms declined to the point where the concentration ratio was high, any significant change in the price or production policies of one major company would have a sharp impact on its competitors. As a result, "administered prices" became the norm in oligopolistic industries. Tacit or explicit decisions to maintain prices at a favorable level for the producer or to follow the leadership of a single firm avoided the traditional form of competition that characterized unconcentrated industries. Businesses competed instead with such weapons as advertising, service, and product variations rather than price.

The Price of Progress

During most of the nineteenth century American entrepreneurship flourished in an environment that supported unfettered capitalistic development. The United States thereby attained world industrial leadership and an enviable standard of living. Yet many Americans grew increasingly uneasy about the extent to which the presence of giant corporations seemed to threaten cherished individualistic values.

In the last two decades of the century, the uneasiness was slowly translated into a movement to establish public oversight of the economy. Countervailing groups formed that were determined to achieve what they saw as a fairer balance between their own goals and those of the business community. In effect, Americans began to wonder whether the economic progress that they were making was worth the price they had to pay.

CHAPTER ELEVEN

Reacting to Industrialism

A story is told that, early in 1890, David K. Watson, attorney general of Ohio, was browsing through some volumes in a Columbus bookstore when he found one entitled *Trusts*, written by a New York lawyer, W. W. Cook. In it, Watson read, supposedly for the first time, the text of the Standard Oil Trust agreement. Watson, it is said, immediately concluded that the intent of the agreement was to establish a petroleum monopoly, and that, as a party to the plan, the Standard Oil Company of Ohio was in violation of its corporate charter. The outcome of Watson's bookshop visit was the filing of a state antitrust suit against the Ohio firm and, indirectly, the entire trust structure.

The suit was concluded with a decision of the Ohio Supreme Court in March 1892. In its finding, the court admitted that Standard Oil may have improved the quality and cheapened the cost of petroleum products. But that was not a sufficient argument to justify a monopoly, since "experience shows that it is not wise to trust human cupidity where it has the opportunity to aggrandize itself at the expense of others." The community must be concerned with the potential power to harm society inherent in any monopoly, whether or not that power was wielded. For the Supreme Court of Ohio, at least, the proper path was clear: "A society in which few men are the employers and the great body are merely employees or servants is not the most desirable in a republic; and it should be as much the policy of the laws to multiply the numbers engaged in independent pursuits or in the profits of production, as to cheapen the price to the consumer."[1]

Just as the Ohio judiciary chose the venerable values of atomistic competition, so did other Americans react to the looming phenomenon of industrialism by making their own choices. As we shall see, most found an answer in a pragmatic middle ground.

The Image of the Businessman

A healthy measure of the difficulty that Americans had in adjusting to industrialism stemmed from their contradictory images of the businessman himself. One aspect of that conflict lay in the sheer diversity of the business community; business executives were not monolithic thinkers. As Sidney Fine writes, "One finds among the businessmen protectionists and free traders, friends of hard money and of soft money, opponents of any real government control of corporate enterprise and advocates of government regulation of corporations as creatures of the state."[2]

The contradictory image of business was also the result of the high esteem in which Americans held those who achieved material success. This esteem was a prime cause of the hospitable climate for capitalism in which ambitious entrepreneurs basked in the United States. The "self-made man," to use Irvin Wyllie's term, was the legendary American hero. Wyllie added: "To most Americans he is the office boy who has become the head of a great concern, making millions in the process. He represents our most cherished conceptions of success, and particularly our belief that any man can achieve fortune through the practice of industry, frugality, and sobriety."[3]

Americans in the Gilded Age thus were hard pressed to understand how the master symbols of the nation's accomplishments could undermine the beliefs and values of their society. There was dismay, for instance, over the unethical conduct of individual businessmen and their companies. Without question, rascals there were, but probably no more than the proportion of scoundrels in the community at large. More likely, an apparent gap between the rhetoric of business leaders and their real-world actions kindled public bewilderment.

Andrew Carnegie was a case in point. Much more inclined to public philosophizing on contemporary issues than were his business peers, Carnegie, in several articles in the 1880s, denounced management intransigence and its use of strikebreakers in labor disputes and stated that he found trade unions "beneficial both to labor and to capital." But, in 1892, Carnegie, in Scotland, turned a deaf ear toward the locked-out workers at his mill in Homestead, Pennsylvania, and he refused to veto the union-busting policy of his partner Henry Clay Frick. The Homestead strike, one of the most infamous in American industrial history, dealt a heavy blow to Carnegie's reputation. Joseph Pulitzer's St. Louis *Post-Dispatch* reflected the tone of the adverse comment when it said: "Three months ago Andrew Carnegie was a man to be envied. Today he is an object of mingled pity and contempt. In the estimation of nine-tenths of the thinking people on both sides of the ocean, he has not only given the lie to all his antecedents, but confessed himself a moral coward."[4] These words were harsh largely because of the disparity between high-sounding rhetoric and industrial reality.

Another cause of the public bewilderment about business ethics related to a failure by management to appreciate the differing impacts of small- and large-scale enterprises. Many of the practices for which corporations were criticized were not new; they had been in the small businessman's bag of tricks for many years. But, when big businesses performed the same marginal deeds, they acquired a much more sinister tone.

Ralph and Muriel Hidy faulted Standard Oil officials for not understanding the difference. "Watching a competitor closely and checking on his activities," they wrote, "were acceptable when the firm was next door or across the street; for a dominant firm to apply that principle in a national market was regarded as espionage and unfair competition." So also with other competitive practices. As Saul Engelbourg has commented: "Large scale enterprises began to be condemned for behavior that had not been challenged previously, and with justice, because now more people were hurt and often more severely."[5]

On an even broader level, the new corporate giants ran afoul of an Anglo-American antimonopoly tradition whose roots lay well before the nineteenth century. Of course, Americans were less than precise in their use of the word "monopoly." Most chose to define it as any large business that appeared to dominate or share dominance in an industry. Indeed, the agonized cries of smaller businessmen often implied that the definition of a monopoly or a trust—the latter word was more in vogue in 1900—was simply any firm larger than their own.

In the Gilded Age, any interest group that was disenchanted with the economic turn of events invoked the antimonopoly tradition. In law, at least, the tradition dated back to fourteenth-century England, when the crown granted one John Peeche, a London merchant, an exclusive right to sell sweet wines in the city. In return for this privilege, he was expected to pay the king a fee of ten shillings on each pipe of wine sold. He was soon accused by Parliament of abusing his privilege by charging unreasonable prices "to the great damage and apprehension of the people." As a result of the indictment, he was jailed for a brief time and ordered "to give satisfaction to the parties complaining of his extortionate prices."[6] At this point, the establishment of the monopoly itself had not been questioned, only the abuse of the economic power that accompanied it.

In the seventeenth century, legal opposition to monopolies was enlarged. In *Darcy v. Allen* (1603), Queen Elizabeth granted Darcy, her groom, the sole right to make or import playing cards in England. Allen, a London merchant, ignored Darcy's monopoly and manufactured and then sold some cards, causing Darcy to bring a legal action charging infringement of his exclusive right. The Court of the King's Bench unanimously held the monopoly void and dismissed the suit. The court, among other wrongs, found that the monopoly encroached on the freedom of Englishmen to engage in the trade of their choice.

Parliament's enactment of the Statute of Monopolies in 1624 further buttressed the court's position. The act declared that all past or future royal monopolies were void—although it exempted patents for inventions, customary monopolies held by towns or guilds, or any monopolies awarded by Parliament. While the Statute of Monopolies was more the product of the tension between Parliament and the Stuart kings than any commitment to free competition, it did contribute to a lasting hostility to all monopolies. This hostility was incorporated into the common law of the American colonies and became an established ingredient of our heritage.

The Prophets of Discontent

The depression of the 1870s precipitated an adverse reaction to industrialism. Many Americans viewed the economic calamity of failed businesses and broken men as a moral judgment that the Almighty had pronounced upon events. A process of soul-searching thus began that culminated in various calls for reform, including new public policies toward business.

The first protests were from farmers. The plain fact, as one agricultural historian concluded, was that "perhaps no development of the nineteenth century brought greater disappointment to American farmers than did their failure to realize the prosperity that they had expected from industrialism."[7] Farmers complained of many problems, but most common were a steady decline in farm prices (the index fell from a high of 161 in 1864 to 72 in 1878), which had the disastrous effect of increasing the burden of mortgage debt; discrimination by the railroads (a problem described in a previous chapter); and unfair practices by agricultural middlemen and food processors.

Agrarian discontent precipitated a series of organizational and political responses—the Grange in the 1870s, the Farmers' Alliance movement of the 1880s, and the People's, or Populist, party in the 1890s. In each instance, the farmers reacted to what they regarded as economic injustices, and they demanded reforms ranging from the reduction of freight rates to the depreciation of the money supply.

The urban counterpart of the farmer's distress was the unrest evident among the new factory proletariat. Data now available indicate that wages rose markedly between 1860 and 1914, while the cost of living declined for most of that period. Real annual earnings in manufacturing increased from just under $300 in 1860 to $425 in 1890 and $500 in 1914. Yet many workers did not see themselves as better off as a result of industrialization. Instead, they saw themselves now as permanent members of a working class. Earlier they might have looked upon their current status as only a passing phase in their lives and believed that opportunities for self-employment awaited them in the future. By the 1870s, however, those opportunities looked more and more unlikely.

They were also dismayed by the growing impersonality of employer-employee relationships in the work place. Workers now faced powerful, industrial corporations that treated labor as another factor of production to be bought as cheaply as possible. Finally, the workingman was haunted by a lack of job security. The depressions of the 1870s and the 1890s were accompanied by substantial unemployment, and, during the entire postwar era, dismal numbers of workers were disabled or killed in industrial accidents.

John Garraty summed up the nature of labor's discontent: "Great mechanized corporations and their multimillionaire masters might in fact be benefiting workingmen by increasing the productivity of labor and creating new job opportunities, but they simultaneously undermined their confidence in their ability to rise and bred envy and resentment."[8] The discontent was vented in often violent strike actions—the railroad strikes of 1877, the Haymarket Square Riot in Chicago in 1886, the Homestead strike of 1892, and the Pullman strike of 1894 were only the four most infamous episodes—and in efforts to organize effective labor unions to serve as collective-bargaining agents for employees.

Joining the farmers and industrial laborers in demanding reforms was a miscellany of popular social critics who reacted in unique ways to industrialism. They included a set of writers and journalists who used fictional and nonfictional prose forms to denounce those evils that they saw as afflicting American society. The fact that they had a substantial readership testified to the strength of popular concern.

Among the most prominent of the late nineteenth-century social critics was Henry George, who proposed, in *Progress and Poverty* (1879), a "single tax" on the "unearned increment" that was derived from the ownership of land. George enjoyed immense popularity; indeed, by 1905, 2 million copies of his book were in circulation. Also prominent was Edward Bellamy, whose fictional work, *Looking Backward* (1888), described a Bostonian, Julian West, who fell asleep in 1887 and awakened in the year 2000 to find an ideal society in place with government owning all the means of production. *Looking Backward* was probably the most popular utopian novel ever published in America. In similar fashion, Henry Demarest Lloyd's *Wealth against Commonwealth* (1894) was a prolonged diatribe against the Standard Oil Company and a call for nationalization of the trusts. After the turn of the century, these Gilded Age authors were joined by Frank Norris, who attacked the Southern Pacific Railroad for its oppressive control of California's economic and political life in his novel *The Octopus* (1901); Ida Tarbell's serialized "History of the Standard Oil Company," which first appeared in *McClure's* in 1902 and later was published in book form; Upton Sinclair's sometimes revolting novel of immigrant life in Chicago packing plants, *The Jungle* (1906); and a host of other muckraking writers.[9]

The academic community played an important role in social criticism. Lester Frank Ward, who was a geologist, paleontologist, and professor of sociology at Brown University, argued against laissez-faire and in favor of positive state action in his principal work, *Dynamic Sociology* (1883), and in other writings. Richard T. Ely led a group of young American economists who challenged the basic tenets of classical economics and founded the American Economics Association in 1885 to promote new thinking. Another rebel in economics was the stormy and acid-tongued Thorstein Veblen, whose most famous work, *Theory of the Leisure Class* (1899), scolded the business elite for their "conspicuous consumption" in the construction of huge mansions or in other showy displays of wealth.

Within some churches in Gilded Age America, critics of the status quo also emerged in what was called the Social Gospel. Such men as Washington Gladden, a Congregationalist minister, maintained that mankind could achieve a Kingdom of God on earth if people believed that current social problems could be corrected. Henry May described the Social Gospel movement "as a widespread, spontaneous response to the challenge of industrial society." He added that its adherents shared two common characteristics: "All were moved by a sense of social crisis, and all believed in the necessity and possibility of a Christian solution."[10]

Business v. Business

Whether it was a Jane Addams from Chicago's Hull House campaigning against the negative impact of industrialism and urbanism on the city's immigrant masses or the populist firebrand Ignatius Donnelly railing against the monied eastern interests, a generation of social critics was aroused by the new concentrations of economic power. But would-be reformers also emerged from a segment of the business community itself.

On this point Robert Wiebe has stated: "Among the components of crisis, none found fuller expression than the belief that great corporations were stifling opportunity, and no one cried his resentment more persistently than the local entrepreneur."[11] Wiebe has divided American businessmen in the period into rival camps of four general types: the first division was along urban versus small-town lines; the second separated businessmen by regions; a third division was according to the size of the firms directed; and the last emphasized the competing functions that they performed in the economy.

In the forefront of advocates of governmental action against discriminatory railroad rates, for example, were Pennsylvania "business shippers who did not qualify for the rebates given to giant corporations" and Iowa river-town grain dealers who found that rail charges from interior towns to their locations on the Mississippi were greater than through rates between the interior and Chicago.[12] Enlisted in the campaign against the trusts were businessmen such as New Yorkers who founded the National Anti-Monopoly League in 1881 and the members of the National Association of Manufacturers, established in 1895, who looked with equal disfavor at big business and big labor.

Of course, a substantial portion of the country's businessmen were appalled by the growing clamor for government regulation of private enterprise. They argued that the proper role of the state was to maintain a hands-off policy with respect to the marketplace. Government was regarded as inefficient and too expensive, and the politicians and bureaucrats who staffed it as weak and corrupt. Furthermore, governmental action was fruitless, a useless interference with inexorable natural laws that governed the economic order. Andrew Carnegie, who held this position, scoffed at politicians for engaging in "Sisyphus' work—ever rolling the stone uphill to see it roll back to its proper bed at the bottom."[13]

Naturally, not all forms of political activity were denounced, for even conservative businessmen were not rigidly doctrinaire. They tended to see no harm in those uses of state power that promoted profits. One example, protective tariffs, had the strong support of most manufacturers, who regarded them as a necessary safeguard against overseas competition.

A sociological version of Darwinism provided pseudo-scientific support for laissez-faire. This argument was derived in large part from the writings of the English social philosopher Herbert Spencer, who attempted to apply Charles Darwin's precepts of biological evolution to human society, claiming that a struggle for existence among individuals ended in a "survival of the fittest." The able would prosper most, the less able the least, and progress would theoretically be the result. This philosophy led Spencer to oppose vehemently any reform efforts as an unjustifiable interference with the natural evolutionary development of a society.

Social Darwinism soon found adherents in the business community. Triumphant entrepreneurs saw it as a rationale for their own success and a defense against soft-headed reformers. Yet, while such business leaders as Carnegie, Rockefeller, and railroad magnate James J. Hill often spoke in the terminology of Social Darwinism, most business-men had not read Spencer. Their position on the issue of government control of business was based instead on the more mundane grounds of simple self-interest.

Regulating an Industry—The Interstate Commerce Act

Public regulation of business in America took two forms: regulation of a specific industry and regulation of competitive behavior. Reg-ulation of an industry was the earliest to develop, and it began with the nation's first big business, the railroads.

Although regulatory commissions existed in four states in 1860, their powers were limited, and none could set railroad rates. The first attempts at serious regulation of freight and passenger charges came in the midwestern states in the 1870s, largely in response to increasing complaints about discrimination against individual ship-pers and localities. Among the most important supporters of regu-lation were the Patrons of Husbandry, or, as they were better known, the Grangers.

Founded in 1867 as a social and educational organization for farm-ers, the Grange soon became more involved in economic issues. Fred Shannon detailed the transition: "The constitution of the Grange prohibited political action, but . . . when a local grange adjourned from its regular meeting, it often resumed activities in the same place as a unit of a farmers' political party. Though many kinds of political and economic reforms were agitated, the chief objective of these third-party organizations was railroad regulation."[14]

Between 1871 and 1874 the joint efforts of the Grangers and their business allies brought about the enactment of such laws in Illinois, Iowa, Minnesota, and Wisconsin. These laws were especially im-portant because they included an innovation that was soon copied elsewhere—the establishment of independent regulatory commis-sions empowered to investigate citizen complaints, to impose rules, and even to set rates for the industry being controlled. Because of the high visibility of the farmers in the movement for public oversight of the railroads, these laws became known popularly as Granger laws, and the subsequent judicial review of those laws was referred to as the Granger cases. Nonetheless, small- and medium-sized business-men, who believed that existing railroad practices placed them at a significant disadvantage, also shared leadership with the Grange in supporting railroad regulation.

The railroads quickly challenged the Granger laws in the state and federal courts. They argued that, by dictating the price that a private business could charge for its services, the state commissions were depriving the firm of property, that is, its profits, without due process of law. State authorities, they contended, were in violation of the Fourteenth Amendment.

The United States Supreme Court eventually heard eight cases. Although the lead case, *Munn v. Illinois*, dealt with a Chicago grain elevator firm rather than railroads, the same issue was at stake in the accompanying seven railroad cases. The Illinois Railroad and Ware-house Commission fixed rates for both types of businesses. The Munn case was argued before the Supreme Court in early 1876, but a decision was not announced until March 1877. Chief Justice Mor-rison Waite delivered the majority opinion in "the Supreme Court's first major statement on the constitutionality of regulating the new industrial capitalism."[15] Waite upheld the state laws in all eight cases, but he did so "in words which gave away half of what he was ap-parently trying to save." He contended that English common law had always accepted state regulation of businesses that were "clothed with a public interest." In Waite's words: "When, therefore, one devotes his property to a use in which the public has an interest, he, in effect, grants to the public an interest in that use, and must submit to be controlled by the public for the common good." Yet, at the same time, as Loren Beth pointed out: "While Waite doubtless meant these observations to illustrate the breadth of the state's power, they had in practice the opposite effect for they implied that purely pri-vate businesses (whatever they might be defined to be) were not subject to regulation."[16]

In later years, business litigants used that opening to besiege the Supreme Court with challenges to all manner of regulatory legisla-tion. And, for a time, more conservative jurists than the Waite Court responded by gradually narrowing the category of "public" enter-prises while widening the private group, thereby giving business an effective defense against regulation.

Along with their court campaign, railroads increasingly turned to direct political action. They supported their own candidates for public office, distributed generous campaign contributions, and, in some instances, resorted to outright bribery. This political involvement did result in some weakening of state laws, but the Supreme Court sounded the death knell of state regulation in *Wabash, St. Louis, and Pacific Railway Company v. Illinois* (1886). The railroad was appealing a state ruling that it could not charge more for a slightly shorter haul between Gilman, Illinois, and New York City than for a shipment sent from Peoria to New York City, eighty-six miles farther. Speaking for the court, Justice Samuel Miller held that Illinois could not regulate rates on interstate shipments, even in the absence of federal regulation on the subject. The Wabash decision removed such regulation from state jurisdiction and made federal action imperative if there was to be any public control at all.

National regulation of railroads had been discussed as early as the 1860s, but Congress was not galvanized into concrete action until the Wabash ruling. The Interstate Commerce Act of 1887 was landmark legislation. It was the federal government's first venture into the regulation of an industry and the source of ample precedents in the future. The new law created a five-person Interstate Commerce Commission (ICC) to oversee enforcement of its provisions, which outlawed pools and required freight and passenger charges to be public, reasonable, and just. The commission was authorized to hear complaints about possible violations, subpoena witnesses, examine records, and issue "cease and desist" orders if unlawful practices were found.

Passage of the Interstate Commerce Act did not mean a sudden repudiation by its supporters of America's traditional doctrine of limited government and unfettered capitalism. Rather, as Marver Bernstein remarked, "In the struggle to use governmental power to promote their private economic interests, these groups were guided more by short-run, common sense considerations than basic notions about the relation of government to economic life."[17] The act did represent a breakthrough in another sense. Congress acknowledged, in establishing the first independent federal regulatory agency, the necessity for technical expertise to solve new economic problems.

Although the Supreme Court did not invalidate any provision of the Interstate Commerce Act, a series of judicial decisions in the decade after the law's enactment in 1887 had the effect of emasculating the ICC's effectiveness. In 1897, in the *Maximum Freight Rate* case, the court denied the ICC's power to prescribe future rates and thus limited its authority to deciding the reasonableness of existing rates. The *Alabama Midland Ry. Co.* case, also in 1897, dealt the commission another blow. Here, the court asserted the right to ignore the ICC's findings of fact and to conduct instead an investigation of its own. The case encouraged the railroads to give the ICC only reluctant cooperation and to rely on a friendly judiciary for protection.

By the beginning of the twentieth century, the Interstate Commerce Commission had become little more than a public-information agency. As a result, the practices that the Interstate Commerce Act of 1887 was intended to prevent—pooling and rebating, for example—were still common. But, as a reform spirit generated momentum after 1900, and especially with the inauguration of Theodore Roosevelt as president in 1901, the loopholes began to be closed.

The Elkins Act of 1903, for example, made the receiver of rebates guilty of violating the law as well as the railroad and made any departure from published rates a misdemeanor, regardless of whether the change injured any other shippers. The Elkins Act was passed with railroad support; company managers felt the need for protection against the pressures applied by large shippers and against their own weaknesses. The most important regulatory legislation of the decade, however, was the Hepburn Act, signed into law by Roosevelt after a protracted struggle in which the president campaigned extensively for public support.

The Hepburn Act gave the ICC, for the first time, effective control of the railroad industry. In its two most important sections, the act gave the commission power to determine rates and ruled that ICC orders were binding upon promulgation. It was now up to the railroad, not the ICC, to appeal to the courts, and the burden of proof fell upon the carrier. The act also extended ICC jurisdiction to include express and sleeping-car companies and petroleum pipelines.

The resurgence of the ICC culminated in 1910 in the passage of the Mann-Elkins Act. The commission received the power to suspend pending rate increases subject to an investigation of their likely effects; it also now possessed enlarged authority over telephone and telegraph companies. With the new law in place, a comprehensive regulatory system had been established over the nation's railroads, but whether the public or the companies themselves were better off for it was another matter.

In the years immediately before American intervention in the First World War, a shipper-oriented ICC, imbued with the reform spirit of the progressive years, repeatedly denied railway requests for rate increases. Albro Martin has argued that those denials contributed to the inability of the nation's rail system to cope with a wartime emergency without federal control. In Martin's words, railroad regulation failed in large part because "the railroad problems of the Progressive era were not those of the Gilded Age, although many people, not surprisingly, continued to think and act as if they were." Facing rising labor and operating costs after 1897 as well as escalating demands for service, the lines urgently needed infusions of new capital and better profits. They received neither in sufficient quantity because of what Martin termed "the archaic Progressives" on the commission and in Congress who refused to appreciate the changing times and the industry's necessity to keep pace.[18]

Whether one accepts Martin's conclusion or not, there is no question that the railroads were ill-prepared for the crisis of the First World War. Even before the United States entered the conflict in April 1917, supplies and war materials were piling up in Atlantic ports while western shippers looked in vain for freight cars to move their goods. Finally, in December 1917, the Wilson administration, ignoring the ICC, assumed the direction of all railroad operations and placed them under a new federal authority headed by Secretary of the Treasury William Gibbs McAdoo.

The Railroad Administration under McAdoo operated the railroads as one consolidated system, which included the shifting of equipment and personnel as needed, the purchase of new rolling stock, and the coordination of scheduling. In the process, a substantial rate increase was decreed without bothering with "tiresome" ICC hearings. The end of an era had been reached, because "in bypassing the ICC, federal control deprived shippers of their power over rates and ended the shipper-dominated Progressive phase of railroad regulation."[19]

Regulating Competition—The Sherman Act

The regulation of competitive behavior—as opposed to the oversight of a specific industry—was the second form of business control that emerged after the Civil War. In the presidential election campaign of 1888, both major parties felt the pressure of an aroused public opinion on the trust issue, and they responded by promising anti-monopoly legislation. The Republicans especially found themselves on the defensive. Democrats claimed that Republican high-tariff policies were an important element in fostering the growth of monopolies, since protectionism reduced or eliminated foreign competition.

When Republican congressional leaders enacted a bill raising tariff rates once again (the McKinley tariff of 1890), it became imperative for them to demonstrate that they could insure competition at home. Senator John Sherman of Ohio thus introduced a bill that gradually gathered support, was significantly rewritten by the Senate Judiciary Committee, and was signed into law by President Benjamin Harrison in July 1890. Sherman expressed displeasure with the final version and claimed that it would be "totally ineffective in dealing with combinations and trusts," but he reluctantly voted for it on the final roll call, and it still bears his name.[20]

Officially titled "An Act to Protect Trade and Commerce against Unlawful Restraint and Monopolies," the substantive provisions of the law were few and brief. Section I declared: "Every contract, combination in the form of trust or otherwise, or conspiracy in restraint of trade or commerce among the several States, or with foreign nations, shall be deemed guilty of a misdemeanor." Another provision of the law empowered United States district attorneys and the attorney general to bring suits against violators and also permitted private parties injured by violations to sue for triple damages.

Overall, the Sherman Act was a cautious legislative step. It only restated some principles, long familiar under common law, and it contained little that was really new. The act's chief contribution was to turn common-law doctrine into offenses against the federal government, to provide for enforcement, and to impose penalties. But perhaps most important of all, it temporarily quieted the public cry for some action against the feared trusts.

The vague language of the statute delegated the interpretation of its meaning to the courts, including the question of whether all combinations were illegal or just those that resulted in great size attained by "unreasonable" means. The first case under the Sherman Act to reach the Supreme Court was decided in 1895, five years after the law's passage. The *United States v. E. C. Knight Co.* dealt with the acquisition of four Philadelphia refineries by the American Sugar

Refining Company, a holding corporation chartered in New Jersey in 1891.[21]

Since the Knight firm and the other three refineries were the Sugar Trust's last significant competitors, word of the acquisitions immediately raised cries of concern across the country, as well as demands that prosecution under the Sherman Act be initiated. The Harrison administration recognized the political necessity for some action and filed suit in May 1892 asking that E. C. Knight and the other parties be enjoined from carrying out the proposed merger.

The Supreme Court's decision in January 1895 shocked those Americans who had looked to the Sherman Act for protection against monopoly power. Speaking for an almost unanimous court (Justice John Marshall Harlan alone dissented), Chief Justice Melville W. Fuller narrowly interpreted Congress' constitutional power to regulate interstate commerce. He differentiated between commerce on the one hand and manufacturing on the other and held that Congress had the power to prohibit monopolies in the first instance but not in the second. In Fuller's famous but questionable dictum: "Commerce succeeds to manufacture, and is not a part of it. . . . The fact that an article is manufactured for export to another state does not of itself make it an article of interstate commerce."[22] Needless to say, antitrust reformers bitterly criticized the ruling.

Four years later the court took a small step toward limiting the scope of the Knight decision. In the *Addyston Pipe & Steel* case (1899), the justices found that a price-fixing agreement involving six cast-iron pipe manufacturers was a violation of the Sherman Act. A critical factor in determining the ultimate ruling was the opinion of William Howard Taft, who then sat on the Sixth Circuit Court of Appeals and heard the case before the Supreme Court. Taft showed that the pipe manufacturers had formed a cartel to control prices in the market, clearly a common-law restraint of trade and a matter of interstate commerce. When the Supreme Court confirmed Taft's ruling, it was evident that manufacturers were not exempt from the Sherman Act's provisions in all circumstances.

Despite the Addyston decision, the 1890s were dismal years for supporters of the antitrust movement. Enforcement was sporadic—only seventeen cases were begun during the administrations of Presidents Harrison, Cleveland, and McKinley, and a number of those were filed against labor unions and not business combinations. Congress supplied no special appropriations for antitrust litigation and no extra personnel to handle the difficult prosecutions. Not until 1903, under Theodore Roosevelt's prodding, was an Antitrust Division formed in the Justice Department with congressionally authorized funds of its own.

Clearly, the Sherman Act did little or nothing to stem the flood of mergers that swept the nation's industrial community at the end of the century. In fact, the Knight decision probably encouraged the merger wave, since it appeared to indicate that, although trust agreements were clearly outlawed, the formation of holding companies was still permissible. It was not until 1904 and the Supreme Court's ruling in the Northern Securities case that the Sherman Act at last came of age and began to make a meaningful difference in the regulation of business enterprise.

The Birth and Death of a Holding Company

The Northern Securities case was the first antitrust action in which all the parties were celebrities. Hence the public attention that was focused on the episode considerably magnified its importance and thereby gave a whole new momentum to the antitrust campaign.

Among the principals was James J. Hill, the one-eyed, dynamic builder of the Great Northern Railroad. Hill's railroad was better designed and constructed than any of the other transcontinental lines, and it never suffered the ignominy of bankruptcy and forced reorganization, as did the others. The Great Northern stretched from St. Paul on the Mississippi to Puget Sound on the Pacific, and, in 1896, Hill further extended his sway in America's Northwest. He took control of the failed Northern Pacific line and established a virtual monopoly of all railroad traffic from the Great Lakes westward.

Pitted against Hill was Edward H. Harriman, a quiet, unprepossessing financier and railroad man, who began his career as a Wall Street office boy and ended it in control of such major companies as the Union Pacific, Southern Pacific, Illinois Central, and Erie. At the time of his death in 1909, his range of interests extended to life insurance, banking, and China's South Manchurian Railway.

Behind the figures of Hill and Harriman stood other powerful individuals. J. P. Morgan was allied with Hill, and Harriman had the support of Jacob Schiff, senior partner of Kuhn, Loeb, and Co. And soon to impose his personality upon the whole cast of characters was the youngest president of the United States, Theodore Roosevelt, New York aristocrat and emerging progressive leader.

The Northern Securities case grew out of a clash between Hill and Harriman over control of the Chicago, Burlington, and Quincy line, or, as it was generally known, the Burlington Road. When Harriman demanded the right to share in Hill's acquisition of the Burlington, a key rail connection to Chicago, Hill refused, and the war was on. Harriman then sought to accomplish his goal by another means— secretly purchasing a majority stock interest in the Northern Pacific. Hill and Morgan soon perceived this maneuver and engaged Harriman in a stock-market scramble in which the price of Northern Pacific stock rose steadily until it briefly touched $1,000 a share. A compromise, engineered by Morgan, finally calmed the Northern Pacific Panic of 1901 in the organization of a gigantic holding company, the Northern Securities Company.

Capitalized at $400 million, incorporated under New Jersey's accommodating laws, and holding the stock of the Great Northern, the Northern Pacific, and the Burlington, it was one of the largest corporations yet formed in the United States. The board of directors included representatives of all the warring interests—Hill, Morgan, and Harriman. An interest that was not represented was that of the public, but the Roosevelt administration in Washington soon assumed that role.

Theodore Roosevelt succeeded the assassinated William McKinley only two months before the organization of the Northern Securities Company. The business community greeted his elevation to the presidency with some anxiety but no real trembling, and Roosevelt's first annual message to Congress in December 1901 only prolonged the uncertain perception. In the message, the president reaffirmed his own Darwinian view of corporate development. Large companies were a natural outcome of America's industrial growth and necessary if the nation was to retain its newly won economic leadership. At the same time, he admitted the possibility of power abuses and urged Congress to enact a federal incorporation law and to establish machinery for the executive branch to investigate the trusts and publish the findings. Publicity was regarded as a reform in itself.

Distinguishing between the good and bad effects of trusts, Roosevelt sought a policy that would enable society to benefit from the productive efficiency of mighty corporations without suffering any harm from unsavory business practices. Finley Peter Dunne's comic character, Mr. Dooley, poked fun at Roosevelt for believing that trusts were "heejous monsthers built up be th'inlightened intherprise iv th' men that have done so much to advance progress in our beloved counthry."[23]

It was, therefore, with considerable shock that the Northern Securities directors greeted the announcement from Attorney General Philander C. Knox—a conservative Republican from Pittsburgh who had once been Andrew Carnegie's lawyer—that the president had directed him to file suit against the railroad combination. Hill, outraged at what he regarded as partisan opportunism, bitingly complained: "It really seems hard, when we look back at what we have done in opening the country and carrying at the lowest rates, that we should be compelled to fight political adventurers who have never done anything but pose and draw a salary." Morgan believed that Roosevelt "had violated the rules of gentlemanly behavior," but invited the president to "send your man to my man and they can fix it up." Roosevelt refused, remarking to Knox: "Mr. Morgan could not help regarding me as a big rival operator who either intended to ruin all his interests or else could be induced to come to an agreement to ruin none."[24]

Nonetheless, there seemed little cause for the directors of the Northern Securities Company to fear any drastic reversal of their plans. The Knight decision offered legitimacy to holding companies, and the dependable Melville Fuller still presided over the Supreme Court. In this instance, however, the court defied predictions. In March 1904, by a five to four vote, the court declared that the Northern Securities company was an unlawful combination within the meaning of the Sherman Act. John Marshall Harlan, the sole dissenter in the Knight case nine years earlier, now pronounced the majority opinion. He denied the contention that a holding company was a mere stock transaction, not in itself interstate commerce and thus beyond the scope of the Sherman Act. Rather, the act was directed at all combinations that restrained trade, since their mere existence "constitutes a menace to, and a restraint upon, that freedom of commerce which Congress intended to recognize and protect."[25] So much for *stare decisis* and the Knight precedent!

The significance of the Northern Securities decision lay in two accomplishments. It first established Theodore Roosevelt's reputation as a "trustbuster" in the popular mind. The Roosevelt administration began over forty prosecutions under the Sherman Act, well beyond the combined total of the three previous presidents, but, during William Howard Taft's four years as Roosevelt's successor, an even larger number of suits were filed. Nevertheless, Roosevelt used this reputation to his political advantage and employed it as a lever to pry the kind of legislation he preferred from a reluctant Congress.

The Northern Securities decision also revitalized the Sherman Act. The damage that the Knight case had done was now overcome, and, as one periodical of the time phrased it, the court's holding "established more firmly than ever the sound political and industrial doctrine that corporations deriving their existence from the hands of the people must submit to regulation by the people." Another journal put it more forcefully: "Even Morgan no longer rules the earth, and other men may still do business without asking his permission."[26]

Paradoxically, what the Northern Securities decision did not do was restore competition among the railroads of the Pacific Northwest. The lines there continued under Hill's control, and a "community of interest" remained between him and Harriman. Furthermore, over a half century later the formal merger that the Northern Securities Company was intended to bring about did take place, possibly to the eternal satisfaction of James J. Hill, by then long departed from the earth.

The Rule of Reason

Much of the legal impact of the Northern Securities victory was sapped by the Supreme Court in a decision seven years later, *Standard Oil Co. v. United States* (1911). The suit began during Roosevelt's second term as an antimonopoly showpiece, an assault upon the nation's most detested industrial combination. As detailed in the previous chapter, the court ordered the separation of the various Standard Oil subsidiaries from their Jersey Standard parent. What eventually overshadowed the dissolution of the Oil Trust, however, was an unexpected and almost irrelevant portion of the decision— the insertion into the majority opinion of what came to be called "the rule of reason."

In 1911, the Supreme Court was headed by a new chief justice, Edward D. White of Louisiana. White inserted into antitrust law the doctrine that, when the Sherman Act prohibited "every" combination in restraint of trade, the words should be understood to mean only those that "unreasonably" restrain trade. Reasonable monopolies were thus presumably legal, and judges had the responsibility to determine those that were in the public interest according to the circumstances of each case and whatever criteria the courts might feel in the mood to apply. Actually, White's position was not far from the view held by some Roosevelt progressives and by the former president himself, who talked of "the inevitableness and the necessity of combinations in business" just three months after the Standard Oil decision.[27]

Three other Supreme Court decisions reaffirmed the rule of reason during the next decade. Only two weeks after the Standard Oil verdict, the court ordered the dissolution of Duke's Tobacco Trust (*United States v. American Tobacco Company*). At the same time, however, the justices restated the principle that, although an unreasonable monopoly was illegal, one that the court found socially and economically acceptable would be a "good" trust and not in violation of the Sherman Act.

The Shoe Trust case (*United States v. United Shoe Machinery Co.*, 1918) and the Steel Trust case (*United States v. United States Steel Corporation*, 1920) produced different immediate results. The court, in an application of the rule of reason, found that neither combination violated the antitrust law. In the second case, the court concluded that the steel giant had not engaged in such tactics as discriminatory freight rebates, predatory price-cutting, or similar acts. Justice Joseph McKenna, speaking for the court, maintained that "the Sherman Act did not make mere size an offense. It, we repeat, requires overt acts and trusts to its prohibition of them and its power to repress and punish them."[28]

In short, although United States Steel was big, it was not bad. The lesson for the business community seemed plain enough. The judiciary was determined not to interfere with the dominant firms in an industry except in extreme cases. The way was now open for another wave of mergers. The mergers of the 1920s took place despite the presence on the statute books of two more pieces of regulatory law, the Federal Trade Commission Act and the Clayton Act. Both were enacted in 1914 in large part because of the leadership of Woodrow Wilson in the White House.

The Federal Trade Commission Act established a five-man body that was empowered to prevent business firms from using "unfair methods of competition." Modeled on the Interstate Commerce Commission, the FTC could receive complaints, hold hearings, and issue cease-and-desist orders if it found illegalities. The new commission was designed to replace the Bureau of Corporations, created during Theodore Roosevelt's first term, which was merely an investigative agency with no enforcement power other than publicity.

The Clayton Act, named for Henry D. Clayton of Alabama, who introduced the legislation in the House of Representatives, declared four anticompetitive acts illegal: price discrimination, tying and exclusive-dealing contracts (sales on condition that the buyer stop dealing with the seller's competitors), corporate mergers, and interlocking directorates. None of these prohibitions was absolute. They were proscribed only when their effect was "to substantially lessen competition or tend to create a monopoly." Other provisions of the Clayton Act allowed judgments in successful government antitrust prosecutions to be used as evidence in private suits against the same defendants, and stipulated that labor unions and farmers' organizations should not be considered conspiracies in restraint of trade. The Clayton Act was a weak weapon in fulfilling the main objective of its framers—counteracting the Supreme Court's rule of reason by enumerating specific unlawful practices. In its final form, the law left as much to the discretion of the courts as before its passage.

Regulation and the American Compromise

Although the regulation of transportation through the Interstate Commerce Commission and the enactment of antitrust laws were the major means by which the federal government responded to a public demand for greater control of big business, there were other exercises of national authority over the marketplace. After 1900, Congress tended increasingly to pass legislation that it viewed as protecting the country's health, morals, and welfare.

The Pure Food and Drug Act of 1906 barred adulterated and misbranded foods from interstate commerce, and the Meat Inspection Acts of 1906 and 1907 did the same for diseased meat. The Federal Employers' Liability Act of 1908 made common carriers liable for the injury or death of any employees engaged in interstate commerce, and the Keating-Owen Child Labor Act of 1916 went perhaps the farthest of all in overseeing business operations. It declared any manufacturer guilty of a misdemeanor if he shipped in interstate commerce products made in factories that employed children under the age of fourteen or required children between fourteen and sixteen to work more than eight hours a day. Only the last of these laws failed to pass judicial scrutiny. In 1918, the Supreme Court found the Keating-Owen Act an unconstitutional extension of congressional power.

The states also broadened their regulatory efforts. By 1917 thirty-seven states had laws banning child labor in manufacturing, and nineteen restricted the working hours of women. Fewer states attempted to regulate the working day for men, but, when they did, the laws were usually confined to hazardous or unhealthy occupations, such as mining. The federal government's first ventures into working-hours legislation for adults were the La Follette Seaman's Act of 1915 and the Adamson Act of 1916, which applied to merchant seamen and railroad workers, respectively. Workmen's compensation laws were on the books in most states by the First World War, and a beginning was even made toward minimum-wage legislation, although it was usually poorly drawn and weakly enforced.

The entry of the United States into the First World War soon blunted the regulatory drive of the progressive era. The struggle against Germany temporarily focused public attention upon international affairs, and the postwar political imbroglio over the Versailles Treaty and the League of Nations turned many disillusioned Americans away from larger concerns to their private interests. Much of the impetus to exert greater societal control over big business dissipated in the years between 1917 and 1920, and it did not reemerge until the bleak days of the Great Depression.

Nevertheless, the call for change was always restrained in the United States, even at the height of reform. Americans have been wary of regulation that is so drastic or so far-reaching that it might impair the country's economic progress. Americans attribute a considerable share of that progress to the free-enterprise system and to the entrepreneurial freedom that forms one of its central supports. Therefore, as Roger Ransom has written: "While concessions might be made to allow for dealing with the more obvious abuses of monopoly power, the underlying structure of production and distribution was to remain unchanged."[29] It was the American compromise with industrialism.

Labor and the Industrialization Process

A manufacturer who lived through the nation's transition to managerial capitalism recalled that when he began his career "I knew every man. . . . I could call him by name and shake hands with him." But, when he retired thirty years later, his firm employed thousands of workers, and one of them "would have stood just about as much chance to get in to see any one with his grievance as he would to get into the Kingdom of Heaven."[30]

The plain-spoken manufacturer was only expressing a clearly observable fact—that the expansion of American industry and the rise of giant corporations had dramatically altered employer-employee relations. The sheer size of the twentieth-century work place reflected the transformation. By the early 1920s half of all industrial laborers were in factories that employed more than 250 persons, and more than 800 plants had in excess of 1,000 men and women on their payrolls. Among the largest, the McCormick plant in Chicago had 4,000 workers in 1900 and 15,000 by 1916. Also in 1916, Henry Ford's works at Highland Park, Michigan, employed a staggering total of 33,000 workers who produced Model T autos.

The anxieties and fears that this new situation engendered were sketched earlier in this chapter. Job insecurity, physical danger, and the loss of individual bargaining power were all present, but added to those was the relentless discipline that new mass-production techniques imposed upon workers. Industrial workers viewed with particular apprehension the rise of a popular new production doctrine, a movement referred to as "scientific management." It was most closely associated with the writings and proselytizing of Frederick W. Taylor, a Philadelphia-born engineer who first came to the attention of his peers when he presented a paper entitled "A Piece Rate System" at a meeting of the American Society of Mechanical Engineers in 1895.

Taylor argued for precise stopwatch studies of time and methods of work to determine the most efficient means of performing a shop task. It would then become the standard for all laborers who performed the same task. He also proposed a "differential piece rate" to accompany the new standards. Workers who failed to meet them would receive a lower wage rate per piece, but those who met the standards qualified for a higher rate. In this way, Taylor expected to eliminate malingering on the job, which he called "soldiering," as well as the randomness with which most factory workers supposedly went about their duties.

Taylor's most famous work, *The Principles of Scientific Management,* was published in 1911. In it, he set forth a series of succinct principles that constituted his system. The first represented the cornerstone of his approach: "Develop a science for each element of a man's work, which replaces the old rule-of-thumb method."[31] The result would be maximum efficiency from each worker.

When Taylor and his various disciples spread the precepts of scientific management throughout American industry, wage earners began to sense that these methods would dehumanize the work place and would drive them to impossible levels of effort. The time-study man—or the "efficiency expert"—and his stopwatch came to be a feared symbol of worker oppression in the new age of mass production. One articulate machinist summed up these feelings in 1914: "We don't want to work as fast as we are able to. We want to work as fast as we think it's comfortable for us to work. We haven't come into existence for the purpose of seeing how great a task we can perform through a lifetime. We are trying to regulate our work so as to make it an auxiliary to our lives."[32]

The response of workers to the threat that they perceived that industrialism posed to their lives and occupations ranged from mute individual protests to organized attacks upon capitalism itself. Such responses might include tardiness, absenteeism, production slowdowns, or, in extreme cases, deliberate sabotage. A more dramatic form of protest was the strike. Sometimes it was a spontaneous work stoppage, as disgruntled factory hands walked off their jobs. In other cases, it was an organized action by a union that attempted to bring pressure upon a recalcitrant employer when bargaining collapsed. On too many occasions, violence accompanied labor's use of the strike, especially when an employer attempted to bring in substitutes, or "scabs," to replace the strikers. Overall, the number of strikes rose with the process of industrialization. The Bureau of Labor Statistics reported almost 10,000 strikes and lockouts in the 1880s alone. But these figures were dwarfed between 1893 and 1904, when over 22,000 strikes took place, involving 4.2 million workers.

The Role of Organized Labor

Unionism has been conventionally regarded as the most important and lasting response of workers to the advent of giant enterprise.

Undoubtedly, the formation of national labor organizations was a significant event in American economic history, but the impact of unions should not be exaggerated. Only a relatively small fraction of the work force ever became union members during this period.

Although organized labor traced its roots to colonial times, as late as the beginning of the Civil War less than 1 percent of the country's laborers were in unions, and these were mainly in trades outside the factory system. After 1865, the union movement grew, but its size was still modest compared to labor in the aggregate. By 1900 membership had reached only 2.7 percent of the work force, and not until the last months of the First World War did it finally exceed 10 percent.

In the last quarter of the nineteenth century, the first major union organization to capture the national attention was the Noble and Holy Order of the Knights of Labor. The Knights and their principal spokesman, Grand Master Workman Terence V. Powderly, preached the concept of "one big union" for all workers, regardless of skill or occupation. A combination of internal squabbles, poor leadership, disunity of purpose, and public hostility—especially after the Knights' tenuous association with the Haymarket Square Riot in Chicago in May 1886—doomed them to extinction as a national movement by 1900.

Samuel Gompers liked to refer to the organizing philosophy of the American Federation of Labor (AFL) as "the new unionism." More often it has been called "business unionism" because of its pragmatic approach and its emphasis on the achievement of immediate economic gains—higher wages, reduced working hours, and employer recognition. The AFL, as is well known, was, in Gompers's time, essentially but not exclusively an alliance of national craft unions. The trade-union ideology that the AFL articulated was another American compromise. As Gerald Grob phrased the terms of the unwritten agreement: "In return for labor nonsupport of revolutionary theories, industry promised the worker a rising standard of living and a respected though subordinate position in the community."[33]

The predominance of skilled workmen, the elite of the labor force, in the AFL helped to insure its stability even in troubled times. From an original membership of less than 50,000 at the time of its founding in the 1880s, the AFL experienced a steady growth. It attained a membership of 250,000 by 1898 and approximately 2 million by the outbreak of the First World War. By 1920 the AFL was, in effect, organized labor in the United States. It claimed 80 percent of all the country's union members, and the railroad brotherhoods were the only significant groups outside the fold.

The growth of organized labor did not go unchallenged by management. Many employers were at first less than ready to accept even the conservative AFL, and so a vigorous—but not unexpected—antiunion counteroffensive occurred in this period. It embodied two very different strategies, one militant and the other benevolent.

In the first, company managers wielded an arsenal of weapons against the upstart labor movement. Blacklists, lockouts, legal injunctions, the hiring of strikebreakers, "yellow dog" contracts (obligating workers not to join a union during the period of their employment), industrial spies, and, at times, open warfare were all thrown into the campaign with considerable effectiveness.

A number of employer organizations assumed leadership, but none was more prominent in the effort than the National Association of Manufacturers (NAM). Predominantly a body of small- to medium-sized producers, the NAM, when it was founded in 1895, focused largely upon the promotion of foreign trade and tariff reform. But the association turned quickly to the matter of unionism and began an aggressive counterattack on organized labor. Its battle cry became "the open shop," a guarantee of the right to work without membership in a union. During the 1920s, the open-shop drive was wrapped in an aura of patriotism by the NAM and renamed the "American Plan." As such, it played no small part in the sharp decline of union membership in the 1920s.

On the other hand, the strategy of benevolence—or, perhaps more accurately, managerial paternalism—was, in its early stage, led by the National Civic Federation (NCF). Formed in 1900 to promote a more conciliatory labor-management relationship, the advisory board included such business leaders as financier August Belmont, industrialist-politician Mark Hanna, and the omnipresent Andrew Carnegie. The Federation's different approach from that of the NAM was highlighted by the election of Samuel Gompers as its first vice-president.

The NCF encouraged the use of mediation as a method of settling labor disputes, and it favored employer recognition of "responsible" unions. It was no surprise that the efforts of the Federation were criticized from both the right and the left. Determined antiunion employers faulted it for being "soft" on unionism, and radicals in the labor movement assailed it for allegedly turning such men as Gompers and United Mine Workers head John Mitchell into appeasers of capitalism.

The organization was also active in fostering a cluster of employee-benefit schemes that often are grouped under the somewhat unflattering label of "welfare capitalism." These included pension and profit-sharing plans, group insurance policies, low-cost cafeterias, recreational or educational activities, and employee-representation programs (which labor derided as company unions). There seems little doubt that the hope of staving off unionization was a prime motive of some firms that instituted all or some of these fringe-benefit schemes.

Nevertheless, humanitarian concerns were certainly evident also in the thinking of many managers. The president of the Studebaker Motor Company manifested such feelings in 1915: "It is the duty of capital and management to compensate liberally, paying at least the current wage and probably a little more, and to give workers decent and healthful surroundings, and treat them with the utmost consideration. If management cannot do this, then it is incompetent."[34]

Unfortunately, for all its good intentions, welfare capitalism had inherent limitations. It was, David Brody reminds us, "a minority phenomenon, limited to the large prosperous firms," and incapable of dealing with such structural problems as technological unemployment.[35] Moreover, the benefit program of many companies was unable to withstand the shock of the 1930s. In the depths of the Great Depression, companies could not bear the added operating costs that welfare capitalism entailed, and many programs were therefore dismantled. Elaborate fringe-benefit systems would not surface again until the Second World War.

The Glass House

More so than ever before, American business after the Civil War lived in a glass house. The rise of large-scale enterprise increased the visibility of business and businessmen enormously and made them subject to unprecedented public examination. When that process identified abuses of power, such as the suppression of competition, Americans demanded corrective action and a redefinition of the functions of government.

Yet, as we have pointed out, the response remained within bounds. Although the role of government was enlarged to incorporate an active regulatory function, the community refused to accept radical solutions to its economic problems. As George Mowry has concluded, "Then and now, for weal or woe, the basic American economic situation, the temper of the great majority of the population, and the character of the political machinery, all seem to prescribe an aptitude for measured social change and to proscribe revolutionary change."[36] This American compromise was and is the reaction to industrialism in the United States.

CHAPTER TWELVE

Business in an Urban Nation

HISTORIAN Carl Degler, in discussing the phenomenon of urbanization in Gilded Age America, related the story of an Irish woman living a poverty-stricken existence in the city who was offered the opportunity for employment and a new life in a rural area. After only a few weeks in the countryside, however, she went back to "her old haunts and miserable circumstances." When asked why she chose to starve once again in the city, she supposedly answered: "Paples is more coompany than sthumps."[1]

There is no doubt that the lure of the city drew great numbers of persons in the years between the Civil War and the First World War. More than half the population of the United States was defined by the Bureau of the Census as urban in 1920, as compared to under one-quarter in 1860. The urban market for the products of American business had grown, in other words, from 6 million to 54 million consumers. In 1860 there were 93 cities of over 10,000 residents; by 1920 there were 752. In some states the proportion of the urban population was overwhelming. Nine of ten people in Massachusetts were city dwellers in 1920, and eight of ten in New York state.

The galloping growth of American cities in these years presented entrepreneurs with a remarkable opportunity, a highly concentrated and accessible mass market. Whole new forms of business and entire industries came into being, as a result, aimed principally at this emergent urban consumer market. This chapter examines businesses and managers that were particularly sensitive to the rise of an era of consumer capitalism.

The Age of the Automobile

A crucial role in the new urban era was assumed by the automobile industry. "The automobile," Henry C. Dethloff has written, "altered the course of America in the twentieth century as the steamboat and the railroad had done in the century before. It made possible the rise of the modern city and its suburbs, and provided the incentive for a revolution in American industry."[2]

In 1900, only 4,192 passenger cars were sold in the United States. In 1985, sales exceeded 8 million units, and General Motors and Ford ranked first and fourth, respectively, in dollar volume of sales among America's largest industrial corporations. Since the embryonic days of the industry, Americans developed a love affair with the automobile, and that affair permanently altered the way they lived and worked.

Before 1945, the automobile industry in the United States evolved in three stages. The first stretched from the advent of the internal-combustion engine to the initial production of Henry Ford's Model T car in 1908. The second phase, the Ford era, continued until the company, faced with a changing market, discontinued the Model T in 1927. During the last phase, the General Motors Corporation assumed leadership in the industry and retained it through the Second World War.

Many historians date the beginning of the auto age in the United States from Charles Duryea's assembling of a gasoline engine car and its first trial runs in Springfield, Massachusetts, in September 1893. Within a matter of months, however, so many others had emulated Duryea's example that the magazine *Horseless Age* in its first issue (1895) proclaimed a new transportation era: "A pleasing prospect it is that rises before us in contemplating this array of horseless vehicles. From the gradual displacement of the horse in business and pleasure, will come economy of time and practical money-saving." The periodical predicted reduced street-noise levels, fewer traffic "blockades," and fewer accidents because "the horse is not so manageable as a mechanical vehicle."[3] The viewpoint of the magazine is more to be noted for its enthusiasm than for its gift of prophecy.

In general, early auto manufacturers came from one of three backgrounds. Some were former bicycle builders; others had produced carriages and wagons; and still others were engineers or master mechanics. What they had in common was a familiarity with factory methods and some technical ability. The infant industry became principally located in Detroit. When asked why, one Detroit civic leader in the 1930s replied that climate was the reason. It was so bad in Michigan that "to defeat the conditions imposed by earth and sky at Detroit, required intensive labor by energetic men who were not tempted by pleasure and play."[4] Miserable Detroit weather aside, the city was already a manufacturing center, situated close to generous copper, lumber, and iron ore resources, and had gained recognition as a focus for bicycle and carriage production.

The industry, however, was circumscribed by the size of its market. As long as the automobile remained a luxury item, priced well beyond the means of all but a small minority of the population, sales were limited. The concept of a car for the masses had not yet been born, except perhaps in the mind of Henry Ford. Ford is one of the most studied and analyzed figures in American business history. Writings about him range from traditional biographical accounts to elaborate and controversial psychological profiles. He is a man about whom it is difficult to be neutral, and many authors are repulsed by the darker side of his personality. As Harold Livesay has said about him, Ford's "intelligence did not expand with his fortune, the foibles of the ordinary nineteenth century rural America—bigotry, ignorance, mulishness—became dogma, then mania as senility set in."[5]

Ford deserted the family farm in Michigan at an early age. He was a born tinkerer and loved to fix things—as small as a watch or as large as a gasoline engine. Inspired by an article in *The American Machinist* in 1896 that contained detailed drawings of a horseless carriage, Ford set out to build an automobile. He was then employed as chief engineer for the Edison Illuminating Company, Detroit's electrical utility supplier. In a brick woodshed behind his house, Ford built his first car, but when he completed it in the early morning of June 4, 1896, he discovered that it was too big to get through the shed door. Without hesitation, he took an axe, knocked down one of the structure's walls, and drove the car out into the street. Three years later, he resigned from his public-utility job to go into the automobile business on a full-time basis. He was thirty-six years old.

After forming two car-building firms and watching them fail—in part because of friction with his financial backers and in part because he did not have the right product—the present Ford Motor Company was incorporated in June 1903. The capital came from a dozen local investors. Ford himself began with only a quarter interest in the business, but within a few years he expanded it to majority control. When he eventually bought out the minority stockholders in 1920, he paid them $105 million for their original combined investment of $33,000. In addition, they had already received $33 million in dividends along the way.

What transformed Ford's third try at auto manufacturing into one of the world's mightiest industrial organizations was the Model T. It was the mechanical embodiment of a strategy that correctly identified a market and determined what potential customers wanted and how much they could pay. It did not come all at once. Ford tried eight different models before—over the objections of the shareholders—he decided to build a "universal car," a low-priced, serviceable automobile intended to appeal to a mass market. In order to be successful, the new car had to be simple in design, standardized in its parts, and produced in high volume. Ford's devotion was to the production function, and it was a production problem his company faced. Cars had to be turned out in large numbers, and at a small enough unit cost, to make possible a vehicle for the masses.

The Model T required innovations in the manufacturing process. Rather than have workers move from point to point to complete the assembly of a car, Ford adopted the principle of taking the work to the man. He first established a straight-line production system with machines placed in a carefully planned sequence. He then added a moving assembly line with a conveyor belt that pulled the individual parts past each worker. After the assembly line was finally perfected in 1914, Ford's Highland Park plant could turn out one thousand cars a day with the average time for assembling a chassis reduced from twelve hours to less than two.

When the Model T was introduced in October 1908, it swept the market. In 1909, over 12,000 were sold, and the number steadily increased from there, reaching 577,000 in 1916. Ford expanded the market by regularly dropping the price as he achieved further production efficiencies. Priced first at $850, by 1916 the Model T Touring Car sold for only $360.

Also part of the Ford innovations was the creation of a dealership network that reached virtually every town in the United States with a population of one thousand or more. Branch assembly plants, which opened in two dozen different cities beginning in 1910, also supplemented operations in Detroit. It was considerably cheaper to ship auto parts—rather than assembled vehicles—from Michigan to various regions of the country.

Ford further startled the nation in 1914 by announcing that he would pay a $5 wage for an eight-hour day to most of his factory hands. The new rate about doubled what had been the standard in the industry. Ford's motives were mixed. In part, the $5 day was simply an attempt to reduce employee turnover, which was on the rise because of the monotonous routine of the assembly line. In part also it seemed a device to undercut any incipient union action. Along with these motives was the clear advantage that the new wage gave Ford in recruiting the best workers and demanding of them higher and higher levels of effort as the speed of the line was gradually increased. Ford himself claimed that the wage was his method of sharing the company's lucrative profits with his employees, but the earnings were shared only with those workers whose personal life-styles were considered appropriate by the company. Investigators from Ford's specially created "Sociology Department" visited employees in their homes, questioned their families and neighbors, and generally sought to assure management that the potential recipients of the $5 wage would not thereafter squander it on wasteful luxuries and intemperance.

In 1916, Ford broke ground for a superplant at River Rouge in Dearborn. The Highland Park works, although then the largest automobile factory in the world, was taxed to capacity. When "the Rouge" was completed in 1927, it was a gigantic integrated marvel, a vast complex of mills, forges, docks, and assembly plants. It made its own steel, glass, paper, and fabric; these materials were turned into automobile components on subassembly lines. Components were then joined to a chassis on the main assembly line or shipped to one of the company's branch assembly plants. And supplying River Rouge were Ford-owned coal mines, iron-ore deposits, rubber plantations, timberland, and steamships. Nothing like the Ford empire had ever been seen before. By 1927, 15 million Model T cars had been sold, half of all the automobiles manufactured in the United States, and Henry Ford stood as a national idol.

Billy Durant and the Rise of General Motors

The year 1908 is noteworthy in automobile history for two reasons. One, as we have seen, was the introduction of the Model T. The other was the organization of General Motors (GM). Its founder was William Crapo Durant—Billy Durant—an extraordinary salesman, but a shaky administrator. The owner of a successful carriage business, he purchased a small bankrupt Flint car firm, the Buick Motor Company, in 1904. Durant redesigned the product, enlarged operations, and, by 1908, was selling more autos than any other American manufacturer, including Ford. He then implemented a plan to unite the resources of the country's most efficient producers and their suppliers into a huge horizontal combination and thereby cut through the thicket of competing firms that had characterized the industry. An early associate described Durant's goal as "having one big concern of such dominating influence in the automobile industry, as for instance, the United States Steel Corporation exercises in the steel industry, so that its very influence would prevent many of the abuses that we believed existed."[6]

It was a visionary scheme and successful only to a limited extent. The General Motors Company erected in 1908 was a holding company for ten car manufacturers (most notably, Buick, Cadillac, Oakland, and Oldsmobile), three truck-building firms, and ten parts and accessories businesses. Negotiations were carried on with Ford, too, but they fell through when Durant offered only GM stock and not cash for the purchase.

Durant's policy of steady expansion left him chronically cash-poor. He expected to cover his bills from sales proceeds, but an unforeseen drop in demand in 1910 made him unable to pay either his suppliers or his employees. Durant secured a substantial loan from a banking syndicate to bail the company out of its predicament, but in return he had to relinquish his own control. The bankers named a new team of officers, including Charles W. Nash, Buick's top manager, as president. Nash was replaced at Buick by Walter P. Chrysler, an engineer trained in locomotive building. In 1921, Chrysler, moving out on his own, took over the failed Maxwell Motor Company, revitalized it, and, in the mid-1920s, renamed it the Chrysler Corporation.

Billy Durant rebounded quickly from his setback. He asked Louis Chevrolet, a Swiss-born racing car driver with some mechanical ability, to design a new low-priced vehicle, and a corporation was established, the Chevrolet Motor Car Company. Actually, Chevrolet's design proved impractical, and he quit the firm in 1913. Bernard A. Weisberger has commented, somewhat wistfully, on his leaving: "And so Louis Chevrolet departed, not too gently, into the peculiar night that enveloped David Buick. Both men would have their names mentioned literally thousands of times a day throughout the United States and parts of the world, but those who spoke their names would rarely have any idea that they once belonged to men."[7]

The Chevrolet Company began to prosper in 1914 with the introduction of new models with considerable popular appeal, and, with his profits, Durant began to buy up General Motors stock to regain control. An alliance forged with members of the du Pont family, led by Pierre S. du Pont, assisted him in the process, and, in the summer of 1916, he reassumed the GM presidency and replaced Charles Nash.

Durant characteristically embarked on another program of expansion. As part of that drive, GM acquired a number of new part and accessory suppliers, including Fisher Body, Hyatt Roller Bearing, Dayton Engineering Laboratories Company (Delco), and the Klaxon Company. Durant also converted the General Motors Company, a New Jersey holding company, into the General Motors Corporation, chartered in Delaware in 1916, with its former subsidiaries transformed into operating divisions.

In the fall of 1920, a sharp downturn in the economy that caused the bottom to drop out of the automotive market disrupted Durant's plans. Serious operating losses forced down the price of General Motors' stock, and, when Durant tried to support it with his personal resources, he became financially overextended. To prevent Durant's own crisis from compounding the corporation's difficulties, the du Ponts, in conjunction with the House of Morgan, bought up his stock and forced him to resign the presidency. Durant was once again ousted from the organization he had created. Years later, Alfred Sloan wrote of the final severing of Durant's GM ties: "That he should have conceived a General Motors and been unable himself in the long run to bring it off or to sustain his personal, once dominating, position in it is a tragedy of American industrial history."[8]

Pierre du Pont succeeded Durant in the GM presidency. A few years earlier, the E. I. Du Pont de Nemours Company had followed up the investment of individual family members by acquiring a quarter interest in General Motors at a cost of $43 million. It now sought to protect that interest with Pierre du Pont as GM's president, and he, in turn, brought a group of his family firm's executives from Delaware to staff key posts in the automobile company.

During the 1920s, the automobile industry faced unique problems. Under du Pont, General Motors made the necessary adjustment; Ford did not do so until it was too late. With the end of the 1920–1921 recession, the demand for passenger cars returned, but by 1924 it had leveled off, and the years of unrelenting growth were over. The demand for automobiles did not increase until after the Second World War. The old strategy of increasing production to meet an ever-expanding market was no longer tenable. Rather, the challenge after 1924 was to become the most efficient competitor in a stable market, since an increase in one firm's share necessarily meant a decline in another's. As Chandler has written, "The underlying marketing problem was no longer to sell an individual his first car but to get the man who already owned one to buy a new car."[9]

Henry Ford did not understand these changes. He assumed that he could continue to sell his low-priced utility car indefinitely—even though a used-car market had developed, and a vehicle could be purchased from it for less than the cost of a factory-fresh Model T. And those consumers who were ready to buy a new auto increasingly preferred to move up from the Model T to something with more style, comfort, and engineering features. Ford was selling a car that was almost twenty years old by 1927. Ford resented any advice to reformulate his basic strategy. He became a lonely, arbitrary, aging leader who either fired many of his old subordinates or caused them to resign. But, by 1927, even Ford himself could not deny the obvious facts. He grudgingly shut down his assembly lines and did not return them to full production for a year. The Model T was at last discontinued and replaced by the Model A.

Although the Model A was a sound car that achieved some initial popularity—it exceeded 1 million units in sales in 1929 and 1930—Ford had lost his leadership position in the industry. General Motors now assumed command, and Ford's market share dwindled from over 50 percent in the early 1900s to only 25 percent in 1931 and 19 percent in 1940. Moreover, the Ford Motor Corporation suffered severe operating losses that, between 1927 and 1932, totaled more than $75 million. The company survived only because of the enormous cash reserves it had built up in its glory days. As John Rae wryly remarked: "Ford provides an excellent illustration of the fact that a really large business organization can withstand a surprising amount of mismanagement."[10] Not until 1945 was Ford belatedly induced to give up the reins to his grandson, Henry Ford II, and only then did a resurgence begin.

Du Pont, Sloan, and the GM Era

One vital human asset that was carried over from the Durant years at General Motors was the presence of Alfred P. Sloan, Jr. Sloan had been the owner of Hyatt Roller Bearing at the time Durant acquired it in 1916. With the sale of his own firm, Sloan transferred his allegiance to GM, where he was made a corporate vice-president.

Although Sloan had been successful as Hyatt's owner-manager, he now found his innately appropriate role as a major executive in a giant bureaucratic enterprise. As Harold Livesay puts it, Sloan was truly "the organization man." Sloan himself later said, "After all, what any one individual can accomplish is not great, but through the power of organization the effect of a few may be multiplied almost indefinitely."[11]

Sloan and Pierre du Pont were a compatible team. Both were MIT graduates; both had restrained, thoughtful, somewhat austere management styles—very few people ever called either man by his first name—and both based policy decisions on hard facts and ascertainable data.

Immediately after Pierre du Pont took over in late 1920, he approved the implementation of an administrative reorganization that Sloan recommended. The plan was embodied in a document, *Organization Study*, that Sloan first prepared for Durant, who had never acted upon it. It was a major document in American business history. It proposed the overall structure under which GM still operates today; moreover, it became the model for a substantial number of managerial enterprises in all industries.

The *Organization Study* set forth two fundamental principles. First, that each operating division should be "complete in every necessary function" and headed by its own chief executive officer, and second, that a central or general corporate office should establish overall policy, coordinate the works of the divisions, and appraise the results. Sloan was, in addition, concerned with clearly defining the lines of authority and communication between the general office and the vertically integrated divisions; he was also concerned with generating "accurate and useful data to flow through these lines."[12] The plan was not perfected overnight. It required continued fine tuning, but the basic concept remained intact—the effective management of a multidivisional, decentralized business organization.

In theory, each GM division operated as a separate company. The yardstick of return on invested capital was used to evaluate its performance. Each division manager submitted monthly reports to the general office, and that data, forwarded in a standardized format, helped determine the rate of return on investment for the division and any needed corrective action.

But developing a new administrative structure was only part of the du Pont-Sloan approach. Another aspect was the implementation of a new marketing strategy. Under Durant, several GM divisions were in direct competition with each other, mainly for the middle-priced car market. Sloan, who was made vice-president for operations by du Pont, rationalized the corporation's product policy by adopting a "full-line" approach. There would be a General Motors car in every price range, from the low-priced Chevrolets through the middle-range Pontiacs, Oldsmobiles, and Buicks, to the luxury level of the Cadillacs. There would be no duplication in the several graded-market steps.

Along with the full-line approach, Sloan also introduced the device of annual model changes, which stressed styling differences to keep the appearance of next year's edition distinctive from the previous year. Also of significance in selling the product was the rapid growth of the General Motors Acceptance Corporation as a mechanism for financing installment-payment buyers. Ford did not offer his customers the same opportunity until 1928.

In 1923, Pierre du Pont turned over the GM presidency to Sloan when he moved up to the post of chairman of the board—a position from which he retired five years later. Symbolically, he retired the year after General Motors wrested the leading position in the industry from Ford. The reorganization engineered by du Pont, Sloan, and their associates during the 1920s had accomplished its purpose.

On the Air

In 1916, a young executive of the Marconi Wireless Telegraph Company of America—a firm that provided maritime radio service—addressed a memorandum to his immediate superior that stated: "I have in mind a plan for development which would make radio a household utility in the same sense as the piano or phonograph." The memo proposed to offer the public a "radio music box" that would bring "music into the house by wireless."[13] David Sarnoff was the author of this idea, and, when he received no response to it, he temporarily put the matter aside. Six years later, however, Sarnoff became general manager of the newborn Radio Corporation of America (RCA), and, in 1930, he moved up to its presidency.

The development of broadcasting as an industry was stalled by the First World War, but by the fall of 1920 it was in motion. Officials of Westinghouse Electric in Pittsburgh were attracted by its commercial possibilities. Among its other products, Westinghouse manufactured radio equipment, and it thus seemed logical that the company would create a larger market for its receivers if it broadcast entertainment programs over its own sending station.

In October 1920, Westinghouse applied to the Department of Commerce for a license to operate a broadcasting service. The Radio Act passed by Congress in 1912 had placed the granting of licenses for wireless transmissions in the Commerce Department, but the concept of broadcasting was hardly envisioned at that point. The department assigned to the proposed Westinghouse station the call letters KDKA and a wavelength for its signal. Then, on the evening of November 2, 1920, from a shack erected on top of one of the plant buildings, KDKA began broadcasting the results of the presidential election held that day. An estimated five hundred persons heard KDKA's first program, but, when the station followed on succeeding evenings with regular entertainment broadcasts, a national mania was born. It quickly became a mark of social sophistication to remark casually that one had "picked up" KDKA (or another of the pioneer stations that were being quickly set up) the previous evening. Electrical shops were deluged with requests for parts, and department stores set up special radio displays. By the end of 1922, the Commerce Department had granted licenses to some six hundred stations, and an estimated four hundred thousand receiving sets were in use in the United States.[14]

Early broadcasters did not establish their stations with the classic economic motive of direct profit maximization. Rather, they sought indirect benefits. The majority of stations were the creation of business firms that were interested in the sale of radio sets. Manufacturers, such as Westinghouse, and retail stores viewed broadcasting as a way to increase public demand for the receiving sets in their inventory, and they anticipated no revenues from the stations themselves. A second group of broadcasters were businessmen who believed that radio could foster community goodwill. Newspapers formed the most numerous element in this category. They looked upon an investment in broadcasting as a part of their promotional activities. Overall, broadcasting was a distinctly urban business in these years, as the bulk of stations were located in larger cities in the most populous states. Rural areas, on the other hand, suffered from a lack of adequate local service until after the Second World War.

Even before KDKA first took the air, maneuvering for dominance in radio had taken place among America's largest corporations in the fields of electrical manufacturing and telecommunications. The Radio Corporation of America was organized in October 1919 to take over the assets of the American Marconi Company—the firm that employed David Sarnoff when he wrote his "radio music box" memorandum in 1916. The possible expansion of American Marconi, a firm controlled by British interests, worried the United States government and especially the Navy Department, who feared so important a technical resource as radio being in non-American hands. Hence, federal officials encouraged a takeover by domestic operations and pressured the British interests to sell out.

RCA was owned largely by a consortium that consisted of General Electric, Westinghouse, and AT&T. Owen D. Young, a General Electric vice-president who negotiated the complicated acquisition of American Marconi, played a central role in RCA's formation. General Electric's own share of RCA stock was eventually 30 percent.

Taking over American Marconi was only part of RCA's mission. It was also intended to be a central participant in a patent pool, or cross-licensing agreement worked out by the interested companies, each of whom possessed some patents important to the future of radio. Under the arrangement, General Electric and Westinghouse manufactured receivers and parts for the market and transmitters for their own use only. On the other hand, AT&T received the exclusive right to make and sell transmitters to nonparticipants in the agreement. RCA, meanwhile, acted as the sales agent for GE and Westinghouse and marketed their products under its trademark. Significantly, Owen Young later claimed that at no time during the planning of all this did the subject of broadcasting arise.

AT&T chose to leave radio in 1926, and it sold its stock in RCA and in a company-owned station in New York City—WEAF. It had provoked a storm of public hostility and ominous discussions of a "radio trust" that might require federal antimonopoly action when it had attempted to prevent new stations from using non-AT&T transmitters—or, at the least, to require them to purchase a license from the telephone giant. AT&T officials, not wishing to risk a backlash and always having regarded radio as a secondary enterprise as compared with its telephone business, decided to withdraw.

Before they did so, however, their New York station broke some important new ground for the infant broadcasting industry. WEAF inaugurated what it called "toll" broadcasting: it carried, for a fee paid to the station, commercially sponsored programs. The toll innovation was an adaptation of the telephone concept to radio; the user of the equipment paid a service charge to the equipment's owner for making it available.

On August 28, 1922, WEAF carried radio's first commercials, a series of short talks by a spokesman for the Queensboro Corporation on behalf of its apartment development on Long Island. The charge for the time furnished by the station was $100, but the result was supposedly several thousands of dollars worth of sales for the sponsor. The next month, WEAF carried sales presentations for two more business sponsors, Tidewater Oil and American Express. Commercial radio was under way.

Opposition to the innovation quickly surfaced. One periodical referred to it as "positively offensive," and the secretary of commerce, Herbert Hoover, complained: "It is inconceivable that we should allow so great a possibility for service to be drowned in advertising chatter."[15] In spite of Hoover's reaction, radio advertising revenue soon opened new commercial vistas for broadcasters.

Along with toll broadcasting, AT&T and WEAF transmitted the first "chain," or network, programs. They had planned a chain of stations stretched across the country, all connected by the telephone company's long-distance lines, that would broadcast identical programs. The idea was first tested on January 4, 1923, when a WEAF program was simultaneously carried by Boston's WNAC. Later in the same year, AT&T formed a chain of stations which it called the Red Network.

The most decisive step toward creating chain broadcasting on a continent-wide scale took place in 1926, when RCA purchased WEAF and then organized a new subsidiary, the National Broadcasting Company (NBC). Since RCA had another New York City station, WJZ, it decided to have NBC form two chains. One was the Red Network, essentially the old AT&T group, and the other was the Blue Network, with WJZ as its flagship.

A major rival to the NBC networks appeared one year later in 1927. The Columbia Phonograph Broadcasting System was formed in April, with primary financial support from the Columbia Phonograph Record Company. The next year, for unexplained reasons, the record firm had second thoughts about the prospects of network radio and pulled out of the venture. William S. Paley of Philadelphia immediately took its place.

Paley's family owned the Congress Cigar Company and had tried some advertising on the Columbia chain. When the results proved impressive in terms of added sales, young Paley, already restless in the family business, decided on a career in radio. He purchased control of the chain, shortened its name to the Columbia Broadcasting System (CBS), and became its new president. With the establishment of network broadcasting, the basic framework of the industry for the next twenty years was in place and was not disturbed until the challenge of television after the Second World War.

Radio was important in a depression-mired America of the 1930s. Social workers reported that poverty-stricken families would surrender an icebox or furniture or even a bed before they would sell their radios. Somehow radio became a lifeline to the outside world that had to be preserved at any cost. The Federal Communications Commission (FCC) later estimated that, during the worst economic crisis in the country's history, the number of radios in use more than doubled, from 18 million in 1932 to 45 million just four years later.[16]

In 1937, the FCC reported that over a thousand factories were engaged in the manufacture of sets, tubes, transmitters, and other equipment; and four thousand retailers were involved exclusively in selling these products to the public. There were also 700 local stations and three national network organizations. The newest and smallest network, the Mutual Broadcasting System, which was started in 1934, was largely under the control of the *Chicago Tribune* and the R. H. Macy Company. While it claimed 107 affiliates, NBC counted 161, and CBS 113. NBC and CBS had most of the more powerful and better-located stations. Together, the three networks transacted almost half of the total business done by America's broad-casters, and, in 1938, their time sales grossed over $46 million.

Government's role in broadcasting during the 1920s and the 1930s focused on the enactment and implementation of two pieces of leg-islation, the Radio Act of 1927 and the Communications Act of 1934. The first act established a five-person Federal Radio Commission; the second replaced it with the Federal Communications Commis-sion. Both bodies operated on the premise that the radio industry was a valuable national resource and that the public owned its various frequencies. They were allocated to private enterprises by means of short-term licenses, which federal authorities granted, and these li-censes would, in theory, remain in effect only as long as their holders followed good engineering practices and adequately served the "public interest, convenience, or necessity."[17] In reality, however, few licenses were ever revoked for failure of stations to live up to their obligations, and, as a result, license holders obtained long-term *de facto* property rights in their operations.

In his able study of the relationship between private broadcasting enterprises and public policy, Philip T. Rosen has written: "Dissen-ters to commercially owned broadcasting have criticized this scheme of things since the beginning, mainly on the grounds that the re-sulting programs lack cultural, intellectual, and aesthetic quality. On the other hand, this arrangement has made the product—radio and later television transmissions—available to the widest possible au-dience of 'consumers' at an extremely low price." And Rosen con-cludes: "On negative and positive counts alike, the structure may be said to be quintessentially American."[18]

Counters and Catalogues—The Mass Retailers

Mass-retailing organizations, like vertically integrated manufactur-ers, bypassed the traditional wholesale apparatus during the last quarter of the nineteenth century. One scholar has calculated that, in 1879, some $2.4 billion in goods reached retailers through the wholesale network, while only $1 billion in goods was purchased directly from manufacturers and processors. But within thirty years that picture was significantly altered. By 1909 the ratio of goods purchased from wholesalers to those bought directly had dropped from 2.40 to 1 to 1.90 to 1 and, only two decades later, to 1.47 to

1.[19] This gradual decline of the middleman role in the distribution system was largely the result of the maturing of three types of retailing enterprises: the department store, the mail-order house, and the chain store.

Department stores developed first, but much of their early history is still murky. Ralph Hower has, however, provided us with an acceptable definition. He described a department store as "a retail institution which is organized by merchandise departments; that is, with administrative subdivisions corresponding to physical segregations of merchandise, each having its own manager and salesforce, with a central accounting system which keeps a record of the income and expense attributable to that particular division of the store."[20]

Although the phrase "department store" was not common until the late nineteenth century, there is little question that some methods associated with this type of mass retailer were in use even before the Civil War. Among these methods were a one-price policy, as opposed to haggling or bargaining with a customer; free entry (the ability of the customer to browse without pressure from a hovering sales person); a truthful presentation of the merchandise; aggressive and interesting advertising; money-back guarantees; sales for cash rather than credit; and, most important, a small markup on goods and a dependence on volume sales to generate profits. In general, store managers sought to create an invigorating, sumptuous atmosphere in which their customers would shop. A writer of that period described the stores as "bringing brightness and change to many who at other times pass their days in the dull monotony of a struggle to live." The surroundings provided, according to the writer, "something to think of and talk over, even if the gorgeous and beautiful trappings seen in the stores are not within the possibility of possession."[21]

Although Robert Hendrickson calls Aristide Boucicaut's Bon Marche in Paris "the first true department store," other writers do not necessarily agree.[22] More likely, a number of stores developed almost simultaneously, each employing the methods and practices mentioned above. A majority evolved from "fancy dry goods" stores, as did Rowland H. Macy's, which opened in New York City in 1858. During the 1860s, Macy began to add new lines of merchandise to the basic dry goods. Drugs, china, glassware, home furnishings, books, and toys were gradually introduced, thereby transforming Macy's into a true department store. When the Straus brothers, Isidor and

Nathan, acquired the store in the 1890s, R. H. Macy and Company was well established as New York's best-known department store.

Meanwhile, in Philadelphia, John Wanamaker was attaining equal renown. In the 1860s, he opened two men's clothing stores that successfully employed new mass-retailing techniques, but not until 1876 did he expand beyond clothing and dry goods. In that year, he purchased an old Pennsylvania Railroad freight building, remodeled it, and began operating a department store. Wanamaker referred to it as a "new kind of store," and one of his biographers later claimed that "it was operated on a different and entirely new basis of storekeeping from any then existing." Nonetheless, his "Grand Depot" operation only copied methods already instituted by Macy and other mass-retailing pioneers.[23] Indeed, a case can be made that these methods were first introduced by Alexander T. Stewart in his "Marble Dry Goods Palace" in New York City in 1848. Stewart, however, confined his stock to textiles and thus did not have a department store. Nevertheless, Wanamaker's Philadelphia store became the largest in the United States, and he remained a potent force in retailing well into the next century.

In general, department stores were made possible by the growing urbanization of the United States. Susan Porter Benson, in her study of department store "counter cultures," has stated that the stores accurately reflected the spirit of the expanding cities of America. In her words: "The congestion, the liveliness, the anonymity, the grand scale, the material promise, and the class divisions of the city, were all distilled into the great stores."[24] Large cities, linked to their downtown shopping areas by street transportation such as the horsecar and the electric trolley, provided the concentrated market necessary to make huge establishments like Wanamaker's Grand Depot possible. Moreover, the department store required a rapid turnover of its inventory to be profitable. The urban mass market made stock-turns as often as six or more times a year possible and a low profit margin feasible. The department store thus succeeded as a business institution.

Rapid inventory turnover and low profit margins were also the merchandising tactics upon which mail-order houses built their enterprises. They were the second of the modern mass retailers to emerge after the Civil War. The earliest was founded by Aaron Montgomery Ward and his brother-in-law George R. Thorne in Chicago in 1872. Ward was a former rural store manager and traveling salesman who was familiar with farmers and their needs. He also recognized the growing importance of a new agricultural organization, the Grange. His plan was simple: he would buy merchandise directly from manufacturers for cash and then sell the articles to farmers, also for cash, and thereby eliminate both middlemen and credit risks.

A farmer ordered the goods by mail, and they were shipped to him via railroad express. Price sheets were issued that instructed farmers about merchandise for sale and how it could be ordered. The sheets depicted Ward's firm as "The Original Grange Supply House" and boasted that "by purchasing with us you save 40 to 100 percent."[25] By the 1880s massive catalogues had replaced the price sheets, and they advertised some ten thousand items that a rural family could purchase.

In the 1890s, a new firm owned by Richard Warren Sears and Alvah C. Roebuck challenged Montgomery Ward's supremacy in the mail-order business. Sears, the driving force in the venture, had begun by selling watches through the mail. Then, in 1893, he joined with Roebuck to create the company that today bears their names, and, at the same time, broadened his merchandise offerings beyond simply watches. Like Montgomery Ward, he located his headquarters in Chicago, the rail center of the United States, and advertised aggressively in rural newspapers and farm magazines; he also published weighty catalogues mailed to farmers for as little as a fifteen-cent fee.

Roebuck, soon weary of the business, sold out to Sears in 1895. His place in the firm was immediately filled by two new investors, Julius Rosenwald, a men's clothing manufacturer, and Aaron Nusbaum, who had accumulated a tidy sum from a soda pop and ice cream concession at the Chicago Columbian Exposition in 1893. Policy differences caused both Nusbaum and Sears himself to resign by 1908, leaving the management to Rosenwald, who directed the company's fortunes until 1925. By then, Sears, Roebuck's sales exceeded $240 million and considerably surpassed its predecessor in the mail-order business, Montgomery Ward, whose own sales totaled $170 million in the same year.

The year 1925 was a turning point in Sears's history. Rosenwald turned over the administration of the organization to a new team led by Charles M. Kittle, former executive vice-president of the Illinois Central Railroad, who now became the Sears president. Kittle's vice-president was Robert C. Wood, who had been Montgomery

Ward's general merchandise manager. Wood fashioned a new marketing strategy. He was impressed by statistical data on the urbanization of America and was aware that the automobile had considerably lessened the isolation of the average farm family. He thus now urged entrance into the retail-store field.

Wood won his point in February 1925, when the first Sears store was opened in Chicago. By the end of the year a total of eight stores were in operation, and rapid expansion followed. By 1929, the company had established over three hundred stores, and, within a few years, they accounted for more than half the Sears, Roebuck sales volume. Montgomery Ward, which had been reluctant to take the same step while Robert Wood was still one of its executives, was now forced to pursue a similar strategy, and it also began a concerted movement into urban retail-store marketing.

In 1928, on the sudden death of Charles Kittle, Wood assumed the vacant presidential chair, which he held until after the Second World War. During his tenure, Sears, Roebuck weathered the depression years in good shape, and, in the wartime period, it exceeded the goal of $1 billion in sales for the first time. Although Montgomery Ward also experienced some growth, it remained firmly lodged in second place.

When Robert Wood first proposed a network of Sears retail outlets, he was actually following the example of a third development in mass merchandising, the chain store. In 1929, the Bureau of the Census defined a chain as a grouping of "four or more stores in the same general kind of business, owned and operated jointly with central buying, usually supplied from one or more central warehouses."[26]

The data that the Census Bureau compiled in 1929 revealed that, while 10.8 percent of all retail units in the nation could be classified as chain stores under the above definition, they accounted for nearly a quarter of total retail sales. In some lines, they thoroughly dominated the trade. About 90 percent of variety-store volume was controlled by chains, about 50 percent among shoe stores, and nearly 40 percent in groceries.

Historians have usually dated chain-store growth in America from 1859, when salesman George Huntington Hartford and leather dealer George F. Gilman organized what they named, ten years later, the Great Atlantic and Pacific Tea Company, or A&P (a name that they chose to celebrate the completion of the first transcontinental railroad in 1869). Hartford and Gilman bought cargoes of tea directly

278 THE AGE OF MANAGERIAL CAPITALISM

from incoming ships and thus allowed their firm to cut costs by eliminating middlemen. This method made the term "cargo pricing" a synonym for low prices. By 1870 they operated eleven stores, but real expansion did not come until the 1880s, when Hartford's sons, George L. and John A., were admitted to the business. By that time, Gilman had retired and the firm was a Hartford family enterprise. Grocery items other than tea were now phased in to each store's stock as part of a new full-line policy.

John Hartford also developed another policy change—a cash-and-carry system rather than home deliveries and credit extension. When his first experiments with cash-and-carry demonstrated the profitability of the policy, the pace of expansion was accelerated even further. In one year during the 1920s, for example, stores were opened at the rate of fifty per week. Five hundred were in place by 1913 and over fifteen thousand by 1930.

The formula was by now well established. A chain such as A&P could accept a smaller profit margin than independent stores, since its total volume was so much greater. Chains possessed a further bargaining advantage in dealing with manufacturers because of their quantity purchases. And, in many instances, they could and did produce their own private-branded mechandise, which further cut their costs.

The example of the Hartfords was soon copied in groceries by Kroger, National Tea, Safeway and others. Another key marketing innovation was that pioneered by a Memphis grocer, Clarence Saunders, in 1916. Saunders introduced into his Piggly Wiggly store the concept of self-service grocery shopping. A customer entered through a turnstile, picked up a wooden basket, walked down store aisles selecting price-tagged items from open display shelves, and then moved to a check-out stand, where the merchandise was paid for. The system was totally different from the traditional practice of customers lining up at a counter to be served by a grocery clerk, who fetched requested items. Saunders's innovation both reduced labor costs for the store owner and stimulated impulse buying (and thus larger grocery bills) on the part of the shopper. There were 1,200 Piggly Wiggly Stores in twenty-nine states by 1922, and Saunders was temporarily a multimillionaire. But in the stock-market hysteria of the late 1920s, Saunders was involved in some ill-fated financial manipulations; he lost control of his company and most of his fortune. Nevertheless, Saunders's fundamental concept was sound, and it was rapidly incorporated into the operations of other chains, becoming the basis for today's self-service supermarkets.

Chain stores also made their appearance outside of the grocery trade. Frank W. Woolworth established the pattern in low-priced variety stores by concentrating upon nonperishable household "smallwares." After some unsuccessful earlier tries, he began earning profits with a "5 and 10 Cent Store" in Lancaster, Pennsylvania in 1879. With his brother Charles, he then began opening similar outlets elsewhere, so that F.W. Woolworth and Company was operating over 1,000 "dime stores" in the United States, Canada, and Great Britain in 1919, the year of the founder's death. More and more, the Woolworth stores dealt directly with manufacturers, eliminating transactions with wholesalers and having goods produced specifically for the chain within its designated price range. The organization's achievements were probably symbolized by its construction of the Woolworth Building in New York City. When it was finished in 1913, it was then the tallest office building in the world. Again, as in the previous cases cited, the Woolworth innovations set an example that was to be emulated by other dime-store chains with names such as Kresge, Kress, and McCrory.

The coming of chain stores also marked the dry goods and drugstore fields in the early twentieth century. James Cash Penney began with a single store in a small Wyoming town in 1902, incorporated under the name J.C. Penney Company in 1913, and moved his headquarters to New York City. By opening new stores and purchasing other chains, the organization was doing $200 million worth of business in 1929. Penney himself remained as chairman of the board until 1946.

A Chicago pharmacist, Charles R. Walgreen, led the way in drugstore chains. His first store was started in 1909. As the chain grew, he stressed the manufacture of his own house-labeled ice cream and drug items, popularized the lunch counter/soda fountain (and supposedly concocted the first malted milk shakes), and relied on a heavy advertising budget to attract business. There were 493 Walgreen stores in 215 cities in thirty-seven states at the time of his death in 1939.

This chain-store momentum did not go unchallenged by small, independent retailers. Antichain measures were frequently debated in state legislatures, especially during the 1920s and 1930s. In Georgia, Maryland, and North Carolina, laws were enacted that imposed punitive taxes on chain units. Although in each case judicial decisions later voided these laws, those legal reversals did little to alter the antichain-store climate of the times.

Inevitably, the wails of threatened smaller merchants reached Washington, and Congress responded with two pieces of special-interest legislation. In 1936, it passed the Robinson-Patman Act. Technically an amendment to Section 2 of the Clayton Act, it sought to reduce the purchasing power of large buyers by limiting the price concessions that a manufacturer could grant to them. Enforcement was placed in the hands of the Federal Trade Commission, and, for a time, the law was the basis for numerous FTC-initiated actions. More recently, however, the Robinson-Patman Act has been so roundly criticized for discouraging price competition and for fostering price uniformity that few FTC actions are brought under it today.

The next year, 1937, Congress pushed protection for the independent merchant even further with the Miller-Tydings Act. It exempted resale price maintenance contracts (or, as they were more commonly know, "fair-trade" agreements) from the penalties of the Sherman Act. As a result of this congressional blessing, over forty states enacted laws permitting many manufacturers to require retailers to sell their products at a preestablished price. Although enforcement varied, prices on many household items, especially drugs and appliances, were thus kept well above competitive levels. Fair trade lost its force soon after the Second World War with the rise of discount stores and, finally, Congress' repeal in 1975 of the Miller-Tydings Act itself.

Whether they were department stores or chain stores, the mass retailers had come into existence when a market large enough to accommodate their high-volume, low-margin strategy developed. Once born, they changed the face of retailing in the United States. In their way, men such as Macy and Sears and Woolworth were as much business pioneers as the magnates of manufacturing who led the process of industrialization.

Advertising—Beyond the Patent Medicine Age

Advertising has been defined as "nonpersonal forms of communication conducted through paid media under clear sponsorship."[27] It is, of course, intended to move merchandise, that is, to stimulate a firm's sales and thereby boost its profits. The English word "advertising" was derived from the French verb *avertir*, which means "to notify." And there has been a great deal of notifying taking place. In 1984 American business spent $88 billion on advertising, the largest share (27 percent) in newspapers and only slightly less (23 percent) on television commercials. The Proctor & Gamble Co. was individually the nation's biggest advertiser in 1984 with expenditures of $872 million, or about 8.5 percent of its total U.S. sales for the same year.

It was not always so, however. While advertising in the United States dates back to the times of Benjamin Franklin and colonial newspapers, the copy was then little more than plain notices of goods available for sale by local merchants. The ads were usually just several lines of ordinary type without any pictures or interesting graphics.

American advertising entered another stage in the nineteenth century with the emergence of the first mass-circulation newspapers and magazines aimed particularly at the new urban population centers. Unfortunately, the leading product group featured by brand names in the advertising of this period was patent medicines. According to one historian of the industry, during the post–Civil War years patent medicines were "the first products to be advertised on a large national scale, the first to aim directly at the consumer with vivid, psychologically clever sales pitches, the first to show—for better or worse—the latent power of advertising."[28] It is estimated that by 1900, gross patent-medicine sales were $75 million in this country. But this long association of popular-press advertising with dubious drug remedies invested the entire advertising community with an unsavory reputation for untruth and chicanery that was not to be quickly, if ever, overcome.

One classic example of a patent medicine that owed its success to a heavy reliance on advertising was Lydia E. Pinkham's Vegetable Compound. Lydia Pinkham herself was involved in the brewing (probably the right word because the mixture had an 18 percent alcohol content) of her tonic for only a few years after it first went on sale in 1875. While she originated the recipe, it was her sons Daniel, Will, and Charles Pinkham who merchandised it successfully. It was touted as "The Positive Cure for All Female Complaints," the catchall Gilded Age phrasing for feminine disorders ranging from painful menstruation to prolapsed uterus.

Both the bottle's label and the advertising copy for the product featured a photograph of Mother Pinkham herself long after she had died in 1883. Biographer Sarah Stage has described the result: "Generations of Americans grew up with Lydia Pinkham. Her face, kindly yet abstracted, her gray hair drawn back into a braided bun, the solid respectability of black silk and white ruching, became as familiar as the daily newspaper or the neighborhood druggist's display. . . . No advertising agent intent on creating the perfect grandmother could have done a better job."[29]

During the early years, the firm, the Lydia E. Pinkham Medicine Company, spent as much as three-quarters of its revenues on advertising. Often it would pay for newspaper space with cases of the product. The publishers, avid to fill their pages with ads, accepted the merchandise as payment and then resold it to local druggists. The advertising generally featured testimonials and what has been called a "pain and agony pitch." Alleged users of the product would describe in rather unpleasant detail their individual symptoms for which the compound had proven exactly the right remedy.

Even Theodore Roosevelt's signing into law of the federal Pure Food and Drug Act in 1906 did not slow the growth of the company. The new legislation only forced the admission on the label of the potent alcohol content of each bottle and caused some minor wording changes in the curative claims being made. Twenty years later, some $3 million worth of yearly business was still being done, and Lydia E. Pinkham's Vegetable Compound would be available for a dwindling number of ever-loyal customers to purchase for decades after that.

As noted, the patent-medicine era in American advertising did not suddenly end with the coming of the twentieth century. Nevertheless, the modern advertising age was well underway by that time. The advent of the mass-market retailers, such as department and chain stores, already discussed, was one causal factor. Another was the need for the new high-volume manufacturers of consumer durables and packaged goods to insure a ready market for the rapidly expanding production of their factories. Both types of businesses were offering legitimate merchandise and not questionable patent-medicine cures. Therefore, both had a vested interest in raising the level of advertising standards so that the public's readiness to believe what was being presented would be enhanced.

Obviously, the new emphasis did not mean shaky product claims would no longer be made. Rather, it became a distinction between outright fraud and what is generally called "puffery." The latter, a common element in most modern advertising, is the seller's claim that a firm's item is simply better or more effective or more satisfying than the competitor's version. Puffery is essentially a professed opinion that may or may not be supported by adequate evidence, and that the consumer must choose to accept or reject when deciding on a purchase. It does not include blatant, intentional falsehood.

As these new types of advertisers came to the fore in the late nineteenth century, professional advertising agencies developed to service them. At first, the agencies were simply independent brokers of newspaper space, who bought in large quantity from publishers and resold in smaller blocks to advertisers for whatever price they could negotiate. Only gradually did the modern, full-service agency— a business that assumed the entire responsibility for an ad campaign (planning, researching, designing, copywriting, and placement) under a standard contract with a client—replace the old-style broker. The first to make the transition was the N.W. Ayer and Son agency.

Founded in 1869 by Francis Wayland Ayer, who named the firm after his father, it pioneered the "open contract." This was an agreement that "bound the agent and advertiser together with both parties knowing the exact financial terms, and with the agent—instead of simply buying space low and selling it high—taking his pay at a set commission, at first 12.5 percent, later 15 percent, of the publisher's fees."[30] The open contract eventually became the standard in the advertising industry. Ayer hired the first full-time copywriter in 1891, and the accounts serviced included Montgomery Ward, Proctor & Gamble, and the National Biscuit Company. It was in 1898 that the Ayer agency undertook for National Biscuit what was probably the first fully integrated national advertising campaign. The million-dollar campaign included the design of a package, the devising of a brand name—Uneeda Biscuit—and a distinctive trademark (a boy in a rain slicker), and the placement of ads in every medium then available. Ayer himself was a sober-sided, Baptist Sunday school superintendent, and he seemed to personify advertising's rising respectability and the demise of the worst hokum of the patent-medicine days.

The First World War offered advertising agency executives an opportunity to show off their expertise within the trappings of wartime
patriotism. Incorporated into the Wilson administration's propa-
ganda campaign as the Division of Advertising of the Committee on
Public Information, agencies contributed their efforts and "mounted
impressive campaigns to sell war bonds, enlist army and navy re-
cruits, enhance worker morale, and promote conservatism of food
and resources." *Printer's Ink*, the industry's principal trade journal,
concluded afterwards that the war years had indeed proven well-
crafted advertising could "sway the minds of whole populations,
change their habits of life, [and] create belief, practically universal,
in any policy or idea."[31]

It was during the decade of the 1920s, however, that the contemporary advertising era actually dawned. In the ten years between
1919 and 1929, total advertising expenditures in the United States
more than doubled, and the ratio of advertising costs to overall distribution costs rose from 8 to 14 percent. And many individual ad
campaigns brought truly impressive results. One of the most famous
was that conducted on behalf of a Lambert Pharmaceutical Company
product, Listerine mouthwash.

Listerine was not a new product in 1920, but its sales were only
a lackluster $100,000 yearly. Then two copywriters named Milton
Feasley and Gordon Seagrove, working for a Chicago agency, fastened upon an old, out-of-use medical term, "halitosis." They introduced it into Listerine ads as a more polite and scientific-sounding
description for "bad breath." Next they created copy that took the
form of miniature social dramas. Gilbert Marchand has described the
ad plots thus: "The heroine or hero of the story invariably possessed
all the qualities needed for success—wealth, good looks, attractive
personality, high social standing. Thus the only possible cause for a
personal failure had to be the inexcusable fault of halitosis." Then
the little dramas repeated the campaign's stern, incessant warning:
"And even your closest friends won't tell you."[32] By 1927 Listerine
sales were exceeding $4 million a year, and Feasley and Seagrove
had gone off to New York to form their own agency.

While not every major agency was based in New York City (N.W.
Ayer and Son was still headquartered in Philadelphia), almost all of
the decade's largest were now there, including the very biggest, the
J. Walter Thompson Company. It was employing a staff of almost
300, and was annually billing clients over $37 million by 1929. Among

the Thompson firm's most effective campaigns of the period were those for Fleischmann's Yeast, Maxwell House Coffee, and Woodbury Facial Soap. The Woodbury campaign focused on the slogan "For the Skin You Love to Touch," and is thought by some observers to have been the initial insertion of implicit sex into modern advertising copy.

By the end of the 1920s, a shorthand reference to the advertising community as "Madison Avenue," after the New York City locale of many of the agencies, had already come into some vogue. And at the same time, Madison Avenue's influence was being more deeply felt than ever before in the fabric of American society and culture.

Commercial Banking in Good Times and Bad

Very important too for the new urban nation's economy were financial institutions. Investment bankers frequently have been referred to as intermediaries between individuals and institutions seeking attractive opportunities in which to invest their funds and capital-hungry enterprises. But there were other intermediaries also, and one of the most vital was commercial banks.

In 1860, there were approximately sixteen hundred state-chartered banks in the United States. They issued notes that circulated as currency in thousands of varieties, but not necessarily at par. The worth of a state bank note might vary from face value to near zero, depending on the known financial strength of the issuing institution. Furthermore, notes that were readily accepted in one region of the country might circulate at a severe discount in another. This variation complicated and impeded interregional trade.

No significant change occurred in this haphazard situation until the Civil War. The National Banking Acts of 1863 and 1864 gave the federal government the authority to establish a new body of "national" banks. Each such bank deposited with the Treasury Department United States government bonds equal to one-third of its starting capital, and, in exchange, it received national bank notes that it could then circulate. The expectation was that these notes would replace the variegated ones that state banks issued and would provide the nation with a uniform paper currency. Moreover, a prohibitive tax was levied on state bank notes that thereby made them unprofitable for the issuers.

The National Banking Acts created a dual system—still in existence today—in which banks operate with either federal or state charters and are subject to different regulatory requirements. As it turned out, many bankers preferred to keep their state charters rather than place themselves under the more restrictive federal rules. Moreover, because of the increased use of checkbook money based on demand deposits, the loss of the note-issuing privilege was no great blow for a state bank. Indeed, in 1913, there were twice as many state banks as national banks.

Actually, as one historian has pointed out, the new national bank system "was not really a system at all but rather a loose body of independent banks responsible only to themselves and responsible only for themselves."[33] Because of the weaknesses in the "system"—especially the absence of any central bank to serve as a stabilizer—periodic financial crises marred the Gilded Age. The worst of these occurred in 1873, 1893, and 1907, always with the effect that "credit would be unobtainable at any price, cash would go into hoarding, and panic conditions would prevail."[34]

The crisis of 1907 prompted another effort at banking reform that culminated in the passage of the Federal Reserve Act of 1913. It is perhaps significant that J. P. Morgan died in the same year that the Federal Reserve System was established. This key figure in American finance passed away at the moment the nation was about to erect a new central banking apparatus. The changes that the Federal Reserve Act brought need not be detailed here. Rather than establishing a single central bank similar to Nicholas Biddle's Bank of the United States, the law created twelve Federal Reserve district banks. Each of the twelve was owned by the "member" banks in its area; all national banks were forced to join and state banks were invited to do so.

Although a Federal Reserve Board based in Washington was formed to exercise some unifying control, the reality of the first twenty years of Federal Reserve operations was that real power resided in the boards of the district banks. Until his death in 1928, the most influential individual in the system was Benjamin Strong, head of the Federal Reserve Bank of New York, rather than any member of the Federal Reserve Board in Washington. Strong, working with Montagu Norman, governor of the Bank of England, kept interest rates low in the United States during the 1920s in order to prevent a further drain of gold from London to New York and a weakening of

Britain's financial stability. Strong was, as his biographer credits him, "a principal architect of world monetary reconstruction after World War I," but his policies also had the effect of stimulating stock speculation here with obviously disastrous consequences in 1929.[35]

At the beginning of the 1920s, there were more than thirty thousand commercial banks in the United States, two-thirds of them state chartered. The majority were of modest size, with assets of less than $1 million, and were located in smaller towns and communities. Actually, the number of banks declined by almost six thousand during the 1920s. One explanation lay in the plight of American agriculture, which was in serious depression ten years before the rest of the nation. The agricultural hard times caused problems for rural bankers, and the decade was marked by a high rate of failure among midwestern and southern banks.

The decline in the number of banks was also caused by the prevailing merger movement in American business. A trend toward concentration appeared in banking as it had in other industries. From 1926 to 1929, for example, bank mergers occurred at the rate of five hundred a year, as bankers sought to attain real or imagined economies of scale and match the increasing size of their business customers.

Although the overall number of banks was dropping, the concept of branch banking became increasingly popular with expansion-minded managers. It was not a nationwide phenomenon. Some states still prohibited banks from spawning branches or, at least, limited their freedom to do so. But in states such as California, where there were few or no legal obstacles, the response was often spectacular. The Bank of America offers the most dramatic example.

Its founder, Amadeo Peter Giannini, was the son of an Italian immigrant, and, at nineteen, he was a partner in his father's produce firm. In 1904, he started the Bank of Italy to serve small businessmen and the workers of San Francisco. By 1918 he had extended his operation to include a chain of twenty-four branch banks stretching southward to Los Angeles, and, when California's economy boomed in the 1920s because of motion pictures, oil, and real estate, Giannini expanded even faster. Through the acquisition of other banks and the opening of more branches, his now renamed Bank of America operated at 453 locations in 1929. Giannini also formed the Transamerica Corporation in 1928 as a holding company for the real estate, insurance, and other financial ventures in which he and his associates were involved.

If the 1920s were troubled times for many bankers, the depression years were absolutely disastrous. Nine thousand banks closed their doors between 1930 and 1933, four thousand in 1932 alone. Nothing demonstrated the depth of the crisis more than Franklin Roosevelt's declaration, one day after his inauguration in March 1933, of a Bank Holiday. All banking operations were shut down until federal authorities could examine and certify as sound each institution in the country.

Banks were faced with a liquidity dilemma. They had to hoard enough reserves to meet any panicky public demands for currency that might occur, but, in order to do so, they had to sell off their securities holdings at depressed prices (thus adding to the downward spiral of the stock market) and contract the extension of credit to their hard-pressed customers. Banks did not receive significant help until the New Deal.

The Reconstruction Finance Corporation (RFC), which began under Herbert Hoover but was broadened in scope by Roosevelt, made loans to, and purchased the bonds of, many banks to keep them afloat. The Banking Act of 1933 eased the fears of the average bank customer by creating the Federal Deposit Insurance Corporation to guarantee deposits up to an original maximum of $2,500. No single legislative step did more to restore calm and reduce the likelihood of further panics.

The Banking Act of 1933 also prohibited commercial banks from simultaneously engaging in investment banking. During the previous decade, a number of the larger commercial banks formed investment affiliates, wholly owned subsidiaries that underwrote new securities issues and retailed the shares to an avid public. In this way, bankers took advantage of the rampaging bull market on the Wall Street exchanges. But some publicized unethical practices of a few affiliates and a general feeling that mixing commercial and investment banking was not in the public interest brought about their permanent separation.

Two years later, the Federal Reserve System was strengthened by further legislation. The Banking Act of 1935 granted more authority to the Federal Reserve Board, now renamed the Board of Governors. The autonomy of the district banks was reduced, and new powers were given to the Board as a means of forestalling repetitions of 1929–1933.

Savings and loan associations also fared poorly in the 1930s. These institutions had enjoyed considerable growth during the preceding ten years because of a surge in real estate and construction. With the onset of the depression, however, their heavy commitments in home mortgages—at a time when many Americans found it impossible to meet the required payments—devastated the industry. Moreover, a persistent withdrawal of savings deposits by unemployed or underemployed workers compounded the associations' difficulties. Even with help from the RFC, a new Federal Home Loan Bank System, and the insuring of deposits by the Federal Savings and Loan Insurance Corporation (formed in 1934), there were still five thousand fewer associations in 1940 than in 1929.

Insurance in an Urban Age

The insurance industry prior to the 1840s was dominated almost exclusively, as we have seen, by companies offering fire and marine hazard protection. There was no significant comparable interest in or demand for life insurance. That fact caused Benjamin Franklin to comment earlier: "It is a strange anomaly that men should be careful to insure their houses, their ships, their merchandise and yet neglect to insure their lives, surely the most important of all to their families and more subject to loss."[36] But that situation was beginning to change dramatically in the years just before and after the Civil War.

Certainly a key factor was the increasingly urban nature of American society, with its reduced devotion to the venerable tradition of agrarian individualism. Just as important, though, was the establishment of a group of vigorous young companies that were exclusively concerned with life underwriting. These companies were able, by means of their aggressive marketing tactics, to successfully remold the way most Americans viewed financial protection.

In the eighteenth century, widows and orphans were informally assisted by friends and neighbors, but in the following century the companies fostered the idea that their policies offered a superior approach. An insurance publication in 1873, for instance, argued thus: "If it were practicable, no system of assurance would be so complete as a common brotherhood. But that which seems to our

moral nature so desirable a consummation is surely never to be realized on earth."[37] The premise was clear—rather than trust the world,
trust the company.

The new insurance firms that came into being in the 1840s and
later were mainly mutual companies. The characteristic principle
under which they were organized was ownership by their own pol-
icyholders, and they were thus dependent upon premium payments
for their working capital. Therefore, to secure the steady cash flow
needed to maintain profitable operations, the companies advertised
extensively in mass circulation periodicals and employed legions of
energetic, ambitious agents who were paid generous commissions
and bonuses on the policies they sold.

At the beginning of the 1840s, there was only a handful of firms
writing a small amount of life insurance. But by the end of the decade
there were nearly fifty companies in the business and some $200
million in policies were in force. The largest single share was gar-
nered by Mutual Life of New York, founded by Morris Robinson in
1843. Even greater growth was to come after the Civil War with the
introduction of "industrial" life insurance.

A British innovation, industrial insurance was designed to tap the
meager savings of those millions of working-class families who could
not afford standard policies. Premiums were collected in small change
as low as ten cents per week by company agents calling door-to-door.
Policies carried very modest face values, and required no health
examinations. The concept was first implemented in the United States
by the Prudential Friendly Society, later the Prudential Insurance
Company of America, which sold its first policies in 1875.

The Prudential was organized by a former Yale University student,
John Fairfield Dryden. He had made a careful study of the British
system and applied the techniques to the American market. Within
fifteen years his company had well over $100 million in policies on
the books, and in 1896 it launched an advertising campaign featuring
a now-famous trademark theme (devised by copywriters at the J.
Walter Thompson agency), "Prudential Has the Strength of Gibraltar." Dryden was elected to the United States Senate from New
Jersey in 1901 and died in 1911. The Prudential example was quickly
copied by other firms, most successfully by the Metropolitan Life
Insurance and John Hancock companies, which also began to concentrate upon industrial insurance. By 1910 Metropolitan was the

country's largest insurer, and had some $2 billion worth of policies in force.

As insurance companies mushroomed in size, their economic power swelled as well. By investing their accumulated premiums in everything from real estate mortgages to railroad and manufacturing stocks, the companies developed close ties with the major Wall Street investment banking houses for whom they became prime customers. As a result, reformers and muckraking journalists of the early twentieth century claimed large insurance firms were very much a part of the so-called Money Trust, the privileged cabal of New York financial potentates who were thought to dominate the nation's capital resources. Moreover, mounting evidence of questionable practices on the part of insurance organizations in their marketing and accounting operations also led to widespread calls for governmental corrective action.

But if any such action was to be undertaken, it would necessarily come at the state rather than the federal level. In an 1868 decision of the United States Supreme Court, *Paul v. Virginia*, the justices had ruled the insurance business was not interstate commerce. Hence later legislation, such as the Sherman Act, could not be brought to bear, and the states were thus required to assume the regulatory lead.

The first important steps came appropriately in the state of New York. An acrimonious and very public feud between the management and the principal stockholders of the Equitable Life Assurance Society led to the governor naming a special investigating body headed by State Senator William W. Armstrong in 1905. The Armstrong Commission, with its chief counsel, Charles Evans Hughes, asking the probing questions that would soon bring him to national prominence, uncovered a mass of detail on general wrongdoing in the insurance industry.

Despite opposition from the major companies, the recommendations for reform made by the Armstrong Commission were eventually enacted by the New York state legislature, and many were then followed by other states. As Harold F. Williamson has said of the commission, its work "led to a housecleaning in the industry that marked the coming of age of the life insurance business. It not only strengthened state insurance supervision but also provided the legal and ethical foundation for the safe and conservative growth of life insurance."[38]

Accident insurance in the United States had its origins in the Civil War period. The first policies were offered by the Travelers Insurance Company of Hartford, Connecticut, in 1863 as protection against railroad hazards. With the coming of the twentieth century, however, automobile insurance soon became a critical need for American drivers. It was in 1912 that James Scott Kemper sold to a customer of his Lumbermen's Mutual Casualty Company what was likely the original motor vehicle liability policy. He set the premium at twice the rate normally charged for a horse-drawn vehicle. Eventually, even more successful in writing this type of insurance was George Jacob Mecherle, who began State Farm Mutual in 1922. Originally concentrating on selling low-cost policies to midwestern farmers, his organization gradually broadened its market until it became, before his death in 1951, the country's largest auto insurer.

In summary, it should be emphasized again that the insurance industry has served two equally powerful functions in the American economy. It has provided necessary protection for individuals and companies against misfortune, and it has been a highly important channel for the flow of investment funds to capital-hungry enterprises. In this latter role, the extent of the industry's potential can be seen from the fact that in 1939, for example, the assets of private insurance companies in the United States constituted some 18 percent of the total assets of all the nation's financial intermediaries. That percentage was exceeded in 1939 only by the commercial banks of the country.

The Business Universe

Along with the surge in the overall population of the United States, the size of the business community grew significantly in the twentieth century. In 1900 there were about 1 million firms; in 1930, 3 million; and after the Second World War, an even larger total. While historical attention inevitably spotlights the progress of those mighty core companies that formed the cutting edge of American industrialization, the others should not be lost sight of in the process.

Thomas C. Cochran has identified three levels of businesses that have coexisted with the corporate giants in the current century.[39] The most basic and the smallest are those myriad proprietorships and partnerships that are owner-managed and employ no outside labor. Unfortunately, the gloomy statistics indicate that the prospects for such "mom and pop" operations are shaky at best, since a majority do not survive two years.

At the next higher level are the firms that require the services of twenty to fewer employees. In 1930, they comprised about two-thirds of the business universe in terms of the total number of enterprises then active. The third level, according to Cochran, are the medium-sized businesses. They counted about 100,000 companies by the end of the 1920s. Employing between twenty and a thousand workers, their owners were, in Cochran's words, "the backbone of chambers of commerce, manufacturers' associations, and service clubs, and some joined with self-employed lawyers in political activities."[40] For many Americans still today, these medium-sized entrepreneurs and not corporate bureaucrats in massive organizations are the quintessential business models for emulation.

CHAPTER THIRTEEN

The Maturing of Corporate Administration

WHETHER most Americans wished it or not, the twentieth century ushered in an age of practiced business administration. Generally, our largest corporate organizations were now professionally managed by teams of career executives who held little or no stock in their companies. They had achieved their positions because of their administrative talents rather than any vested ownership interests. It was the administrators of these modern "managerial enterprises" who were called upon to formulate the business strategies needed to meet the fast-rising challenges of diversification, multinational operations, depression, war, and evolving public demands and expectations.

In previous chapters, we have referred to the business strategies that various firms have employed, either successfully or unsuccessfully. We should say a bit more at this point about the general concept of strategic design in management and will adopt the definition suggested by Thomas J. McNichols in *Policy-Making and Executive Action.* McNichols defines strategy in the context of business as: "The science and art of employing the skills and resources of an enterprise to attain its basic objectives under the most advantageous conditions."[1]

The strategy of a firm can be determined either by conscious decision or by simply drifting along in the stream of customary practice. The strategy of drift is not a true policy. An explicit management decision, on the other hand, sets basic guidelines for the future and implements this root strategy through a series of subsequent steps. In this process, the firm commits its resources and skills, appraises the effectiveness of its performance in achieving the desired objectives, modifies specific operations, or even, if necessary, reformulates the original strategic design.

Establishing overall strategy is an elite function that is reserved for the highest levels of management. In theory, top management alone has the advantage of perspective and can view the company, no matter how large, as a single coordinated unit. In practice, however, executive officers are sometimes overly wedded to the functional specialties (sales or production or finance, for example) in which they had spent a large portion of their careers. This "functional emotionalism" may impede effective decision making. The ideal top managers are those who feel no special allegiance to particular functions or specialties.

In this chapter, we will look at a number of strategic decisions that have been made within managerial enterprises in this century. These include decisions to diversify operations by producing entirely new products for the domestic market, to expand overseas and take on a multinational character, and to react creatively to unexpected developments in whatever form they might take.

Professionalizing American Management

The career executive was not a new figure in American business. He appeared as early as the beginning of the industrial revolution in the United States, but in the twentieth century he truly came into his own. As the number of managers in large businesses multiplied, a substantial degree of specialization also developed. Functions such as accounting, finance, and marketing now offered attractive career opportunities to men and women who could acquire expertise in one of those areas. No longer was the ladder of success limited to the management of production alone. Specialization in turn promoted professionalization, as businessmen adopted many of the trappings of such fields as law and medicine. These included the formation of professional societies and associations, the publishing of journals and other periodicals, and the establishment of schools of business within universities to teach the new administrative techniques.

Those professional groups that existed by 1929 included, among others, the American Association of Public Accountants (later the American Institute of Accountants), the Society for the Promotion of the Science of Management (later the Taylor Society, and, still later, the Society for the Advancement of Management), and the American Management Association. Professional periodicals abounded, such as *Accounting Review*, the *Journal of Marketing*, and *Management and Administration*. And an active movement began during the early twentieth century that was aimed at introducing both individual courses and entire schools of professional management into American colleges and universities.

During the preceding century, the teaching of business methods was confined to private commercial schools in larger cities (for a short time in 1855, John Rockefeller attended one in Cleveland that still exists today) and to classes offered in some public high schools. That pattern began to change in 1881, when a Philadelphia financier-manufacturer, Joseph Wharton, donated $100,000 to the University of Pennsylvania to endow the first collegiate school of business. He intended to provide students with "a training suitable for those who intend to engage in business or to undertake the management of property." By 1895 the Wharton School of Finance and Commerce offered a four-year curriculum that included courses in accounting, banking, insurance, production, and "private secretaryship."[2] In 1898, the University of Chicago and the University of California added similar programs. Two years later, the Amos Tuck School of Administration and Finance at Dartmouth College offered the first postgraduate training in management. It preceded the Harvard Graduate School of Business Administration, which opened in 1908. Altogether, thirty university-level business schools were operating by 1911.

The work of these schools was supplemented by the research and writings of a variety of theorists, of whom Frederick Taylor was only one. Another was Alexander H. Church whose book, *The Science and Practice of Management* (1914), was the first attempt by an American to explore the principles of management and to relate them to a coordinated whole. In France, Henri Fayol addressed the same issues in a comprehensive theory of management. But his major work, *General and Industrial Management* (1916), was not published in the United States until 1949, and Fayol's ideas, although important, were not widely known in America until then.

As industrial stocks began to be publicly and widely traded, many observers also described the increasing separation of corporate ownership from actual control in managerial enterprises, especially after the publication in 1933 of a study by two Columbia University faculty members, Adolf A. Berle and Gardiner C. Means, entitled *The Modern Corporation and Private Property*.[3] Their depiction of the diffusion of stock ownership in major corporations and the rise of a new class of professional managers captured popular attention, but their comments on other implications of managerial enterprises were equally thought-provoking. Berle and Means maintained that control of a large firm was no longer exercised solely in the interests of its owners, as the classical business ideology had always ordained. That classical view emphasized profit maximization and the unrestrained freedom of owners to do with their property as they saw fit.

Instead, a new managerial ideology manifested itself. Career executives in top policy-making positions now viewed their responsibilities more broadly; rather than a single-minded dedication to the interests of stockholders, they saw their role as managers as trustees for several interest groups. In 1923, in an article in *Management Review*, this emerging philosophy was summed up: "We are beginning to regard those who occupy executive positions in industry as having something in the nature of quasi-public responsibility. The war merely emphasized a tendency to consider those in charge of various industries as trustees not merely for the owners of the particular industry but for the national community as well."[4]

Corporate executives were now expected to balance several competing interests—investors, employees, customers, society in general—and to view business problems in a broader perspective than the entrepreneurs of the past. The stress was placed on longer-range policies of steady, reasoned growth, not on maximizing short-run profits. It also meant that the new professional managers were often less aggressive risk-takers and more inclined to make decisions that promised not to disrupt a pattern of smooth and orderly development. The term "industrial statesman," heard on many occasions in the 1920s, symbolized this new managerial ideology.

Departments and Divisions—Administering Modern Business

In one of the seminal books in American business historiography, Alfred Chandler wrote: "The historical record certainly does suggest that structure does follow strategy, and that the different types of expansion brought different administrative needs requiring different administrative organizations.''⁵ This interrelationship between what Chandler has identified as strategy and structure explains to a considerable extent the background of the two main plans of organization that have characterized the administration of large business firms in the present century.

The first of the two to develop was the centralized departmental structure, in which activities such as purchasing, production, sales, and finance are each treated as large single-function departments in an integrated firm. Members of the du Pont family used this administrative form to organize the operations of a large company. In 1902, three young du Pont cousins—Coleman, Alfred, and Pierre (who has been discussed in a previous chapter in connection with General Motors)—took over the century-old family business. Under their guidance, competitors were quickly bought out and a new corporation was formed, E. I. Du Pont de Nemours Powder Company, that consolidated the old firm and its recent acquisitions. This new firm controlled about two-thirds of the explosives industry in the United States.

In order to smooth the integration process, various centralized departments were formed, each headed by a vice-president who also served as a member of the company's executive committee. The committee's members thus had twin responsibilities; they managed their own departments, and they set grand strategy for the entire enterprise. In addition to this departmental structure, the du Pont cousins and their associates installed the elaborate accounting and control systems that were later introduced at General Motors.

But the structure contained a flaw. The ability of the functional vice-presidents to face in two directions—toward the departments for which they were responsible and toward the executive committee of which they were members—often was limited. Functional emotionalism caused them to focus on the day-to-day concerns of running a manufacturing or sales department and to give less thought to long-range planning and policy. They frequently viewed the firm's operations from the vantage point of their own specialty rather than taking a corporation-wide perspective.

Although it was flawed, the centralized departmental structure perfected at Du Pont became a model for other large, integrated industrial corporations. Companies that produce a single line of products still find the form useful today. However, those other firms, which, after 1920, consciously adopted a strategy called diversification, discovered that they had to devise an entirely new structural form if their new policy was to be implemented successfully.

Diversification is the production of dissimilar products by similar processes or the marketing of dissimilar products through the same distribution facilities. One writer has singled out these different types of diversification: (1) internal development—producing new products by utilizing the firm's own special competence in research and technology; (2) acquired technology—the purchase of needed competence by the acquisition of other companies; (3) homogeneous markets—firms that are oriented toward marketing can sell unrelated, nationally advertised and branded consumer goods because of their mass-merchandising expertise; (4) conglomeration—diversification into totally unrelated fields and industries. The last phenomenon began in the 1950s, often because the original business of a company was no longer as profitable as it once had been. In other instances, this diversification was simply empire building or securities manipulation on the part of some hard-charging and ambitious entrepreneur.[6]

The first type of diversification, internal development, created the initial pressures for another administrative form. Du Pont again led the way. The company emerged from the First World War with a vastly expanded production capacity and a greatly increased work force as a result of tremendous wartime demands for explosives. In order to make use of that excess capacity after 1918 when military contracts were canceled, Du Pont embarked upon a program of rapid diversification.

The company moved into artificial leather, chemicals, dyestuffs, paints and varnishes, and rayon, among other fields. But this massive diversification program increased the strain on Du Pont's administrative structure and its officers. Executives with experience in explosives now made decisions about a wide variety of products. Coordination within and between departments became difficult, and the executive committee was soon overwhelmed by the complexity of evaluating the performance of departments that operated in several different fields simultaneously.

Du Pont responded to these problems by developing a decentralized multidivisional organization, the second main structural plan identified by Chandler. Product rather than function now became the cornerstone of the structure. Autonomous, integrated product divisions were created to handle the manufacture and marketing of individual lines. A general corporate office was created that was concerned with appraising the success of the divisions and deciding upon the future allocation of the company's resources in the light of its overall plans. The executives in the general office were relieved of everyday managerial duties in the different divisions. The new form allowed the general-office personnel to concentrate on what can be called strategic responsibilities—such as planning, coordinating, and evaluating—while middle-level managers focused on the operational problems of the self-contained product divisions.

By late 1921 the revamped structure was in place at Du Pont. At the same time, General Motors, under Pierre du Pont and Alfred Sloan, was erecting a remarkably similar structure, though for somewhat different reasons. Thus these two major industrial corporations were the pathbreakers in the development of a far-reaching administrative design. And, clearly, the connection between the two was personified in Pierre du Pont, who engineered the diversification program in his family firm that led to its administrative reorganization, and then later presided over a similar reorganization at General Motors. As his biographers have said of him: "Because he understood and accepted the technological and managerial imperatives of an industrial economy, he created two of the most successful of the nation's modern corporations."[7]

Leadership in diversification was assumed by those large firms that already had a research and technical base established and, in addition, had the financial resources (accumulated profits, primarily) to develop and market new products. Electrical manufacturers such as Westinghouse and General Electric followed Du Pont into diversification by branching out from producers' goods into consumer durables, such as washing machines, refrigerators, and other household appliances. During the 1930s, General Motors began producing airplanes, aircraft engines, diesel locomotives, tractors, and home appliances; and, in the same decade, food companies such as General Mills and Borden's used their existing distribution channels to offer new items to the public.

The Second World War accelerated the trend toward diversification. Meeting wartime demands for sophisticated electronics equipment, synthetic rubber, and other defense-related products fitted companies with the skills, resources, and appetite for pursuing new civilian opportunities after 1945; and the depression-free years of the following decades blessed diversification strategies with success.

The favorable results had the effect of institutionalizing research and development (R&D) as key elements in a modern corporation's plans for future growth.

In order to accommodate the new strategic plans, corporations increasingly adopted the multidivisional structure pioneered by Du Pont and General Motors in the early 1920s. In Chandler's words: "By the nineteen fifties diversification and decentralization had become the compelling fashion in American industry."[8]

Business in the Multinational Arena

A number of American companies also extended their operations geographically by crossing national frontiers. Even though the United States was a net debtor nation before 1914—that is, there was more total foreign investment in the country than Americans invested outside their borders—American businessmen and investors were committing an increasing volume of dollars in other areas of the world.

In 1914, the foreign investments of American residents totaled $3.5 billion, but that sum should be divided into two separate categories. Approximately $1 billion was in "portfolio" investments— the ownership of foreign securities. The remainder, some $2.5 billion, represented "direct" investments—the establishment of foreign branches, subsidiaries, or similar business units by American corporations. Direct investments meant that American companies acquired an international, or, as it would later be called, a multinational, character.

At first, progress was slow. A small number of American firms engaged in foreign ventures prior to 1914, and those that did tended to concentrate upon the two closest neighbors of the United States, Canada and Mexico. Over half of the direct foreign investment in 1914 was lodged in those two nations. Mira Wilkins has pointed to a significant fact, however. The total amount invested in international activities by American business in 1914 represented about 7 percent of the gross national product. Fifty years later, when the absolute number of dollars invested was about twenty times as much as in 1914, the portion of GNP was still the same 7 percent.[9]

There is general agreement that Singer Sewing Machine was America's first multinational company. It established branch sales offices and, later, factories in the British Isles and on the European continent during the 1860s, and, by the following decade, Singer sold over half its machines abroad. Other large American corporations, including Standard Oil, International Harvester, Eastman Kodak, American Tobacco, and Westinghouse Electric, soon followed the Singer example. A firm usually sold its products initially through independent agents in foreign countries; then later employed its own salaried sales managers and established its own sales office; and finally erected a manufacturing or assembly plant to meet the demands of a foreign market.

Some corporate managers expanded overseas because they believed the potential of the home market was nearly exhausted. The depression of the 1890s, in particular, fostered a growing belief that the nation was destined to have a chronic overproduction problem unless new trading opportunities were developed.

Many businessmen looked to the Orient and especially to the 400 million potential customers in China. Dreams of the great China market proved to be a persistent economic mirage. H. Wayne Morgan has aptly commented that enthusiasm outran the facts of the situation: "Few of the alleged 400,000,000 customers lived within the reach of traders. No transportation system penetrated the vast back-country. . . . Western goods were not suited to oriental needs. . . . And however much they might want to buy, the Chinese were simply poor."[10] Exports to China still only accounted for 6 percent of total American exports in 1914.

The First World War ended America's debtor-nation status. As European-held investments in United States companies were sold to finance the war, and as Americans made new portfolio investments, primarily in private loans to the Allied powers, the United States moved into a net-creditor position for the first time. Total American international investment reached $7 billion by 1919, more than twice the level of foreign capital invested in the United States. Direct American investment accounted for nearly $4 billion of that total.

New foreign interests were usually in less-developed areas of the world, especially Latin America, where oil and an assortment of minerals (copper, tin, nitrates) attracted attention. During the 1920s, direct investment by American business continued its climb to a peak of over $7 billion in 1929, and South America now replaced Europe and Canada as the largest recipient of United States capital. The movement of South America into first place signaled that American companies increasingly sought supply sources rather than new markets.

The depression years after 1929 obviously brought a sharp contraction in the foreign activities of American business. Some overseas operations were shut down or sold, and plans for future projects were canceled. Those few new investments that were made were usually motivated by an attempt to circumvent Canadian and European tariffs that were erected in retaliation for our own highly protectionist Smoot-Hawley tariff of 1930. By building factories in those countries, firms evaded tariffs and products remained competitive, since they were technically not imports.

However, open hostility to a flood of goods produced by American businesses overseas had already surfaced. In England, for instance, a "Buy British" campaign was well under way even before 1930. As Mira Wilkins has observed: "U.S. companies were resented for their size, their power (or potential power), their profits (which were assumed to be enormous), and for their just being alien enterprises."[11]

Despite the significant overseas involvement of American firms prior to the Second World War, the modern multinational corporation (MNC) is largely a post-1945 phenomenon. Several factors accounted for its postwar appearance. One was the willingness of the principal trading nations of the world to adopt freer commercial and investment policies and to abandon the isolationist economic practices of the 1920s and 1930s. The recent breakup of the old colonial empires also spurred demands from the now-independent countries of Asia and Africa for commodities and capital equipment that an enterprising MNC would be ready to supply. Moreover, the process of rebuilding the war-ravaged European continent and Japan provided an additional opportunity for MNC investment.

American corporations were in the best position to take advantage of these developments. They had seen massive increases in their capacity and output during the 1939–1945 years. In meeting the wartime needs of the United States and our Allies, American business had not only earned handsome profits, it had generated whole new product lines and technologies born out of the conflict itself. These could now be marketed for peacetime uses.

Furthermore, with the gradual emergence of the Cold War and the perceived threat from Soviet expansionism, governmental policy in the United States became directly supportive of American Business's international operations. The Commerce and State Departments and new federal instruments, such as the Agency for International Development, which made loans available to United States companies ready to invest in less-developed countries, all endorsed the principle that the solid presence of private American economic interests abroad was in the national public interest as well. During the 1950s, especially, encouraged by a friendly Eisenhower administration in Washington, overseas direct investment spurted ahead. Its book value in 1960 quadrupled the 1940 figure, and by 1970 the value was twice that of 1960.

The Case of Middle East Oil

Leading the way in multinational operations after the Second World War were technology-based firms and resource companies. Petroleum was one case in point. In 1945 American oil corporations were being drawn to the vast production potential of the Middle East and the looming opportunity to replace waning British influence in the region. In the process, they would receive backing from officials in Washington, who often viewed the major United States–owned international oil companies as quasi-partners in attaining American foreign policy objectives.[12]

Prior to Pearl Harbor, the Western Hemisphere had been the center of the world's petroleum activity, as it accounted for 75 percent of all production. The United States alone both produced and consumed 60 percent of the world output. The Middle East in the 1930s, despite its enormous reserves, was still just a minor player in the oil scene.

But the Second World War was to change that picture rather dramatically. As a result of the physical destruction of their coal fields during the war years, European recovery depended upon a new reliance on imported oil. Furthermore, the postwar period was also expected to see rapid growth in the energy demands of worldwide air and automobile transportation, thereby adding even greater pressures on existing Western Hemisphere production. Middle East oil offered the most obvious solution.

In the Middle East in 1945, Great Britain was the leading producer (80 percent), primarily through its Anglo-Iranian Oil Company (later renamed British Petroleum). United States firms, on the other hand, could claim just 15 percent of the region's output. The only significant concession held by American companies was in Saudi Arabia, where Standard Oil of California and Texaco were united in a joint venture formed in the 1930s as the California-Arabian Standard Oil Company. The real development of the concession was delayed, however, by the onset of the war. In 1946 the joint venture was broadened by the inclusion of two more American companies, Jersey Standard and Socony (New York Standard), and the enterprise had been retitled the Arabian-American Oil Company (ARAMCO). It was ARAMCO that constructed the 1,000-mile-long Trans-Arabian Pipe Line to Lebanon, completed in 1950, to facilitate oil shipments to Europe.

In a geopolitical sense, though, there was an even more significant joint venture than ARAMCO, one that joined the major American oil firms with the United States government. Under its unwritten terms, it became the companies' responsibility to produce the low-cost oil necessary for European postwar recovery. Since expanded production necessarily required new marketing and refining facilities in Western Europe too, that meant substantially increased foreign investment on the part of the companies. The record thus shows that the bulk of the overall capital outflow American corporations sent abroad in the immediate postwar years was the result of petroleum industry activity.

At the same time, it became Washington's responsibility to offer the industry diplomatic support and military protection, if need be, against possible Arab radicalism and Soviet ambitions in the Middle East. In Iran, for instance, a nationalist government under Premier Mohammed Mossadegh came to power in 1951 and immediately confiscated the Anglo-Iranian Oil property and operations there. In retaliation, Great Britain organized a boycott of nationalized Iranian oil; the United States assisted and demanded that Mossadegh compensate the British or return the property. When Mossadegh, unwilling and unable to do either, indicated he might seek Soviet aid, the CIA backed a coup that toppled him and installed a royalist government in 1953. A year later, an Iranian Consortium was fashioned that received managerial control of the oil fields. While Iran retained the title, actual authority was now in the hands of the companies making up the consortium. And though Iran had been a British preserve prior to 1951, the consortium was marked by the now equal participation of the major American firms.

At approximately this same time, the United States government rendered the oil companies another significant service. It agreed to treat the royalty payments made by them to the various Arab states as the equivalent of income tax payments to Washington. The effect was to greatly reduce their United States tax liability, while simultaneously serving as a form of unofficial foreign aid program designed to help keep the Arab states in the pro-Western orbit. The companies were thus able to offer generous royalty terms to the rulers of those states without suffering any great loss of profits themselves. The tax credit arrangement also provided a tremendous incentive for American firms to invest in even more production facilities outside the United States.

For a quarter-century after the Second World War, the system built around the expansion of Middle East oil production seemed to provide an era of stability. Prices were relatively low and supplies were abundant. This international oil system was presided over by the so-called Seven Sisters, seven giant, often interlocked, firms—Jersey Standard (today named Exxon), Socony (today named Mobil), Standard Oil of California, Texaco, Gulf, British Petroleum (the former Anglo-Iranian Oil Company), and Royal Dutch/Shell. The first five, of course, were and are American.

Only gradually did the host nations begin to think in terms of their own joint action to deal more effectively with the Seven Sisters and with the oil-consuming countries in which they were headquartered. Though it was little noticed at the time, representatives from the Arab states plus Venezuela met at Baghdad in 1960 and established the Organization of Petroleum Exporting Countries (OPEC). Ironically, as Edward W. Chester has pointed out, "it would appear that the cartel policies of the major oil companies in the Middle East during the 1950s and 1960s served as models for the oil-producing countries."[13] The world would hear much more from OPEC during the 1970s.

Structure and Debate

Any administrative decision to engage in worldwide operations meant the adoption of a strategy that necessarily had structural ramifications. It was logical for corporate managers, soon after embarking upon foreign investment policies, to form international divisions within their organizations to supervise the overseas business. But as the volume of that business grew and as product lines proliferated, the single international division structure proved inadequate and too isolated in many cases.

Therefore, in corporations in which multiple domestic product divisions were already in place, foreign operations frequently were turned over to those divisions, which now became global in their responsibilities. An alterative to that trend was seen in some corporations whose businesses were focused upon specific commodities, such as petroleum. In those instances, the pattern was to set up geographical area divisions, of which one was the United States, headed by area managers reporting directly to top management at corporate headquarters. Whatever the structural choice, however, the multinational companies faced the same fundamental imperative, "the simultaneous need to be globally competitive and nationally responsive," a very delicate balancing act.[14]

As more and more American firms pursued a multinational strategy after the Second World War, they began to succeed rather too well for many Europeans. Of the $78 billion in United States direct investment in 1970, fully a quarter of the total was in Europe, and that was regarded by concerned observers there as a disturbing situation. In a widely read 1968 book, *The American Challenge*, French journalist and political figure Jean Jacques Servan-Schreiber warned his countrymen and a general European audience of the formidable economic invasion from the United States. While the threat may have seemed genuine at the time, in fact the impressive performance of American multinationals was fostering eager emulation by non-American corporations. The result, one analysis has determined, was that by "somewhere in the mid-1970s the total overseas investments from firms outside the United States surpassed the foreign holdings of American MNCs. In succession, the major firms of a resurgent Europe and, more recently, Japan, matched and then overtook the foreign stake of U.S. MNCs."[15]

Indeed, the intervening years have left Japan, now a global economic force, in much the same position within the United States as Servan-Schreiber had envisioned America in his own country twenty years ago. A leading business periodical recently reported on a "wave of Japanese investment . . . sweeping across America."[16] The evidence was not hard to find. Today Sony manufactures television sets in San Diego and compact disks in Indiana; Honda assembles automobiles in Ohio and Nissan does the same in Tennessee; and Japanese bankers are providing financing for everything from floundering American steel companies to ailing city governments in Middle America.

Yet, while "Japan, USA" has become a heatedly discussed topic, the modern multinational enterprise raises other conspicuous issues for public debate too. The MNCs have been described as "firms of truly cosmopolitan outlook, not just national firms operating abroad."[17] As such, they are sometimes seen as spawning a revolutionary type of corporate manager. One best-selling critique has claimed that the MNCs have given birth to "the first entrepreneurial class with the practical potential to operate a planetary enterprise." These new "global managers," according to the critics, are demanding "the right to transcend the nation-state, and in the process, to transform it."[18] Whether such hyperbole has any real substance remains a matter of conjecture and debate. Certainly, the argument over the multinational corporation and its role in the American and the world economy promises to continue for some time to come.

Business and Public Policy, 1917–1945

During the last three-quarters of a century, unforeseen events and new pressures have brought American business under much closer public control than ever before in the nation's history. While the United States has hardly become a command economy in the Soviet or socialist sense, it has moved significantly from the unregulated marketplace model of Adam Smith. The term "mixed economy" is commonly used now to describe the contemporary American system. The mixture is the interrelationship between the private free-enterprise sector and the public governmental sector. Within the past seventy-five years, there has been substantial growth in the latter, both in terms of its share of the country's gross national product and in the novel regulatory responsibilities that it has assumed.

Two causes have chiefly propelled government into taking on those responsibilities. One has been the dictates of two world wars. The second has been domestic economic crisis—the calamitous depression of the 1930s and periodic painful recessions. Other factors have contributed to the expansion of the public sector too, but they have not matched in impact the twin shocks of war and economic crisis.

In order to better understand the mixed economy climate in which American business lives and works today, it is necessary to discuss how each of the shocks has contributed to the evolving, complicated relationship between government and the business community.

THE LESSONS OF ALMOST TOTAL WAR, 1917–1918

The armed conflict fought between the summer of 1914 and the fall of 1918 was much closer to total war than anything mankind had seen before. Because the First World War was more mechanized than any previous struggle among nation-states, it required both a massive industrial effort and considerably greater centralized planning on the part of governments, including that of the United States. It has been estimated, for instance, that the weight of metal fired in just one 1918 offensive in France probably matched the entire amount expended by the Union Army during the Civil War. Such a prodigious consumption of munitions demanded cooperation between government and industry if the production of war supplies was to be at all adequate for the country's needs.

Even before the United States Congress declared war on Germany in April 1917, the economic effect of the war raging in Europe was being felt here. An increasing proportion of the armaments used by the belligerents were coming from American factories. In 1915 Bethlehem Steel received a British ammunition contract worth over $80 million. The next year Du Pont was awarded a $96 million contract for powder. Our overall trade with the Allied Powers alone, which stood at a total of $825 million in 1914, swelled to $3.2 billion in 1916. As a result, the American economy reached the full-employment level months before the United States officially entered the war in 1917.

The country's leaders faced a monumental allocation problem. Existing production facilities were functioning at full capacity, yet the nation faced an immediate need to equip the American armed forces as well as to continue supplying the Allies. In addition, there was an unprecedented civilian demand for consumer goods. Inevitably, the Wilson administration was compelled to step in and provide unparalleled centralized direction of the economy. Over the course of the next year, it proceeded to establish thousands of agencies and offices, usually staffed with "dollar-a-year men" on loan from private enterprise. But their authority and responsibilities frequently conflicted, and effective overall coordination was lacking until a War Industries Board (WIB), chaired by the millionaire Wall Street speculator Bernard M. Baruch, was given powers sufficient to rationalize the mobilization effort.[19]

The scope of WIB orders was staggering to many laissez-faire–minded businessmen. The board, among its many actions, forced manufacturers to reduce the yardage in men's clothing by eliminating some outside pockets, forbade the production of bronze or copper coffins, and banned the use of metal ribs in women's corsets (to conserve steel). It had the power, if necessary, to seize a factory when a company's management seemed to be impeding the war effort, and to operate the facility in the national interest. When steel executives proved recalcitrant on prices, Baruch threatened them with such a stroke. After the war, the arch-conservative Elbert Gary, United States Steel's board chairman, claimed "subversive influences in the government had sought to nationalize the steel industry as the first step toward undoing America's free enterprise system." The unforgiving Gary saw Baruch and the WIB as that sinister influence.[20]

Actually, most of the business community probably approved of the board's intervention as necessary in order to match available supplies with wartime demands, especially if profits were assured in the process. As an example, the WIB persuaded the Du Pont organization to construct and operate a huge government smokeless powder plant near Nashville. The company took on the assignment with a negotiated guarantee of a $2 million compensation over and above its costs. At the end of the war, the Old Hickory complex, as the company was known, which had employed 30,000 workers in 1918, was simply closed down, even though building it represented an $85 million expenditure of public funds. Most war contracts were let on this cost-plus basis, causing one industrialist to comment somewhat ruefully: "We are all making more money out of this war than the average human being ought to."[21]

The centralized decision making of the period was undoubtedly necessary if a rapid mobilization of the nation's resources were to be achieved. Even so, America's conversion to a wartime footing was still incomplete when the Armistice ended the fighting in November 1918. Nevertheless, in the general euphoria of the victory over Germany, there was a tendency on the part of Wilson administration officials and businessmen alike to exaggerate the effectiveness of the collaboration between government and private enterprise that the country had just witnessed.

Woodrow Wilson's personal commitment was to a traditional competitive marketplace, and he tolerated the economic controls his administration exercised only as emergency measures. Within weeks of the Armistice, therefore, he had already abolished most of them, despite the strong urging from a number of his own advisors to continue the system during demobilization and reconversion to a peacetime economy.

The memory of the unprecedented economic structure of the First World War persisted, however, long after the special boards, offices, and quasi-public corporations that were its instruments had ceased to exist. Many would reappear in modified form as New Deal agencies during the 1930s, often with the same individuals serving again in positions similar to those they had held less than two decades before. Given the urgency of the crisis in 1933, it was entirely reasonable for those faced with the challenge of surmounting the debacle of the 1929 stock market crash and the ensuing depression to look back to the last emergency the country had weathered for lessons to be followed. In that way, the legacy of the First World War became a key element in the evolution of business-government relations in the United States.

THE NEW DEAL AND BUSINESS HOSTILITY

Franklin Roosevelt entered the White House in March 1933 prepared to fight a war. As he described the crisis facing American society that year: "The whole of the country has a common enemy; industry, agriculture, capital, labor, are all engaged in fighting it. Just as in 1917 we are seeking to pull in harness; just as in 1917, horses that kick over the traces will have to be put in a corral." The analogy to the First World War experience permeated the thinking and the economic strategy of many Roosevelt administration officials. Historian William E. Leuchtenburg wrote: "The commandants of New Deal agencies thought of themselves as soldiers in a war against depression."[22]

For FDR in 1933, the concept of a nation pulling "in harness" meant the teaming of all economic sectors, with needed direction coming from Washington. It meant no sector, and particularly not the business community, would be singled out as the scapegoat for the calamitous circumstances in which the country was mired. Roosevelt would not come into office deliberately seeking to score political points off business leadership's failure to maintain America's economic equilibrium. Rather, in those early months he was as anxious to hold the allegiance of businessmen as any other group in society.

Because of his desire to create an all-class alliance, the first two years of the Roosevelt New Deal have been characterized as "interest-group democracy." The president would be an "honest broker" mediating between the various interest groups of the nation, offering something to each.[23] Business was very much a part of Roosevelt's coalition, sharing a position of equality with labor and agriculture in his mind.

Why, therefore, if business was represented in this team attack on the depression, should virulent hostility develop between business and the Roosevelt New Dealers to the extent that it did in the 1930s? Part of the answer lies in the preceding decade. During the 1920s, businessmen enjoyed a position of supremacy in the economic hierarchy and in the attentions of the federal government. Indeed, the Republican presidents of the 1920s have been said to have conducted "single-interest administrations," with that one interest being business prosperity. At the time, the *Wall Street Journal* had observed: "never before, here or anywhere else, has a government been so completely fused with business."[24]

Operating from such a preferred position during the Republican era of the 1920s, it was understandable that business leaders would have difficulty accepting Roosevelt's different concept of their role. Even a standing equal to that of other interest groups in 1933 still embodied a retreat from the preeminence of a few years before. Therefore, despite Roosevelt's references to a "partnership between Government and farming and industry and transportation" and his ringing declaration that "we move as one great team to victory," important business elements gradually began to secede from the New Deal coalition.[25]

The stresses of making the transition from the single-interest policies of the Republican 1920s to FDR's interest-group democracy were sharpened considerably by specific features of the early New Deal program for which many businessmen showed an aversion. The National Industrial Recovery Act of 1933 was the primary weapon of the early New Deal war on the depression. It established the

National Recovery Administration (NRA), which was to supervise the drafting of "codes of fair competition." The over 500 codes, drawn up primarily by business executives from their respective industries, once accepted by NRA officials, bound all firms in the industry to specific practices regarding pricing, output, wages, working conditions, and collective bargaining. Significantly, administration of the NRA was given to General Hugh S. Johnson, an associate of Bernard Baruch on the War Industries Board in 1918.

At another time, the codes might have been regarded as illegal price-fixing and collusive cartel activities. Under the NRA's auspices, though, they were exempt from antitrust action. FDR defended the exemption in a May 1933 "fireside chat" radio speech, saying the antitrust laws were "never intended to encourage the kind of unfair competition that results in long hours, starvation wages, and overproduction."[26]

But much to the dismay of business, one effect of the NRA endeavor seemed to be the encouragement of a growing militancy on the part of unions. Section 7(a) of the act creating the NRA guaranteed labor the right to organize and to bargain collectively through representatives of its own choosing. Further, there was considerable public feeling that small and medium-sized businesses were being unduly penalized by the operations of the NRA codes. The Roosevelt administration was accused of adopting a policy of throwing the neighborhood entrepreneur to the economic wolves in the interest of getting big business to subscribe to the NRA program.

Couple these with other concerns, such as the degree of power and influence supposedly wielded now in Washington by college professors and intellectuals (the conservative *Saturday Evening Post* warned in 1934 that the country was becoming a "laboratory for a small group of professors to try out experiments that bid fair to result in an explosion and a stink"), plus the fact that the crisis of 1933 had passed and the glimmerings of some recovery were appearing upon the horizon, and you have much of the explanation for the rise of business hostility to the New Deal.[27] As 1934 became 1935, the White House found the bridges it had sought to build to business being inexorably dismantled by the growing vehemence of the latter's opposition.

Under pressure from neo-populists on the left, such as Senator Huey Long, under attack from an increasing number of businessmen on the right, and hearing the constant urging of progressives within the administration's own ranks, FDR largely abandoned the all-interest group coalition strategy of 1933–1934 and adopted a more frankly reformist stance. Rhetoric now took on a distinctly anti-business tone. He spoke of "economic royalists" and "privileged princes . . . thirsting for power."[28] And the direction change was made all the easier by Supreme Court decisions voiding key parts of the early New Deal legislative program, including the NRA itself, in May 1935.

Despite business lobbying against their passage, more stringent regulatory measures became law. Examples include the Public Utility Holding Company Act of 1935, intended to break up the pyramided firms that controlled most of the country's electric power; the National Labor Relations Act, a strongly prolabor bill setting up the permanent National Labor Relations Board and seeking to promote an equality of bargaining power between management and workers; banking and securities legislation that tightened governmental oversight in both systems; and a more steeply graduated income taxation schedule that included a tax on corporate profits. A sharp recession in 1937 gave further impetus to this policy change that historians have often called the Second New Deal. The unexpected and politically embarrassing economic slump forced the administration to offer an explanation, and it quickly blamed big business. The New Dealers claimed "administered prices" and a "strike of capital" had caused the recession. They argued that monopolistic pricing decisions of corporations had stymied the recovery, and the business establishment had deliberately chosen not to invest its funds in order to undermine Roosevelt's popular support.

Early in 1938, FDR appointed a colorful, voluble, and energetic Yale Law School professor to head the Antitrust Division of the Justice Department. Thurman Arnold used that post to revitalize what had become a musty backwater within the Washington bureaucracy. Within a year, he doubled the size of the division, and he pumped new life into it by recruiting young and dedicated legal talent to carry on the campaign that he envisioned. He added economists to the staff for the first time, and he made sure the activities of the division were given considerable publicity.

Prosecuting several industries at a time, Arnold focused particularly on protecting consumers and on increasing their purchasing power. He instituted cases against firms in the aluminum, automobile, construction, movie, petroleum, and shoe industries. Unlike many antitrusters, however, he found nothing essentially holy about small-scale enterprises, and he prosecuted small firms that violated the antitrust laws as well as large ones. His approach was more pragmatic than ideological, and he was a distinct puzzle to many observers. A 1939 magazine article said of him: "He enjoys the distinction of being the only New Dealer who is also an Elk, and very likely the only Elk who is also an iconoclast."[29]

Arnold was not predictable. One historian has written about him: "Just when big business was convinced of his unquenchable hostility, Arnold launched a massive suit against labor unions with the same intensity that he demonstrated in his direction of the proceedings against the petroleum industry."[30] He regarded the Sherman Act as an instrument that only required a willingness to use it on the part of the responsible public authorities.

Arnold eventually resigned his post at the Justice Department in 1943 when he accepted a presidential appointment to the United States Circuit Court of Appeals. His new appointment had been recommended by several of FDR's advisors who had come to believe that Arnold's antitrust campaign was interfering with the nation's war effort. Although Arnold argued strenuously that antitrust actions could aid mobilization by preventing profiteering, members of the president's cabinet, led by Secretary of War Henry Stimson, charged Arnold with impeding production by frightening the business community. Years later, Arnold, still bitter over being eased out of the Antitrust Division, grumbled: "FDR, recognizing that he could have only one war at a time, was content to declare a truce in the fight against monopoly."[31] Nevertheless, when he left the Justice Department in 1943, Thurman Arnold could point to a remarkable record of having filed more than half of all the suits by the federal government during the entire history of the Sherman Act to that time.[32]

To summarize, with the New Deal the regulatory role of the federal government expanded considerably and permanently. While the economic controls of the First World War years were far-reaching and influential, they disappeared after the Armistice. On this point, Thomas K. McCraw has elaborated: "By the end of the 1930s, a bewildering maze of new government organizations had sprung up as if by magic. Four new federal commissions were born, surpassing the total number that had appeared in all the years before 1933. These were the Securities and Exchange Commission, the Federal Communications Commission, the National Labor Relations Board, and the Civil Aeronautics Authority. Almost as significant, all existing agencies were given new responsibilities or additional industries to regulate or both."[33] This regulatory apparatus, put in place in the 1930s, became a part of the fabric of the American economic system for decades to come.

Overall, the New Deal left business to operate in an economy that was still basically market-oriented, though monitored more closely by government than ever before. The systemic changes the New Deal years saw were not radical. If FDR had wanted to pursue truly fundamental changes, he probably could have secured the popular support sufficient to nationalize all banking in the United States and possibly some other vital industries too. He chose not to do so. He believed instead that private enterprise should be preserved, and he sought, in his view, to strengthen it by the enactment of necessary reforms. He was convinced the legislation of his presidency did just that, and he felt business should have appreciated that fact.

TOTAL WAR AND BUSINESS RESURGENCE

For those fortunate enough to have survived it, James Oliver Robertson has observed, the Second World War was "the great American success story." It "brought revival to the economy, victory to the military and renewed esteem to American business."[34] The New Deal, despite its legislative fireworks, had not ended the depression. As late as 1940, there was still a disturbing 14.6 percent of the labor force who were unemployed, a number almost as high as in 1931.

The unfolding of the mobilization process, however, dramatically changed that situation. Lingering depression was transformed into a soaring business resurgence and an astounding industrial production record. Economic historian Jonathan Hughes has termed it "the full Keynesian message illustrated: government expenditures, utilizing deficit spending, could and did wipe away the depression."[35] Each of America's major wars required greatly increasing expenditures from the federal treasury—the Civil War cost the Union some $3.2 billion; the First World War multiplied that expense by a factor of ten to $33 billion; and the Second World War once again multiplied the last total by another ten, with the final outlays for the four years between 1941–1945 being approximately $321 billion. During the course of the war, the gross national product of the United States doubled, reaching $213.6 billion in 1945, with almost half that amount being government purchases.

American business could rightly pride itself on the production miracles it worked with the spur provided by lucrative defense contracts. In the five years after the fall of France in 1940, the nation's factories turned out 300,000 airplanes, 86,000 tanks, 2.6 million army trucks, and nearly 20 million small arms. Steel production, always an important barometer of the economy's health, rose from 47 million tons in 1939 to 80 million tons in 1944. In the same year, 1944, unemployment stood at an almost incredibly low 1.2 percent, and the average work week in manufacturing, with generous amounts of overtime being accumulated by employees, increased from 38 hours in 1940 to 45 hours just four years later.

Symbolic perhaps of the industrial resurgence was the performance of Henry J. Kaiser, who became something of a national folk hero during the war. A construction contractor and cement manufacturer prior to the war, his firm had helped build the Hoover, Bonneville, Grand Coulee, and Shasta dams in the West and the Golden Gate Bridge in San Francisco. But it was his shipbuilding feats during the war that captured public attention. Kaiser-operated shipyards in California and the Northwest turned out 1,490 vessels, ranging from aircraft carriers to landing craft. Most were workhorse cargo vessels, called Liberty ships, and were built using prefabrication and assembly-line techniques. The average delivery time of a Liberty ship had been 355 days; Kaiser cut that to just 56 days, and he completed one ship in less than two weeks. The admiring publicity his production record attracted, and his close ties to the Roosevelt administration, led FDR to regard Kaiser as a possible vice-presidential running mate in the 1944 election.[36]

Kaiser saw himself as a model product of the free enterprise system. Historian John Morton Blum put Kaiser's accomplishments in a more objective light when he commented: "Energy, ability, ambition, those things Kaiser had; but government supplied his capital, furnished his market, and guaranteed his solvency on the cost-plus formula—and so spared him the need for cost efficiency, rewarded speed at any price, and came close to guaranteeing his profits. . . . The loose rhetoric of American business culture described it as free enterprise."[37]

After the war, Kaiser branched out even further. With a partner, he launched a short-lived and unsuccessful attempt to enter the automobile industry, marketing cars under the name Kaiser-Frazer until the early 1950s. With much more success, he bought two government-built aluminum plants near Spokane, Washington, and later extended those operations by adding additional plants in Louisiana and West Virginia. He also built a steel mill at Fontana, California, the first west of the Rockies, and maintained its viability in spite of fierce competitive attacks from eastern manufacturers. Kaiser, pursuing a personal vision, pioneered in the establishment of group health care facilities, the forerunner of today's spreading health maintenance organization systems. Kaiser retired from active business responsibilities in 1954 and died in 1967.

American industry's prodigious wartime production record could not have been set without Washington-based planning and prodding. The nation's industrial output had to be converted from civilian goods to defense requirements, and at first business executives were not particularly anxious to make that change for several reasons. For one thing, many were still distrustful of, if not hostile to, a Roosevelt administration whose New Deal reforms they had stridently opposed just a few years before. Second, corporation heads feared being labeled "merchants of death," the stigma popularly applied to the munitions makers of the First World War. During the 1930s, a congressional investigating committee chaired by Senator Gerald P. Nye of North Dakota had generated widely reported unpleasant revelations about the wartime activities of those firms.

Moreover, with the economic stimulation of the first phases of mobilization already being felt in revived consumer purchasing power, many businesses were seeing their sales climbing again and were thus not happy about the prospect of interrupting a long-awaited upward trend. Finally, corporate managers were worried about the danger of excess capacity. If they expanded their plants to meet current demands for war goods, would they be left with unneeded facilities in the event of a sudden end to the fighting? They well remembered the Wilson administration's abrupt cancelling of contracts immediately after the 1918 Armistice.

In convincing business to make the necessary conversion, Roosevelt tried to strike a policy balance that was part persuasion and part dictation. The persuasion, besides straightforward appeals to the patriotism of the business community, took the form of some attractive incentives. Among them was the ability to amortize the costs of plant expansion over an accelerated tax depreciation period of just five years. Just as important, the "cost-plus" contract was used even more extensively than it had been during the First World War. It effectively shifted the risks of doing business to the federal government and assured companies at least a reasonable profit. Also noteworthy was the fact that new antitrust prosecutions were virtually halted, much to the chagrin of Thurman Arnold, as we have seen. More of an olive branch than an incentive, but nonetheless welcome, was Roosevelt's willingness to put aside the New Deal reform agenda for the duration of the war in the interest of forging a better working relationship with business leadership. As FDR explained it in December 1943, the services of "Dr. New Deal" were no longer required, and he had been replaced by "Dr. Win-the-War."[38]

The dictation side of the federal government's mobilization program was essentially a reflection of the size of the job to be done. In order to successfully fight a two-ocean war, centralized planning and control were imperative to insure a maximum utilization of the nation's resources. During the Second World War, the direction was provided by a bewildering maze of Washington boards and bureaus, which together had the power to determine what would be produced, for whom, by whom, and at what price. It was an extension of governmental authority well beyond the First World War's mobilization mechanisms.

At the beginning of the war, the head of the Bank of England remarked to the United States ambassador in London, Joseph P. Kennedy, that probably only God Almighty would be capable of organizing American industrial mobilization.[39] There were times, early in the war especially, when he seemed very close to being right. As early as August 1939, Roosevelt had begun the process by creating a War Resources Board, and it was succeeded by other pre–Pearl Harbor agencies, all intended to facilitate defense production. None proved particularly effective and confusion reigned.

Finally, in January 1942, a month after the Pearl Harbor attack, FDR established the War Production Board (WPB) with Sears, Roebuck executive Donald M. Nelson as its head. The board was given broad powers to coordinate overall industrial production, including the administration of priorities and the allocation of materials and manufacturing facilities. At the same time, though, WPB power was somewhat diminished by the formation of several autonomous agencies, each presided over by its own "czar," with authority over particular problem areas, such as petroleum and rubber. Nevertheless,

Nelson's board could still take actions as sweeping as prohibiting any further production of civilian automobiles after the beginning of February 1942. The automobile industry from 1942–1946 was converted entirely to military needs. Chrysler built tanks; Ford was the country's largest producer of bombers; and General Motors received $14 billion in assorted war orders, the most of any single corporate organization.

Even after the WPB was set up, the structure of the government's war bureaucracy was the object of further reshuffling. There were key areas of the economy over which the WPB had little control. In order to provide broader coordination, Justice James F. Byrnes resigned from the Supreme Court in October 1942 to accept a presidential appointment as head of the Office of Economic Stabilization (renamed the Office of War Mobilization and Reconversion in 1944). Byrnes, a former senator, appeared to exercise such wide authority that he became known in press reports as the "assistant president." Actually, his role was not so much administrative as it was political conciliation, refereeing the in-fighting that frequently erupted between rival agencies. In the fall of 1944, Byrnes's office was given the additional assignment of developing a plan for postwar conversion back to a peacetime economy.

United States output of war goods by 1944 doubled that of our enemies, Germany, Italy, and Japan, but we could not have attained that level with just the plant capacity that existed at the time of Pearl Harbor. Therefore, the construction of new manufacturing facilities was essential, and most of it was done with government financing under War Production Board supervision. When the war ended, it was found the federal government owned 90 percent of the plant capacity for turning out planes, ships, and synthetic rubber, and at least half of the facilities for the manufacture of aluminum and machine tools. Disposing of these properties after the end of the war proved a difficult problem.

Harold G. Vatter, in his 1985 study of the American economy during the Second World War, has pointed out some consequences of the war that had important implications for the future of business in the United States. One was the introduction of a number of "war-induced new products, industries, and activities."[40] The most obvious breakthrough was in the development of atomic power, but radar, synthetic rubber, and jet propulsion were among the others, as well as such laboratory-generated products as penicillin and DDT. Scientific research in general was given an enormous boost by the war, so much so that the National Research Council reported almost 2,500 industrial laboratories in operation in 1947, employing twice the number of people as in 1940.

Significant too was the fact that business was able to successfully use the war years to regain the public esteem it had lost during the depression. The production miracle of the early 1940s was the best possible public relations campaign business could have mounted to counter the tarnished image of the previous decade. Moreover, Roosevelt, concerned with the need to enlist industry in the mobilization effort, had not only muted harsh New Deal rhetoric for the duration of the war, he had also invited such prominent business executives as Donald Nelson, William S. Knudsen of General Motors, and Charles Wilson of General Electric, among others, to administer key segments of the program. The "dollar-a-year men" had returned to Washington in force. The resurgence in business's reputation with the public and the regaining of its influence in the federal government had two effects. It reduced the likelihood of any further unsettling New Deal reform legislation, and it marked the genesis of what would eventually be identified as the "military-industrial complex" in the United States. Hence for American business, the Second World War was very much of a success story.

A New Era

The experience of the Second World War confirmed the coming of a new era in business-government relations. Its dawn had been America's entrance into an earlier war in 1917, but the crisis circumstances of the New Deal and Second World War years insured it would be a permanent characteristic of America's mixed economy system. Business executives henceforth knew their managerial decisions would be affected, directly or indirectly, by possible governmental action, and thus those decisions had to be shaped with that fact in mind.

It became routine for large companies to have staff employees whose primary duties were the interpretation and implementation of federal regulations. In addition, corporations often found it necessary to hire their own Washington lobbyists or even open a company office in the capital, frequently headed by a vice-president, especially if they were heavily dependent upon government contracts or they operated in a closely regulated industry, such as telecommunications. It was also not uncommon for a lobbyist or the Washington office head to have been a former public official whose connections and knowledge of the federal bureaucracy were his or her principal qualifications.

The traditional functions of any organizational administrator had previously included such standard responsibilities as planning, staffing, controlling, and the like. After 1945, however, for a professional manager in a business enterprise of any size, dealing with government had to be added to the list.

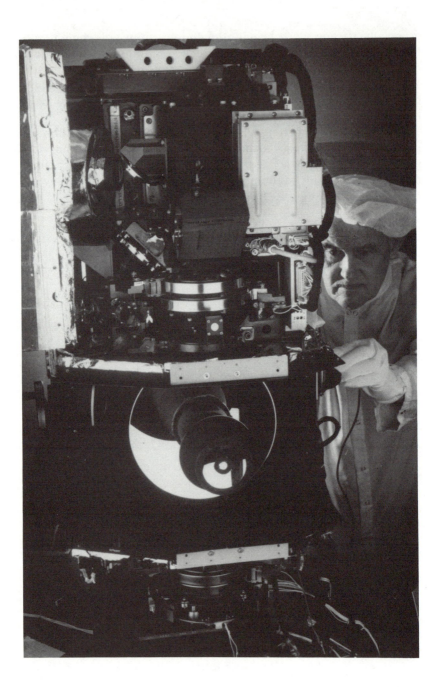

CHAPTER FOURTEEN

Industries and Policy in the Modern Era

In 1945, the final year of the Second World War, David E. Lilienthal, head of the federal government's massive Tennessee Valley Authority and soon to be the first chairman of the United States Atomic Energy Commission, confidently predicted: "There is almost nothing, however fantastic, that . . . a team of engineers, scientists, and administrators cannot do today."[1] Lilienthal was also expressing the optimistic views of most business leaders in that year of wartime victory, and for a quarter of a century afterwards their optimism seemed well-founded. American industrial performance was the envy of the world, and journalistic references to the new "affluent society" in the United States were commonplace. Those twenty-five years saw the nation catapulted into an exciting age of nuclear power, ambitious space programs, and computer technology.

Yet, that American preeminence was seriously undermined in the decade and a half after 1970. Declining industrial productivity, the dislocations in the domestic economy resulting from intervention in Vietnam, rising competitive challenges from aggressive European and Asian companies, notably in Germany and Japan, and the twin shocks of the 1973 and 1979 oil embargoes all combined to create a radically altered situation from the one David Lilienthal had foreseen in 1945. The turnabout's dimensions were perhaps reflected in the very different kind of "optimistic" prediction made by a major business periodical in January 1987: "Don't hold your breath. Don't bet the ranch. Don't uncork the champagne—just yet. But it does look as though maybe, just maybe, the nation's long-suffering basic manufacturing sector is turning around."[2]

This chapter will explain something of the story of American business enterprise in the past forty years through a series of brief updates illustrating the experience of some key American industries and a discussion of federal regulatory policy in the same period. In chapters 10 and 12, we examined the early development of five key post–Civil War industries—steel, petroleum, telephone, automotive, and broadcasting. We will begin this chapter by carrying forward to the present each of their individual histories, which have taken quite divergent paths.

Industry Updates: Steel, Oil, Telecommunications

STEEL

At the end of the Second World War, America's steel industry was the most powerful in the world. It accounted for 60 percent of the total international crude steel output, and, in view of the devastated condition of both the European and Japanese competition, it seemed to face a profitable future. The reality of the next twenty-five years, however, was quite different. By 1960 American steel companies produced only a quarter of the world's output, and by the last half of the 1970s their share had fallen to less than 20 percent. The steel industry in the United States had not only ceased to grow, it was retiring more capacity than it was building.

The decline in the fortunes of American steel began in the 1950s, if not before. The industry's giant, the United States Steel Corporation, was experiencing multiple problems even before Pearl Harbor. Elbert H. Gary, its board chairman until his death in 1927, stressed a policy of avoiding too much size for fear of an adverse antitrust action (we have discussed earlier U. S. Steel's judicial escape in 1920 because of a divided Supreme Court and the rule of reason), and he emphasized instead good relations and cooperation with other companies in eliminating price competition. In his presidential address to the American Iron and Steel Institute in 1910, Gary spoke of: "Real, hearty, cheerful and continued cooperation. . . . Frank and friendly intercourse; full disclosure of his business by each to the others, . . . and conduct founded on the belief that healthy competition is wiser and better than destructive competition."[3]

While U. S. Steel pursued its policy of benign restraint, rivals like Bethlehem, Republic, and National strengthened their own industry positions by acquiring smaller firms. U. S. Steel was also hurt by a demand shift from heavier items, such as rails and structural shapes, to sheets and strips. The corporation's capacity was deeply committed to the heavier products, and making the transition was painful and slow. By the mid-1980s U. S. Steel's share of total raw steel output was less than 20 percent, a far cry from the dominance it held when J. P. Morgan brought it to life in 1901.

The turning point for the industry was 1959. In that year, it was hit by a long and expensive strike at the very time that the Japanese were beginning their own expansion. Imports rose dramatically and never again returned to their pre-1959 level as Japan bought its way into the American market with its lower-priced products. Japan, with larger and more modern plants, could boast of the world's most efficient steel industry, while the United States even today relies mainly on tired facilities that predate the Second World War.

Equally revealing was a 1980 congressional report that found the steel industry in the United States had been lagging in research and development expenditures as compared to its foreign rivals. American firms in recent years have invested only about 0.5–0.6 percent of their sales in R&D, while Japan, for example, has averaged over 1 percent. Any new technology was usually developed outside the United States, and American steel manufacturers lagged behind in adopting it. The basic oxygen furnace, which gradually replaced the open-hearth process, is an example of this trend. It was invented in Europe in 1950, but was not adopted by major American firms until the 1960s.

Today the United States, once the world's leading steel producer, ranks fourth in raw steel output, trailing the Soviet Union, the European Economic Community, and Japan. Currently, the single largest steelmaking company is Nippon Steel, and the tonnage produced by that Japanese corporation more than doubles the output of its foremost American competitor. Moreover, the United States has become the world's principal importer of steel; the foreign-made product, which represented only a 5 percent share of our market in 1960, claimed a 25 percent share of the steel consumed here in the mid-1980s. The reaction of American firms to the rising import threat has been an incessant demand for government protection. They have usually charged foreign nations with unfair trade practices and cited

severe wage disparities—a $3 per hour labor cost in Korea, for in-
stance, versus $20 per hour in the United States—as the heart of
their competitive problem. Washington's response has been the ne-
gotiation of a variety of "voluntary" import restraint agreements
with important steel-exporting nations, but even these quotas have
not rescued a domestic industry whose problems go well beyond just
imported steel.

In 1986 alone a softening market for steel inflicted a $4 billion
net loss on the industry, and during the first half of the 1980s three
major companies filed for reorganization under Chapter 11 of the
federal bankruptcy law. Retrenchment has been one of the key strategies adopted by steel managers as a reaction to their industry's
decline. Since 1981 they have closed over 15 percent of their plant
capacity and slashed employment rolls, thereby wreaking a great
deal of human hardship on laid-off workers and the communities in
which they live. Some measure of the extent of the retrenchment
can be seen in the drop in membership strength of the United Steel-
workers of America. The union counted 1.3 million members as recently as 1979; but in 1986 there were just 700,000.

One thought-provoking alternative to simply laying off workers
was tried in 1984 in Wierton, West Virginia. There the National Steel
Corp., rather than simply closing an unprofitable facility, agreed to
sell it to the company's own employees. The long-term future of the
now employee-owned plant is still uncertain, however, and thus far
no other steel firms have chosen to follow National's example when
shutting down operations.

Particularly noteworthy have been the recent actions of the country's best-known producer, U. S. Steel. It suddenly announced in
July 1986 that it was changing its corporate name. Henceforth it
would be called USX Corp. The "X" in the name was derived from
the long-time use of that symbol as the company's designation on
the New York Stock Exchange ticker.

More than just a simple adoption of a new name, the step reflected
a fundamental restructuring of the organization that had already taken
place. During the 1980s, the corporation has pursued a vigorous
diversification strategy, especially by moving into the energy field.
It purchased Marathon Oil for $6 billion in 1982, and four years
later it acquired Texas Oil & Gas for another $3 billion. The result
has been that steel production now accounts for only 30 percent of
USX's sales. Indeed, given the condition of the industry, there has

been speculation that the company might actually withdraw from steel altogether. At the time of the name change, a cartoon in a Pittsburgh newspaper depicted a steelworker lamenting: "I think we're the 'EX' in USX."[4] It would be difficult to conceive of a more telling comment about the reversal of fortunes in the American steel industry in the century since the halcyon days of Andrew Carnegie, when it was a mighty engine for industrial progress in the United States.

OIL

Petroleum, from the time of John D. Rockefeller, has always been a headline-making industry, and that tradition has been borne out in the last fifteen years of recurring energy crises. But, to appreciate recent developments, one must understand those that occurred even before the dissolution of the Standard Oil family of companies in 1911.

The transformation of the industry began when Anthony Lucas, an engineer and former Austrian naval officer, set up a rotary drilling rig on a hill near Beaumont, Texas. He called the site Spindletop because of some scrawny pine trees nearby. On January 10, 1901, Lucas's well blew in with the mightiest gusher ever seen, and it continued to stream oil for nine days before it was finally capped.

Out of the Spindletop strike emerged two major petroleum companies. One was formed when Lucas was bought out by his financial backers, a group that included the Mellon Bank of Pittsburgh. They then organized a new company, which they called Gulf Oil. At the same time, another investors' syndicate headed by a former Texas governor, James H. Hogg, bought some Spindletop leases and started drilling. When the wells came in, the investors incorporated themselves as the Texas Company (later shortened to Texaco). After the Spindletop field played out in 1903, Gulf and Texaco extended their operations to other areas and successfully challenged Standard Oil's longtime grip on an industry that would never again be the same.

The second major development that transformed the industry was the arrival of the automobile age. As Ford, General Motors, and the other car companies sold the American public on the horseless carriage, the petroleum industry was swept along by the craze. The quantity of gasoline produced between 1901 and 1919 illustrates this point. In the first year, 54.3 million gallons were refined in the

United States, while, in 1919, the total exceeded 3.9 billion gallons. Contributing to the huge increase was the invention of the thermal pressure cracking process by chemists at Standard Oil of Indiana. This process significantly increased the amount of gasoline that could be obtained from any given quantity of refined oil. Noting the many changes in his industry, one prominent oil man observed in 1923 that "the petroleum industry of the gasoline age is no more the petroleum industry of the kerosene age than the great automobile industry is the multiplication of the old village wheelwright, laboriously fashioning a democrat wagon."[5]

During the late 1920s, with new discoveries in California, Oklahoma, and Texas, overproduction and an oil glut that depressed prices soon became the problem. The situation worsened in 1930 when another East Texas strike proved the most productive that the industry had yet seen. By 1931 the new field was pouring out a million barrels a day, enough to meet one-third of the entire requirement of the United States.

Crude-oil prices fell as low as ten cents a barrel, and the state governments of Oklahoma and Texas stepped in to restore some sort of order. They imposed a rationing system on all producers, which limited total output and allocated quotas, and even called out the National Guard to enforce the controls. The states also appealed to Washington for help, but, as Gerald Nash has written, "the collapse of the industry evinced no energetic response from President Hoover, who maintained a sphinxlike pose."[6]

The incoming Roosevelt administration provided better controls. Section 9(c) of the National Industrial Recovery Act of 1933 prohibited the interstate shipment of contraband or "hot oil," that is, oil produced in violation of a state quota. Section 9(c) failed to survive the judicial gauntlet, however, when the Supreme Court ruled in January 1935 that federal officials lacked the power to enforce production quotas set by state agencies. This was the first piece of New Deal legislation that the court found unconstitutional, and it was the beginning of Franklin Roosevelt's troubles with the judiciary branch.

Immediately following the hot-oil decision, the administration and Congress collaborated on a more carefully drawn version of Section 9(c). It was embodied in the Connally Act of 1935, which again prohibited hot-oil shipments across state lines. This time, though, there was no veto from the Supreme Court, which by the late 1930s was taking a more benign view of New Deal legislation.

The Second World War greatly increased oil imports into the United States, but the inflow of foreign oil did not decrease after 1945. Crude-oil imports swelled from 272,000 barrels a day in 1947 to 900,000 in 1956, as the federal government encouraged the development of foreign sources with no barrier to imports. There were two reasons for this policy—a fear of eventual depletion of domestic reserves and anti-Communism. Substantial imports from nations in the Middle East appeared to be a way to tie their interests to those of the anti-Communist West.

But the Middle Eastern countries soon took some action of their own. As we have already seen, in 1960 they formed OPEC. Its initial members were Iran, Iraq, Kuwait, and Saudi Arabia, together with Venezuela from the Western Hemisphere. Later more members were added until the cartel reached thirteen in number. Their aim was to press for a larger royalty payment from the oil companies that held concessions on their soil, but OPEC did not achieve a solid enough bargaining position to accomplish its goal until the 1970s.

Until then, the West had taken it for granted that the oil companies, and in particular the Seven Sisters, held the necessary power to limit OPEC aspirations. But the situation changed when both American and world consumption of oil started to run well ahead of predictions by 1970, and imports attained an all-time high of 28 percent of the oil used in the United States. OPEC, under the leadership of the Saudi oil minister, Sheikh Ahmed Zaki Yamani (a Harvard graduate), shrewdly chose this moment to insist not only on an increase in the price of oil—and thereby an increase in the payments its members received—but also on a "participation" in the ownership of the companies that held leases in member countries. In view of the growing dependence of the West on oil imports, the companies agreed to the OPEC demands.

Then the outbreak of another Arab-Israeli war in October 1973 brought even more drastic OPEC action. The Arab bloc within the cartel announced a cut in production, a unilateral price hike of 70 percent, and an embargo of shipments to the United States because of its support of Israel. Imports from the Arab OPEC countries dropped from 1,175,000 barrels a day in October 1973 to only 18,000 barrels daily the following February. Filling stations in the United States ran out of gasoline; motorists drove for miles to find fuel, and then lined up for an hour or more to purchase it at a much higher price than they had ever paid before. The public immediately suspected that the oil corporations were manipulating the crisis and blamed them more than the Arabs. The denunciations intensified as the companies announced record profits in their quarterly reports. The embargo ended in March 1974, but the OPEC-dictated price increases remained. Although OPEC oil had soared from $1.79 a barrel in 1970 to over $13 in 1974, still higher prices were to come. The economic consequence, in the words of one scholar, was "a massive and immediate transfer of funds from oil consumers to oil producers."[7]

The Iranian revolution in 1979 that saw the ousting of the shah and the coming to power of the anti-American Khomeini regime set off a second round of steep oil price increases. Iran, under its new radical leadership, joined with OPEC's other price "hawks," notably Iraq, Libya, and Algeria, to reduce production, force a tight market, and then boost prices sharply. Saudi Arabian light crude, the benchmark used to measure oil prices, soared to over $30 a barrel by the end of 1980.

The oil price increases dealt American economic growth a devastating blow. Inflation rose above 10 percent (it is usually thought that any $5 increase in crude prices represents a 1 percent rise in the inflation rate), and what amounted to a new wealth tax was levied on oil consumers. On the other hand, oil companies in the 1970s had a quite different experience. As one study has pointed out: "When OPEC raises the price of crude oil, it increases the value of oil in the ground everywhere, including oil in the ground that is owned or controlled by vertically integrated majors. To this extent, the majors have interests in common with the OPEC cartel."[8]

In 1970 the net income of the five leading United States oil companies (Exxon, Gulf, Mobil, Chevron, and Texaco) totalled $3.6 billion, but by 1980 that figure had quadrupled to $14.5 billion. In fact, overall oil industry profits in 1980 represented 25 percent of the net earnings of the entire manufacturing sector of American business. In the first quarter of that year, Exxon's profits of $1.9 billion were more than any other corporation had ever earned in a single quarter. Sometimes, oil companies used these accumulated funds to purchase unrelated acquisitions—Reliance Electric by Exxon and Montgomery Ward by Mobil, for example—and thereby added to the fiery debate over the industry's "windfall" profits. Oil-company managers, of course, argued that their earnings made possible the expensive search for new energy resources, and that only by discovering them could the United States guard its national security and prevent future attempts at economic blackmail.

But the exceptionally high prices came back to haunt OPEC. They encouraged conservation, fuel switching, and more production from areas outside OPEC's control (Alaska, Mexico, and the North Sea). Demand for petroleum in the non-Communist world shrank from 51 million barrels in 1978 to 46 million in 1985, and production in non-OPEC countries grew by 28 percent over the same period. In the United States, conservation and the heavier use of other fuels reduced oil's share of American energy consumption from 47 to 43 percent during the first half of the 1980s. All of these factors contributed to a startling reversal in the oil price trend.

From their historic highs, prices started down in 1981. By 1985 they were under $25 a barrel and under $20 in 1986, thereby creating economic havoc in the so-called oilpatch states of the Southwest. Employment rolls of oil companies were slashed (300,000 industry workers were laid off between 1982 and 1987), refineries were closed, many smaller firms dropped out of the business, and expenditures for exploration and development fell from $40 billion in 1982 to only $12 billion a few years later. At less than $20 a barrel, the incentive for keeping marginal wells pumping or for drilling in new areas was lacking. A recent *Fortune* magazine discussion of the industry's condition described the resulting plight of the oilpatch: "Today geologists step lively as bellhops in Houston hotels, and unemployed drill hands have either drifted into other fields or resorted to poaching game to feed their families. The stream of professionals entering the business is drying up. Last year 192 students were enrolled in petroleum engineering at the University of Texas, down from 1,112 in 1982."[9]

As this is written in 1987, however, another price reversal may just have taken place. Crude prices have regained the $20 plus level, and the average cost of a gallon of gasoline at a service station has inched over $1.00 again. Many objective analysts regard this as a welcome occurrence. There are perils associated with oil that is too cheap beyond just a considerable loss of profits for the industry itself. Very low prices encourage excessive national consumption and discourage conservation and the use of alternative energy sources. They make domestic production uneconomic and cause the United States to be too dependent on imported petroleum, especially from the Middle East, where the costs of production are much less. Given the volatility and the unpredictability of Middle Eastern politics, any reliance on a continuity of supply from that region is a roll of the dice.

TELECOMMUNICATIONS

At the outbreak of the Second World War in 1939, the Bell System that had been forged by Theodore Vail was a formidable entity. AT&T had assets of $5 billion and supplied over 80 percent of all telephones in service in the United States, about 16 million altogether. Moreover, it was owned by some 637,000 stockholders who held an average of less than thirty shares each. The separation of ownership from actual control, a twentieth-century corporate phenomenon that developed with the widespread public purchase of securities, was never better exemplified than in the case of AT&T.

The 1940s and 1950s brought both progress and problems for Bell. On the one hand, the firm made important technical advances. Microwave radio channels for domestic long-distance telephone transmissions, coaxial cables for television signals, the direct-dialing system, the laying of a transatlantic cable for overseas phone calls, and the transistor were just some of the achievements of AT&T's Western Electric and Bell Laboratories subsidiaries.

But, on the other hand, AT&T had to defend itself against a government antitrust prosecution. The Justice Department, in a suit filed in January 1949 under the Sherman Act, charged Western Electric with maintaining a monopoly control of the telephone-equipment market and sought to separate the manufacturing subsidiary from its AT&T parent. The case dragged on for years until 1956, when the Eisenhower administration, encouraged by the Defense Department, which depended on the Bell System for critical military assistance, entered into a consent decree with the corporation.

Under the complicated terms of the agreement, AT&T retained Western Electric, made available its eight thousand patents to all comers on a royalty-free basis, and promised not to engage in any business other than common-carrier communications. The 1956 settlement had two important consequences. First, it sacrificed any structural reform by accepting AT&T's integrated holding-company organization, and, second, it prevented the corporation from entering the blossoming computer industry. The latter was ironic, since the Bell Labs played a key role in developing the semiconductor, which is the heart of any computer unit.

The telephone industry changed little over the next two decades. In 1974, the Bell System was responsible for 80 percent of all telephone service in the United States, essentially the same proportion it had in 1939. Its local operating companies provided nearly 100 million telephones, whereas its nearest competitor, General Telephone and Electronics (GTE), accounted for less than 10 million, or 8 percent, of the nation's total.

AT&T, of course, not only controlled its local phone companies, it also owned Western Electric, from whom the locals purchased most of their equipment requirements, and the Bell Telephone Laboratories, the research and development arm of the organization. The Bell Labs have a deserved international reputation for inventions and product development, as well as for basic research of substantial importance. And the Long-Lines Division of the Bell System structure continued to handle 90 percent of the country's long-distance service. Such was the AT&T organization in 1974 when the Justice Department again filed an antitrust suit against the telephone giant.

This time the department sought to sever from the parent corporation not only Western Electric but also the local operating companies. The suit, like the earlier action begun in 1949, lingered in the courts for years until, in January 1982, it was abruptly settled by another consent decree. But, this time, the terms of the decree came as a staggering surprise to the business community and the public.

After eight years of litigation and an estimated $360 million in legal fees, AT&T shocked the nation by announcing that it had agreed to divest itself of its twenty-two local phone companies, while retaining the Long-Lines Division, Western Electric, and Bell Labs. The federal government in turn agreed to allow the corporation to enter other markets, such as those for computers and office equipment. The *Wall Street Journal* termed it "the most important antitrust development since the Supreme Court ordered the dissolution of the Standard Oil Trust in 1911," and it concluded that "by agreeing to divest itself of its twenty-two local telephone operating companies, AT&T has traded its 100-year-old role as the main supplier of basic telephone service to the nation's homes and offices for a new and largely uncharted course as a high-technology, innovative competitor in the marketplace."[10]

The historic divestiture took place at the beginning of 1984. Instead of AT&T's former local phone companies, seven huge regional corporations were formed, all completely independent both of AT&T and each other. Popularly known as the "Baby Bells," the seven new organizations and their respective regional headquarters are: Ameritech (Chicago), Bell Atlantic (Philadelphia), Bell South (Atlanta), Nynex (New York City), Pacific Telesis (San Francisco), Southwestern Bell (St. Louis), and U. S. West (Englewood, Colorado). The Baby Bells continue to provide the usual local phone service, but under the terms of the original 1982 consent decree they could not either engage in long-distance telephone operations or manufacture equipment. At the same time, AT&T created separate administrative divisions to manage the varied fields in which it was free to engage after 1984. Thus AT&T Communications became the long-distance unit; AT&T Network Systems would be Western Electric's successor as the supplier of equipment to other phone companies; and AT&T Information Systems was to be the vehicle that would carry the company into the promised land of unregulated, high-technology businesses.

The years since 1984 have seen a number of developments, some anticipated and some not. As expected, long-distance telephone charges have gone down, but by a surprisingly steep 30 percent. Two reasons account for the sharp drop. Before 1984 those rates had been kept artificially high in order to keep local residential rates low, a subsidy practice that was possible in a near-monopoly environment in which AT&T could lose money in one area but make it up in another. But with the breakup of the old Bell System, the rationale for that pricing policy disappeared.

Second, the long-distance marketplace was now highly competitive. There had been some competition ever since the mid-1970s, when the FCC and the courts finally permitted other firms, led by MCI Communications Corp. and using such technologies as inexpensive microwave radio transmission and satellites, to make direct connections for customers through local Bell phone companies. Nevertheless, the pre-1984 competitors had done little to lessen AT&T's dominance, which amounted to 95 percent of long-distance traffic, because they shared a common handicap. To make a call, their users had to dial into a computer first, a procedure requiring the dialing of as many as twenty-four digits. Only AT&T had the "1-plus-area code" capability.

That handicap was removed by the consent decree, which stipulated that local phone customers should choose a long-distance carrier and dial into its system in the same manner as they had with AT&T. What followed was a gradual city-by-city ballot process, called an "equal access" referendum, that has been described as "the most elaborate exercise in U.S. regulatory history."[11] The balloting exercise, still going on, has proved to be disappointing for the AT&T challengers. After enormous advertising campaigns by the major contenders, relying heavily on television commercials featuring show-business celebrities, AT&T still retained some 80 percent of the long-distance market, a figure well above what many had thought would be the outcome of the voting. In addition to aggressive advertising, AT&T had also cut its rates, lessening the difference between it and its competitors. The costs of that competition have been so great, that the two next-largest companies in the long-distance telephone business, MCI and U. S. Sprint Communications Corp., each incurred 1986 dollar losses running into the hundreds of millions.

Another unanticipated development following the 1984 breakup of the Bell System has been the performance of the seven regional companies. The Baby Bells have been acting in a very adult manner. As *Business Week* commented: "They were supposed to be caretakers, making sure Grandma and Grandpa got a dial tone, while AT&T was freed to become a highflier in the fast-moving information industry. But somebody forgot to tell the Bell executives."[12] Not willing to settle for the relatively slow growth and modest prospects of the conventional local telephone-service business, the Baby Bells soon adopted ambitious diversification strategies. While still drawing the great bulk of their revenues from their traditional operations, the Baby Bells have been venturing into everything from chains of retail computer stores to publishing and commercial real estate. Moreover, they have been seeking the agreement of the Justice Department and the federal court to a revision of the consent decree that would permit them to enter the long-distance service field. If granted, competition in that market will become even more heated, and AT&T's 80 percent share should certainly decrease.

Many analysts have expressed concern about the activities of the Baby Bells because of the potential effect on local phone-service charges. Without the pre-1984 Bell System subsidy, those charges have already risen over 40 percent since 1984, as most industry observers predicted they would. They might go up even more if possible losses suffered by the regional companies in unsuccessful diversification ventures were allowed by state regulatory authorities to be passed on to local phone customers in the form of further rate increases.

Finally, the recent experience of AT&T itself has been a mixture of success and sluggishness. While its long-distance market share has held up better than many expected, and it has continued to do well selling equipment to the Baby Bells, it has had a great deal of difficulty in the computer and business-telephone systems fields. Faced with the rather daunting problems of competing with such established powerhouses as IBM, the administrative puzzle of adjusting to a new internal organizational structure, and other troubles, AT&T's Information Systems division has suffered significant losses. In 1986, AT&T overall saw its profits decline by 80 percent from the previous year. The current consensus within the industry is that AT&T's transformation into a high-tech superstar will take a good deal more time, and that for the next several years its profits will still be coming primarily from its storied long-distance service. Meanwhile, the debate continues among a still somewhat confused general public and in the popular press—did it make sense to break up the Bell System?

More Industry Updates: Autos and the Electronic Media

THE AUTOMOTIVE INDUSTRY

Despite its recent well-publicized troubles, the automobile industry remains a very important sector in the American economy. In 1986, General Motors ranked first in sales revenue among all American industrial corporations, and Ford ranked third on the list. The Chrysler Corporation, which had teetered on the brink of oblivion at the beginning of the 1980s, was eleventh in sales, earned some $1.4 billion in net profits, and had its colorful chief executive officer, Lee Iacocca, considered for a time as a possible future occupant of the White House. Yet, the industry's history during the past forty years has been anything but an uninterrupted triumphal march.

During the Second World War, as we saw, the industry performed wonders of production and rolled out millions of tanks, trucks, aircraft, guns, and engines; it was converted entirely to the war effort, and ordinary passenger car output suspended. At the end of the war, as the auto companies retooled for peacetime, prospects were bright. Pent-up consumer demand was extremely high, and the economy was charging ahead.

A change in leadership had just occurred at Ford which would finally pull that firm out of its doldrums. The company had been badly managed for years, and not until September 1945 could the family at last persuade the aging founder to turn over the reins of the corporation to his grandson, Henry Ford II (whose father, Edsel Ford, had died in 1943). After assuming the presidency, the younger Ford fired most of his grandfather's cronies and brought in Ernest R. Breech, president of Bendix Aviation, a GM subsidiary, as Ford's executive vice-president.

Breech found his new company saddled with "rundown plants, obsolete products, almost nonexistent financial control, an inadequate engineering staff, . . . the worst labor relations in the industry, and a poor public image."[13] Breech raided General Motors for dozens of its executives and installed the GM management system at Ford. During his tenure, which lasted until 1960 when he left to take over Trans World Airlines, Breech propelled the company back into second place in the industry and probably prevented it from collapsing altogether.

A turning point of sorts occurred in the industry in 1957. In the early fall of that year, Ford unveiled with enormous fanfare a new car line, the Edsel, supposedly the ultimate in engineering design and styling. It was the wrong car at the wrong moment. The public, in the late 1950s, was beginning to seek out economy as represented by smaller, simpler vehicles, and the Edsel seemed to be Detroit at its gaudiest and worst. Shortly after the Edsel appeared, the Soviet Union launched the first *Sputnik* satellite into orbit and temporarily shattered American perceptions of technical superiority. According to one theory, *Sputnik* precipitated a revolt against Detroit frills. Americans "put themselves on a self-imposed austerity program. Not buying Edsels was their hairshirt."[14]

After two disastrous years, Ford dropped the Edsel at an estimated loss of $350 million. The debacle seemed to signal a new and distressful era in the industry's history. The following years were marked by growing competition from European and Japanese imports, public concern about safety and environmental factors, and a general belief that American-made automobiles were not delivering the quality and value that consumers should expect.

The Volkswagen "Beetle" was the first of the imports to make a significant impact in the American market. It was introduced into the United States in the 1950s, and, by 1970, it had sold 4 million units, largely due to its high standards of workmanship and low price. Other small foreign cars appeared by the early 1960s and increased the market share of imported makes from 5 percent in 1963 to over 11 percent in 1970 (and 30 percent in 1986). American companies have fought back with small vehicles of their own, but without great success, as the above figures indicate.

The automobile industry was buffeted during the 1960s by the issues of safety and air pollution. The publication in 1965 of Ralph Nader's book, *Unsafe at Any Speed: The Designed-in Dangers of the American Automobile*, attracted considerable public attention, since it charged Detroit with "subordination of safety to styling in automotive design." The industry had supposedly taken the position that "safety doesn't sell."[15]

When the auto companies appeared to drag their feet on the issue, the federal government stepped in with the National Traffic and Motor Vehicle Safety Act of 1966. The act established a new agency, the National Highway Traffic Safety Administration, within the Department of Transportation to determine the safety features needed on new automobiles. The first safety standards went into effect in 1968 and called for seat belts for all passengers, impact-absorbing steering columns, dual braking systems, and padded instrument panels. The agency also had the authority to require companies to make public announcements of any recalls of vehicles to correct defects. The framers of the law hoped that this open admission of car defects would goad manufacturers into improving their products, but the results of this act are open to question.

As air quality began to deteriorate measurably in the 1960s, Americans mindful of the environment pressed the issue of atmospheric pollution. They usually singled out the automobile as the principal culprit. Studies attributed from 60 to 80 percent of the pollution problem to the internal combustion engine. Especially high levels of pollutants were recorded in smog- and car-ridden urban areas such as Los Angeles; when the industry failed to take any noticeable action, the state of California reacted with the first legislation to reduce auto emissions by requiring the installation of exhaust-control devices on all cars sold in the state.

The federal government followed a few years later with the Motor Vehicle Air Pollution Act of 1965 and the Clean Air Act of 1970. These laws imposed standards similar to those in effect in California, and the responsibility for enforcement was given to the Environmental Protection Agency when it was created in 1971. Despite initial balking by the industry, the acts have made some progress in reducing pollution from motor vehicles.

After the first oil crisis in 1973, considerable pressure was brought by Washington upon United States automakers to produce cars that were more fuel-efficient. The Energy Policy and Conservation Act of 1975 specifically required a company's new vehicles to gradually reach an average fuel-consumption standard of not less than 27.5 miles per gallon over the next ten years. Administration of the law was given to the Environmental Protection Agency, and as a result, EPA mileage ratings became an ever-present feature of automobile marketing.

There was little public clamor for small fuel-efficient cars until the Iranian Revolution in 1979 brought on the second oil crisis of the 1970s. Industry historian John B. Rae, terming the event a watershed in American automobile history, described the aftermath: "Large cars became unsalable, and there was a stampede toward compacts, which the domestic manufacturers could not satisfy because they had not anticipated any such drastic changes in demand."[16] As a result, buyers quickly turned to foreign-made automobiles, and the import share of the United States market jumped to an unprecedented 27 percent. The next few years were very difficult for the three principal American producers, General Motors, Ford, and Chrysler.

In the case of Chrysler, the company came very close to not surviving. In late 1978 it was painfully announcing the largest operational losses in the corporation's history at the same moment it was undergoing a management transition. Joining Chrysler was the man who had just been fired as the president of Ford Motor Corp., Lido Anthony "Lee" Iacocca. Born in Allentown, Pennsylvania, in 1924, Iacocca earned engineering degrees at Lehigh and Princeton before joining Ford in the late 1940s. He first came to national attention when, as head of the Ford car division, he oversaw the design and production of the spectacularly successful Mustang model, brought out in 1964. Why Iacocca was fired by Henry Ford II in 1978 is still a matter of argument among industry insiders, but there is a strong likelihood the reasons involved, in part, the personality and background differences between the two men.

Six years later, in his autobiography, which became a publishing sensation because of its long tenure on the best-seller list, Iacocca wrote: "What I found at Chrysler was a state of anarchy." He immediately began a sweeping reorganization of the company that included ruthless administrative personnel changes. "Over a three year period I had to fire thirty-three out of the thirty-five vice-presidents," he later recalled.[17]

A critical component in the fight to save Chrysler was government assistance. Company officials lobbied hard and successfully for $1.5 billion in federal loan guarantees (they originally had wanted tax credits, not guarantees), which were received in 1980 despite considerable political and press opposition. Iacocca himself later contended: "Believe me, the last thing in the world I wanted to do was turn to the government. Ideologically, I've always been a free enterpriser, a believer in survival of the fittest. Once the decision was made, however, I went at it with all flags flying."[18]

By the mid-1980s, the Chrysler situation was very different. It had repaid its government-backed loans; new lines of restyled front-wheel-drive cars had proven to be marketplace winners; significant profits were again being earned; and the company had reclaimed a good deal of its share of United States automobile sales, mostly at the expense of General Motors. Iacocca, principally because of his television commercial appearances, had become America's best-known businessman. In one recent account of the Chrysler struggle, Iacocca's role has been contrasted with that of the industry's legendary Alfred Sloan: "Though Sloan's contributions to General Motors had certainly been recognized by every student of American business, they were concealed from the public. . . . He had not tied his face, his demeanor, and his style to the public image of General Motors. Iacocca, however, had become synonymous with Chrysler. He . . . had succeeded in tying his name more closely to the health of the company than any man since Walter Chrysler and had added further proof to the advertising homily that personalities differentiate companies."[19]

On the other hand, the trend at General Motors in the decade since 1978 has not been as favorable for the company. In the late

1970s it was selling over half the cars purchased in the United States, and it was earning record profits. Moreover, it was about to embark on one of the most audacious business strategies ever conceived in the industry—GM would invest its vast financial resources in a redesign of all its cars and a reequipping of its factories. A new fleet of fuel-saving, down-sized cars would pour out of integrated, high-technology plants utilizing the latest in computers, lasers, and robots.

Ten years later, it has become clear the plan did not work. General Motors' market share is down to 40 percent and might well drop even lower, despite an estimated investment of $40 billion or more in new technology between 1978 and 1988. One top GM executive sadly commented: "Only a few years ago, we were so successful and so powerful in the marketplace, we were worried about antitrust. Now we're running for our lives."[20]

What went wrong? A variety of factors have been cited by industry analysts. The company was expecting gasoline prices to continue their rise; instead they dropped and there was a resurgence in demand for larger automobiles at the very time GM was bringing out its new smaller vehicles. Styling was a serious problem too. Recent GM models have been called "monumentally mundane," all looking too much alike, while Ford was introducing a sleek line of distinctive, European-looking cars.[21] In addition, the swollen bureaucracy of the huge GM organization has slowed its ability to react to market changes and to cut costs.

Particularly important, though, is the fact that the massive capital spending program did not pay its anticipated dividends. It has been shown that many of GM's expensive automated factories are not much more efficient than the old ones. In fact, an ironic lesson was learned in Fremont, California, the location of a nonautomated plant that is a joint venture of GM and Toyota. Work there on a restyled Chevrolet Nova, a copy of the Toyota Corolla, was organized using Japanese management techniques. Despite having only a fraction of the money invested in it as in the high-tech plants, Fremont's productivity was one of the highest in the GM system, and the quality of its products earned the highest marks from customers. The company is now attempting to apply the Fremont lessons in other plants. At this time the direction of General Motors' future is indefinite. The corporation's management, led by board chairman Roger B. Smith, is determined to regain the organization's lost respect, but how soon that can be accomplished, if ever, remains to be seen.

In 1986 there were over 16 million cars and trucks sold in the United States, the most ever. The problem, however, for American automakers is that they sold a smaller percentage in the nation's market than ever before, only about 70 percent. Besides Japanese and European imports, cars are now coming into the country from Brazil, Canada, Mexico, South Korea, and Taiwan. Just as troubling, in a 1986 poll of new-car owners that rated thirteen brands as above-average in consumer satisfaction, only two brands, Lincoln and Mercury, were American, while five were Japanese and six were European. Obviously, the job facing American auto manufacturers, if they intend to improve their position in the market or even retain it in the years ahead, is no small assignment.

THE ELECTRONIC MEDIA

In June 1941, the Federal Communications Commission reported that 915 radio stations were in operation or under construction; four years later, the number remained relatively unchanged, as the FCC banned the licensing of new stations for the duration of the war in order to conserve essential electronic materials. The ownership of a station in these years was a bonanza; revenues from advertising-time sales for all networks and local stations surged from $117 million in 1938 to $288 million six years later. Sponsors seemed to be throwing money at broadcasters in order to keep their product names before the public in preparation for the postwar years, even though the actual items were often unavailable during the war itself.

The postwar era began for radio in October 1945, when the FCC resumed consideration of new station applications. The phenomenal earnings of the war years and the hiatus in the normal expansion of the industry had combined to build up an enormous pressure that rapidly increased the size of the industry. There were over two thousand AM broadcasters by June 1948, plus something new in the air—some one thousand FM licensees and one hundred television stations, which were the wave of the future.

"No one created the American television system," it has been said. "It evolved in a series of patchwork progressions, affected variously by governmental regulations, corporate aims, technological advances, advertising and marketing requirements, and to some degree, by public reaction."[22] Television, as a potential mass-communications medium, had existed for almost as long as radio. An experimental television program in which Secretary of Commerce Herbert Hoover participated was transmitted in 1927, and, twelve years later, NBC telecast the New York World's Fair. The diversion of electronic parts and equipment to military needs stalled television's development for several years after 1939, but, by 1946, there were thirty-four stations operating in twenty-one cities with about 1 million sets in use.

In most cases, the owners of the pioneering TV stations also held AM licenses and used their radio profits to meet the heavy development costs of television. *Fortune* magazine estimated in 1949 that the minimum possible investment in TV within a metropolitan area for a would-be owner was $400,000, and that was spent before a camera was turned on. The National Association of Broadcasters adhered to a "two by four" formula, which set TV expenses at from two to four times those of radio. It, therefore, took some degree of courage and vision for radio broadcasters to accept "the grim insecurity of plowing in hundreds of thousands of dollars without an immediate, countable, clear return at hand."[23] Not until 1954 did gross revenues from television-time sales finally surpass those taken in by radio. By that time, in comedian Fred Allen's words, stars and sponsors were deserting radio "like bones at a barbecue."[24]

It was clear from the first that the major radio networks would attempt to form television chains, too. NBC took the lead when it connected twenty-five affiliates by 1949, the year in which network television effectively began. As television grew, network radio shrank to little more than a news service.

Television had established its clear ascendancy by 1960. Over five hundred stations were in operation, and time sales reached $1.6 billion, or some 13 percent of all advertising expenditures, regardless of medium. In contrast to the perils of 1948, the ownership of a television station in a sizable market area was now regarded as a key to the mint.

In the years since 1960, broadcasting witnessed a number of developments that affected the economics and the structure of the industry. For example, radio discovered a second life, even in an era of television ascendancy, by transforming itself from a network-programmed, mass-entertainment medium to a local music and information service. Specialized program formats became the rule, with each station targeting a particular segment of the listening audience and tailoring its sound and personalities to that age or ethnic group's tastes.

An extraordinary variety of radio formats, ranging from "Top 40" music, first programmed at midwestern and southern stations managed by Robert Todd Storz in the early 1950s, to "all-news" information, first successfully introduced in 1966 at WINS, the Westinghouse station in New York City, as well as many other format variations, appeared in this period. Furthermore, when stereo sound was added to FM transmission in the 1960s, the result made that hitherto neglected service at least the equal of AM radio in listener popularity. Of the 8,800 commercial radio stations on the air in 1987, about 45 percent are FM, and in many communities they are the ratings leaders. Overall, for a form of broadcasting many supposedly knowledgable observers were consigning to the grave in the 1950s, radio is enjoying a very robust life. The total number of stations in the country has tripled in the past forty years, and they are earning a highly respectable 25 percent (about $5 billion) of all commercial broadcast advertising revenues in the 1980s.

In the world of television, a startling development since the late 1970s has been the decline in network dominance. Where once the three national networks—NBC, CBS, and ABC (the latter formed in 1945 out of the old NBC Blue chain)—commanded a 90 percent share of the viewers in the evening prime-time hours, since the mid-1980s that number has plummeted to 75 percent and less. In part, inroads into the traditional network share of the prime-time audience have been made by aggressive "independent" stations (ones not affiliated with any network) and by viewers who are watching motion pictures or pretaped programming on video cassette recorders (VCRs). VCRs, the electronic toys of the 1980s, can now be found in nearly half the TV homes in the United States.

The supremacy of the three networks has also been lessened by the appearance in 1986 of a fourth television chain. Fox Broadcasting, a property of Australian-born publishing magnate Rupert Murdoch, is the first significant attempt at establishing a true national programming service since the 1950s. Fox is proceeding cautiously at this point, concentrating on the prime-time hours, when viewing is at its highest, and introducing its program schedule one evening at a time. But its own ultimate economic success, especially in light of the increasing diffusion of the TV audience today, remains in doubt.

Probably most instrumental in reducing the three-network audience share has been the emergence of cablecasting. It was known as "community antenna television" when it was first seen in the 1950s, when enterprising small-town businessmen would erect large antennae atop nearby mountains or tall buildings so that television signals could be picked up from distant cities. The signals received would then be sent to TV sets in the homes of system subscribers, who paid for the service. During the 1960s, cable television moved into many of the country's major cities, but it was not until the following decade that the business began to achieve any real profits.

Cable's turning point came in 1975, when Home Box Office, a subsidiary of Time, Inc., initiated the first national, satellite-delivered programming service. Local cable-system operators were now able to promise subscribers a channel of commercial-free, recent motion pictures and other entertainment features. When more "premium" channels replicated the HBO innovation, cable television offered an attractive alternative to the conventional network program fare. By the mid-1980s, well over 40 percent of American television homes were wired for cable, and the industry's revenues totaled $4 billion and were still climbing.

While the three established networks were encountering this new competition, they were experiencing their own internal adventures as well. The ownership of two of the networks changed hands within a matter of months in 1985–1986. General Electric bought RCA, and with it GE thereby acquired RCA's subsidiary NBC, the country's top-rated TV network. Interestingly, GE had been one of the original owners of RCA sixty years earlier, and had then been forced by the Justice Department to divest itself of those holdings under the terms of a 1932 antitrust consent decree. In an even more unexpected takeover, ABC was acquired by Capital Cities Communications, Inc., an important owner of broadcasting stations but not a corporation previously thought capable of such a giant step. The third network, CBS, barely managed to escape a hostile takeover attempt in 1985 by the flamboyant Ted Turner, the Atlanta-based cable "superstation" entrepreneur. These ownership changes or attempted changes were other clear indications that the old days of a rock-solid three-network domination were indeed over.

A final development affecting the electronic media since the 1970s has been the deregulation movement. The American broadcasting system is anchored in private enterprise, but a central principle of its existence since the 1920s has been the concept of public responsibility. In the words of a 1966 federal court decision written by then Judge Warren Burger, later chief justice of the Supreme Court: "A broadcaster seeks and is granted the free and exclusive use of a limited and valuable part of the public domain; when he accepts that franchise it is burdened by enforceable public obligations."[25]

The advocates of deregulation have been the first to seriously question that venerable philosophy. Their leading governmental spokesman was Mark S. Fowler, whom President Reagan appointed to chair the FCC in 1981. Fowler was able to eliminate many minor procedural rules that unduly burdened radio and television operations, but he created storms of controversy when his FCC sought to substitute broad-brush, unfettered marketplace concepts for long-standing regulations grounded in the public responsibility standard. When Fowler resigned from the FCC in 1987, some of the momentum seemed to temporarily drain from the deregulation drive. It may be that Fowler's inability to more completely dismantle the regulatory system he abhorred proves the validity of a recent observation about the abruptness of the deregulatory effort: "The stake this country has in broadcast communications seems too precious to be subjected to drastic actions that may not allow for gradual modification of the system to deal with new conditions."[26]

"High Tech": From ENIAC to the Personal Computer

In recent years, a chorus of voices acclaimed the wonders of high technology and hailed it as the cure for all the economic woes of the nation. It would revitalize the "rustbelt" cities of the East and put millions of unemployed Americans back to work, said its enthusiasts. Of course, their expectations were complicated by the fact that there was no consensus on an exact definition of high technology. A Westinghouse executive, for instance, defined it as "any technology with a high rate of change," while a New England state official described it simply as "any industry that is going to create jobs in the 1980s and 1990s."[27]

The Bureau of Labor Statistics, however, has been more specific. It classifies an industry as high technology if its R&D expenditures and number of technical employees are double the average for all

American manufacturers. Although various industries qualify as "high tech" under the standard, most Americans tend to equate the term with computers. Therefore, as an example of a post-1945 industry, we will briefly examine the business of computers.

Charles Babbage, an early nineteenth-century Cambridge University professor, is usually cited as "the father" of the computer, since he devised many of the principles upon which it is based. Babbage never completed the "Analytical Engine" that he had conceived, a massive steam-powered mechanical contraption that employed punched cards similar to modern punched cards, but his concepts are remembered.

During the Second World War, two faculty members at the University of Pennsylvania's Moore School of Engineering, J. Presper Eckert and John W. Mauchly, collaborated to build an electronic digital computer that they christened ENIAC (the Electronic Numerical Integrator and Computer). It used vacuum tubes, occupied some fifteen thousand square feet of floor space, and was first put into service in the federal government's Los Alamos Laboratories in late 1945. Eckert and Mauchly left the university in 1946 to form their own commercial company; they planned to sell their computers to whatever governmental agency or private corporation might be interested.

They undertook the assembly of a new machine to replace the ENIAC. It was called UNIVAC (Universal Automatic Computer), and the first was to be delivered to the Bureau of the Census. But when development costs exceeded the resources of their small firm, the two pioneer computer men were forced to seek outside financial support. They found it in James H. Rand, board chairman of the Remington Rand Corporation, a large manufacturer of office equipment. Eckert and Mauchly sold their company to Rand, who did not hold the prevailing opinion that the market for computers would be limited to a half-dozen customers at the most.

The first UNIVAC was shipped to the Census Bureau in June 1951 and immediately placed Remington Rand in the forefront of computer technology. Eckert and Mauchly accepted positions in the company, which in 1955 merged with the Sperry Corporation to become Sperry Rand. For a while in the 1950s, the name UNIVAC was a generic term for computers because the Eckert-Mauchly-Rand product dominated the emerging industry. That dominance soon ended when International Business Machines (IBM) entered the field.

Thomas J. Watson, Sr., was first employed by the National Cash Register Company (NCR) in 1895; by 1914, he had become one of its top executives. He was then fired by NCR's eccentric czar, John H. Patterson. Watson, however, had learned his business skills from Patterson, who, for all his arbitrary and dictatorial behavior, can probably be regarded as the originator of modern salesmanship.

Although many businesses treated their salesmen as necessary evils, Patterson regarded them as his key employees, and he trained them accordingly. The training included memorizing a company primer, *How I Sell a Cash Register*, and the posting of a variety of slogans, the most prevalent of which was the single word THINK. More important, Patterson guaranteed his salesmen exclusive territories, and he allowed them to earn high incomes if they sold successfully. Watson copied Patterson's methods when he had a company of his own.

After he was fired in 1914, Watson sought a new business opportunity, and particularly one in which he would be the principal decision maker. His search ended when he took over a hitherto shaky firm with the ungainly name of the Computing-Tabulating-Recording Company that made accounting machines, time clocks, and butchers' scales. Under Watson's management, new office machines were introduced and successfully marketed, and earnings gradually rose to more than respectable levels. In keeping with the strengthened standing of the company, it adopted a new corporate signature in 1924: International Business Machines, or IBM.

Watson employed Patterson's techniques and added some of his own to motivate IBM employees. The company had its own songbook, which featured such inspirational pieces as "Ever Onward IBM," and it hosted an annual three-day military-style encampment for salesmen who achieved 100 percent of their assigned quotas. The festivities featured "band music, displays of flags and fireworks, awards for gallantry in commercial combat and endless St. Crispin's Day speeches by company brass."[28]

By 1939 IBM's revenues reached $39 million and its profits $9.1 million. In the office-machine industry, its sales were exceeded only by Remington Rand, but its profits were far ahead of any competitor. The decision to enter the computer field, though, was not that of Watson. It seems to have hinged upon the return of Watson's son, Thomas, Jr., from wartime service in 1945. The younger Watson moved rapidly up the executive ladder and was groomed to take over the entire operation. He assumed the IBM presidency in 1952. It was Thomas, Jr., who first became convinced that there was a substantial market for computers awaiting the right machines, and he convinced his father to commit the company to their development.

The first IBM computer, the 701, was delivered in 1953. Although it was intended primarily for scientific users, the 702 followed soon afterward to compete with the UNIVAC in the business market. The first 702 was installed in 1955 by Monsanto Chemical. Even before then, however, IBM had announced that two newer machines were being developed, the 704 as a scientific replacement for the 701, and the 705 as a further improvement on the recently produced 702. Such advance announcements were later the focus of vigorous competitor complaints and legal actions, since they caused potential customers to decide against a rival machine already available and to wait instead for the well-advertised IBM product to come.

With the 704 and 705, IBM assumed the leadership in the industry. Within a decade, it had firmly established its first-place position; it controlled 65 percent of the market in 1965, while Sperry Rand, in second place, had only 12 percent. The shift was not the result of the superiority of IBM hardware. Although the 704 and 705 were excellent computers for their time, the UNIVACs were essentially their technical equals. The difference lay in marketing. According to one industry observer: "UNIVAC salesmen, well primed in the special features of their equipment, visited company presidents and talked learnedly of dual circuitry, metal tape and mercury delay lines; IBM salesmen promised that their computer would get the payroll out two days early and save vast sums of money in the process; and there was no question whose argument was more persuasive."[29]

During the 1960s, the industry's structure became characterized as IBM and the Seven Dwarfs (IBM was never called Snow White, especially not by its competition). The dwarfs at that time were Sperry Rand, Control Data Corporation, Honeywell, RCA, NCR, General Electric, and Burroughs. When GE and RCA later dropped out of the computer business (RCA in 1971 after losses of over $250 million), their places were taken by Xerox (only temporarily until it, too, bowed out in 1975) and Digital Equipment Corporation (DEC), a manufacturer of smaller minicomputers.

Computer development has passed through multiple stages or generations since the 1950s. The first generation employed vacuum tubes in massive banks of black boxes. The second generation replaced tubes with a foot-long array of transistors, and the third generation, which appeared in the mid-1960s, substituted integrated circuitry for transistors.

IBM's third-generation machines were the 360 series, so named because they were said to encompass the entire spectrum, 360 degrees, of modern computer technology. They were brought out in 1965 following a stupendous investment of $5 billion in their development. After some initial problems were solved, the series was a huge success and shaped the direction of the industry for a decade afterward. In Robert Sobel's words: "In the history of computers, everything is pre-360 or post-360."[30]

By 1980 Americans were spending over $55 billion a year on data processing, and they spent a third of that figure on new hardware. Of the money expended for general-purpose computers, IBM's share continued at over 60 percent. One measure of the company's success is the fact that an investment of only $20,000 in IBM stock in the early 1950s, before the corporation produced its first computer, would have grown to over $1 million by 1980, and the shareholder would also have collected more than $400,000 in dividends along the way.

IBM has also survived periodic antitrust bouts both with the Justice Department and with its competitors. The latest was a suit filed by the Justice Department in 1969 that charged IBM with attempting to monopolize the industry. The case ended in a complete victory for the company when the department dropped the suit in January 1982 and admitted that it was without merit. The withdrawal came after uncounted hours of legal research and preparation by both sides, and interestingly, almost simultaneously with the AT&T consent-decree agreement discussed earlier in this chapter.

An economic study of the first thirty years of the computer era has made the point that the period was one "of continual, rapid, often unanticipated technical change."[31] Furthermore, what was true for the 1950s through the 1970s has certainly held true for the 1980s. The advent of the microcomputer, a relatively low-cost desktop machine with the computational and information-processing power of the room-sized marvels of a quarter of a century ago, ushered in the age of the personal computer. No longer is sophisticated computer technology confined to corporate offices. Personal computers have become an essential part of the educational process in elementary and secondary schools, and they have become an everyday accessory in a growing number of American homes, where they balance checkbooks, play games, and write novels.

In reality, the birth of the age of the personal computer corresponds to the birth of Apple Computer, Inc., an enterprise that celebrated just its tenth anniversary as a corporation in January 1987. As a 1985 *Newsweek* article stated: "The story of Apple Computer is not just another garage-to-gigabucks, brainstorming-to-burnout, high-tech tale. It has become *the* success story of the generation. Two scruffy kids . . . combine some technical genius and marketing flair and spawn a billion dollar company."[32] In the process, the personal computer industry came into being.

The "two scruffy kids" were a pair of college dropouts from Cupertino, California, Steven B. Jobs, who has been called "the Johnny Appleseed of personal computing," and Stephen Wozniak, who would be the chief hardware engineer on the early Apple products. Actually, their initial "business" venture together was wiring and selling "little blue boxes" that made it possible for university students at Berkeley to place long-distance telephone calls without the nuisance of paying AT&T. They began assembling the first Apple units in the Jobs family garage in 1976, marketing their small output to local hobbyists and computer shops.[33]

The technical excellence of the Apple II, a more advanced version of the very first machines the team built, quickly attracted the attention of computer enthusiasts and of some knowledgeable financial backers in the Silicon Valley, the cluster of high-tech communities in northern California near San Francisco. As a result, the Jobs-Wozniak partnership was succeeded by a better-capitalized corporation, Apple Computer, Inc., formed in 1977. The immediate growth of the company after that was phenomenal. In 1978 sales totalled $7.8 million; just two years later sales had soared to $117.9 million and Apple earned a $11.7 million profit. Jobs and Wozniak, still in their twenties, were overnight folk heroes as well as multimillionaires, and Apple Computer took less time to reach the *Fortune* 500 list of the nation's largest industrial corporations than any other new company in the history of that index.

Until 1981, the emerging personal computer industry in the United States was clearly led by the Cupertino comet, but that was the year IBM chose to introduce its answer to the Apple II, the PC. With IBM's well-proven marketing and service expertise added to the high quality of the PC as a machine, it rapidly became the personal computer of choice in the country's business offices. Apple found itself still leading only in the less lucrative educational and home markets, in which IBM showed little interest.

Several critical developments occurred within the Apple organization during the next several years. A new president was named in 1983, when Steve Jobs, now chairman of the board, personally recruited John Sculley from the soft drink industry, where he had been heading Pepsi-Cola's operations. It became Sculley's responsibility to be the company's chief administrative officer, while Jobs concentrated on the design and production of the Macintosh, the new computer Apple was counting on to win back first place from IBM.

When the Macintosh was unveiled in 1984, it sold well to individuals, but it proved to have drawbacks as a business computer. By 1985 Apple could claim only 24 percent of the microcomputer market, as compared with 40 percent for IBM, and in the spring of that year Apple reported its first-ever quarterly loss. In addition, its stock, which had traded at a high of $63 in 1983, was selling for only $14 in June 1985. With continuing problems in the Macintosh division apparent, Sculley convinced the Apple directors to strip Jobs of all his operational authority, leaving him with just the honorary title of chairman. Jobs then resigned in September 1985, severing his ties with the company that had begun in his garage less than a decade before, and soon organized a new educational computer firm named, appropriately, Next, Inc. Wozniak, the other cofounder, had withdrawn from active participation in the business some time before.

During 1986, Apple Computer sales reached $1.9 billion and its profits were up over the previous year. Yet the Macintosh still had not overtaken the PC in sales to commercial customers, and in early 1987 Apple's goal became all the harder to attain when IBM announced its new Personal System/2 model, the PC's successor. Nevertheless, even in second place, Apple Computer in its ten-year life as a corporation represents an American business success story worthy of a Horatio Alger novel.

The Military-Industrial Complex

On January 18, 1961, in a "farewell" speech to the nation, President Dwight Eisenhower issued a warning. He first noted that, "until the latest of our world conflicts, the United States had no armaments industry. American makers of plowshares could, with time and as required, make swords as well. But now we can no longer risk emergency improvision of national defense; we have been compelled to create a permanent armaments industry of vast proportions." Then he added his now famous caveat: "In the counsels of government we must guard against the acquisition of unwarranted influence, whether sought or unsought, by the military-industrial complex. The potential for the disastrous rise of misplaced power exists and will persist."[34]

In singling out the "military-industrial complex" as an area for public concern, Eisenhower gave a name to a debate that began before his speech and has continued long afterward. Of course, the term itself has acquired an unfavorable tone, so those who are directly involved usually refer instead to the "defense industry." By whatever name, however, the concept denotes an alliance of the interests of Pentagon officials, corporate contractors, and funded university research faculty. But, in a larger sense, it also includes anyone who has a material or philosophical stake in an elaborate defense establishment—politicians (national, state, and local), labor unions, newspapers, and even ordinary citizens in any community where significant work is being done for the military.

During the 1960s, as an example of this larger involvement, a bitter battle was waged over a $7 billion contract to build a new Air Force plane, the TFX (Tactical Fighter, Experimental—now called the F-111). The two final bidders were Boeing, whose headquarters were in Seattle and who planned to build the plane in Wichita, and General Dynamics, whose corporate offices were then in New York and whose production facilities were in Fort Worth. Before Secretary of Defense Robert McNamara finally awarded the contract to General Dynamics, the competition became an outlandish geographical and political struggle between influential political leaders, well-connected businessmen, and other prominent citizens in all the affected states, each seeking to bring to bear on the Defense Department whatever pressure they could muster. Later, after the TFX developed numerous operational problems when put into actual service by the Air Force, a congressional investigating committee questioned whether it should have been built at all.

At one time, military spending was a tiny part of the federal budget, but that is no longer the case. In the past forty years, the United States has expended over $2 trillion on war and defense require-

ments, a figure that is almost incomprehensible to the human mind.
On an annual basis defense spending has grown from $1.9 billion in
1939 to $300 billion in 1987. Indeed, under the Reagan adminis-
tration in the 1980s, there has been the longest and largest peacetime
arms buildup in American history. The Reagan approach to defense
spending has been described as "theological," in the sense that it is
grounded in a generalized belief that the nation must demonstrate
to our adversaries a willingness to expend vast sums to maintain
military parity, if not supremacy. Less important is the matter of
what the sums of money will actually buy.[35]

From another perspective, however defense expenditures have not
risen at all. In 1987, they accounted for 28 percent of total federal
spending, down from 29 percent in 1974 and 40 percent at the
height of the Vietnam War. Meanwhile, spending on social or "human resources" programs has increased to over 50 percent of the
budget.

Nevertheless, the defense industry plays an important role in the
American economy. It employs between one-fifth and one-third of
all American engineers and scientists, and over 10 percent of the
country's factory labor force. It is not, however, an especially concentrated industry. The top five firms control only about 20 percent
of the business, and the top twenty-five have just half the total
"sales"—not exactly oligopolistic proportions. Indeed, the principal
contractors, cognizant of the many pitfalls that a company can encounter in the defense industry, have tended to reduce their dependence on such work. But a corporate strategy of less reliance on
Pentagon business is something easier to preach than to practice. At
General Dynamics (GD) in the 1970s, for example, top management
stated its objective was an increase in civilian work (then running
about 40 percent of GD's sales) "as a hedge against fluctuations in
the defense market."[36] Nevertheless, by 1985 government contracts
were 88 percent of GD's revenues, a higher proportion than ever
before.

Why does a McDonnell Douglas, a Lockheed, a Boeing, or a General Dynamics stay involved at all? Jacques S. Gansler has recently
offered several explanations. He cites the fact that the government
pays for R&D expenses—and there is a history of eventually transferring that technology into the civilian sector; that a sizable volume
of business is usually available for a protracted five- to ten-year period
once the development contract for a weapons system is awarded;

and that it offers the "experience of managing large, high-technology programs."[37]

By staying in, however, those companies have opened themselves to a certain amount of criticism and even social stigma (Du Pont dropped out when it was denounced for manufacturing napalm in the 1960s). They have been accused, among other charges, of deliberately submitting unrealistically low bids to win contracts—and thus later incurring skyrocketing cost overruns—and of employing former military and civilian Pentagon officials in order to parlay their influence into stronger negotiating positions when competing for defense largesse. On the matter of high costs, one industry executive claims that, "from the days of the Wright brothers' airplane to the era of the modern high-performance fighter aircraft, the cost of an individual aircraft has unwaveringly grown by a factor of four every ten years." He wryly adds: "In the year 2054, the entire defense budget will purchase just one tactical fighter."[38]

Both the boons and the pitfalls of being a prime defense contractor can be found in the recent history of the General Dynamics Corporation, an organization that has been called "the world's most diverse arms company."[39] It is also quite probably this country's most controversial one. Unlike most other weapons suppliers, GD has strong links to all three United States military services: it builds Trident nuclear submarines for the Navy, F-16 fighter planes for the Air Force, and the M-1 battle tank for the Army, among other armament systems. In 1986 it ranked first among the Pentagon's largest defense contractors, and its overall sales of $9.2 billion (of which more than $8 billion was government business) put it in thirty-sixth place on the *Fortune* 500 list. Yet, the company has lately endured accusations, investigations, fines, and suspensions, and to many Americans it is the corporate embodiment of waste and corruption in military spending.

General Dynamics' origins date back to 1900, when a little firm named the Electric Boat Company sold the United States Navy its first workable submarine for $150,000. Electric Boat, located in Groton, Connecticut, was the base upon which General Dynamics was built. The second piece was the Consolidated Aircraft Corporation (later Consolidated Vultee or Convair), begun in 1923. During the Second World War, the various Convair plants built 33,000 military aircraft, nearly 13 percent of the total American production between

1941 and 1945. Electric Boat and Convair merged in 1954, and the resulting entity was the General Dynamics Corporation.

David S. Lewis, Jr., a native of South Carolina, earned his degree in aeronautical engineering from Georgia Tech in 1939. He joined the McDonnell Aircraft Corporation in St. Louis (now McDonnell Douglas) in 1946 as chief of aerodynamics, and in 1962 he was named its president and chief operating officer. But when founder James McDonnell showed no willingness to retire and open the way for Lewis to take over the company, he chose in 1970 to accept an offer from General Dynamics to be its chairman of the board and CEO. It was Lewis who paid Lee Iacocca $350 million in 1982 for Chrysler's defense products division, which held a valuable contract with the Army for the new M-1 tank. Iacocca's urgent need for cash at the time to keep Chrysler afloat worked to GD's advantage. General Dynamics now became the only defense firm with multibillion dollar weapons contracts with all three military services, and in 1983 it alone accounted for over 5 percent of all Pentagon prime contracts.

At that moment when Lewis's GD seemed atop the defense world, he and the company were rocked by sensational charges of fradulent and improper business practices. A Justice Department investigation of GD had actually started during the days of the Carter administration in the 1970s, but it was terminated in 1981 without any formal action being taken against the corporation. The probe was reopened in 1984, however, because of the revelations of a former GD executive vice president, P. Takis Veliotis, who had been the manager of the Electric Boat division. Veliotis fled the country in 1983 to avoid prosecution for his role in an alleged kickback scheme with a subcontractor. Then, from a plush villa in Athens, Veliotis, a Greek citizen, bargained for a grant of immunity from prosecution by offering the Justice Department information that GD had supposedly defrauded the government by giving the Navy false financial data about cost overruns on Trident submarines, for which the company was reimbursed.

The Veliotis allegations spurred a broader Justice Department examination and also some well-publicized congressional inquiries. Their findings ranged from charges that GD had deliberately submitted unrealistic bids to the Navy in order to win submarine contracts, a practice known as "buying in," to the fact that over the years the company had given Admiral Hyman Rickover, the Trident program head, gifts worth $67,000, including a pair of diamond earrings for the admiral's wife. The jewelry's cost was then concealed in the regular expense records of the corporation. Other unpalatable stories told of an $18,000 country club initiation fee that was billed to the government, of negotiating possible GD employment with an assistant secretary of the Navy while he was still in his post at the Pentagon and awarding contracts, and a good deal more.

David Lewis denied that the company had intentionally acted improperly. Lewis told a congressional committee in February 1985: "We do many things well and we make our share of mistakes. But those are human errors. I refuse to accept any portrayal of our company or its people as being dishonest or lacking integrity in our dealings with the United States Government or our many other valued customers."[40]

The Navy, at least, was not convinced. Twice during 1985 it temporarily suspended General Dynamics from bidding on new contracts. In addition, the corporation was fined $676,000, a figure arrived at by multiplying the value of the Rickover gifts by a factor of ten. According to the secretary of the Navy, GD had been guilty of pervasive misconduct. The suspensions were lifted only after GD agreed to reform its procedures along lines prescribed by the Defense Department, and after David Lewis promised to retire before the end of the year. In reality, it had proved difficult for the Navy to get along without such a key supplier, and in one instance bidding on a contract was postponed until GD was again eligible.

Taking over as Lewis's replacement at the beginning of 1986 was Stanley C. Pace, who had been president of TRW, Inc., a Cleveland automotive and electronics firm that was also in the defense business. Among other actions, Pace distributed to all of GD's 103,000 employees a twenty-page ethics booklet, established ethics "hotlines" so that workers could report any illegal practices, and hired a University of Chicago business school dean to conduct in-house ethics seminars for management personnel. The company tightened its rules, so much so in fact that one manager informed his staff: "If your neighbor is a supplier or a military person, we don't even want you exchanging Christmas gifts."[41]

It was with some sense of vindication that GD received the news on May 19, 1987, that the Justice Department was terminating its three-year-old investigation and would not seek any indictments against the company. After examining over 40,000 documents and quizzing 120 executives, Justice admitted it lacked enough evidence for a successful prosecution. In St. Louis, GD's headquarters, a spokesman said the decision in Washington "gives us comfort after the years of allegations, accusations, and adverse publicity."[42]

Not everyone was satisfied with the result. A commentary in *Business Week* termed the Justice Department withdrawal "a bad precedent" and claimed the government had "left the impression that breaking the often-incestuous relationship between military contractors and their Pentagon overseers isn't a top priority."[43] Moreover, congressional critics of General Dynamics pledged to continue pressing their own investigations, so the company may not yet have put its troubled past behind it.

For all the debate over the military-industrial complex, both conservatives and liberals concede that there is no immediate alternative to high levels of defense spending. The threat of war is a reality in the modern world and necessitates a national security response. The argument, therefore, is over degrees of protection rather than the basic decision to have a strong defense force. While there has long been sentiment that the existing defense-procurement process can and should be reformed, whether the reformers will ever be able to make any significant changes in a system that even its ardent advocates concede contains a healthy measure of inefficiency, waste, and conflict of interest remains to be seen.

The Regulatory System—Old and New

As we have seen in previous chapters, the scope of the American regulatory system has been considerably widened in the half century since Franklin Roosevelt entered the White House. The government is no longer confined to policing the competitive practices of business and removing imperfections in the market system, although that role, what has been termed the "old regulation," certainly continues. A "new regulation" emerged with the Roosevelt programs of the 1930s, in which the federal government took on the responsibility for stabilizing the economy and promoting economic growth, guaranteeing economic security for all Americans, and extending its authority into other unexplored areas of governmental action.

The Employment Act of 1946 acknowledged this stabilization role. The act pledged that the government would "promote maximum employment, production, and purchasing power." The Council of

Economic Advisers was created within the executive branch and the Joint Economic Committee in Congress; both had the duty of monitoring the progress of the economy in relation to the overall goals set by the act.

In addition to macroeconomic stablization, another part of the new regulation has been the government's guarantee of individual economic security. The enactment of programs such as social security and unemployment insurance in the 1930s and of various kinds of welfare and health insurance after the Second World War have all served to form what President Reagan has called a social safety net. There is a consensus among Democrats and Republicans alike about the urgent need to maintain the security provided by this safety net, although the total funding of many social programs has been reduced in the 1980s.

Furthermore, the new regulation extends federal intervention into such problems as environmental pollution, consumer protection, occupational safety, urban blight, and affirmative action in employment. The expense imposed upon businesses in complying with a huge outpouring of regulatory requirements has been heavy. Companies have had to spend perhaps an additional $100 billion or more on compliance, and the consumer has absorbed the entire expense in the form of higher prices on products and services.

On the other hand, the fate of the old regulation can be seen best by tracing the antitrust story since the resignation of Thurman Arnold from the Justice Department in 1943. Undoubtedly, Arnold's most important single victory came in a case that was not settled until 1945, two years after he had taken his seat on the federal bench. The government's conduct of the *United States v. Aluminum Company of America* action resulted in the first noteworthy modification of the rule of reason since that doctrine had been articulated in 1911. The case was decided by the distinguished jurist Learned Hand in the Second Circuit Court of Appeals when the Supreme Court was unable to muster a quorum of six justices to hear the case. Hand's ruling was thus treated as the equivalent of a Supreme Court decision.

Hand found that Alcoa manufactured more than 90 percent of the virgin aluminum ingot used in the United States, and he concluded that this constituted a monopoly under Section 2 of the Sherman Act. The defense of good behavior proved unavailing. Although the corporation was shown not to be abusing its dominant market position, Hand negated the thirty-year-old rule of reason by holding that the Sherman Act "did not condone 'good trusts' and condemn 'bad' ones; it forbade all."[44] Thus, rather than focusing on the defendant's abusive practices (since none were in evidence), the judge emphasized market structure and potential power.

The decision, at the time, seemed to open a new antitrust era, but this did not occur, even though the Alcoa verdict was followed in 1950 by the Celler-Kefauver Amendment to Section 7 of the Clayton Act, which closed the so-called assets loophole. Under the original wording, a firm was forbidden to acquire the stock of another company if such an acquisition markedly reduced competition in an industry. The law of 1950 also prohibited mergers by the purchase of assets rather than capital stock, if that step reduced competition or created a monopoly.

A vigorous period of antitrust litigation failed to develop, in part, because business managers took greater care to avoid possible Sherman Act violations; the Justice Department was more willing to settle matters out of court; and new business combinations—specifically the proliferation of conglomerate mergers—"made antitrust legislation appear antiquated and inadequate, if not irrelevant."[45]

Horizontal mergers of anything but the most trivial type still seemed likely to run aground in the courts. In *United States v. Von's Grocery Co.* (1966), the Supreme Court stopped a "baby" merger of Von's, a retail grocery chain in Los Angeles that had only 4.7 percent of all area sales, and an even smaller chain. Together they would have accounted for only 7.5 percent of all grocery sales in Los Angeles. Vertical mergers (those between suppliers and customers) were also regarded with growing disfavor. In 1962, in the first case decided under the Celler-Kefauver Amendment, the Supreme Court blocked a proposed merger of a manufacturer, the Brown Shoe Company, with a retail chain, Kinney Shoes, although Kinney sold less than 2 percent of all shoes retailed in the nation. The court feared foreclosure of the Kinney outlets to other manufacturers, even though they were minimal in terms of the total industry.

In spite of the above cases and the Celler-Kefauver Amendment, a new merger wave swept the business community in the 1950s and 1960s. It differed from the earlier waves of mergers at the turn of the century and in the 1920s in that it lasted longer and was precipitated more by aggressive corporate managers than by investment bankers. Conglomerate mergers, in which the two parties were neither direct competitors nor related as supplier and customer, were the most prevalent and accounted for over 50 percent of all mergers in the 1950s and more than 60 percent in the following decade. High stock prices assisted these mergers because it was easier for conglomerates to pay for acquisitions with their own inflated-price securities than with cash.

The conglomerates that attracted the most attention, almost frantic at times, were International Telephone and Telegraph (ITT), Litton Industries, Ling-Temco-Vought (LTV), and Textron. Each was headed during its vigorous years by one dominant figure: Harold S. Geneen (ITT), Charles "Tex" Thornton (Litton Industries), James Ling (LTV), and Royal Little (Textron). "Almost to a man," business historian Robert Sobel has written, "the major conglomerators were classic outsiders." Sobel drew the following profile of them: "Some were foreign born, most were Jewish or Catholic, and many came from areas of the country not known for producing major businessmen, namely the South and the Far West. Their education was scanty, and these men were poorly connected with the old establishments, which in some cases rejected them out of hand, and considered them somewhat barbaric."[46] Not surprisingly, therefore, the conglomerate makers were ready to disregard traditional rules and to devise their own instead.

We will not trace the expansion of each of the major conglomerates, but we can note that Royal Little showed the way in the 1950s when he suddenly transformed Textron, his medium-sized, rather ordinary textile company into a wildly diversified corporate giant. Seeing but dim prospects for significant growth in the textile industry, between 1954 and 1961 Little increased Textron's indebtedness from $4 million to $92 million and used the funds to buy fistfuls of unrelated firms. They produced everything from bathroom accessories to chain saws, and from golf carts to helicopters. At one point, he even purchased an old Navy vessel and remodeled it into a cruise ship to carry tourists to Hawaii. Little retired from Textron in 1962 after pioneering the conglomerate movement in the United States. Ironically, after all the maneuvering and with revenues of well over a billion dollars a year, the one industry Textron was not in by the mid-1960s was textiles, its original base.

At ITT, it was English-born Harold Geneen, a hard-driving manager with a night-school accounting degree, who forged the conglomerate strategy. For years, ITT had been a foreign twin of AT&T,

because it operated communication systems and telephone equipment plants in other countries. Geneen, who had specialized in financial administration at such corporations as Jones & Laughlin and Raytheon, joined ITT as its new CEO in 1959. Dubious about the future of his organization's overseas enterprises, he determined on a policy of substantially increasing ITT's domestic business through aggressive diversification. In the period between 1961 and 1968 alone, he acquired fifty-two companies with combined assets of $1.5 billion, including such established names as Avis (rental cars), Continental Baking (Wonder Bread, Twinkies, etc.), William Levitt & Sons (home construction), and the Sheraton Corporation (hotels).

As a result, ITT's original telecommunications line by 1974 amounted to only 20 percent of its total revenues. The rest was derived from such varied fields as banking, electronics, finance, hotels, insurance, and residential construction. The Justice Department halted ITT's attempt to buy the American Broadcasting Company in 1968, thus preventing ITT from becoming a major force in the electronic media. The department approved a takeover of Hartford Insurance in 1971 only after Geneen agreed to divest his conglomerate of Avis, Levitt, and some other acquisitions made earlier.

The conglomerate movement reached its peak in 1968. After that date, a combination of factors reversed its course. The Justice Department, following a decade of uncertainty, began to challenge some takeovers. More important was the fact that major conglomerates failed to translate their acquisitions into higher profits. Litton Industries, for example, had purchased ninety-seven small companies between 1958 and 1969, and its common stock had soared from $6 a share in 1960 to over $100 in early 1968. But poor earnings reports after that time drove the price back down so that, in 1974, it was selling for less than $3. Other conglomerates had the same experience.

In addition, several important business and financial periodicals began to banner stories that exposed questionable methods employed by some conglomerates to improve their earnings and boost their stock prices. One critic concluded: "The new conglomerate managers did not discover new management techniques, but rather a seemingly endless number of tax, accounting, and financial gimmicks that favored merger over internal growth."[47] Finally, the economic slowdown of the 1970s was another test of conglomerate management, which many failed.

The Fourth Wave

The advent of the 1980s has produced new questions about the status of United States antitrust policy. The fourth great merger wave of the twentieth century has swept over American business without any perceptible reaction from Justice Department antitrust enforcers. The wave reached a peak in 1985, when the total value of the fifty largest mergers and acquisitions was $94.6 billion. That year saw Philip Morris acquire General Foods for $5.7 billion, and General Motors buy Hughes Aircraft for $4.7 billion, but even those transactions were dwarfed by Chevron Corp.'s $13.2 billion purchase of Gulf Oil in 1984. The takeovers continued in 1986—General Electric bought RCA, USX acquired Texas Oil & Gas, and Burroughs merged with Sperry, among many others. *Business Week* termed the convulsions "deal mania" and described the tempo as "frantic."[48]

This fourth merger tide was precipitated by several factors, including a modest inflation rate and a soaring stock market. Particularly important, though, was a relaxed regulatory environment and an easing of antitrust constraints under the Reagan administration. One scholar has characterized the philosophical climate in the administration as a "latter-day Economic Darwinism" that has been translated into a policy approach of tolerating increases in business concentration, especially if the new combinations appear to improve American competitiveness in the world market.[49] Significantly, the principal academic critic of the antitrust laws was law school professor Robert H. Bork, whose 1978 book, *The Antitrust Paradox*, made a vigorous case against their use. Bork was appointed a federal appeals court judge by President Reagan, and then in the spring of 1987 was nominated for a seat on the United States Supreme Court.

The merger wave of the 1980s has also been marked by the appearance of a new business figure, the corporate raider. The typical tactic of the raider is to fasten upon a company whose stock is not performing well on the exchange. The raider will buy a small stake in the company, and then make a tender offer to the other shareholders for enough additional stock to gain a controlling interest in the firm. The tender offer will generally be entirely or largely financed with borrowed money. Once the raider secures control, the assets of the company, its various operating divisions, can be sold off individually to pay down the takeover loans. In many cases tender offers never ended in an actual control change, because before that happened, the threatened management of the targeted firm paid a huge premium to buy the raider's stock, a practice that has come to be known as "greenmail."

More recently, some companies have staved off raiders by adopting elaborate antitakeover devices, mainly financial and procedural mechanisms that are informally referred to as "shark repellants," and a number of state legislatures have assisted by passing laws making it more difficult to execute a hostile takeover. Meanwhile, the debate goes on as to the real economic impact of the turmoil.

Carl Icahn, who made millions in raids on companies such as Phillips Petroleum and B.F. Goodrich, and who gained formal control of TWA in 1985, defines himself as a "concerned shareholder," not a raider.[50] According to Icahn, too many corporations have become bloated and inefficient, and thus are not operating up to their potential. Icahn sees raiders as beneficial for the economy, since they are the only force capable of ousting poor managements from otherwise entrenched positions in those companies. The same views have been expressed by another prominent raider, T. Boone Pickens, a Texas oil man who established Mesa Petroleum in 1964. In his autobiography, published in 1987, Pickens wrote: "For more than thirty years I had witnessed mismanagement in American corporations. . . . And the nation's economy was suffering as a consequence. There had to be some way to mobilize against this powerful enemy."[51] To Icahn and Pickens, their actions were rendering a critically important service to other stockholders and to the country by enforcing a stricter accountability on corporate managers.

But the arguments against Icahn and Pickens have been strongly voiced too. Managers have complained bitterly that they are forced to ignore the legitimate interests of customers and employees and the long-range future of their companies in order to ward off raiders. They are compelled to emphasize short-run profits, and this often means unwise cutbacks in research programs or the hasty laying off of workers in order to shrink operating costs, boost immediate earnings, and appease dissatisfied stockholders. In effect, they can be so busy fighting raiders that they cannot fight Japanese competitors.

Moreover, since takeovers are usually financed with borrowed dollars, frequently generated by the selling of "junk" bonds (very high-yield, speculative-grade bonds), there has been an enormous accumulation of debt in the corporate sector in the past several years. Some of this debt has been deliberately accumulated by would-be target companies, who hope thereby to make their balance sheets look less attractive to prospective raiders. Firms burdened with extremely heavy debt commitments are obviously in a much less favorable position to survive a severe downturn in the economy. The ultimate consequences of raiding, therefore, may not be determined until the nation's next sharp recession.

In the debate over raiding, who is right? Both sides are to some degree, since it clearly depends upon one's vantage point—that of the raider or that of the beseiged corporate manager. One thing is certain, however: administering a big business in the turbulent world of the 1980s is a much less secure vocation than it once was.

Prospects

Historians are understandably reluctant to make predictions about things to come. They realize their province is the past, not the future, and they tend to believe history repeats itself in only the broadest fashion. Thus we might look to examples of good journalistic speculation for some insights into the years ahead. One of the best recent forecasts was *Fortune's* special report, in February 1987, on the American economy in the 1990's.

It is *Fortune's* projection that we should not expect any spectacular developments. Instead, there will be "solid growth of the most benign kind, growth without enormous swings from boom to bust."[52] The American per capita gross national product should increase an average of 2 percent per year, well below the 4 percent annual rise in the GNP the nation enjoyed from 1948 to 1968, but at least above the lackluster 1.4 percent of the past twenty years.

During the 1990s, about 13 million new jobs will probably be created, and a startling 90 percent of them will be in service industries. It is also anticipated that 80 percent of those new jobs will be filled by women, minorities, and immigrants. The 1990s should see more women than ever before in top-level management posts. Studies indicate about 37 percent of all corporate managers now are women, as compared to 24 percent a decade ago. Significant for the future, too, is the fact that over one-third of the 70,000 MBA students graduating from the nation's business schools today are women, while they were an almost invisible 2 percent in 1967. The economy's shift to more service industries employment, a business sector that accepted women executives earlier than manufacturing, should also assist in opening the way for more females to become CEOs than there are now.

It is likely that manufacturing, smokestack America, will retain its 20 percent share of the GNP, but with fewer workers and fewer plants. One study has predicted that there will be no more than 10 percent of the work force in manufacturing in the early twenty-first century; the figure is 16 percent in 1987. Moreover, quite a few of the plants operating in the 1990s will be foreign-owned or joint ventures with overseas firms. In the automobile industry, for example, the current production of 600,000 cars from foreign-owned facilities in the United States will probably be at least doubled.

Within the large American corporation, "demassing" has lately become a popular catchword. It means simply that great numbers of middle managers and administrative staff personnel, as well as production-line workers, have either lost their jobs through layoffs or been demoted to more workaday duties. The process will probably continue into the 1990s, as companies fight to remain competitive by cutting costs, and as advances in computer networking make it possible for machines to do staff work more cheaply than people in many cases. One worrisome aspect of demassing is the fact that the baby-boom generation of the post–World War II years is maturing and will be ready to move into managerial slots in the 1990s, yet there will be fewer of those opportunities available. The result could be frustration and serious internal morale problems.

If the 1980s are any guide, the 1990s will see their share of business fads too. The 1980s have reflected what has been derisively called "management by best-seller." A succession of trendy books, each offering its special prescription for American business ills, whether it be fostering a "corporate culture" or "management-by-walking-around," has been snapped up by readers searching for instant solutions. The best-sellers have recommended adopting Japanese management methods (William Ouchi's *Theory Z*), introducing entrepreneurial projects within the large corporation (Gifford Pinchot III's *Intrapreneuring*), and staying close to your customer (Peters and Waterman's *In Search of Excellence*), to give just a few examples. The authors have almost always followed up the publication of their books with lucrative lecture tours and high-priced seminars offered to business groups. Surveying the phenomenon with some dismay, *Business Week* concluded: "Business fads are something of a necessary evil and have always been with us. What's different—and alarming—today is the sudden rise and fall of so many conflicting fads and how they influence the modern manager."[53]

In the area of governmental policy towards business, the Reagan years have been the era of deregulation. It was the explicit objective of the Reagan conservatives to replace what they regarded as the dead head of regulation with the invisible hand of free market competition. We have already discussed the implementation of that philosophy in broadcasting and telecommunications, but it was introduced in other regulated industries as well, notably airlines, railroads, and trucking. The deregulation campaign has given us mixed results and is now the focus of some sharp debate among academic and business economists.

In the case of the airlines, where deregulation actually began during the Carter presidency, passenger fares have declined from their 1970s levels, especially for travel between major cities. But the declining fares have been accompanied by a striking increase in industry concentration, which may eventually offset the gains achieved. A series of mergers and acquisitions has produced a situation in which the six largest carriers now control over 80 percent of the market, and some analysts predict the number will be 90 percent in the 1990s.

The Department of Transportation has endorsed virtually every proposed airline merger of the 1980s, and it apparently has not been disturbed by the current concentration ratio in the industry. Nevertheless, mounting criticisms of airline operations, as evidenced by the staggering increase in consumer complaints about delays, poor service, questionable pricing policies, and safety issues, has begun to generate calls for some form of "reregulation." Certainly, the outcome of the 1988 presidential election will be a key factor in determining whether the regulatory pendulum will swing back in the other direction during the 1990s.

One final comment is perhaps in order. More than a decade ago, Peter Drucker pointed out that America had become a "society of organizations," and it was thus incumbent upon the managers of those organizations, including business managers, to "hold themselves accountable for the quality of life and . . . to make the fulfillment of basic social values, beliefs, and purposes a major objective of their continuing normal activities rather than a social responsibility that restrains or that lies outside of their normal main functions."

By grounding their authority in such a moral commitment, managers earn an indispensable legitimacy, for as Drucker warned then: "Authority without legitimacy is usurpation."[54] What was true in the 1970s, when Drucker wrote those words, is still true today, and it will also be so in the 1990s and beyond.

SOME SUGGESTIONS
FOR FURTHER READING

SINCE one of the purposes of this book was to whet the reader's appetite for further servings of American business history, the following suggestions should provide a reasonable menu. Many of the best works in the field were cited in the footnotes of the preceding text, so the reader is encouraged to refer to those notes as well for guides to where he or she might pursue a favorite topic.

There are several survey works that deal with the history of business in the United States from the colonial era to the present. These include two by Thomas C. Cochran: *Two Hundred Years of American Business* (1977), and his earlier *Business in American Life* (1972). The latter takes more of a "business in society" approach, while the former is especially strong in comparing American business to developments in other countries. Herman E. Krooss and Charles Gilbert, *American Business History* (1972); Elisha Douglass, *The Coming of Age in American Business* (1971)—although it stops in the year 1900; Keith L. Bryant and Henry C. Dethloff, *A History of American Business* (1983); James Oliver Robertson, *America's Business* (1985); and Mansel G. Blackford and K. Austin Kerr, *Business Enterprise in American History* (1986) are all recommended as supplements to this text. For American business since 1900, see Cochran's *American Business in the 20th Century* (1972) and Robert Sobel's *The Age of Giant Corporations* (1972). Although they are more specialized, two works by Alfred D. Chandler, Jr., *The Visible Hand: The Managerial Revolution in American Business* (1977) and *Strategy and Structure: Chapters in the History of American Industrial Enterprise* (1962), are enormously valuable for delineating the relationship between business operations and administration. Two collections of cases dealing with specific episodes in the evolution of business in the United States are the recent *The Coming of Managerial Capitalism* (1985), edited by Alfred D. Chandler, Jr., and Richard S. Tedlow; and *American Business History: Case Studies* (1987), edited by Henry C. Dethloff and C. Joseph Pusateri.

There is a wealth of information about business in the essays contained in the three-volume *Encyclopedia of American Economic History* (1980), edited by Glenn Porter. The same can be said about the older multivolume series, *The Economic History of the United States.* Especially useful in that series are two studies of the nineteenth century, George Rogers Taylor's *The Transportation Revolution, 1815–1860* (1951) and Edward C. Kirkland's *Industry Comes of Age: Business, Labor, and Public Policy, 1860–1897* (1961). Stuart Bruchey's concise and interpretative book, *The Roots of American Economic Growth, 1607–1861* (1965), while also concerned primarily with the broad landscape of economic history, has good insights into business movements.

For a biographical approach to historical matter, there are a few collections of short essays on the careers of individual businessmen: Harold Livesay's *American Made: Men Who Shaped the American Economy* (1979), Jonathan Hughes' *The Vital Few: American Economic Progress and Its Protagonists* (1986), and Robert Sobel's *The Entrepreneurs: Explorations within the American Business Tradition* (1974). Although designed for classroom discussion use, N. S. B. Gras and Henrietta M. Larson, *Casebook in American Business History* (1939), still offers some good introductions to specific businessmen and their firms. There are far too many worthy full-length biographies to list here. But four, at least, should be mentioned as prime examples of the business biographer's art: Alfred D. Chandler, Jr., and Stephen Salsbury, *Pierre du Pont and the Making of the Modern Corporation* (1971); Allan Nevins, *Study in Power: John D. Rockefeller, Industrialist and Philanthropist* (2 vols., 1953); Joseph Frazier Wall, *Andrew Carnegie* (1970); and Maury Klein, *The Life and Legend of Jay Gould* (1986).

Company histories have always been a mainstay of the business historian and are the most prevalent works in the field. Actually, studies of individual firms take a wide range of forms—they may be "puff pieces" pasted together by a public-relations department, often to celebrate a business anniversary of some sort; or they may be "authorized" histories, which, while more restrained in tone, are often uncritical; or they may be serious, scholarly treatments of the life and times of a business. Although some information is better than none at all, we will only mention the last form here. Among the best of this genre are the three-volume *History of the Standard Oil Company (New Jersey)*, especially the first volume, written by Ralph and Muriel Hidy; William T. Baxter, *The House of Hancock: Business in Boston, 1724–1775* (1945); Boris Emmet and John E. Jeuck, *Catalogues and Counters: A History of Sears, Roebuck and Co.* (1950); Ralph M. Hower, *History of Macy's of New York, 1858–1919* (1946); Richard Overton, *Burlington Route: A History of the Burlington Lines* (1965); and Edwin J. Perkins, *Financing Anglo-American Trade: The House of Brown, 1800–1860* (1975).

Some business historians have examined whole industries rather than single firms. These studies may trace the entire life of the industry or focus upon a particularly critical time segment. Excellent examples of such histories are Erik Barnouw, *A History of Broadcasting in the United States* (3 vols., 1966–1970); Vincent Carosso, *Investment Banking in America* (1970); Fritz Redlich, *The Molding of American Banking, 1781–1910* (1947); John F. Stover, *The Life and Decline of the American Railroad;* Peter Temin, *Iron and Steel in 19th Century America* (1964); Harold F. Williamson et al., *The American Petroleum Industry* (2 vols., 1959–1963); Mary Yeager, *Competition and Regulation: The Development of Oligopoly in the Meat Packing Industry* (1981); and John B. Rae, *The American Automobile Industry* (1984).

The subject of business-government relations is always a key area of interest for historians, and thus it has produced a sizable number of superior works, including the following: Carter Goodrich, *Government Promotion of American Canals and Railroads, 1800–1890* (1960); Bray Hammond, *Banks and Politics in America: From the Revolution to the Civil War* (1957); Ellis W. Hawley, *The New Deal and the Problem of Monopoly* (1966); William Letwin, *Law and Economic Policy in America* (1965); Albro Martin, *Enterprise Denied: Origins of the Decline of American Railroads* (1971); Thomas K. McCraw, *Prophets of Regulation* (1984); Hans B. Thorelli, *The Federal Antitrust Policy: Organization of an American Tradition* (1955); and Robert H. Wiebe, *Businessmen and Reform: A Study of the Progressive Movement* (1962).

The business mind has been another area of fruitful research for scholars. They have studied how businessmen saw themselves, the ethical systems that they developed, and the professionalization of management thought. Recommended on this topic are: Saul Engelbourg, *Power and Morality: American Business Ethics, 1865–1914* (1980); Claude S. George, *The History of Management Thought* (1968); Morrell Heald, *The Social Responsibilities of Business: Company and Community, 1900–1960* (1970); Edward C. Kirkland, *Dream and Thought in the Business Community, 1860–1900*; Daniel Nelson, *Frederick W. Taylor and the Rise of Scientific Management* (1980); and Francis X. Sutton et al., *The American Business Creed* (1956).

Finally, how the American public has viewed the business community, as opposed to how businessmen viewed themselves, is equally interesting and important. For this topic, the reader has an abundance of possibilities from which to choose, including: Sigmund Diamond, *The Reputation of the American Business Man* (1955); Sidney Fine, *Laissez Faire and the General Welfare State* (1956); Louis Galambos, *The Public Image of Big Business in America, 1880–1940* (1975); Leo Marx, *The Machine in the Garden: Technology and the Pastoral Ideal in America* (1964); and Irvin G. Wyllie, *The Self-Made Man in America: The Myth of Rags to Riches* (1954).

The above suggestions, together with other works cited in the notes to the text, should provide an ample introductory bibliography for the subject of American business history. It is hoped the reader will use this bibliography to delve deeper into the story of enterprise and entrepreneurs in the United States.

APPENDIX A

A Chronology of American Business

IMPORTANT events in the history of American business are listed below by the year in which they occurred. Not listed are well-known dates in the general history of the United States that should already be familiar to the reader—for example, the signing of the Declaration of Independence, presidential elections, and the outbreak of wars. The following chronology should be useful in establishing a business-history time line.

1607 Jamestown colony established by a chartered joint-stock company, the Virginia Company of London.

1613 John Rolfe in Virginia successfully cures tobacco grown from West Indian seeds, thereby creating America's first important export commodity.

1624 Virginia Company forced into bankruptcy—first major business failure in American history.

1639 Merchant Robert Keayne accused of overcharging on goods sold in the Massachusetts Bay Colony.

1643 First successful ironworks in American colonies established on the Saugus River near Lynn, Massachusetts.

1660 British Parliament passes Enumerated Products Act designating certain colonial products that could only be exported to England.

1663 Parliament's Staple Act requires all goods being transported to colonies from Europe to be cleared first through a port in England.

1669 Parliament's Woolens Act prohibits the export of woolen cloth beyond a colony's borders.

1670 First Merchants' Exchange founded in New York City.

1732 Parliament's Hat Act prohibits exportation by water of beaver hats from their colony of origin.

1750 Parliament's Iron Act prohibits colonial production of finished iron products.

1757 Thomas Willing founds first marine insurance company in America.

1765 Stamp Act provokes the first of a series of colonial boycotts of imports from England.

1768 First Chamber of Commerce organized in New York City.

1773 Tea Act allows British East India Company to sell its tea through its own agents in the colonies, rather than at auction, where it was usually bought by American merchants.

1782 Bank of North America, the nation's first commercial bank, opens its doors.

1784 1. The ship *Empress of China* sails from New York harbor for China, beginning American trade with that country.

   2. Bank of New York, the second commercial bank in the United States, is founded with a state charter drafted by Alexander Hamilton.

1789 First tariff on imports enacted by Congress.

1790 Samuel Slater's mill in Rhode Island begins operations, inaugurating the industrial revolution in the United States.

1791 1. The First Bank of the United States, a national bank proposed by Secretary of the Treasury Alexander Hamilton, is chartered by Congress.

   2. Hamilton's *Report on Manufactures* is presented to Congress.

1792 A guild of security dealers is formed under a Wall Street buttonwood tree. It would evolve into the New York Stock Exchange.

1793 Eli Whitney invents the cotton gin.

1794 The Lancaster Pike, an improved road or turnpike owned by a private company, is completed between Philadelphia and Lancaster, Pennsylvania, inaugurating an era of "turnpike fever."

1798 The Treasury Department contracts with Eli Whitney for the manufacture of four thousand muskets.

1807 1. President Thomas Jefferson's Embargo Act severs American trade with all foreign countries.

   2. Robert Fulton successfully demonstrates the commercial feasibility of steamboats by making an upriver trip on the Hudson between New York City and Albany.

1808 John Jacob Astor organizes the American Fur Company.

1811 1. The New York legislature enacts the first general incorporation law, though it is limited only to manufacturing firms.

   2. Nicholas Roosevelt's *New Orleans*, the first steamboat to operate on the Ohio and Mississippi rivers, is constructed.

1813 The Boston Manufacturing Company is incorporated by Francis Cabot Lowell and the Boston Associates.

1814 Production commences at Waltham, Massachusetts, in the nation's first integrated factory.

1816 First protective tariff enacted by Congress in response to a flood of British manufactured goods following War of 1812.

1818 The Black Ball Line, organized by New York merchants, inaugurates first successful Atlantic packet service.

1819 The Supreme Court's decision in the *Dartmouth College v. Woodward* case holds that a corporation charter is protected by the contract clause of the Constitution.

1824 The Supreme Court's decision in the *Gibbons v. Ogden* case upholds federal supremacy in the regulation of interstate commerce.

1825 The Erie Canal is completed, opening a new era in interregional trade in the United States.

1827 The Baltimore & Ohio Railroad is incorporated.

1832 President Andrew Jackson vetoes the bill rechartering the Second Bank of the United States.

1837 The Supreme Court decision in the *Charles River Bridge v. Warren Bridge Co.* case reasserts the right of a state to promote economic development and narrows the Dartmouth College ruling.

1839 The Supreme Court decision in the *Bank of Augusta v. Earle* case holds that a corporation can do business under interstate comity within other states.

1842 The first mutual life insurance company, Mutual Life of New York, begins doing business.

1844 First telegraph line is completed and operating between Washington and Baltimore.

1846 Pennsylvania Railroad Company is incorporated.

1848 1. Cyrus Hall McCormick moves his reaper factory from Virginia to Chicago, a shift that will transform it into a major American business.

2. The Chicago Board of Trade is organized to regularize the buying and selling of agricultural commodities.

3. Alexander Turney Stewart opens his Marble Dry Goods Palace in New York City.

1853 New York Central Railroad incorporated.

1854 Clipper ship *Flying Cloud* sets a speed record of 89 days, 8 hours for a voyage between New York and San Francisco.

1856 Western Union Company incorporated.

1858 Rowland H. Macy opens a "fancy dry goods" store in New York City, the forerunner of his department store.

1859 Edwin Drake strikes oil at Titusville, Pennsylvania, by drilling the world's first producing well.

1861 Jay Cooke & Co. banking house founded.

1862 Pacific Railway Act becomes law, chartering the Union Pacific Railroad Company and providing financial aid for the building of the first transcontinental railroad.

1863 1. National Banking Act becomes law, establishing a system of federally chartered banks to parallel the state bank system.

   2. Brotherhood of Locomotive Engineers, the first railroad labor union, is formed.

1867 Cornelius Vanderbilt gains control of the New York Central Railroad.

1869 1. Completion of the first transcontinental railroad is accomplished when the Union Pacific and the Central Pacific lines meet in Utah.

   2. N. W. Ayer & Son, the first modern advertising agency, is founded by Francis Wayland Ayer.

1870 The Standard Oil Company of Ohio is incorporated by John D. Rockefeller and his associates.

1871 Drexel, Morgan & Co., the predecessor of J. P. Morgan & Co., is established at 23 Wall Street.

1872 1. Andrew Carnegie decides to concentrate his business activities upon the manufacture of steel.

   2. Aaron Montgomery Ward founds the first mail-order house, retailing goods to a largely rural market.

1873 Jay Cooke & Co. fails, precipitating a financial panic and depression.

1876 1. Alexander Graham Bell patents the telephone.

   2. Thomas Edison establishes the first industrial-research laboratory at Menlo Park, New Jersey.

   3. Gustavus Swift starts a meat-packing business in Chicago.

4. John Wanamaker opens his Grand Depot store in Philadelphia.

1877 1. Extensive and bloody railroad strikes take place and halt service on a number of lines.

2. The Supreme Court's decision in the Granger cases (led by *Munn v. Illinois*) upholds state regulation of railroads.

1879 1. Thomas Edison invents the incandescent light.

2. Standard Oil Trust organization devised by Samuel C. T. Dodd and used to consolidate a near monopoly in petroleum refining.

1880 Edison Electric Illuminating Company lights New York City's financial district.

1881 Joseph Wharton donates $100,000 to the University of Pennsylvania for the endowment of the first collegiate school of business.

1885 American Telephone and Telegraph (AT&T) is incorporated.

1886 1. American Federation of Labor (AFL) founded, and Samuel Gompers becomes its first president.

2. The Supreme Court's decision in the *Wabash Railroad* case negates the effectiveness of state regulation.

3. A bomb explodes in Chicago's Haymarket Square; a riot ensues, and a wave of antiunion hysteria is unleashed.

1877 Interstate Commerce Act becomes a law, the first significant federal regulation of an industry.

1889 The state of New Jersey amends its corporation laws to permit holding companies.

1890 1. Five major cigarette manufacturers combine to form the American Tobacco Company, with James Buchanan Duke as its president.

2. Sherman Antitrust Act becomes law.

1892 1. General Electric Company organized, the product of a merger of Edison General Electric and Thomson-Houston Electric.

2. A strike at the Homestead, Pennsylvania, mill of the Carnegie Steel Company results in violence and damages Carnegie's reputation as an industrial statesman.

1893 1. Sears, Roebuck & Co. established.

2. James J. Hill's Great Northern Railroad reaches Puget Sound, completing a line from St. Paul to Seattle.

1894 Pullman strike brings a major intervention by the federal government, effectively breaking the American Railway Union's struggle with railroad management.

1895 1. The Supreme Court's decision in the *E. C. Knight* case appears to nullify the Sherman Act almost completely by excluding manufacturing from interstate commerce.

2. National Association of Manufactures is founded to deal with foreign labor matters.

1901 1. Andrew Carnegie sells out, and his company becomes the key component in the new United States Steel Corporation, organized by J. P. Morgan.

2. The Spindletop oil strike in east Texas produces 17 million barrels in its first year alone.

1902 Three du Pont cousins—Alfred, Coleman, and Pierre—take over the family business.

1903 Wright brothers, Orville and Wilbur, make the world's first powered flight in a heavier-than-air machine at Kitty Hawk, North Carolina.

1904 The Supreme Court's decision in the *Northern Securities Company* case dissolves a Hill-Harriman railroad combination, establishes Theodore Roosevelt's reputation as a trustbuster, and revitalizes the Sherman Act.

1905 The Armstrong Committee investigation of life insurance practices brings reforms in the industry.

1906 The Hepburn Act gives new authority over railroads to the Interstate Commerce Commission.

1908 1. Henry Ford begins producing the Model T.

2. William C. Durant organizes General Motors.

1911 1. The Supreme Court's decision in the *Standard Oil* case forces the dissolution of the holding-company structure headed by New Jersey Standard. The same decision, and that in the *American Tobacco* case soon after, promulgates a "rule of reason" in antitrust law.

2. Frederick Winslow Taylor's *The Principles of Scientific Management* is published.

1913 The Federal Reserve Act establishes the country's first central banking system since the demise of the Second Bank of the United States in the 1830s.

1914 The Clayton Act becomes law, and the Federal Trade commission is created; both are intended to strengthen antitrust enforcement.

1917 The federal government assumes control and operation of the nation's railroads for the duration of the First World War. They are not returned to private control until 1920.

1920 1. The United States Steel Corporation is found by the Supreme Court not to be in violation of the Sherman Act under a rule of reason interpretation of the law.

2. Pierre du Pont replaces Billy Durant as president of General Motors.

3. The nation's first broadcasting station, Pittsburgh's **KDKA**, owned by Westinghouse Electric, goes on the air.

1923 Alfred Sloan becomes president of General Motors, and Pierre du Pont moves up to chairman of the board.

1924 Thomas Watson, Sr., renames his growing office-equipment company International Business Machines (IBM).

1925 Both Montgomery Ward and Sears, Roebuck branch out from their mail-order businesses by opening retail stores.

1926 The National Broadcasting Company (NBC) is established as a subsidiary of RCA, beginning network domination of radio.

1927 Henry Ford discontinues the Model T and shuts down operations for a year in order to retool for the Model A. In the meantime, industry leadership is lost to General Motors.

1929 The plummeting of stock prices that begins with the October crash will continue for more than three years and be accompanied by a decade-long depression.

1932 The Reconstruction Finance Corporation is established by Congress and the Hoover administration to assist ailing financial institutions and other important business units.

1933 1. The Banking Act creates the Federal Deposit Insurance Corporation and orders a separation of commercial and investment banking.

   2. The National Industrial Recovery Act attempts unsuccessfully to promote recovery by means of cooperative planning by government and the business community.

1934 The Communications Act establishes the Federal Communications Commission to regulate the broadcasting industry.

1935 The Wagner Act establishes the National Labor Relations Board and gives new protection to labor unions.

1936 The Congress of Industrial Organizations (originally the Committee for Industrial Organization) is broken off from the AFL and undertakes its own campaign to organize the country's mass-production industries.

1937 General Motors, Chrysler, and the United States Steel Corporation are all successfully unionized by the CIO.

1938 1. Thurman Arnold becomes chief of the Justice Department's Antitrust Division.

   2. The Fair Labor Standards Act establishes the first national minimum wage and maximum work week.

1941 The Ford Motor Company finally, under governmental pressure, agrees to unionization.

1944 The federal government's military expenditures reach a wartime high of $87.4 billion, and unemployment falls to an all-time low of 1.2 percent.

1945 1. Henry Ford II succeeds his grandfather, who reluctantly steps down as president of a struggling Ford Motor Company.

2. Judge Learned Hand's decision in the *Alcoa* antitrust case reverses the 1911 rule of reason.

3. ENIAC, the first electronic digital computer, is put into actual service.

1946 Employment Act commits the federal government in principle to the promotion of "maximum employment, production, and purchasing power."

1947 Taft-Hartley Act places restrictions upon unions and prohibits closed shops.

1950 The Celler-Kefauver Amendment strengthens the antimerger section of the Clayton Act.

1953 The first IBM computer, the 701, is introduced.

1955 1. The AFL and CIO merge.

2. Ray Kroc and the McDonald brothers begin franchising hamburger drive-ins, providing the model for an emerging fast-food industry.

1957 Ford introduces the Edsel, which soon proves to be a $350 million bust.

1959 A 116-day steel strike is the longest in the industry's history and marks the beginning of its decline.

1960 The Organization of Petroleum Exporting Countries (OPEC) is formed.

1961 President Dwight Eisenhower warns the nation of the dangers of the "military-industrial complex."

1968 The Pennsylvania and New York Central railroads merge into the Penn-Central. Two years later, in 1970, the merged entity collapses in a spectacular bankruptcy.

1971 1. President Richard Nixon orders a wage-price freeze to halt the economy's inflationary momentum. Controls are not entirely removed until 1974.

2. Most of the nation's rail-passenger service becomes the responsibility of the federally operated National Railroad Passenger Corporation, later known as Amtrak.

1973 The outbreak of war in the Middle East results in an Arab embargo on oil shipments to the United States (ended in 1974) and the beginning of a drastic increase in oil prices.

1976 Conrail (the Consolidated Railroad Corporation) takes over operation of 17,000 miles of line in the Northeast by means of a government-sponsored merger of six bankrupt companies.

1978 Airline Deregulation Act provides for gradual elimination of federal control over fares and routes.

1979 A serious reactor leak at the Three Mile Island, Pennsylvania, nuclear plant raises doubts about the future of the nuclear-power industry.

1982 AT&T and the Justice Department arrive at a consent agreement ending an antitrust prosecution begun a decade before with the corporate giant agreeing to divest itself of twenty-two regional telephone companies.

1983 The Dow-Jones Industrial Average of stocks listed on the New York Exchange surpasses the 1200 mark.

1984 1. The divestiture of AT&T is carried out, and the seven "Baby Bells" begin operations.

2. Chevron Corp.'s $13.2 billion acquisition of Gulf Oil is American business's biggest merger ever.

3. Lee Iacocca's autobiography, a publishing sensation, begins its long run on the best-seller list.

1985 Coca-Cola announces the scrapping of its ninety-nine-year-old formula in April, then, under intense consumer pressure, brings it back three months later as "Classic Coke."

1986 1. U.S. Steel changes its corporate name to USX.

2. In the biggest corporate merger outside the oil industry, General Electric acquires RCA (and its NBC subsidiary) for $6.3 billion.

1987   1. The Dow-Jones Industrial Average zooms past the 2500 level, more than twice as high as its peak just four years before.

2. The Dow-Jones Industrial Average falls 508 points on October 19, and a period of uncertain volatility sets in, fueled by increasing concerns over the budget and trade deficits.

APPENDIX B

The Twenty-five Largest Industrial Corporations

BELOW is a list of the twenty-five largest industrial corporations in three different years in the twentieth century: 1917, 1957, and 1986. Similar data for the period prior to 1917—for example, the nineteenth century—are not available. Corporations are ranked here by their reported assets. The reader should particularly note the changes in the ranking of various firms over the entire sixty-nine year span between 1917 and 1986.

Table 1. 1917

Rank	Name in 1917	1917 Assets (000)
1.	United States Steel Corp.	$2,449,500
2.	Standard Oil Co. of N.J. (Exxon)	574,100
3.	Bethlehem Steel Corp.	381,500
4.	Armour & Co.	314,100
5.	Swift & Co.	306,300
6.	Midvale Steel & Ordinance Co.	270,000
7.	International Harvester Co.	264,700
8.	E. I. Du Pont de Nemours & Co.	263,300
9.	United States Rubber Co.	257,500
10.	Phelps Dodge Corp.	232,300
11.	General Electric Co.	231,600
12.	Anaconda Copper Mining Co.	225,800
13.	American Smelting & Refining Co.	221,800
14.	Standard Oil of N.Y. (Mobil)	204,300
15.	Singer Manufacturing Co.	192,900
16.	Ford Motor Co.	165,900
17.	Westinghouse Electric Co.	164,700
18.	American Tobacco Co.	164,200
19.	Jones & Laughlin Steel Co.	159,600

20.	Union Carbide Corp.	155,900
21.	Weyerhaeuser Timber Co.	153,200
22.	B. F. Goodrich Co.	146,100
23.	Central Leather Co.	145,300
24.	Texas Co. (Texaco)	144,500
25.	Pullman Co.	143,300

Source: This list was taken from a compilation contained in Thomas R. Navin, "The 500 Largest American Industrials in 1917," *Business History Review* 44 (Autumn 1970): 360–86.

Table 2.   1957

Rank	Name in 1957	1957 Assets (000)
1.	Standard Oil Co. of N.J. (Exxon)	$8,712,387
2.	General Motors Corp.	7,498,008
3.	United States Steel Corp.	4,372,770
4.	Ford Motor Co.	3,347,645
5.	Gulf Oil Corp.	3,240,571
6.	Socony Mobil Oil (Mobil)	3,105,252
7.	E. I. Du Pont de Nemours	2,755,547
8.	Texas Co. (Texaco)	2,729,095
9.	Standard Oil Co. (Indiana)	2,535,023
10.	General Electric Co.	2,361,319
11.	Bethlehem Steel Corp.	2,260,340
12.	Standard Oil of California	2,246,296
13.	Phillips Petroleum Co.	1,519,631
14.	Chrysler Corp.	1,496,605
15.	Sinclair Oil Co.	1,480,616
16.	Union Carbide Corp.	1,456,353
17.	Shell Oil Co.	1,407,444
18.	Westinghouse Electric Co.	1,400,683
19.	Western Electric Corp.	1,328,922
20.	Aluminum Co. of America	1,315,569
21.	Cities Service Corp.	1,292,561
22.	International Business Machines	1,153,969
23.	Anaconda Copper	1,029,562
24.	International Harvester Co.	1,021,117
25.	Republic Steel	980,379

Source: Fortune, July 1958, pp. 131f.

Table 3. 1986

Rank	Name in 1986	1986 Assets (000)
1.	General Motors Corp.	$72,593,000
2.	Exxon Corp.	69,484,000
3.	International Business Machines	57,814,000
4.	Mobil Corp.	39,412,000
5.	AT&T	38,883,000
6.	Ford Motor Co.	37,933,000
7.	Texaco Inc.	34,940,000
8.	General Electric Co.	34,591,000
9.	Chevron	34,583,000
10.	E. I. Du Pont de Nemours	26,733,000
11.	Shell Oil Co.	26,214,000
12.	Amoco	23,706,000
13.	USX	21,823,000
14.	Atlantic Richfield Corp.	21,604,000
15.	Tenneco, Inc.	18,021,000
16.	Philip Morris	17,642,000
17.	Occidental Petroleum Corp.	17,467,000
18.	RJR Nabisco	17,019,000
19.	Standard Oil (Ohio)	15,955,000
20.	Chrysler Corp.	14,463,000
21.	Proctor & Gamble	13,055,000
22.	International Telephone & Telegraph	12,920,000
23.	Eastman Kodak Co.	12,902,000
24.	Phillips Petroleum Co.	12,399,000
25.	Dow Chemical Co.	12,242,000

Source: Fortune, April 27, 1987, p. 364.

Note: The above lists include only industrial corporations. Banks and public utilities, for example, are not shown. In the 1917 and 1957 listings, AT&T did not appear because it was not classified as an industrial corporation at that time.

APPENDIX C

A Roster of Fifty Major Business Leaders

CHOOSING the fifty most important individuals in American business history is an invitation to disagreement. Nevertheless, the choices of this writer are presented here to provide a handy reference for the reader and, perhaps, to stimulate some discussion. For each person this list gives birth and death (if deceased) dates and a capsule identification. The absence of any women on the roster is, regrettably, a testament to the historic male dominance of the business world's higher echelons, a discrimination which is only now being remedied.

Astor, John Jacob: b. 1763, d. 1848; fur trader (American Fur Company), merchant, real estate speculator; New York's foremost landlord by the time of his death.

Biddle, Nicholas: b. 1786, d. 1844; banker, president of the Second Bank of the United States; America's first great central banker.

Carnegie, Andrew: b. 1835, d. 1919; steel industrialist (Carnegie Steel) and philanthropist; a brilliant manager whose constant emphasis on achieving greater efficiencies created the world's greatest steel company.

Chrysler, Walter P.: b. 1875, d. 1940; automobile manufacturer (the Chrysler Corporation), particularly noted for his engineering innovations in passenger cars.

Cooke, Jay: b. 1821, d. 1905; banker-financier (Jay Cooke & Company). The eventual failure of his firm precipitated the Panic of 1873.

Duke, James Buchanan: b. 1856, d. 1925; tobacco industrialist (American Tobacco Company). "Buck" Duke made the cigarette part of everyday life.

Du Pont, Pierre S.: b. 1870, d. 1954; industrialist (president of both Du Pont and General Motors); in many ways, the architect of the modern American corporation.

Edison, Thomas Alva: b. 1847, d. 1931; America's foremost inventor, a less successful organizer of companies to market his inventions.

Field, Marshall: b. 1834, d. 1906; department-store founder (Marshall Field & Company, Chicago).

Ford, Henry: b. 1863, d. 1947; pioneer automobile manufacturer (Ford Motor Company) who made the passenger car, and especially his Model T, an integral element of American society.

Ford, Henry, II: b. 1917, d. 1978; grandson of founder of Ford Motor Company, assumed the presidency of the family business in 1945 and brought it back from the brink of corporate oblivion.

Giannini, Amadeo Peter: b. 1870, d. 1949; banker and financier (Bank of America and Transamerica Corporation); established first statewide (California) branch banking system in the United States.

Girard, Stephen: b. 1750, d. 1831; merchant, financier, philanthropist; his private bank was the largest of its time.

Gould, Jay: b. 1836, d. 1892; financier and railroad magnate; probably comes the closest of any Gilded Age business leader to fitting the stereotype of "robber baron."

Hancock, Thomas: b. 1703, d. 1764; foremost American merchant of the eighteenth century. Based in Boston, he was the uncle of revolutionary leader John Hancock, who succeeded him as owner of his mercantile house.

Harriman, Edward H.: b. 1848, d. 1909; railroad magnate and financier; controlled most of the railroad systems of the West and Southwest as well as investments in banking, insurance, and marine shipping.

Hearst, William Randolph: b. 1863, d. 1951; publisher; built an empire that included eighteen newspapers, nine magazines, and news and photo services.

Heinz, Henry John: b. 1844, d. 1919; agricultural products processor and distributor (H. J. Heinz Co.); first used the "57 Varieties" slogan in 1896.

Hill, James J.: b. 1838, d. 1916; railroad magnate (Great Northern Railway—the only transcontinental line to remain financially stable and prosperous).

Hilton, Conrad N.: b. 1887, d. 1979; hotel chain owner (Hilton Hotel Corporation); by the 1960s, the Hilton group included more than sixty hotels in the United States alone.

Huntington, Collis P.: b. 1821, d. 1900; railroad builder and magnate; one of the Central Pacific's "Big Four"; later controlled the Southern Pacific and other lines.

Iacocca, Lee: b. 1924; automobile manufacturer; president of Ford Motor Company, 1970–1978; chairman of the board, Chrysler Corp., 1978–present.

Kaiser, Henry J.: b. 1882, d. 1967; multi-industry manufacturer; active in aluminum, automobiles, cement, shipbuilding, and steel; also established the country's most successful health maintenance organization.

Lowell, Francis Cabot: b. 1775, d. 1817; pioneer textile manufacturer (Boston Manufacturing Company); was responsible for the establishment of the first integrated factory in the United States.

Luce, Henry: b. 1898, d. 1967; founder, editor, and publisher of the *Time, Life, Fortune, Sports Illustrated* empire.

Macy, Rowland H.: b. 1822, d. 1877; department store founder; arguably his New York enterprise was the first full-fledged department store in America by 1870.

McCormick, Cyrus Hall.: b. 1809, d. 1884; agricultural implement manufacturer; his reaper helped revolutionize agriculture in the United States, and his company (McCormick Harvester) dominated the industry in the nineteenth century.

Mellon, Andrew: b. 1855, d. 1937; banker (Mellon National Bank), financier-industrialist (Alcoa, Gulf Oil), and secretary of the treasury in the Harding, Coolidge, and Hoover administrations.

Morgan, J. Pierpont: b. 1837, d. 1913; premier investment banker in American history (Drexel, Morgan & Company, later J. P. Morgan & Company, one of the world's leading banking houses).

Morris, Robert: b. 1734, d. 1806; banker-financier (Willing, Morris, and Company) and superintendent of finance during the Revolutionary War.

Paley, William S.: b. 1901; broadcasting network magnate; acquired control of Columbia Broadcasting System in 1929 and built it into a major force in the industry. Stepped down as chairman of CBS board in 1983.

Patterson, John H.: b. 1844, d. 1922; business-equipment industrialist (National Cash Register Co., later NCR); probably the pioneer in developing modern salesmanship techniques.

Penney, James Cash: b. 1875, d. 1971; department-store chain founder (J. C. Penney Company) with over 3,000 stores by the time of his death.

Rockefeller, John D.: b. 1839, d. 1937; petroleum industrialist and philanthropist; a brilliant organizer whose Standard Oil combination dominated the industry to such an extent that it was the principal cause of an antitrust movement that developed in the United States.

Rosenwald, Julius: b. 1862, d. 1932; retailing executive; he assumed the management of Sears, Roebuck when its founder retired and guided it to a leadership position in mass merchandising.

Sarnoff, David: b. 1891; d. 1971; broadcasting leader; president or board chairman of the Radio Corporation of America (RCA) from 1930 until his retirement in 1970.

Schiff, Jacob: b. 1847, d. 1920; investment banker; after Schiff joined Kuhn, Loeb & Co. in 1874, it became a major force in American financial capitalism.

Slater, Samuel: b. 1768, d. 1835; pioneer textile manufacturer; his Rhode Island mill, built in 1790 with the financial assistance of Moses Brown, inaugurated the industrial revolution in the United States.

Sloan, Alfred P.: b. 1875, d. 1966; automobile executive (president and later board chairman of General Motors in the 1920s and 1930s); an organizational genius and an outstanding administrator.

Stewart, Alexander T.: b. 1803, d. 1876; pioneer dry-goods retailer; his Marble Dry Goods Palace (1848) incorporated many of the techniques used by later department-store managers.

Swift, Gustavus F.: b. 1839, d. 1903; pioneer meat-packer (Swift & Co.); responsible for the development of vertical integration in the industry.

Thomson, J. Edgar: b. 1808, d. 1874; railroad leader (Pennsylvania Railroad); built what, at his death, was the largest transportation company in the world, with over six thousand miles of track, or nearly 10 percent of the nation's total.

Vail, Theodore: b. 1845, d. 1920; telephone executive (AT&T); general manager of American Bell Telephone Co. in the 1880s and president of AT&T from 1907 to retirement shortly before his death; was primarily responsible for the existence of the modern Bell System.

Vanderbilt, Cornelius: b. 1794, d. 1877; steamship and later railroad magnate (New York Central system).

Wanamaker, John: b. 1838, d. 1922; department-store founder; while not the first, his Grand Depot store in Philadelphia, opened in 1876, became the largest and probably the best-known department store in the United States; later expanded operations to New York City.

Ward, Aaron Montgomery: b. 1843, d. 1913; mail-order house founder (Montgomery Ward & Co.); conceived the idea of buying merchandise in large quantities from manufacturers and selling it by mail to farmers.

Watson, Thomas J., Sr.: b. 1874, d. 1956; office-products industrialist; in 1914, he became president of a company that became International Business Machines Corp. (IBM) in 1924, and brought out its first computer in 1953.

Westinghouse, George: b. 1846, d. 1914; inventor and manufacturer, invented the air brake for railroads, introduced alternating current for electric-power transmission, built a system for conducting natural gas to homes, and organized the Westinghouse Electric Co.

Whitney, Eli: b. 1761, d. 1825; inventor and manufacturer; invented the cotton gin in 1793 and later popularized interchangeable-parts manufacturing through his production of arms for the federal government.

Woolworth, Frank W.: b. 1852, d. 1919; variety-store chain founder (F. W. Woolworth Co.); opened his first "dime store" in Lancaster, Pennsylvania, in 1879, and was operating six hundred by the time of his death.

NOTES

Chapter 1: The Entrepreneur

1. John D. Rockefeller, *Random Reminiscences of Men and Events* (New York: Doubleday, Page & Company, 1909), 20, 22.

2. Allan Nevins, *Study in Power: John D. Rockefeller*, 2 vols. (New York: Charles Scribner's Sons, 1953), 1:328.

3. Nevins, *John D. Rockefeller: the Heroic Age of American Enterprise*, 2 vols. (New York: Charles Scribner's Sons, 1940), 2:712.

4. Thomas C. Cochran, *Business in American Life: A History* (New York: McGraw-Hill Book Company, 1972), 1.

5. U.S., Bureau of the Census, *Statistical Abstract of the United States, 1986* (Washington, D.C.), 517.

6. *Fortune*, April 27, 1987, 359–364.

7. Peter Kilby, *Entrepreneurship and Economic Development* (Englewood Cliffs, N.J.: The Free Press, 1971), 1.

8. Henry W. Spiegel, *The Growth of Economic Thought* (New York: Prentice-Hall, Inc., 1971), 260.

9. Joseph Schumpeter, *Theory of Economic Development* (Cambridge, Mass.: Harvard Economic Studies, 1934; Galaxy Book Paperback, 1961), 61.

10. *Ibid.*, 75.

11. Herman E. Kroos and Charles Gilbert, *American Business History* (Englewood Cliffs, N.J.: Prentice-Hall, Inc., 1972), 3.

12. Arthur H. Cole, *Business Enterprise in Its Social Setting* (Cambridge, Mass.: Harvard University Press, 1959), 7–9, 233.

13. Peter F. Drucker, *Innovation and Entrepreneurship: Practice and Principles* (New York: Harper & Row, 1985), 27, 151.

14. *Ibid.*, 28, 34–35, 149.

15. Harold Geneen, *Managing* (Garden City, N.Y.: Doubleday & Company, Inc., 1984), 29–30.

16. *Ibid.*, 17–18.

17. Miriam R. Beard, *A History of Business*, 2 vols. (Ann Arbor: The University of Michigan Press, 1938; Ann Arbor Paperbacks, 1962), I, 2–3.

18. Robert L. Heilbroner, *The Making of Economic Society* (Englewood Cliffs, N.J.: Prentice-Hall, Inc., 1980), 56.

19. David C. McClelland, "The Achievement Motive in Economic Growth," in Kilby, *Entrepreneurship and Economic Development*, 110.

20. McClelland, *The Achieving Society* (Princeton, N.J.: D. Van Nostrand Company, Inc., 1961), 210.

21. Thomas C. Cochran, *200 Years of American Business* (New York: Basic Books, Inc., 1977), 7.

22. Cochran, *Business in American Life*, 96–97.

23. Cochran, *200 Years of American Business*, xiv.

Chapter 2: The Stages of American Capitalism

1. Edwin J. Perkins, *The Economy of Colonial America* (New York: Columbia University Press, 1980), 96.

2. N. S. B. Gras and Henrietta M. Larson, *Casebook in American Business History* (New York: Appleton-Century-Crofts, Inc., 1939), 9.

3. *Ibid.*, 12.

4. Jonathan Hughes, *The Vital Few: American Economic Progress and Its Protagonists* (Boston: Houghton Mifflin, 1966), 4.

5. *Ibid.*

6. Hughes, *The Vital Few: The Entrepreneurs & American Economic Progress*, 2d ed., exp. (New York: Oxford University Press, 1986), 455–461.

7. Alfred D. Chandler, Jr., *The Visible Hand: The Managerial Revolution in American Business* (Cambridge, Mass.: Harvard University Press, 1977), 3.

8. Chandler, and Richard S. Tedlow, *The Coming of Managerial Capitalism* (Homewood, Ill.: Richard D. Irwin, Inc., 1985), 396.

9. Chandler, *The Visible Hand*, 492.

10. Chandler, "The United States: Seedbed of Managerial Capitalism," in *Managerial Hierarchies: Comparative Perspectives on the Rise of Modern Industrial Enterprise*, ed. Alfred D. Chandler, Jr., and Herman Daems (Cambridge, Mass.: Harvard University Press, 1980), 3.

Chapter 3: Old-World Origins

1. George G. Coulton, *Medieval Village, Manor and Monastery* (New York: Columbia University Press, 1925; Harper Torchbooks, 1960), 393.

2. Gabriel Le Bras, "Conceptions of Economy and Society," in *The Cambridge Economic History of Europe*, vol. 3: *Economic Organization and Policies in the Middle Ages* (Cambridge, Eng.: Cambridge University Press, 1963), 566.

3. Heilbroner, *The Making of Economic Society*, 47.

4. Fernand Braudel, *Civilization and Capitalism, 15th–18th Century*, vol. 1: *The Wheels of Commerce* (New York: Harper & Row, 1979), 85.

5. O. Verlinden, in *The Cambridge Economic History of Europe*, 3:127.

6. Raymond de Roover, "The Organization of Trade," in *Cambridge Economic History of Europe*, 3:45.

7. *Ibid.*, 3: 46.

8. E. Victor Morgan, *A History of Money* (New York: Penguin Books, 1965), 129.

9. *The World of Business*, ed. Edward C. Bursk, Donald T. Clark, and Ralph W. Hidy, vol. 1 (New York: Simon and Schuster, 1962), 91.

10. Beard, *A History of Business*, 1: 167.

11. *The World of Business*, 1: 231.

12. Melvin Kranzberg and Joseph Gies, *By the Sweat of Thy Brow* (New York: G. P. Putnam's Sons, 1975), 66.

13. Jurgen Kuczynski, *The Rise of the Working Class* (New York: McGraw-Hill Book Company, 1967), 29.

14. Henri Pirenne, *Economic and Social History of Medieval Europe* (London: Routledge and Kegan Paul, Ltd., 1936), 186.

15. A. Rupert Hall, "Early Modern Technology to 1600," in *Technology in Western Civilization*, ed. Melvin Kranzberg and Carroll W. Pursell, Jr., vol. 1 (New York: Oxford University Press, 1967), 95.

16. J. H. Parry, "Transport and Trade Routes," in *The Cambridge Economic History of Europe*, vol. 4: *The Economy of Expanding Europe in the Sixteenth and Seventeenth Centuries* (Cambridge, Eng.: Cambridge University Press, 1967), 191.

17. Shepard B. Clough, *European Economic History* (New York: McGraw-Hill Book Company, 1968), 158–59.

18. *Ibid.*, 161.

19. E. L. J. Coornaert, "European Economic Institutions and the New World: The Chartered Companies," in *Cambridge Economic History of Europe*, 4:240.

20. Braudel, *The Wheels of Commerce*, 234–238.

21. *Ibid.*, 600.

Chapter 4: New-World Beginnings

1. Louis B. Wright, *The Dream of Prosperity in Colonial America* (New York: New York University Press, 1965), 30.

2. T. H. Breen, *Tobacco Culture: The Mentality of the Great Tidewater Planters on the Eve of Revolution* (Princeton, N.J.: Princeton University Press, 1985), 57.

3. Hughes, *The Vital Few*, 22.

4. Louis B. Wright, *The Atlantic Frontier: Colonial American Civilization, 1607–1763* (Ithaca, N.Y.: Cornell University Press, 1947), 221.

5. Hughes, *The Vital Few*, 61.

6. Stuart Bruchey, *The Colonial Merchant* (New York: Harcourt, Brace and World, Inc., 1966), 2.

7. Bernard Bailyn, *The New England Merchants in the Seventeenth Century* (Cambridge, Mass.: Harvard University Press, 1955), 20.

8. Bruchey, *The Colonial Merchant*, 103.

9. Bailyn, *The New England Merchants . . .*, 43.

10. *Ibid.*, 39–40.

11. Thomas J. Wertenbaker, *The Puritan Oligarchy* (New York: Charles Scribner's Sons, 1947), 202.

12. Dorothy Gregg, "John Stevens, General Entrepreneur," in *Men in Business*, ed. William Miller (Cambridge, Mass.: Harvard University Press, 1952; Harper Torchbook, 1962), 120.

13. William T. Baxter, *The House of Hancock: Business in Boston, 1724–1775* (Cambridge, Mass.: Harvard University Press, 1945), 185.

14. *Ibid.*, 216.

15. Stuart Bruchey, "Success and Failure Factors: American Merchants in Foreign Trade in the Eighteenth and Early Nineteenth Centuries," *Business History Review* 32 (Autumn 1958), 279.

16. Paul G. E. Clemens, *The Atlantic Economy and Colonial Maryland's Eastern Shore* (Ithaca, N.Y.: Cornell University Press, 1980), 121.

17. Richard Hofstadter, *America at 1750* (New York: Alfred A. Knopf, 1976), 75.

18. Perkins, *The Economy of Colonial America*, 81.

19. Carl Bridenbaugh, *The Colonial Craftsman* (New York: New York University, 1950; Phoenix Books, 1961), 154.

20. *Ibid.*, 108.

21. *Ibid.*, 132.

22. W. J. Rorabaugh, *The Craft Apprentice: From Franklin to the Machine Age in America* (New York: Oxford University Press, 1986), 15.

23. Brooke Hindle, "The Artisan During America's Wooden Age," in *Technology in America: A History of Individuals and Ideas*, ed. Carroll W. Pursell, Jr. (Cambridge, Mass.: The MIT Press, 1981), 8.

24. Alice Hanson Jones, *Wealth of a Nation to Be: The American Colonies on the Eve of Revolution* (New York: Columbia University Press, 1980), 298–300, 341.

Chapter 5: Business in a Revolutionary Era

1. Gary M. Walton and James F. Shepherd, *The Economic Rise of Early America* (Cambridge, Eng.: Cambridge University Press, 1979), 153–154.

2. John J. McCusker and Russell R. Menard, *The Economy of British America. 1607–1789* (Chapel Hill, N.C.: University of North Carolina Press, 1985), 15.

3. Walton and Shepherd, *The Economic Rise of Early America*, 161.

4. Carl Ubbelohde, *The American Colonial and the British Empire, 1607–1763* (Arlington Heights, Ill.: Harlan Davidson, Inc., 1968), 66.

5. Benjamin W. Labaree, *Patriots and Partisans: The Merchants of Newburyport, 1764–1815* (New York: Harvard University Press, 1962; Norton Library, 1975), 16–18.

6. Labaree, *The Boston Tea Party* (New York: Oxford University Press, 1964), 13.

7. Arthur Meier Schlesinger, *The Colonial Merchants and the American Revolution, 1763–1776* (New York: Frederick Ungar Publishing Co., 1957), 283.

8. Bernhard Knollenberg, *The Growth of the American Revolution* (New York: The Free Press, 1975), 100.

9. Schlesinger, *The Colonial Merchants and the American Revolution*, 605.

10. Curtis P. Nettels, *The Emergence of a National Economy, 1775–1815* (New York: Holt, Rinehart and Winston, 1962), 40.

11. Robert A. East, *Business Enterprise in the American Revolutionary Era* (New York: Columbia University Studies, 1939; AMS Press, 1969), 90.

12. Nettels, *The Emergence of a National Economy*, 15.

13. Clarence L. Ver Steeg, *Robert Morris, Revolutionary Financier* (Philadelphia: University of Pennsylvania Press, 1954), 40–41.

14. Forrest McDonald, *We the People: The Economic Origins of the Constitution* (Chicago: University of Chicago Press, 1958), 375.

15. *Ibid.*, 382.

16. Gordon S. Wood, *The Creation of the American Republic, 1776–1787* (Chapel Hill, N.C.: University of North Carolina Press, 1969), 514.

17. *United States Constitution*, Article I, Sections 8 and 10.

18. Broadus Mitchell and Louise P. Mitchell, *A Biography of the Constitution of the United States* (New York: Oxford University Press, 1975), xi.

Chapter 6: The Twilight of the All-Purpose Merchant

1. Spiegel, *The Growth of Economic Thought*, 245.

2. *Ibid.*, 246.

3. The data in this discussion are based mainly on *Historical Statistics of the United States: Colonial Times to 1970* (Washington: Bureau of the Census, 1975), and Moses Abramovitz and Paul A. David, "Reinterpreting Economic Growth: Parables and Realities," *American Economic Review 63 (May 1973): 430*.

4. Peter Temin, *Causal Factors in American Economic Growth in the Nineteenth Century* (New York: The Macmillan Press, 1975), 16.

5. Paul A. David, "The Growth of Real Product in the United States Before 1840: New Evidence, Controlled Conjectures," *Journal of Economic History* 27 (June 1967): 186–188.

6. Samuel Eliot Morison, *Maritime History of Massachusetts, 1783–1860* (Boston: Houghton Mifflin Co., 1921), 125.

7. Douglass C. North, *The Economic Growth of the United States, 1790–1860* (Englewood Cliffs, N.J.: Prentice-Hall, Inc., 1961), 49.

8. Stuart Bruchey, *Cotton and the Growth of the American Economy, 1790–1860* (New York: Harcourt, Brace & World, Inc., 1967), 45.

9. Jonathan Hughes, *American Economic History*, 2d ed. (Glenview, Ill.: Scott, Foresman and Co., 1987), 181.

10. Vincent P. Carosso, *Investment Banking in America: A History* (Cambridge, Mass.: Harvard University Press, 1970), 6.

11. This discussion is based on Edwin J. Perkins, *Financing Anglo-American Trade: The House of Brown, 1800–1880* (Cambridge, Mass.: Harvard University Press, 1975).

12. *Ibid.*, 45.

13. Bray Hammond, *Banks and Politics in America: From the Revolution to the Civil War* (Princeton, N.J.: Princeton University Press, 1957), 66.

14. Fritz Redlich, *The Molding of American Banking* (New York: Johnson Reprint Corporation, 1968), 17.

15. Hammond, *Banks and Politics in America*, 226.

16. Chandler, *The Visible Hand*, 42.

17. Redlich, *The Molding of American Banking*, 118.

18. Robert V. Remini, *Andrew Jackson and the Bank War* (New York: W. W. Norton & Company, Inc., 1967), 176.

19. Marquis James, *Biography of a Business: Insurance Company of North America, 1792–1942* (New York: The Bobbs-Merrill Company, 1942), 21.

20. William H. A. Carr, *Perils: Named and Unnamed, The Story of the Insurance Company of North America* (New York: McGraw-Hill Book Company, 1967), 7.

21. Elisha P. Douglass, *The Coming of Age of American Business: Three Centuries of Enterprise, 1600–1900* (Chapel Hill, N.C.: The University of North Carolina Press, 1971), 156–159.

22. Robert Sobel, *The Big Board: A History of the New York Stock Market* (New York: The Free Press, 1965), 22.

23. Robert Sobel, *The Curbstone Brokers: The Origins of the American Stock Exchange* (New York: The Macmillan Company, 1970), 13–14.

24. Cochran, *Business in American Life*, 147.

25. Chandler and Tedlow, *The Coming of Managerial Capitalism*, 55.

26. Paul Chrisler Phillips, *The Fur Trade*, vol. 2 (Norman, Okla.: University of Oklahoma Press, 1961), 119.

27. Kenneth W. Porter, *John Jacob Astor, Business Man*, vol. 2 (Cambridge, Mass.: Harvard University Press, 1931), 664.

28. *Ibid.*, 665.

29. *Ibid.*, 620, 912.

30. Gras and Larson, *Casebook in American Business History*, 97.

Chapter 7: Innovations in Transportation and Distribution

1. Harold D. Woodman, "Economy from 1815 to 1865," in *Encyclopedia of American Economic History*, ed. Glenn Porter, vol. I (New York: Charles Scribner's Sons, 1980), 67.

2. Robert A. Lively, "The American System: A Review Article," *Business History Review* 29 (March 1955): 86.

3. Douglass C. North, *Growth and Welfare in the American Past* (Englewood Cliffs, N.J.: Prentice-Hall, Inc., 1966), 100.

4. Stuart Bruchey, *The Roots of American Economic Growth, 1607–1861* (New York: Harper Torchbooks, 1968), 129.

5. R. Kent Newmyer, *The Supreme Court under Marshall and Taney* (Arlington Heights, Ill.: Harlan Davidson, Inc., 1968), 59.

6. Stanley I. Kutler, *Privilege and Creative Destruction: The Charles River Bridge Case* (Philadelphia: J. B. Lippincott Company, 1971; Norton Library, 1978), 160–161.

7. George Rogers Taylor, *The Transportation Revolution, 1815–1860* (New York: Holt, Rinehart and Winston, 1951), 58.

8. Jeremy Atack et al., "The Profitability of Steamboating on Western Rivers: 1850," *Business History Review* 49 (Autumn 1975): 350–354.

9. Julius Rubin, "An Innovating Public Improvement: The Erie Canal," in *Canals and American Economic Development*, ed. Carter Goodrich (New York: Columbia University Press, 1961; reprint ed., Kennikat Press, 1972), 15.

10. Gras and Larson, *Casebook in American Business History*, 353.

11. Taylor, *The Transportation Revolution*, 112.

12. The following discussion is based on John G. B. Hutchins, *The American Maritime Industries and Public Policy, 1789–1914* (Cambridge, Mass.: Harvard University Press, 1941), and Robert G. Albion's article on Collins in the *Dictionary of American Biography* (New York: Charles Scribner's Sons, 1958), 2: 305–306.

13. Glenn Porter and Harold C. Livesay, *Merchants and Manufacturers: Studies in the Changing Structure of Nineteenth Century Marketing* (Baltimore: Johns Hopkins Press, 1971), 8.

14. Porter and Livesay distinguish between a factor/broker and a commission merchant by designating the former as a wholesaler who never took title to the goods he handled, while the latter traded partly on his own account and partly as a factor/broker.

15. The following discussion is based on Harold D. Woodman, *King Cotton and His Retainers* (Lexington, Ky.: University of Kentucky Press, 1968), and Bruchey, *Cotton and the Growth of the American Economy, 1790–1860*.

16. Ralph W. Haskins, "Planter and Cotton Factor in the Old South: Some Areas of Friction," in *The Changing Economic Order*, ed. Alfred D. Chandler, Jr., Stuart Bruchey, and Louis Galambos (New York: Harcourt, Brace, & World, Inc., 1968), 104.

17. Woodman, *King Cotton and His Retainers*, 13.

18. The following discussion is based principally on Lewis E. Atherton, "The Pioneer Merchant in Mid-America," *The University of Missouri Studies*, vol. 14 (April 1939), and John G. Clark, *The Grain Trade in the Old Northwest* (Urbana, Ill.: University of Illinois Press, 1966).

19. *Ibid.*, 6.

20. Morton Rothstein, "The International Market for Agricultural Commodities, 1850–1873," in *The Changing Economic Order*, 318.

21. Jonathan Lurie, *The Chicago Board of Trade, 1859–1905* (Urbana, Ill.: University of Illinois Press, 1979), 24–25.

22. Porter and Livesay, *Merchants and Manufacturers*, 28–29.

23. *Ibid.*, 36.

24. Chandler, *The Visible Hand*, 38.

25. H. Thomas Johnson, "Early Cost Accounting for Internal Management Control: Lyman Mills in the 1850s," *Business History Review* 46 (Winter 1972): 467.

26. Chandler, *The Visible Hand*, 38.

27. Wayne E. Fuller, *The American Mail* (Chicago: The University of Chicago Press, 1972), 64–65.

28. James H. Madison, "Communications," in *Encyclopedia of American Economic History*, 2:338.

29. Robert Luther Thompson, *Wiring a Continent: The History of the Telegraph Industry in the United States, 1832–1866* (Princeton, N.J.: Princeton University Press, 1947), 442–443.

Chapter 8: The Industrial Revolution in America

1. T. S. Ashton, *The Industrial Revolution, 1760–1830* (New York: Oxford University Press, 1948), 58.

2. Peter Lane, *The Industrial Revolution: The Birth of the Modern Age* (New York: Barnes & Noble Books, 1978), 1.

3. Melvin Kranzberg, "Prerequisites for Industrialization," in *Technology in Western Civilization*, 1: 218.

4. *Ibid.*, 228.

5. David J. Jeremy, "Damming the Flood: British Government Efforts to Check the Outflow of Technicians and Machinery, 1780–1843," *Business History Review* 51 (Spring 1977): 2.

6. Thomas C. Cochran, *Frontiers of Change: Early Industrialism in America* (New York: Oxford University Press, 1981), 10.

7. Victor S. Clark, *History of Manufactures in the United States,* vol. 1 (New York: McGraw-Hill Book Company, 1929), 442.

8. Gras and Larson, *Casebook in American Business History*, 210.

9. James B. Hedges, *The Browns of Providence Plantations: The Nineteenth Century* (Providence, R.I.: Brown University Press, 1968), 162.

10. *Ibid.*, 163.

11. Barbara M. Tucker, "The Merchant, the Manufacturer, and the Factory Manager: The Case of Samuel Slater," *Business History Review* 55 (Autumn 1981): 300. See also by the same author, *Samuel Slater and the Origins of the American Textile Industry, 1790–1860* (Ithaca, N.Y.: Cornell University Press, 1984).

12. Robert K. Lamb, "The Entrepreneur and the Community," in Miller, *Men in Business*, 97.

13. David J. Jeremy, *Transatlantic Industrial Revolution: The Diffusion of Textile Technologies between Britain and America, 1790–1830s* (Cambridge, Mass.: The MIT Press, 1981), 95.

14. George S. Gibb, *The Saco-Lowell Shops: Textile Machinery Building in New England, 1813–1949* (Cambridge, Mass.: Harvard University Press, 1950), 14.

15. Caroline F. Ware, *The Early New England Cotton Manufacture: A Study in Industrial Beginnings* (Boston: Houghton Mifflin Company, 1931: reprint ed., New York: Russell & Russell, 1966), 61–62.

16. Robert B. Zevin, "The Growth of Cotton Textile Production after 1815," in *The Reinterpretation of American Economic History*, ed. Robert W. Fogel and Stanley L. Engerman (New York: Harper & Row, Publishers, 1971), 141.

17. Thomas Dublin, *Women at Work: The Transformation of Work and Community in Lowell, Massachusetts, 1826–1860* (New York: Columbia University Press, 1979), 40.

18. Robert S. Woodbury, "The Legend of Eli Whitney and Interchangeable Parts," in Robertson and Pate, *Readings in United States Economic and Business History*, 208.

19. Constance McL. Green, *Eli Whitney and the Birth of American Technology* (Boston: Little, Brown and Company, 1956), 61–62.

20. Merrit Roe Smith, "Eli Whitney and the American System of Manufacturing," in Pursell, *Technology in America*, 47.

21. David A. Hounshell, *From the American System to Mass Production, 1800–1932* (Baltimore, Md.: The Johns Hopkins University Press, 1984), 28.

22. Nathan Rosenberg, "Technological Change," in Lance E. Davis et al., *American Economic Growth: An Economist's History of the United States* (New York: Harper & Row, Publishers, 1972), 257.

23. Alfred D. Chandler, Jr., "Anthracite Coal and the Beginnings of the Industrial Revolution in the United States," *Business History Review* 46 (Summer 1972): 180.

24. The following discussion is based principally on Peter Temin, *Iron and Steel in Nineteenth Century America: An Economic Inquiry* (Cambridge, Mass.: The MIT Press, 1964), and the chapter, "The Merchant in Operation: The Marketing of Iron," in Porter and Livesay, *Merchants and Manufacturers*.

25. Paul W. Gates, *The Farmer's Age: Agriculture, 1815–1860* (New York: Holt, Rinehart, and Winston, 1960), 285.

26. William T. Hutchinson, *Cyrus Hall McCormick*, vol. 1 (New York: The Century Company, 1930; reprint ed., New York: Da Capo Press, 1968), 17.

27. Robert Sobel, *The Entrepreneurs: Explorations within the American Business Tradition* (New York: Weybright and Talley, 1974), 60.

28. Harold D. Livesay, *American Made: Men Who Shaped the American Economy* (Boston: Little, Brown and Company, 1979), 73.

29. Carroll W. Pursell, Jr., ed., *Readings in Technology and American Life* (New York: Oxford University Press, 1969), 97–98.

Chapter 9: Railroads and the Challenge of Big Business

1. Taylor, *The Transportation Revolution*, 75.

2. The discussion of railroading in the decade of the 1850s is based in good part on John F. Stover, *Iron Rails to the West: American Railroads in the 1850s* (New York: Columbia University Press, 1978), and Stewart H. Holbrook, *The Story of American Railroads* (New York: Crown Publishers, 1947).

3. Irene D. Neu, *Erastus Corning, Merchant and Financier* (Ithaca, N.Y.: Cornell University Press, 1960; reprint ed., Westport, Conn.: Greenwood Press, Inc., 1977), 168–70.

4. James A. Ward, *J. Edgar Thomson, Master of the Pennsylvania* (Westport, Conn.: Greenwood Press, Inc., 1980), 4, 91.

5. See, for example, Albert Fishlow, *Railroads and the Transformation of the Antebellum Economy* (Cambridge, Mass.: Harvard University Press, 1965), and Robert W. Fogel, *Railroads and American Economic Growth: Essays in Econometric History* (Baltimore, Md.: Johns Hopkins Press, 1960).

6. Jeffrey G. Williamson, *Late Nineteenth Century American Development: A General Equilibrium History* (Cambridge, Eng.: Cambridge University Press, 1974).

7. John F. Stover, *The Life and Decline of the American Railroad* (New York: Oxford University Press, 1970), 78.

8. Edward C. Kirkland, *Industry Comes of Age: Business, Labor, and Public Policy, 1860–1897* (New York: Holt, Rinehart, and Winston, 1961), 53.

9. Charles Francis Adams, Jr., and Henry Adams, *Chapters of Erie* (Ithaca, N.Y.: Cornell University Press, 1956), 95.

10. James A. Ward, "Image and Realty: The Railway Corporate-State Metaphor," *Business History Review* 55 (Winter 1981): 494.

11. Oscar A. Winther, *The Transportation Frontier: Trans-Mississippi West, 1865–1890* (New York: Holt, Rinehart, and Winston, 1964), 93.

12. Alfred D. Chandler, Jr., *The Railroads: The Nation's First Big Business* (New York: Harcourt, Brace, & World, Inc., 1965), 9.

13. The following discussion draws on Alfred D. Chandler, Jr., "The Railroads: Pioneers in Modern Corporate Management," *Business History Review* 34 (Spring 1965), and Chandler, "The Railroads: Innovators in Modern Business Administration," in *The Changing Economic Order.*

14. Chandler, "The Railroads: Innovators in Modern Business Administration," 235.

15. Carosso, *Investment Banking in America*, 13.

16. Edwin P. Hoyt, Jr., *The House Of Morgan* (New York: Dodd, Mead & Company, 1966), 160.

17. Gras and Larson, *Casebook in American Business History*, 557.

18. Hughes, *The Vital Few*, 423.

19. John R. Commons et al., *History of Labour in the United States*, vol. 2. (New York: The Macmillan Company, 1918), 63.

20. Robert V. Bruce, *1877: Year of Violence* (New York: The Bobbs-Merrill Company, Inc., 1959; Chicago: Quadrangle Books, Inc., 1970), 38.

21. For the most detailed accounts of the Pullman story, see Almont Lindsey, *The Pullman Strike* (Chicago: The University of Chicago Press, 1942), and the more recent Stanley Buder, *Pullman: An Experiment in Industrial Order and Community Planning, 1880–1930* (New York: Oxford University Press, 1967).

22. Gerald G. Eggert, *Railroad Labor Disputes: The Beginnings of Federal Strike Policy* (Ann Arbor: the University of Michigan Press, 1967), 1.

23. *Ibid.*, 214.

24. Stover, *The Life and Decline of the American Railroad*, 85.

25. Thomas C. Cochran, *Railroad Leaders, 1845–1890: The Business Mind in Action* (Cambridge, Mass.: Harvard University Press, 1953), 138.

26. Albro Martin, *Enterprise Denied: Origins of the Decline of American Railroads, 1897–1917* (New York: Columbia University Press, 1971), 17.

27. Henry Adams, *The Education of Henry Adams: An Autobiography* (Boston: Houghton Mifflin, 1918), 240.

Chapter 10: Industrialization: Expansion and Extension

1. Henry Demarest Lloyd, *Wealth against Commonwealth* (New York: Harper & Bros. Publishers, 1894), 494.

2. Louis M. Hacker, *The World of Andrew Carnegie, 1865–1901* (Philadelphia: J. B. Lippincott Company, 1968), xxvii, 5. For Charles Beard on the same topic, see his and Mary R. Beard's *The Rise of American Civilization* (New York: Macmillan Company, 1927; rev. ed., 1937), chap. 18.

3. Thomas C. Cochran, "Did the Civil War Retard Industrialization?," *Mississippi Valley Historical Review* 48 (September 1961): 197–210. Also see Robert E. Gallman, "The Pace and Pattern of American Economic Growth," in *American Economic Growth*, 15–60.

4. Paul Uselding, "Manufacturing," in *Encyclopedia of American Economic History*, 1:408.

5. Douglass, *The Coming of Age of American Business*, 432.

6. Douglas Alan Fisher, *The Epic of Steel* (New York: Harper & Row, Publishers, 1963), 122.

7. Jeanne McHugh, *Alexander Holley and the Makers of Steel* (Baltimore, Md.: The Johns Hopkins University Press, 1980), 190.

8. Livesay, *American Made*, 103.

9. Joseph Frazier Wall, *Andrew Carnegie* (New York: Oxford University Press, 1970), 311.

10. Quoted in Porter and Livesay, *Merchants and Manufacturers*, 149.

11. Harold F. Williamson and Arnold F. Daum, *The American Petroleum Industry: The Age of Illumination, 1859–1899* (Evanston, Ill.: Northwestern University Press, 1959), 75.

12. *Ibid.*, 82.

13. Ralph Hidy and Muriel Hidy, *Pioneering in Big Business, 1882–1911: History of Standard Oil Company (New Jersey)* (New York: Harper & Brothers, 1955), 6.

14. *Ibid.*, 9.

15. Rockefeller, *Random Reminiscences of Men and Events*, 111.

16. Nevins, *Study in Power: John D. Rockefeller . . .*, 2:426, 433.

17. John Brooks, *Telephone: The First Hundred Years* (New York: Harper & Row, Publishers, 1975), 60.

18. For the most satisfactory biography of Bell, see Robert V. Bruce, *Bell: Alexander Graham Bell and the Conquest of Solitude* (Boston: Little, Brown and Company, 1973).

19. George David Smith, *The Anatomy of a Business Strategy: Bell, Western Electric, and the Origins of the American Telephone Industry* (Baltimore, Md.: The Johns Hopkins University Press, 1985), 157.

20. Sobel, *The Entrepreneurs*, 245.

21. Alfred D. Chandler, Jr., "The Beginnings of Big Business in American Industry," *Business History Review* 33 (Spring 1959): 1–31. For a concise treatment of the same matter, see Glenn Porter, *The Rise of Big Business, 1860–1910* (Arlington Heights, Ill.: Harlan Davidson, Inc., 1973).

22. Mary Yeager, *Competition and Regulation: The Development of Oligopoly in the Meat Packing Industry* (Greenwich, Conn.: JAI Press, Inc., 1981), 1.

23. For further detail on the United Fruit story, see Charles M. Wilson, *Empire in Green and Gold: The Story of the American Banana Trade* (New York: Holt, Rinehart & Winston, 1947), or Stacy May and Galo Plaza, *The United Fruit Company in Latin America* (Washington: National Planning Association, 1958).

24. Maurice P. Brungardt, "The United Fruit Company in Colombia," in *American Business History: Case Studies*, ed. Henry C. Dethloff and C. Joseph Pusateri (Arlington Heights, Ill.: Harlan Davidson, Inc., 1987), 236.

25. Patrick G. Porter, "Origins of the American Tobacco Company, *Business History Review* 43 (Spring 1969): 59–76.

26. For further detail on the early Singer firm, see Robert B. Davies, " 'Peacefully Working to Conquer the World': The Singer Manufacturing Company in Foreign Markets, 1854–1959," *Business History Review* 43 (Autumn 1969): 299–325, and Peter Lyon, "Isaac Singer and His Wonderful Sewing Machine," *American Heritage* 9 (October 1958): 34–38, 103–109.

27. *Ibid.*, 104.

28. Wyn Wachhorst, *Thomas Alva Edison, An American Myth* (Cambridge, Mass.: The MIT Press, 1981), 13.

29. Robert Friedel and Paul Israel, *Edison's Electric Light: Biography of an Invention* (New Brunswick, N.J.: Rutgers University Press, 1986), 222.

30. Ronald W. Clark, *Edison: The Man Who Made the Future* (New York: G. P. Putnam's Sons, 1977), 161.

31. Harold C. Passer, *The Electrical Manufacturers, 1875–1900* (Cambridge, Mass.: Harvard University Press, 1953; reprint ed., New York: Arno Press, 1972), 206.

32. Naomi R. Lamoreaux, *The Great Merger Movement in American Business, 1895–1904* (Cambridge, Eng.: Cambridge University Press, 1985), 187–188.

33. Porter, *The Rise of Big Business*, 81.

Chapter 11: Reacting to Industrialism

1. *State of Ohio v. Standard Oil Company*, 49 Ohio 137 (1892).

2. Sidney Fine, *Laissez Faire and the General-Welfare State: A Study in Conflict in American Thought, 1865–1901* (Ann Arbor: The University of Michigan Press, 1956; Ann Arbor Paperbacks, 1964).

3. Irvin G. Wyllie, *The Self-Made Man in America: The Myth of Rags to Riches* (New York: The Free Press, 1966), 6.

4. Quoted in Robert Green McCloskey, *American Conservatism in the Age of Enterprise, 1865–1910.* (Cambridge, Mass.: Harvard University Press, 1951; New York: Harper Torchbooks, 1964), 151.

5. Hidy and Hidy, *Pioneering in Big Business*, p. 716; Saul Englebourg, *Power and Morality: American Business Ethics, 1840–1914* (Westport, Conn.: Greenwood Press, 1980), 8.

6. William Letwin, *Law and Economic Policy in America* (New York: Random House, 1965), 20, 22.

7. Theodore Saloutos, "The Agricultural Problem and Nineteenth Century Industrialism," *Agricultural History* 23 (July 1948): 156.

8. John A. Garraty, *The New Commonwealth, 1877–1890* (New York: Harper & Row, Publishers, 1968), 140.

9. For a discussion of all three authors plus more, see Daniel Aaron, *Men of Good Hope: A Story of American Progressives* (New York: Oxford University Press, 1951).

10. Henry F. May, *Protestant Churches and Industrial America* (New York: Octagon Books, Inc., 1963), 163.

11. Robert H. Wiebe, *The Search for Order, 1877–1920* (New York: Hill and Wang, 1977), 45–46.

12. Wiebe, *Businessmen and Reform: A Study of the Progressive Movement* (Cambridge, Mass.: Harvard University Press, 1962; Chicago: Quadrangle Paperbacks, 1968), 10–15; George H. Miller, "Origins of the Iowa Granger Law," *Mississippi Valley Historical Review* 40 (March 1954): 661–62.

13. Edward Chase Kirkland, *Dream and Thought in the Business Community, 1860–1900* (Ithaca, N.Y.: Cornell University Press, 1956), 122.

14. Fred A. Shannon, *The Farmer's Last Frontier: Agriculture, 1870–1897* (New York: Holt, Rinehart and Winston, 1945), 309.

15. C. Peter Magrath, "The Case of the Unscrupulous Warehouseman," in *Quarrels That Have Shaped the Constitution*, ed. John A. Garraty (New York: Harper & Row, Publishers, 1962), 122.

16. *Munn v. Illinois*, 94 U.S. 113 (1877); Loren P. Beth, *The Development of the American Constitution, 1877–1917* (New York: Harper and Row, Publishers, 1971), 169, 171.

17. Marver H. Bernstein, *Regulating Business by Independent Commission* (Princeton, N.J.: Princeton University Press, 1955), 21–22.

18. Martin, *Enterprise Denied*, 354–55.

19. Ari Hoogenboom and Olive Hoogenboom, *A History of the ICC: From Panacea to Palliative* (New York: W.W. Norton & Co., Inc., 1976), 85.

20. Letwin, *Law and Economic Policy in America*, 94.

21. For a detailed discussion of the origins and history of this firm, see Alfred S. Eichner, *The Emergence of Oligopoly: Sugar Refining as a Case Study* (Baltimore, Md. The John Hopkins Press, 1969).

22. *United States v. E.C. Knight Co.*, 156 U.S. 1 (1895).

23. William H. Harbaugh, *The Life and Times of Theodore Roosevelt*, new rev. ed. (New York: Oxford University Press, 1975), 154.

24. Albro Martin, *James J. Hill and the Opening of the Northwest* (New York: Oxford University Press, 1976), 494; R. W. Apple, Jr., "The Case of the Monopolistic Railroadmen," in *Quarrels That Have Shaped the Constitution*, 168.

25. *Northern Securities Co. v. United States*, 193 U.S. 197 (1904).

26. Apple, "The Case of the Monopolistic Railroadmen," 175; George E. Mowry, *The Era of Theodore Roosevelt and the Birth of Modern America* (New York: Harper & Brothers, 1958), 131.

27. Bruce Bringhurst, *Antitrust and the Oil Monopoly: The Standard Oil Cases, 1890–1911* (Westport, Conn.: Greenwood Press, 1979), 161; Letwin, *Law and Economic Policy in America*, 265; Mowry, *The Era of Theodore Roosevelt*, 55.

28. *United States v. United States Steel Corp.*, 251 U.S. 417 (1920).

29. Roger L. Ransom, *Coping with Capitalism: The Economic Transformation of the United States, 1766–1980* (Englewood Cliffs, N.J.: Prentice-Hall Inc., 1981), 81.

30. David Brody, *Workers in Industrial America: Essays on Twentieth Century Struggle* (New York: Oxford University Press, 1980), 9.

31. Frederick W. Taylor, *The Principles of Scientific Management* (New York: Harper & Bros., 1911), 36–37; see also Daniel Nelson, *Frederick W. Taylor and the Rise of Scientific Management* (Madison: The University of Wisconsin Press, 1980), 168–74.

32. Daniel T. Rodgers, *The Work Ethic in Industrial America, 1850–1920* (Chicago: University of Chicago Press, 1978), 168.

33. Gerald N. Grob, *Workers and Utopia: A Study of the Ideological Conflict in the American Labor Movement, 1865–1900* (Evanston, Ill.: Northwestern University Press, 1961; Chicago: Quadrangle Paperbacks, 1969), 9.

34. Morrell Heald, *The Social Responsibilities of Business: Company and Community, 1900–1960* (Cleveland: The Press of Case Western Reserve University, 1970), 36.

35. Brody, *Workers in Industrial America*, 59.

36. George E. Mowry, *The Progressive Era, 1900–1920: The Reform Persuasion* (Washington: The American Historical Association, 1972), 36.

Chapter 12: Business in an Urban Nation

1. Carl N. Degler, *Out of Our Past: The Forces That Shaped Modern America* (New York: Harper & Row Publishers, Harper Colophon Books, 1962), 307.

2. Henry C. Dethloff, *Americans and Free Enterprise* (Englewood Cliffs, N.J.: Prentice-Hall, Inc., 1979), 213.

3. Allan Nevins, *Ford: The Times, the Man, the Company* (New York: Charles Scribner's Sons, 1954), 165.

4. Robert Lacey, *Ford: The Men and the Machine* (Boston: Little, Brown and Company, 1986), 65.

5. Livesay, *American Made*, 163.

6. James J. Flink, *America Adopts the Automobile, 1895–1910* (Cambridge, Mass.: The MIT Press, 1970), 310.

7. Bernard A. Weisberger, *The Dream Maker: William C. Durant, Founder of General Motors* (Boston: Little, Brown and Company, 1979), 167.

8. Alfred P. Sloan, Jr., *My Years with General Motors*, (New York: Macfadden-Bartell Corporation, 1965), 4.

9. Alfred D. Chandler, Jr., *Giant Enterprise: Ford, General Motors, and the Automobile Industry* (New York: Harcourt, Brace & World, Inc., 1964), 13.

10. John B. Rae, *The American Automobile: A Brief History* (Chicago: University of Chicago Press, 1965), 115.

11. Livesay, *American Made*, 228.

12. Alfred D. Chandler, Jr., *Strategy and Structure: Chapters in the History of American Industrial Enterprise* (Cambridge, Mass.: The MIT Press, 1962), 133.

13. Elliott N. Sivowitch, "A Technological Survey of Broadcasting's Pre-History, 1876–1920," *Journal of Broadcasting* 15 (Winter 1970–1971): 16–17.

14. For a discussion of KDKA and broadcasting's beginnings, see Erik Barnouw, *A History of Broadcasting in the United States*, vol. 1: *A Tower in Babel* (New York: Oxford University Press, 1966), and Gleason Archer, *History of Radio to 1926* (Washington: American Historical Society, 1938).

15. William Peck Banning, *Commercial Broadcasting Pioneer: The WEAF Experiment, 1922–1926* (Cambridge, Mass.: Harvard University Press, 1946), 90–93. See also Charles H. Wolfe, *Modern Radio Advertising* (New York: Funk and Wagnalls Company, 1949), 622.

16. Barnouw, *A History of Broadcasting in the United States*, vol. 2: *The Golden Web* (New York: Oxford University Press, 1968), 6; Federal Communications Commission, *Report on Social and Economic Data Pursuant to the Informal Hearing on Broadcasting, Docket 4063* (Washington, D.C., July 1, 1937), 5.

17. *Documents of American Broadcasting*, ed. Frank J. Kahn (New York: Appleton-Century-Crofts, 1973), 69.

18. Philip T. Rosen, *The Modern Stentors: Radio Broadcasters and the Federal Government, 1920–1934* (Westport, Conn.: Greenwood Press, 1980), 3.

19. Harold Barger, *Distribution's Place in the American Economy since 1869* (Princeton, N.J.: Princeton University Press, 1955), 69–71.

20. Ralph W. Hower, *History of Macy's of New York, 1858–1919* (Cambridge, Mass.: Harvard University Press, 1946), 68.

21. Susan Porter Benson *Counter Cultures: Saleswomen, Managers and Customers in American Department Stores, 1890–1940* (Urbana, Ill.: University of Illinois Press, 1986), 17.

22. Robert Hendrickson, *The Grand Emporiums: The Illustrated History of America's Great Department Stores* (Briarcliff Manor, N.Y.: Stein and Day, 1979), 29.

23. Joseph H. Appel, *The Business Biography of John Wanamaker, Founder and Builder* (New York: The Macmillan Company, 1930), 92.

24. Benson, *Counter Cultures*, 8.

25. Boris Emmet and John E. Jeuck, *Catalogues and Counters: A History of Sears, Roebuck and Company* (Chicago: University of Chicago Press, 1950), 20.

26. Theodore N. Beckman and Herman C. Nolen, *The Chain Store Problem: A Critical Analysis* (New York: McGraw-Hill Book Company, Inc., 1938),

3, 37. See also Godfrey M. Lebhar, *Chain Stores in America, 1859–1950* (Chain Store Publishing Corporation, 1952).

27. Quoted in Roland Marchand, *Advertising the American Dream: Making Way for Modernity, 1920–1940* (Berkeley, Ca.: University of California Press, 1985).

28. Stephen Fox, *The Mirror Makers: A History of American Advertising and Its Creators* (New York: William Morrow and Co., 1984), 16.

29. Sarah Stage, *Female Complaints: Lydia Pinkham and the Business of Women's Medicine* (New York: W.W. Norton & Co., 1979), 17.

30. Fox, *The Mirror Makers*, 21.

31. Marchand, *Advertising the American Dream*, 6.

32. *Ibid.*, 18–19.

33. Robert Craig West, *Banking Reform and the Federal Reserve, 1863–1923* (Ithaca, N.Y.: Cornell University Press, 1974), 29.

34. Herman E. Krooss and Martin R. Blyn, *A History of Financial Intermediaries* (New York: Random House, 1971), 99.

35. Lester V. Chandler, *Benjamin Strong, Central Banker* (Washington: The Brookings Institution, 1958), 3.

36. Cited in Harold F. Williamson, "Insurance," in *Encyclopedia of American Economic History*, 3:729.

37. Viviana A. Rotman Zelizer, *Morals and Markets: The Development of Life Insurance in the United States* (New York: Columbia University Press, 1979), 95.

38. Williamson, "Insurance," 3:733.

39. Thomas C. Cochran, *American Business in the Twentieth Century* (Cambridge, Mass.: Harvard University Press, 1972), 57–58.

40. *Ibid.*, 58.

Chapter 13: The Maturing of Corporate Administration

1. Thomas J. McNichols, *Policy-Making and Executive Action* (New York: McGraw-Hill Book Company, 1977), 3–6.

2. James P. Baughman, "Management," in *Encyclopedia of American Economic History*, 2:839.

3. Adolf A. Berle and Gardiner C. Means, *The Modern Corporation and Private Property* (New York: The Macmillan Company, 1933).

4. Heald, *The Social Responsibilities of Business*, 64–65.

5. Chandler, *Strategy and Structure*, 49.

6. Jon Didricksen, "The Development of Diversified and Conglomerate Firms in the United States, 1920–1970," *Business History Review* 46 (Summer 1972): 210–19.

7. Alfred D. Chandler, Jr., and Stephen Salsbury, *Pierre S. du Pont and the Making of the Modern Corporation* (New York: Harper & Row, Publishers, 1971), 604.

8. Alfred D. Chandler, Jr., "The Large Industrial Corporation and the Making of the Modern American Economy," in *Institutions in Modern America: Innovations in Structure and Process*, ed. Stephen E. Ambrose (Baltimore,

Md.: The Johns Hopkins Press, 1967), 99. See also Chandler's "The Structure of American Industry in the Twentieth Century: A Historical Overview," *Business History Review* 43 (Autumn 1969): 255–98.

9. Mira Wilkins, *The Emergence of Multinational Enterprise: American Business Abroad from the Colonial Era to 1914* (Cambridge, Mass.: Harvard University Press, 1970), 201–202.

10. H. Wayne Morgan, *Unity and Culture: The United States, 1877–1900* (Baltimore, M.d.: Penguin Books, 1971), 138.

11. Mira Wilkins, *The Maturing of Multinational Enterprise: American Business Abroad from 1914 to 1970* (Cambridge, Mass.: Harvard University Press, 1974), 158.

12. The following discussion is based in large part on Steven A. Schneider, *The Oil Price Revolution* (Baltimore, Md.: The Johns Hopkins University Press, 1983) and Edward W. Chester, *United States Oil Policy and Diplomacy* (Westport, Conn.: Greenwood Press, 1983).

13. *Ibid.*, 37.

14. Chandler and Tedlow, *The Coming of Managerial Capitalism*, 720.

15. Leonard Glynn, "Multinationals in the World of Nations," in *The Multinational Enterprise in Transition*, ed. Phillip D. Grub et al. (Princeton, N.J.: The Darwin Press, Inc., 1986), 17–18.

16. *Business Week*, July 14, 1986, 45.

17. Phillip H. Trezise, "Some Policy Implications of the Multinational Corporation," *Department of State Bulletin*, May 24, 1971, 670.

18. Richard J. Barnet and Ronald E. Muller, *Global Reach: The Power of the Multinational Corporations* (New York: Simon and Schuster, 1974), 14–16.

19. Page Smith, *America Enters the World* (New York: McGraw-Hill Book Company, 1985), 569–571.

20. Edward Robb Ellis, *Echoes of Distant Thunder: Life in the United States, 1914–1918* (New York; Coward, McCann, & Geohagan, 1978), 381.

21. *Ibid.*, 386.

22. William E. Leuchtenburg, "The New Deal and the Analogue of War," in *Change and Continuity in Twentieth Century America*, ed. John Braeman et al. (New York: Harper & Row Publishers, 1966), 123, 131.

23. Leuchtenburg, *Franklin D. Roosevelt and the New Deal* (New York: Harper & Row Publishers, 1963), 87–88.

24. Arthur M. Schlesinger, Jr., *The Age of Roosevelt*, vol. I: *The Crisis of the Old Order, 1919–1933* (Boston: Houghton Mifflin Company, 1957), 61.

25. *The Public Papers and Addresses of Franklin D. Roosevelt*, comp. Samuel I. Rosenman, 13 vols. (New York: Random House, 1938–1950), 2:156, 164.

26. U.S., Congress, House of Representatives, *Congressional Record*, 73rd Cong., 1st Sess., May 8, 1933.

27. Editorial, "Smilin' Through," *Saturday Evening Post*, September 22, 1934.

28. Rosenman, *The Public Papers. . .*, 5:232.

29. Joseph Alsop and Robert D. Kintner, "Trust Buster—the Folklore of Thurman Arnold," *Saturday Evening Post*, August 12, 1939.

30. Gene M. Gressley, "Thurman Arnold, Antitrust, and the New Deal," *Business History Review* (Summer 1964), 214–231.

31. Thurman Arnold, "Must 1929 Repeat Itself?" *Harvard Business Review* (January 1948), 43.

32. Ellis W. Hawley, *The New Deal and the Problem of Monopoly* (Princeton, N.J.: Princeton University Press, 1966), 441.

33. Thomas K. McCraw, *Prophets of Regulation* (Cambridge, Mass.: Harvard University Press, 1984), 210.

34. James Oliver Robertson, *America's Business* (New York: Hill and Wang, 1985), 217–218.

35. Hughes, *American Economic History*, 483.

36. Mark S. Foster, "Giant of the West: Henry J. Kaiser and Regional Industrialization," *Business History Review* 59 (Spring 1985): 1–23.

37. John Morton Blum, *V Was for Victory: Politics and American Culture During World War II* (New York: Harcourt, Brace, Jovanovich, 1976), 115.

38. Richard Polenberg, *War and Society: The United States, 1941–1945* (Philadelphia: J.B. Lippincott Co., 1972), 73.

39. John Chamberlain, "A History of American Business, Part 13: The New World of Enterprise," *Fortune*, May 1962, 146.

40. Harold G. Vatter, *The U.S. Economy in World War II* (New York: Columbia University Press, 1985), 146.

Chapter 14: Industries and Policy in the Modern Era

1. Cited in Arthur M. Johnson, *The American Economy* (New York: The Free Press, 1974), 5.

2. *Business Week*, January 12, 1987, 66.

3. Quoted in C. Joseph Pusateri, *Big Business in America: Attack and Defense* (Itasca, Ill.: F. E. Peacock Publishers, 1975), 82.

4. *Business Week*, July 21, 1986, 71.

5. Harold F. Williamson et al., *The American Petroleum Industry: The Age of Energy, 1899–1959* (Evanston, Ill.: Northwestern University Press, 1963), 205.

6. Gerald D. Nash, *United States Oil Policy, 1890–1964* (Westport, Conn.: Greenwood Press, 1968), 117.

7. E. Anthony Copp, *Regulating Competition in Oil: Government Intervention in the U.S. Refining Industry, 1948–1975* (College Station, Tex.: Texas A&M University Press, 1976), 192.

8. Walter S. Measday and Stephen Martin, "The Petroleum Industry," in *The Structure of American Industry*, ed. Walter Adams, 7th ed. (New York: Macmillan Publishing Co., 1986), 59.

9. John Paul Newport, Jr., "Get Ready for the Coming Oil Crisis," *Fortune*, March 16, 1987, 49.

10. *Wall Street Journal*, January 11, 1982, 1.

11. *Time*, August 25, 1986, 44.

12. *Business Week*, December 2, 1985, 95.

13. Livesay, *American Made*, 251. See also Nevins and Hill, *Ford: Decline and Rebirth*, 312–345.

14. John Brooks, "A Net Loss of $350 Million," in *Great Business Disasters*, ed. Isadore Barmash (Chicago: Playboy Press, 1972), 132, 141.

15. James J. Flink, *The Car Culture* (Cambridge, Mass.: The MIT Press, 1975), 215–216.

16. John B. Rae, *The American Automobile Industry* (Boston: Twayne Publishers, 1984), 142, 145.

17. Lee Iacocca, "Iacocca: An Autobiography," *Newsweek*, October 8, 1984, 62.

18. *Ibid.*

19. Michael Moritz and Barrett Seaman, *Going for Broke: Iacocca's Battle to Save Chrysler* (Garden City, N.Y.: Anchor Press, 1984), 303.

20. Anne B. Fisher, "GM Is Tougher Than You Think," *Fortune*, November 10, 1986, 56.

21. *Ibid.*

22. Les Brown, *Television: The Business Behind the Box* (New York: Harcourt Brace Jovanovich, Inc., 1971), 61.

23. *Fortune*, July 1949, 73–74, 144.

24. Barnouw, *The Golden Web*, 290.

25. Cited in R. Terry Elmore, *Broadcasting Law and Regulation* (Blue Ridge Summit, Pa.: TAB Books, 1982), 21.

26. Erwin G. Krasnow, Lawrence D. Longley, and Herbert A. Terry, *The Politics of Broadcast Regulation*, 3rd ed. (New York: St. Martin's Press, 1982), 284.

27. *Business Week*, March 28, 1983, 85.

28. Katharine Davis Fishman, *The Computer Establishment* (New York: McGraw-Hill Book Company, 1981), 76.

29. *Ibid.*, 44.

30. Robert Sobel, *IBM: Colossus in Transition* (New York: Truman Talley Books, 1981), 232.

31. Franklin M. Fisher, James W. McKie, Richard B. Mancke, *IBM and the U.S. Data Processing Industry: An Economic History* (New York: Praeger Publishers, 1983), IX.

32. *Newsweek*, September 30, 1985, 47.

33. Bro Uttal, "Behind the Fall of Steve Jobs," *Fortune*, August 5, 1985, 20. See also Michael Moritz, *The Little Kingdom: The Private Story of Apple Computer* (New York: William Morrow and Co., Inc., 1984).

34. Speech reprinted in James L. Clayton, ed. *The Economic Impact of the Cold War* (New York: Harcourt, Brace, & World, Inc., 1970), 242–243.

35. William J. Weida and Frank L. Gertcher, *The Political Economy of National Defense* (Boulder, Colo.: Westview Press, 1987), 20–22.

36. Jacob Goodwin, *Brotherhood of Arms: General Dynamics and the Business of Defending America* (New York: Times Books, 1985), 242.

37. Jacques S. Gansler, *The Defense Industry* (Cambridge, Mass.: The MIT Press, 1980), 41.

38. *Time*, March 7, 1983, 23.

39. Roger Franklin, *The Defender: The Story of General Dynamics* (New York: Harper & Row Publishers, 1986), IX.

40. Goodwin, *Brotherhood of Arms,* 11.

41. Ford S. Worthy, "Mr. Clean Charts a New Course at General Dynamics," *Fortune,* April 28, 1966, 74.

42. *Wall Street Journal,* May 20, 1987, 12.

43. Paula Dwyer and Seth Payne, "The General Dynamics Case Sets a Bad Precedent," *Business Week,* June 8, 1987, 41.

44. *United States v. Aluminum Co. of America,* 148 F. 2nd 416 (1945).

45. Robert Sobel, *The Age of Giant Corporations: A Microeconomic History of American Business, 1914–1970* (Westport, Conn.: Greenwood Press, Inc., 1972), 191.

46. Robert Sobel, *The Rise and Fall of the Conglomerate Kings* (New York: Stein & Day, 1984), 20.

47. Willard F. Mueller, "Conglomerates: A Nonindustry" in *The Structure of American Industry,* 354.

48. *Business Week,* November 24, 1986, 74.

49. Walter Adams, "Public Policy in a Free Enterprise Economy" in *The Structure of American Industry,* 402–403.

50. *Newsweek,* October 20, 1986, 50.

51. T. Boone Pickens, Jr., *Boone* (Boston: Houghton Mifflin Co., 1987), 282.

52. Michael Brody, "The 1990s" *Fortune,* February 2, 1987, 22.

53. *Business Week,* January 20, 1986, 53.

54. Peter F. Drucker, *Management: Tasks, Responsibilities, Practices* (New York: Harper & Row, Publishers, 1974), 34–35, 809.

A GLOSSARY OF AMERICAN BUSINESS TERMS

AT each point in the text where a new business or economic term is introduced, an effort has been made to define it properly. But, as the narrative proceeds, terms recur which may have appeared pages or chapters before. Hence this glossary is provided as a quick reference for the reader who wishes to recall the exact meaning of some word or phrase.

administered price   A price that is set by management and held rigid without normal consideration of the forces of supply and demand in the marketplace.

antitrust   A governmental policy intended to prevent individual companies or combinations of companies from gaining or maintaining monopolies and restraining free trade and commerce.

assembly-line production   A method of manufacturing in which the worker performs a single specialized task. The materials and parts are normally conveyed on mechanical belts, and the worker accomplishes the task as the material moves past his or her place on the line.

assets   The property or economic resources owned by a business. These include cash, amounts owed to the business by its customers for goods and services sold to them on credit, merchandise held for sale by the business, supplies, equipment, buildings, and land.

backward integration   The extension of a firm's operations toward its source of supply or raw materials.

balance sheet   A financial statement of a business on a specific date listing assets, liabilities, and the equity of the owner or owners.

bank notes Paper currency issued by banks.

bill of exchange A written order addressed by one party (the drawer) to another party (the drawee) instructing the latter to pay a specific sum of money to a third party (the payee).

board of directors Persons elected by the stockholders of a corporation to serve as its governing body.

capital In accounting, the net worth of a business; that is, the excess of its assets over its liabilities. In economic terms, the collection of machines, buildings, and other durable assets used in the process of production.

capital intensive A production process that uses a high amount of capital relative to other inputs.

capital stock The shares of stock that represent the ownership of a corporation.

cartel An association of business organizations whose purpose it is to corner a market or establish a monopoly in some particular sector of the economy.

central bank The official financial institution of a government which controls the monetary system by regulating credit conditions and supervising the creation of a nation's money supply.

common stock A share in the ownership of a corporation. Common stockholders have the right to vote for the directors of the company, but in the event of liquidation have only a residual claim on its assets after the claims of creditors and preferred stockholders have been met.

competition The rivalry between firms active in selling to the same general market. In a state of perfect competition, which ordinarily exists only in an economics classroom, no single firm is large enough to influence the price or output of goods.

concentration ratio The measure of the degree of control of an industry by the leading firms (usually the four or eight largest).

conglomerate A combination of firms that produce goods or services in unrelated industries.

cost externalities Reductions in the average costs of a firm that result from actions taking place outside its own operations.

consumer goods Items purchased by a consumer for his or her personal or household use.

corporation A form of business organization that operates under a charter or articles of incorporation granted by a state government or, in selected instances, the federal government. It is recognized as a legal entity or person apart from its shareholders.

demand The quantity of a good or service that buyers stand ready to purchase at any given price.

demand deposits Money on deposit in banks subject to withdrawal by check; that is, checkbook money.

department An organizational term referring to a division of activity within a firm over which a manager has authority for the performance of specified tasks.

distribution The transporting and/or marketing of goods to buyers.

dividend A periodic distribution of earned profits by a corporation to its shareholders.

durable goods Items such as industrial equipment or large household appliances that have an expected service life of several years.

economies of scale Increased efficiency, as measured by a reduction in the average unit cost of a product, resulting from a growth in the size of operations.

entrepreneur An individual or group of associated individuals who undertake to initiate, maintain, or aggrandize a profit-oriented business unit.

equity The net worth of a business.

firm A business enterprise. It may be a sole proprietorship, a partnership, or a corporation.

forward integration The extension of a firm's operations toward the purchasers of its products, usually by acquiring control over the channels of distribution and marketing.

function In business terms, a specific activity or division of responsibility.

greenmail The management of a corporation buys its own shares from a raider for more than the going price to stop the threat of a hostile takeover.

holding company A corporation (parent) formed for the purpose of buying stock in other companies, and usually thereby controlling the other companies (subsidiaries).

horizontal combination The combining of firms that produce at the same state of production in the same industry.

innovation Applied invention; also the introduction of a new production technique, a new organizational form, or a new product.

interlocking directorates Instances in which the same individuals appear on the boards of directors of different and, usually, competing corporations.

interstate commerce Business conducted between two or more states and usually subject to federal regulation.

investment Business expenditures for new capital equipment; also can refer to the ownership of a stock or bond; also the owner's equity in a business.

investment banker A financial intermediary who underwrites and markets new security issues to dealers or the public.

jobber A wholesaler who buys from manufacturers or importers and sells to retailers.

junk bond Very high-yield, below investment-grade bonds issued by many corporations and raiders to finance acquisitions and hostile takeovers.

labor intensive A production process that employs a large amount of labor relative to other inputs.

laissez-faire An economic policy characterized by little or no government regulation or intervention.

liability The debts of a business, including amounts owed to creditors for goods and services bought on credit, salaries and wages due employees, and taxes, notes, and mortgages payable.

leveraged buyout An acquisition of a public company by a small group of investors, typically including the company's management, who then take the company private. Most of the purchase price is financed with borrowed money.

management The group of persons within a business who have decision-making and supervisory authority; also the process of planning, organizing, staffing, directing, controlling, and representing in a business enterprise.

managerial capitalism According to Chandler, a business system in which the core enterprises are administered at the top and middle levels by salaried, professional managers and not the nominal owners of a corporation.

market A set of buyers and sellers who exchange goods or services.

market economy An economic system in which the basic decisions regarding production and distribution are made without significant government intervention.

mass production Large-scale production employing a substantial investment in equipment, standardized parts, and specialized labor.

merger The joining of two or more business enterprises into one entity.

middleman A businessman who buys from the manufacturer or importer and sells to consumers or retailers; usually a wholesaler.

mixed economy An economic system in which decisions regarding production and distribution are made by both free-market forces and government intervention.

monopoly A market in which there is a single seller of a product, for which there are no close substitutes.

monopoly power The ability of a seller to restrict output or increase prices in a particular market in much the same way as a pure monopoly.

multinational corporation A firm that has active business operations in two or more countries.

national banks In the United States, banks chartered by the federal government.

net worth The remaining value after liabilities are subtracted from assets; the equity of the owner or owners.

oligopoly A market dominated by a small number of firms selling similar products.

overhead A cost of doing business not specifically identifiable with the production of a good or service offered by a firm.

partnership A business form in which ownership is vested in two or more persons who are joint owners and are each legally responsible for all debts of the firm.

plant The standard production unit in a manufacturing enterprise. A large firm will operate multiple plants.

pooling Competing firms joining together in written or unwritten agreements to set prices, restrict output, or divide the market, thereby reducing competition between themselves.

preferred stock The class of stock that carries the right to receive dividends before common stockholders, and likewise to receive a prior share to the assets of the corporation in the event of liquidation.

productivity The efficiency of the production process, measured by the ratio of output in relation to input over a given period of time.

profit The earnings or return to a business enterprise and its owners; the excess of a firm's revenues over its expenditures.

proprietorship A business form in which all of a firm's assets are owned and controlled by a single individual.

raider An investor who buys a large block of stock in a public corporation, attempting a hostile takeover.

rate of return The percentage of an investment yielded as profit.

retailing The business activity concerned with selling products to their final consumers.

specie Hard money, gold or silver.

speculator An individual who is willing to assume an above-average risk on a business or security transaction in hopes of gaining a larger-than-normal return.

supply The quantity of a good that sellers are willing and able to offer for purchase at any given price level.

takeover A move by an outside group to take control of a public corporation. The takeover can be friendly or hostile, depending upon whether the incumbent management supports the attempt or opposes it.

tariff A tax on imported goods, intended either to generate a revenue or to protect domestic industries from foreign competition.

tender offer A public offer to shareholders to buy a corporation's stock. It is usually priced above the market to get shareholders to sell their stock to the bidder.

trust A form of business organization popular in the last decades of the nineteenth century in which firms turned over their voting stock to a board of trustees in return for trust certificates. Outlawed by the Sherman Act, the word itself continued to be used loosely to describe any business organization that appeared to dominate an industry.

unit cost The expense of producing a single product item, usually an average figure.

vertical integration The combining of firms that operate at various stages of production and distribution within a single industry.

wholesaling The business activity of selling goods to others, usually retailers, who are buying for resale to their own customers.

working capital The excess of current assets over current liabilities.

yield The rate of return on a given investment.

INDEX

Accident insurance, 292
Accounting practices, 40, 134
Accounting Review, 297
Achievement, need for, 12
Acquired technology, 300
Adams, Charles Francis, 179
Adams, Henry, 194
Adams, John, 155
Adams, John Quincy, 90
Adams, Sam, 79
Adamson Act (1906), 250
Addams, Jane, 235
Addyston Pipe & Steel case, 243
Advertising agencies, 283–85
Advertising industry, growth of,
  280–85
AFL-CIO, 384
Agency for International Development
  (AID), 305
Aggregate demand, 95
Agrarian discontent, and formation of
  the Grange, 233
Agricultural processing firms, 216
Airline Deregulation Act, 385
Airline industry, deregulation of, 369
Air pollution, 340–41
Alabama Midland Railway Co. case
  (1897), 240
Albert, Prince, 163
Alcoa, 361
Alcoa case, 384
Alexander Brown and Sons, 100
Alger, Horatio, 4
Algerian pirates, 89
Allen, Fred, 345

All-purpose merchant
  in colonial period, 56–64, 127
  decline of, 93, 95–112
  replacement of, by specialist, 20–21
Almy, Brown, and Slater, 145
Almy, William, 145
America, insurance of, 106–7
American Association of Public
  Accountants, 296
American Bell Telephone Company,
  211
American Broadcasting Corporation,
  364
American capitalism, stages of, 17–29
American Challenge, The (Servan-
  Schreiber), 308
American Economics Association, 235
American Express, 271
American Federation of Labor (AFL),
  253, 380
American Fur Company, 111, 377
American Institute of Accountants, 296
American Iron and Steel Institute, 326
American Management Association, 297
American Marconi Company, 270
American Plan, 254
American Railway Union (ARU),
  188–89, 190, 381
American Society of Mechanical
  Engineers, 251
American Stock Exchange, 109
American Sugar Refining Company,
  242–43
American system of manufacturing, 156

A History of American Business, Second Edition, was copyedited by Anita Samen and proofread by Martha Kreger. Production manager was Brad Barrett. The index was compiled by Schroeder Editorial Services. Type was set by Impressions, Inc., and the book was printed and bound by Edwards Brothers, Inc.

Text and cover design by Roger Eggers.